Controversial Issues in Child Development

Controversial Issues in Child Development

Doria Pilling
and
Mia Kellmer Pringle

SCHOCKEN BOOKS · NEW YORK

First published by SCHOCKEN BOOKS 1978

© National Children's Bureau 1978

Library of Congress Cataloging in Publication Data

Pilling, Doria.
    Controversial issues in child development.

    Bibliography: p.
    Includes index.
    1.   Child development.   2.   Education of children.
3.   Parent and child.   4.   Socially handicapped
children.   I.   Pringle, Mia Lilly Kellmer, joint
author.   II.   Title.
HQ767.9.P54 1978   301.42'7   78–1353

Manufactured in Great Britain

Contents

Acknowledgements

The four official readers of *The Needs of Children* were invited jointly by the Department of Health and Social Security and the Bureau to comment on the text. They were Professors David Donnison, Michael Rutter, Gordon Trasler and Bill Wall. All of them did so with the greatest care and we are deeply grateful for their constructive and detailed comments and criticisms which led to many improvements.

Invaluable help in obtaining material for the reviews and in checking references was given by the Bureau's librarians, Ian Vallender and Biddy Cunnell. The typing and collation of the various drafts was undertaken with great skill and intelligence by Penny Harrington of whose painstaking work we cannot speak too highly. Roz Treadway kindly assisted with much of this work at the early stages.

Many colleagues at the National Children's Bureau have made helpful suggestions on the manuscript. We are particularly grateful to Harvey Goldstein, then head of the Statistics and Data Processing Section (now Professor of Statistics and Computing, Institute of Education, University of London), for his help with Part IV. He commented on the statistical analyses in *Pygmalion in the Classroom* by Rosenthal and Jacobs, and the re-analysis of the data in this study presented by Elashoff and Snow in *Pygmalion Re-considered*.

We would also like to thank Dr Joan Tough of the Institute of Education, University of Leeds, and Dr Barbara Tizard of the Thomas Coram Research Unit, Institute of Education, University of London, for allowing us to use their unpublished papers.

The agreement of the publishers of *The Needs of Children*, Hutchinson Publishing Group, to use quotations from that book is gratefully acknowledged.

Finally, and most important, we must thank the Department of Health and Social Security for their sponsorship and support of this literature review. Also, the many helpful suggestions made on the manuscript by the Department were much appreciated.

While many people gave generous help, the responsibility for any omissions or weaknesses which remain, as well as for the interpretations and conclusions, must be ours.

D. P. and M. K. P.

February 1978

How the book came to be written ... Mia Kellmer Pringle

In 1973 the Department of Health and Social Security commissioned the preparation of a document to assist in formulating possible measures for disseminating knowledge about child development and parenthood within a broad general context. The terms of reference were as follows:

"To prepare a comprehensive document about the developmental needs of all children, about the ways in which these needs are normally met and about the consequences for the emotional, intellectual, social and physical growth and development of children when, for one reason or another, these needs are not adequately met."

The resulting report, *The Needs of Children* (Hutchinson, 1974; paperback, 1975 and Schocken, 1975), was based on findings from the Bureau's research work as well as my own experience, research and knowledge. Because I offered my own interpretations of the policy and the practical implications of available knowledge, I sub-titled the book 'A personal perspective'. The time scale stipulated for preparing the report – six months – made it impossible to carry out a comprehensive, systematic review of all the literature. Therefore, the Department agreed to the Bureau's undertaking such a review subsequently. This book is the outcome.

The same constraints which I had to impose on *The Needs of Children* apply to this work: it is concerned only with conditions in developed, Western societies; the main emphasis is on children's psycho-social needs; and the development and needs of the younger age group are given the major attention. Most of the research reviewed is based on British and American work.

Overview
by Mia Kellmer Pringle

Reasons for choosing particular issues

Each of the five issues we have chosen for review is and remains, to a greater or lesser extent, the subject of controversy – hence the title of the book. This may be so because they are bound up with three major aspects of contemporary life: first, the parental role and women's liberation; second, the role of education, and teachers in particular, in enhancing or hindering the life chances of pupils; and third, the problems of disadvantage and the feasibility of intervention to prevent, minimise or eliminate its long-term consequences for children's development. The five issues chosen were: the impact of very early life experiences on development; shared care; the father's role in the family; teachers' expectations and pupil performance; and disadvantage and intervention. Most of the research reviewed is based on British and American work, and hence should be found equally useful on both sides of the Atlantic.

The parental role and women's liberation

In a largely man-made and male-orientated society, home-making and child-rearing have traditionally, with but a few exceptions, been assigned low status. The necessary and justified aim of the women's movement to raise the consciousness and sense of personal identity of women has to a very considerable extent led to a further devaluing of mothering and to a misleadingly biased portrayal of young children. This is doubly unfortunate. It deprives many a young woman of a sense of joy and achievement when she creates a nurturing and happy environment for her family because she is made to feel that she is 'wasting' her abilities. And young babies are presented as mind-blowingly boring rather than as engagingly individual, rapidly developing, though inevitably immature personalities.

Early child care and education

To understate the importance of early infancy at the present time is all the more regrettable since it is only recently that the pre-school years have been given relatively greater attention, in research as well as in social policy debates both in Britain and the USA. Until then, they had been the most neglected. For example, since the war there have been public

1

enquiries in Britain into the needs of all age groups from university students downwards (Robbins, Crowther, Newson and Plowden) except the under-fives; and there has been continuing under-provision for the care and education of the very young compared with the greatly expanded facilities for students and sixth-formers (11th grade) which took place during the sixties. Thus – possibly unwittingly – the women's movement may well be putting the clock back just when recent research is showing how early 'early' is and when the significance of even the first few weeks of life is being documented.

Full-time caring is unique in the sense that the mother has the time, and hence the patience, to develop sensitivity to her baby. This enables her to recognise and adapt to his very individual needs. To be so closely involved and to participate in her child's earliest learning is extremely difficult for those mothers who can give only hurried and preoccupied attention. In Western society, at any rate, no adequate substitute has been found for the one-to-one, loving, mutually enjoyable relationship which is the essence of maternal care, particularly during the first few years of a child's life.

Of course, none of this implies that mothering should or need be carried out single-handed for twenty-four hours a day by the mother herself. There is some evidence that more fathers are now actively participating in the care of their infants and more might well be willing to do so if their hours of work made this easier. Also, most mothers welcome and benefit from sharing this role either informally with relatives and friends; or on a more organised basis with playgroups, one-o'clock clubs (i.e. lunch-time playgroups held in public parks), kindergartens, nursery schools or classes. Many three- to five-year-olds are ready for such shared care on a regular basis for several hours several times a week or even daily. However, this is very different from the all-day group care provided for ten or more hours in day nurseries and crèches or by child minders.

In Britain at present, a small minority of mothers are forced by economic circumstances to seek full-time employment because they are the sole breadwinners. Among them are women who have a chronically sick or handicapped husband, those who have been deserted by their spouses, or who have never been married. Until such time as an agreed, statutorily prescribed minimum income is available to all families who need one – whether one- – or two-parent families and whether it is the mother or father who undertakes the care of the children – it will be necessary to provide substitute day care practically from birth onwards for the children. The basis on which such care is provided needs to be re-examined (*Early Child Care in Britain*, Pringle and Naidoo, 1975).

Traditionally, there are two strands of pre-school provision, care and education, which function quite separately. Whether care is provided in a day nursery or by a child-minder, the emphasis is essentially on physical aspects, though some opportunities may be provided for mothering and for learning. Pre-school education, on the other hand, is essentially geared to learning, albeit in the wider sense of the term though mothering and physical care do play some part. Yet there are no theoretical or practical justifications for perpetuating this artificial distinction between care and education. Moreover, it is both socially divisive and paradoxical. It is divisive because a much higher proportion of middle-class parents make use of nursery schools and classes; whereas day nurseries and child-minders are used primarily by poorer, working-class mothers. It is paradoxical because a charge is made for the latter but not for the former; and also while primary schools have for long been practically comprehensive and secondary education may soon become so for the majority, pre-school provision has remained quite rigidly stratified.

The ideal solution would be for all types of pre-school provision to be available free of charge according to the child's needs and parental wishes. If for the time being the economic situation makes this impracticable then would it not be fairer to provide free services for those in need and charge the others according to ability to pay? Equally important, all the advantages would seem to lie in setting up integrated, multi-purpose, pre-school centres on a neighbourhood basis, to provide both care and education. Such centres would offer much greater flexibility and thus be able to take account of changes in family circumstances, whether these are intentional or accidental. The most suitable programme for any one child at any particular time could be worked out on the basis of careful initial observation and assessment. The appropriate balance between physical care, mothering, stimulation, self-directed exploration and adult-directed learning activities could be determined and re-adjusted in the light of progress made; so could the frequency and length of time the child attends.

The degree and nature of the mother's (and father's) participation in the centre's activities could similarly be flexible but would always be actively encouraged. In this way, pre-school centres would combine the best features of day nurseries, nursery schools and playgroups; they could also be available for use by child-minders.

The double bind of social and economic pressures

Ironically, the movement to liberate women is currently imposing the worst of all worlds on them. If they decide to have a career and not children, most have to withstand powerful social and family pressures. If they decide to become mothers, then their contribution as home-maker with a young family is grossly undervalued. Those who opt for combining a family with full-time paid work outside the home are made

3

to feel guilty, especially when they can only find unsatisfactory substitute care for thier children.

In addition, to cope adequately, a working mother needs inexhaustible energy as well as superb organising ability. Of course, the task is much easier when, for example, one, if not both, parent is a university teacher whose pattern of work is not only largely at his or her own discretion but also allows parents to devote a great deal of time, especially during lengthy vacations, to their family (if they choose to do so). Some media people, especially those doing free-lance work, and certain self-employed professional groups enjoy a similarly privileged position. Their situation is totally different from and bears no comparison with that of the vast majority of mothers who work outside their home in tedious, semi-skilled or unskilled occupations for long hours, with but a few weeks' holiday; at the same time, they have to carry the entire responsibility for home-making without the support of a resident *au pair* girl or a daily help. If able to work part-time only, the burden is, of course, eased to some extent.

The demand for greatly increased facilities for the all-day substitute care of pre-school children is a facet of the denigration of the value of mothering. It is claimed that these are essential because of the vast increase in the proportion of working mothers. Such a statement is in fact rather misleading. It is true that in the UK the proportion of working mothers with dependent children has increased from 27 per cent to 40 per cent between 1961 and 1971. However, the proportion who work full-time (i.e. thirty-five hours or more a week) has decreased, from $13^1/_2$ per cent in 1961 to 10 per cent in 1971; this means that of the total number working, only a quarter did so full-time in 1971, compared with half in 1961.

Another even more significant fact is that the younger the children, the lower the proportion of mothers who work full-time; only a tiny minority of those with under-fives do so $- 5^1/_2$ per cent, which rises to 18 per cent for those with children aged over eleven years.

In the United States there has been a similar increase in the number of working mothers. Whereas in 1948, 26 per cent of those with children of school age (six to seventeen years) were part of the labour force, in 1975, 52 per cent were working or looking for work. About two-thirds of married mothers were working full-time. Of mothers with children under six years of age, 37 per cent were working outside the home, a proportion three times higher than that in 1948. (Current Population Report of the Bureau of the Census, US Department of Commerce; and Special Labor Force Reports of the US Department of Labor). It is evident that a higher proportion of mothers enter the labour market in the United States than do in Britain.

Some would counter that these numbers would be swollen by those who would choose paid employment if substitute care were more readily available. Against this, it could be argued that many women with young children would prefer to be full-time mothers if child-rearing and home-making were accorded the status their importance deserves; and consequently, if adequate financial support were available as of right for all who need it. This is all the more important in times of stringency which are likely to increase financial pressures on mothers to seek paid employment, especially those with very young children, in view of the effect of each new arrival on the family budget. At a time of inflation, the family's economic need is particularly pressing.

In Britain, family allowances, tax benefits and preferential housing allocations are all designed to ease the cost of dependent children. However, this financial help is too limited in relation to actual expenditure. It fails to accept that child-rearing is both a vital and demanding job which deserves adequate remuneration. Its unique contribution to the community should be recognised, which would also help to raise its status. In fact, until adequate financial support for child-rearing becomes available to all mothers as of right, women's true preferences in relation to caring for their very young children themselves or accepting full-time paid employment cannot be known.

In America, mothers whose husbands have the lowest incomes were most likely to work and this held true whatever their educational level. The only exceptions were mothers who did not complete high school. This may be because their lack of schooling possibly prevented them from qualifying for jobs that would bring sufficient incomes to outweigh the expenses of child care and going to work. On the other hand, the highest proportion of working mothers was found among single parents. Almost three-quarters of those with school-age children and some 56 per cent of mothers with those aged under six years were employed outside the home, over 80 per cent working on a full-time basis.

'Nearly 30 per cent of America's youngest children live in families whose ability to rear them is severely crippled by the lack of money. At least another 5 per cent of all pre-school children have parents who have slightly higher income levels only by spending so much time and energy in work outside the home that the children are deprived of vital human attention from their parents – a response to economic pressure that may be as harmful to children as low income. ... Policies that provide minimal levels and security of income may improve the chances that a two-parent family will remain a suitably warm and nurturing environment for children. ... The Committee concludes therefore, that an essential component of social policy to enhance child development – a necessary though not sufficient condition – is to ensure that every American family has an income sufficient to enable parents to provide the basic necessities for their children. ... To date relatively little of the redistributed cash benefits have gone to working, poor families with children. Such families have benefitted from educational programs and school lunch programs but these are among the least rapidly growing of the social welfare programs. In other words, while redistribution has been practised on a large and growing scale, the groups towards which it is directed exclude millions of children in poor and near poor families, leaving them drastically disadvantaged in pursuing the opportunities available in our society. .... If the family — the front-line institution in child development — is not enabled to use all its considerable strength, the task of raising children is too big and too difficult for any forces outside the family to cope with.' (*Toward a National Policy for Children and Families*, National Academy of Sciences, Washington DC, 1976). Meanwhile the 'Aid to families with dependent children' program is a major component of the policy of economic assistance to children of the poor. Food stamps and the 'Women's, Infants' and Children's Special Nutrition Program' provide additional ways of attempting to supply the necessities of life to all children (*Early Child Care in the USA*, Robinson, H. B., *et al*, 1973).

There is little doubt that many mothers enjoy caring for their infants, finding it an emotionally satisfying and enjoyable task. And why not? Surely it is more varied and creative than the type of work available to the vast majority of women (and men for that matter too). Yet the demotion of mothering and home-making, the social isolation arising from urban re-housing and, all too often, sheer economic necessity, have persuaded many a woman to seek as a desirable alternative the heavy burden of two roles, worker and home-maker.

In an increasingly materialistic society, where salary levels are important status symbols and where not to be 'unionised' means remaining at the bottom of the heap, the home-maker has lost out even more than before. How much this is so is evident, for example, from the extremely small child benefits now being introduced in the UK (though they will at last be paid also for the first-born child); and the fact that they have never been linked with increases in the cost of living. Thus they lag far behind increases in other benefits, such as old age pensions, which have been increased much more frequently, so as to take account of inflation. The low priority given to children by society is reflected in both the low level of benefits and the failure to link them to the cost of living.

Recognising the value of mothering

Mothering should be recognised as the important, skilled and demanding job it is. (Incidentally, it is almost the only responsible job in our society which everyone is thought capable of undertaking without preparation or inclination). Adequate financial reward should be provided so that no mother of children of under five has to go out to work for financial reasons. Husbands should have to acknowledge the value of looking after young families by sharing their incomes with their wives as of right. Also, the state should pay a salary to mothers, whether married or single. This is already done in France and Hungary, the amount being related to the pay of trained teachers and being highest for infants under three years. In Sweden, either parent may take seven months' leave on full pay after the birth of a child and about 6 per cent of fathers do so now. It is proposed to extend the period by a further five months. The longer term aim is that children should be able to spend the first three years at home with one or other parent.

It has been argued that the view that very young children require full-time mothers is merely an ideological basis for the discouragement of day-care services. Might it not make more sense to turn this thesis on its head and ask: what are the ideological reasons prompting those who argue for vastly increased group care for the very young when countries such as Russia and Hungary who introduced such care are now reversing this very policy?

There would appear to be at least four reasons for this reversal. First, group care is considered to be a very costly provision especially if it is to be of good quality. Second, it is no longer regarded as being beneficial to children's emotional or intellectual development. For the under-threes at least, it is thought to be much better to be cared for by one and the same person, either their own mother or by what the Swedes call 'day mothers', a more accurately descriptive term than child-minders which implicitly devalues the importance and scope of the job.

Third, most mothers were found to prefer looking after their very young children themselves when given financial support to do so. Fourth, it was hoped that the falling birth rate might be arrested, or even take an upward trend, if mothers were paid a salary to enable them to remain at home. This did in fact happen. For example, a programme of child care aid was introduced in Hungary in 1966 under which mothers received the equivalent of half the starting salary of a teacher for three years for each child (and double this amount for twins); within three years, the birth rate was beginning to show an upward trend.

In the United States, the Advisory Committee on Child Development of the Department of Health, Education and Welfare, came to not dissimilar conclusions in their recently published report (*Toward a National Policy for Children and Families*, National Academy of Sciences, 1976). The Committee concluded that 'existing scientific knowledge about the fundamental processes of child development, along with evidence of existing needs of families and children, provides a sound basis for describing the elements of an adequate system of child care services.' Basic to such a system is, in the Committee's view, 'a guaranteed minimum income system to ensure that all families have sufficient income for one or the only parent to choose not to work outside the home, without sacrifice to family or children.' This conclusion in turn led the Committee to make four recommendations about child care, summarised in what follows.

'Parents should have the option, first and foremost, of raising their children at home, without sacrificing a reasonable standard of living. For those families designated as "high risk", this will require a substantial program of family income support.

'For those families who, out of necessity or preference, elect some form of substitute care, a range of alternatives should be available. These should include in-home care, family day care, center-based day care programs, and pre-kindergarten and nursery schools. The programs should be available free or at costs that do not require the sacrifice of other essential goods and services.

'Mechanisms should be established to ensure that alternative care arrangements meet minimum federal and state standards based on research findings of the effects of daytime care and on experience in the administration of such programs. These standards include continuity of care, a high ratio of adults to children, cleanliness and nutritional adequacy, safety, health services and a stimulating environment.

'Parents should have sufficient information regarding available alternatives in child care services to enable them to make reasonable choices and to shift from one alternative to another as their needs or preferences change.'

There is a need for wide-ranging and long-term cost-benefit studies of the respective advantages of paying a salary to mothers on the one hand, or, on the other hand, encouraging women to work full-time, while providing good quality child-care facilities. These might well confirm the Russian and Hungarian view that 'upgrading' the status of mothering is the more cost-effective alternative in more senses than one.

Once children go to school, women who want to return to paid employment need to be provided with three facilites: child-rearing experience to be recognised as having enhanced – or at least not retarded – their career prospects where it is relevant to the career in question; training opportunities or refresher courses; and shorter, more flexible working hours so that mothers (or fathers for that matter) can see their children off to school and be home when they return, as well as unpaid leave during their holiday periods and sickness.

Two even more radical options are available to all couples. The first is to choose childlessness. There is evidence of a continuing trend towards smaller families and towards deferred but compressed fertility (i.e. child-bearing starting later in marriage but ending earlier). Thus the decision to have, say, two children and not to resume full-time work until both are attending school means that the mother devotes between six and ten years (depending on the spacing of the children) to their care, leaving some thirty years for paid employment. Despite this, some women will feel that even six years of home-making and child-rearing are an unjustified imposition on their personal independence and individual fulfilment, or an unacceptable interruption of their professional career. For them, would it not be a more realistic option to resolve not to have a family at all?

The second option would be to translate into reality that parenting should be a shared task. To make it truly so would mean rotating the home-making role, each parent in turn undertaking it for, say, a three- or four-year period. The mother would probably opt for the child's early care, to consolidate the initial bond created at birth. Many occupations lend themselves quite readily to such interchangeability: work in shops, factories and offices; jobs in transport, whether driving or conducting; work in the catering and hotel industry; appointments in teaching, social work, nursing, medicine and the law — to name just a few. Indeed, in many of these professions, newly trained workers rarely stay as long as four years in their first jobs.

Those who opt for a lifestyle of shared parenthood may well establish a more durable and satisfying union because the greater interweaving of experiences, both inside and outside the home, should foster better mutual understanding. The children would benefit too since they would get to know their fathers on a day-to-day basis, rather than only in the evenings and at weekends. Such radical changes in family relationships and sex roles would seem to fit in with other social trends in contemporary Western thinking: the questioning of the 'rat race' and of the dogma of economic growth as the overriding objectives; as well as the acceptance that personal relationships, rather than material possessions, are more likely to bring contentment and a sense of fulfilment.

The impact of very early life experiences on development

Doria Pilling's review of the recent literature on this topic tends to confirm my view that the attention and emphasis now being given to the earliest years, indeed months, of life, are entirely justified. This is because early childhood experiences have long-lasting effects which are difficult to alter subsequently. Of course, this does not mean that those occurring later in a child's life may not also have marked or lasting consequences for later development.

The interaction between mother and infant satisfies primarily his basic physical and psychological needs. It has to be a two-way process, since it is the one-to-one relationship and its continuing and reciprocal nature which promote maximal learning and progress. It mediates between the

9

child and the outside world, providing a buffer, a filter and a bridge. It fulfils the irreplaceable function of laying the basis for the adjustment of the individual within society. Thus the capacity for integration, co-operation and creativity has its roots in family living.

'Early experience' means in fact from birth onwards. Equally early is the interaction between nature and nurture, and of the mother's attitudes and handling of the child on the one hand, and the baby's reactions and responsiveness on the other. Moreover, there are marked individual differences in the extent and pace of children's intellectual, educational, emotional and social development, just as there are of physical development. In my view, therefore, it follows that methods of child-rearing must take individual differences more into account than hitherto. It is the quality of parents' understanding – often intuitive, rarely fully explicit – which can best guide them in the upbringing of a particular child. From a general knowledge of the principles of child-rearing, parents need to fashion a method 'tailor-made' for each particular child at each particular stage of his development and suited to his particular environment.

Secondly, if each child in a family is to be treated appropriately, it is never possible to treat two children alike. Moreover, a given family is not psychologically the same for each child: partly because the family constellation is different in respect of each member of the family; for example, in respect of the parents' age and the child's position in the family; and partly because of the interaction between the parents' personalities and that of the child.

Thirdly, allowance should be made for the fact that just as physical endowment ranges from the resilient to the delicate, so children differ genetically in their intellectual and emotional constitution and susceptibility to stress. Nevertheless, environmental influences also come into play at birth and in some respects from conception onwards and have potentially a far greater effect than has been generally realised.

Shared care

In introducing this topic, Doria Pilling comments that 'despite continuing controversy on whether care of the child can be safely or even beneficially shared between the mother and other adults, there is a surprising lack of research evidence'. Then she concentrates on reviewing available literature on the effects of various types of substitute care, in particular day-care centres and nursery schools. The vast majority of studies quoted relate to mothers who are in part- or full-time employment outside the home. Again and again, two factors become clear: first, that the evidence is both thin and inconclusive; and second, that it is often contradictory. Moreover, in many studies carried out in the UK, samples have been relatively small.

The position is very similar regarding conclusions which can be drawn from American investigations. Reviewing *Research on the Effects of Day Care on Child Development*, Bronfenbrenner comments in relation to the effects on intellectual development as follows: 'First, the results are based on only a few studies. Second, the day care centres represented are small in number and of high quality. Third, and most serious, the available data on possible long-range effects are limited to a single study with the single measure (IQ) based on a sample of only eleven pairs of children and providing information only through the fifth year of life. ... Given these uncertainties, no firm conclusions can be drawn about the impact of day versus home care on the cognitive development of children. All that can be said is that the existing evidence does not justify claims for the superiority of one setting over another insofar as intellectual growth during the pre-school years is concerned.' (in: *Toward a National Policy for Children and Families*, National Academy of Sciences, 1976.)

On the issue of day care and attachment, Bronfenbrenner concludes in the same article that 'Paradoxically, the evidence on the effects of day care is least conclusive with respect to attachment behaviour – the issue of greatest initial concern and the one to which most attention has been given in research. ... Prudence dictates that the possibility of negative emotional consequences of extended group care for children under three years of age be considered in public policy and practice and that programs be designed to foster the development of stable emotional relationships between children and their principal care takers.'

Thirdly, summarising the effects on motivation and social behaviour, Bronfenbrenner concludes that 'the most clear and consistent differences between home-reared children and those receiving day care appear in motivation and social behaviour in group settings. ... Studies show that, depending on the goals and methods involved, group upbringing can lead to a variety of consequences, ranging from delinquency and violence at one extreme to unquestioning conformity at the other. The existing research suggests that peer groups in the United States while far from either pole, are closer to the former than the latter end of the continuum. It is of interest that in contrast with American specialists, professionals and parents in the Soviet Union and in Sweden, two countries in which full-day group care facilities are widespread, have expressed concern about possibly deleterious effects of extended care. In the light of these findings, a re-examination of current American practices in group day care is clearly indicated.'

One conclusion does, nevertheless, seem justified from UK and US research, namely that it is the quality of substitute care as well as its stability which are of crucial importance. However, too little attention is

11

being given to what the cost of ensuring the necessary high quality would be. It must include providing a far higher staff-child ratio than is currently available in group care settings and a more realistic salary scale for those who staff them; as well as training for child-minders, who care for other people's children in their own homes, together with adequate remuneration so that these jobs become attractive alternatives to other employment. Thus the additional finance required would be very considerable. Even then, stability and hence continuity for substitute day care would not be easily assured.

With regard to children growing up in the Israeli kibbutz, it is generally conceded that this is the only Western child-rearing pattern where upbringing is truly shared from the earliest months of life, between the child's parents and professional educators, the latter undertaking the major part of the daily care, training, teaching and disciplining. This means that the parents' role is different but in terms of the sheer time spent with the child, it is probably greater than is normally the case in Western societies. Parental concern and involvement remain paramount; the choice of the caring personnel, as well as the pattern of care, are decided and supervised by the parents themselves. Each child spends three or more hours daily with his parents who during this time are free to devote their whole attention to playing with, talking to and enjoying their children. This is very different from the kind of half-attention usually given for part of or throughout the day in our society to pre-school children by mothers who are unavoidably busy with cleaning, shopping and cooking. Thus it is a very specific way of dividing the parental role which is unique in developed societies.

More recent evidence available to me (personal communication) indicates that there is now a gradual return to more traditional family life in a growing minority of cases. In over 25 per cent of kibbutzim, the children not only sleep in their parents' home but also take at least one meal with them there; this continues until the age of seven — the start of compulsory schooling — and often later. This trend is on the increase as is the tendency for young kibbutz-reared women to prefer looking after their children and family themselves, rather than undertaking other work in the kibbutz. However, it must be remembered that only a tiny minority (about 3 per cent) of the Israeli population live in kibbutzim.

With regard to the presence or absence of brothers and sisters, no major new evidence has emerged. Hence the effects of family size on the social and educational development of children are clear and unequivocal, namely that the dice are loaded in favour of the first-born. The findings from the Bureau's National Child Development Study show that even at birth family size begins to exert an influence, higher perinatal mortality being associated with high parity. The overall picture clearly indicates that by the time they are seven or eight years old, children from large families are at a considerable disadvantage physically, educationally and in social adjustment. These effects are found to operate irrespective of social class.

The father's role in the family

Pilling's review demonstrates the relative scarcity of investigations into the father's role in the child's development compared with that of the mother's. Furthermore it is not as yet possible to answer specific questions about exactly how and when the father's influence makes itself felt. Thus there is a need for more research as well as for improvements in methodology and conceptualisation.

Pilling comments as follows:

'Overall, research findings using different approaches are consistent enough to justify the conclusion that the father has a direct influence – in addition to his indirect influence, as the mother's economic and emotional support – on the child's development, probably from the earliest years. ... Insufficient longitudinal data and a number of studies with subjects of one sex only, leave much in doubt though about the timing of the influences exerted by the father's behaviour and the apparently differential effect on the sexes.'

My belief is that the father's part in fostering the child's development is to provide the child with a second adult model so that a boy can identify with a member of his own sex, and a girl can also learn at first hand about the behaviour and attitudes of the opposite sex. Secondly, better progress appears to be made when praise and recognition come not only from the mother but also from another person, preferably of the opposite sex.

There is a third likelihood for which there is not yet research evidence: the mother herself probably receives reassurance from her husband's support so that he 'reinforces' not only the child's but her own feelings of adequacy and self-esteem; this, in turn, increases her confidence in her mothering which communicates itself to the child. The same may well be true in relation to the mother, conveying both to father and child the value of the paternal role.

With regard to the father's absence, in the light of the research review which follows in this book, Pilling states that:

'On the whole, the studies of father absence suggest that lack of a father-child relationship has relatively little effect on the child's cognitive, emotional and social development when the material deprivations of father absence have been taken into account. ... However, there remain some adverse effects of father absence for which the most plausible explanation does appear to be the lack of father-child relationship itself. The greater effect of father absence on the educational attainment of boys than of girls, and the difficulties experienced in opposite sex relationships by girls whose fathers have died, as well as those whose fathers have left the family, are examples.'

Perhaps at this stage of research into the paternal role, it can only be concluded that insufficient is as yet known. My own inclination would be to attach rather more significance to the absence of a father but I accept that the evidence is somewhat inconclusive. More and better research is required, especially of a longitudinal kind, to elucidate the father's influence on his children's development and the specific nature of the ill-effects of his prolonged absence from the family. Meanwhile, as Pilling argues:

'Most essential is the acknowledgement that the father needs opportunities to develop a continuing and sympathetic relationship with the child. The evidence from research gives some indication that an affectionate but hardly-ever-at-home father is insufficient for the development of good adjustment, particularly for boys.'

Conclusion

Eventually, when research has succeeded in establishing the impact of very early life experiences on development; when a sufficient number of varied pre-school settings – both in institutions providing group care and in substitute family day care – have been monitored and evaluated to indicate to what extent they can succeed in complementing and supplementing parental care for children and at what ages; and when the father's influence on child development has been more clearly delineated, both within the current prevalent family structure and in homes where he is truly sharing the child's care with his wife – then, and only then, will it be possible for women, couples, local authorities and central government to make with greater assurance the necessary decisions which will affect children's development and well-being for at least a generation to come. For individuals, they are decisions about their personal life-style. For government, central and local, they are decisions about supporting the family so as to make possible the optimal care of children; and determining the best – or perhaps more realistically, the least detrimental – type of care and educational provision for those under-fives whom it is necessary to compensate for parental care which is to some extent inadequate.

The role of education, and of teachers, in enhancing pupils' life chances

The past quarter of a century has seen what might almost be called a transformation of Britain's education system. It was a period of high hopes and expectations. Education was seen to be the way through which to achieve a more egalitarian, socially less divisive and open society in which merit and not wealth would determine children's life and career chances. It was sparked off by the 1944 Education Act which replaced the previous elementary school system with a new pattern of primary schooling; provided free and reorganised secondary education for all and made available grammar school places on grounds of ability rather than parental income, as had largely continued to be the case before.

The building of schools proceeded apace to accommodate the steeply rising number of pupils caused by the 'baby boom' of the immediate post-war years. Whereas the total school population in England and Wales had been about six million in 1952, it had risen to over nine million by the end of 1976. During this period the number of teachers doubled, not only in order to deal with this increase but also in the hope of reducing the size of classes and to enable the school leaving age to be raised. These aims materialised albeit at a slower rate than envisaged; the statutory leaving age became fifteen in 1955 and sixteen years in 1974.

During this twenty-five-year span, secondary education underwent two major reorganisations. These were brought about by the decision to abolish the examination held at eleven years for the purpose of selecting those pupils able to follow an academic education; and instead to make comprehensive education the general pattern across the country. Teacher training also experienced wide-ranging changes. First, the two-year, non-graduate training course was lengthened by one year; second, a vast expansion of training was decreed by central government, to be reversed by an equally drastic cut-back in facilities by the end of this period; then it was also decided to change the nature of the great majority of colleges of education by converting them into institutes of higher education which would cater for a broader range of professional training. If, as some claim, standards of teacher training have fallen, is it not likely that a succession of sudden major policy changes, with consequent repercussions on staffing and morale, must bear a large share of the responsibility for it?

The proportionately even greater expansion of further and higher education in the 1960s led to something like a seven-fold increase in the places available to young people in universities, polytechnics, teacher training and other further education colleges. Then disenchantment began to set in, born perhaps of disappointed hopes, which had been unrealistically high; perhaps in part a reflection of the general climate of the times which questioned and indeed resented authority; which was growing suspicious of intellectual excellence, partly because it was viewed as an aspect of unfashionable elitism and partly because scientific advances were being seen as a much more mixed blessing than had

15

hitherto been the case. No doubt many other strands contributed to this mood of disillusion which showed itself in such unexpected phenomena as unfilled university places for which previously there had been fierce competition. Also in the mid-sixties the birth rate was slowing down, leading to what is now somewhat over-dramatically called 'the birth dearth'. Coinciding with an increasingly severe economic recession, 1976 saw Education faced with cuts so savage as to have been unimaginable even five years ago.

In the United States remarkably similar trends can be discerned in the role of education and public attitudes towards it. In an historical overview entitled *America's Unsystematic Education System*, Graham comments: 'The American "system of education" is an organisational nightmare but a functional triumph. It nearly defies explanation as a coherent enterprise but persons regularly emerge from their encounters with it more knowledgeable than when they entered it. If it is to be judged on the educational attainments of the entire American public, then its success is real. However, few American institutions have suffered as much criticism, particularly in the last twenty-four years, as have those concerned with education. The paradox of functional success but massive criticism raises perplexing questions about this enigmatic enterprise.' (*200 Years of Children*, US Department of Health, Education and Welfare, 1976.)

The author argues that the most serious problem faced by the educational system is the gap between public expectations of it and its performance so that it has remained 'the imperfect panacea'. These expectations have been both academic and social. Too often the latter have been so overwhelming that schools have been unable to cope successfully with the academic expectations. During the early fifties in particular vociferous demands were made for more rigorous academic programmes even though expectations continued that the educational system should bring about greater justice, affluence and personal fulfilment. Nevertheless such characteristics as race, class and sex, as well as less tangible influences such as motivation and teacher expectations continued to affect academic success and intellectual development.

Graham summarises the position thus: 'Over thirty years ago, George S. Counts asked "dare the schools build a new social order?" He had hoped for an affirmative answer but the reply then and now is negative. ... Statistically children from middle class homes are over-represented in the college population in the United States and this is particularly true of male children from middle-class homes. Thus whereas women currently constitute more than 50 per cent of the nation's population, they represent only a little more than 44 per cent of the undergraduate enrolment. Bright girls from economically depressed circumstances form the largest category of persons who might be expected to profit from college but who do not do so. The male-female discrepancy is even greater at the doctorate level, where women currently receive only about 18 per cent of the doctorates awarded annually. Until recently blacks did not attend college in anything like their proportion in the population, but in the last few years the undergraduate enrolment proportion has come closer to approximating their proportion of the population. They are still far behind at the doctorate level, however, receiving less than 1 per cent of the doctorates awarded annually, although they constitute over 11 per cent of the population.

'Although our educational system clearly has serious limitations as a vehicle for social mobility, it is noteworthy that the most prestigious universities in this country have not limited their enrolments particularly at the graduate level, to children of the upper middle class. ... One of the most persistent tensions in school systems has been that between parents of school children and the policy makers of the schools, whoever they have been. Generally parents have played a rather small role in setting priorities for the schools, and when the schools did not seem to be educating their children satisfactorily, they have complained. Such parental dissatisfaction was evident during the 1950s in the denunciation of progressive education by the Council for Basic Education, a group that included many parents who were not educators. More recently the school decentralisation controversy in New York City has been marked by vivid complaints from some parents that the centrally controlled schools were not responsive to the needs of their children.

'Dissatisfaction with the schools is endemic. Ever since there have been schools there has been criticism of them. It comes from parents who blame the schools for the inadequacies they find in their own children. It comes from employers who find their employees ill-prepared (somehow young people are always better prepared a generation ago when the employer was young). It comes from teachers who find their students unco-operative (again, a generation ago, when the teachers were young the students were better). And it comes from the students who find the schools dull (as students always have).

'With the American educational system – as with most systems – the halcyon days always seem to be in the past. Its contemporary triumphs are often obscure, particularly to persons currently struggling with it. Since education has become so widespread in America today – and that, of course is one of its principal accomplishments – higher proportions of Americans are directly concerned with how it fares. Many of them believe the past to be preferable to the present; what survives from the past tends to be the successes of the past, not the failures. What troubles us in the present are our difficulties, not our achievements. It is to our credit that we are dissatisfied with the present, then our future may be even better.'

Both in Britain and the USA gradual disenchantment about the role and value of education has been accompanied by an increasingly vocal lobby criticising the level of educational standards. At its most extreme, this lobby claims that they have now declined even among the most highly educated minority, including university graduates. That some standards have risen in Britain is beyond doubt. For example, the proportion of the age group obtaining a first degree has increased about fourfold; and there has been an even greater increase in the proportion of pupils who successfully take some examinations before leaving school. A more widely held criticism is directed against what are claimed to be the deteriorated scholastic attainments of the minority of pupils who do not manage any examination successes nor even achieve full mastery in the basic subjects of reading, writing and arithmetic.

Whether or not standards in the three 'Rs' have fallen is in fact a longstanding controversy informed by more heat than light. There is no reliable research evidence to make a sound judgement; nor does a dependable baseline exist from which a start could now be made. Indeed, the complaints that standards are 'low', 'falling', or 'not high enough' have been voiced for at least a hundred years though perhaps more loudly during the past twenty-five. For example, the 1952 Annual Report of the then Ministry of Education in Britain stated: 'The misgivings most often voiced during the year concerned standards and attainments in the three "Rs", especially reading and writing'.

In the United States, knowledge about the trends in the educational achievement of pupils seems to be similarly lacking. Thus the authors of a wide-ranging review of available data concluded that it is 'nearly impossible to obtain definitive evidence regarding such a simple question as: "are children reading better or worse now than ten or twenty years ago?" Though one can easily find cabinets full of test scores in virtually every school system in this country, these sources generally turn out to contain little information relevant to the issue of the longitudinal monitoring of performance.' (*Reading Achievement in the United States: Then and Now*, Farr *et al.*, 1974; a report prepared for the Office of Education.)

In Britain, some argue that it reflects a signal failure of the education system that despite the great investment of recent years and the undoubted expansion in terms of manpower and financial resources, some young people continue to emerge from eleven years schooling almost illiterate. On the other hand, it can be argued that this is not unexpected since the investment has been relatively smallest in the primary sector and virtually non-existent for the pre-school stage.

Yet it is during the early years of schooling that the foundations are laid for the mastery of the basic tools of learning. Nor is it only a question of priorities regarding the age group to which the greatest resources are devoted. Prestige and status are likely to be involved too. It remains as true as ever that the most intellectually promising university students are expected to teach older pupils on the (usually tacit) assumption that the younger the child the less need to have able, highly trained teachers. It is also paradoxical that classes become smaller the older the pupils when it is the youngest who require the greatest amount of individual attention. Also the total capitation allowance (for books and equipment) for each child during the junior school stage in 1977 was in the region of £10.26 per annum, compared with the annual allowance for secondary pupils of £20.42.

Inflated and probably unrealistic expectations of what schools might be able to do to improve the quality and prosperity of society have led to a backlash of disappointment. In particular, they have prompted a search for factors which might explain the continued educational shortcomings of pupils from socially disadvantaged home backgrounds. Singled out for scape-goating have been so-called 'progressive' or 'child centred' (as against 'subject centred') teaching methods; the imposition of middle-class aims and values on working-class children; and teachers' attitudes towards and beliefs about the abilities of disadvantaged pupils.

These three issues have been hotly debated for the past fifteen years and attitudes about them have to some extent become identified with left- and right-wing ideologies. Any research findings which lend support to either side are not only accorded wide publicity but they also prompt further research designed to refute or confirm its validity. The work of Basil Bernstein in Britain on the sociology of language in the early 1960s; Rosenthal and Jacobson in the US on teacher expectation and pupils' intellectual development in the late 1960s; and Neville Bennett's in Britain on teaching style and scholastic progress in the mid 1970s, are examples of this.

Because *Pygmalion in the Classroom* (Rosenthal and Jacobson) aroused so much hostility as well as a spate of research on teachers' expectations, we decided that the time was ripe for a critical look at the current state of the evidence.

Teachers' expectations and pupil performance

I have argued in *The Needs of Children*, 1974 that:

'The child's progress will come to be powerfully affected by his teachers' attitudes, values and beliefs; some of these will be overt and deliberate; others may be implicit and incidental; still others may well be unconscious but just as powerful in influencing his learning. ... Teachers have an unrivalled opportunity not only to establish a favourable attitude to learning in general and scholastic progress in particular; but also, where necessary, to improve or entirely rebuild

19

the foundation of a child's self-esteem and hence his attitude to learning.

'To succeed in this, a teacher has to act on the assumption that every pupil possesses an as yet unrealised potential for development; that an appropriate "diet" can succeed in improving intellectual or emotional "under-nourishment"; and that rather than accepting previous assessments or test results or even the parents' judgement of the child's abilities, the teacher should try to "beat prediction" even though he may not always succeed. ... Such a positive and optimistic attitude communicates itself very readily.'

Then I quoted five recently completed studies to document these views. Their findings seemed to me to underline 'the truth of the saying "give a dog a bad name"; labelling a child "slow" (or "bright") becomes a self-fulfilling prophecy. And this is as powerful in affecting the teacher (and parent) as it is in affecting how the child feels about himself, whether he thinks he is stupid or capable, and how hard he tries; self-confidence and motivation are fostered or extinguished by the way teachers think about and treat their charges.'

One of these studies – that of Rosenthal and Jacobson, 1968 – was the first to claim that it provided measurable experimental evidence to show that teachers' attitudes and beliefs about the level of their pupils' ability affected their actual attainments. This report led to prolonged and passionate controversy, primarily because of the implication that teachers might be responsible to some extent – however unintentionally – for the poor scholastic performance of socially and culturally disadvantaged children.

In reviewing the literature, Pilling paid special attention to those researchers who had attacked Rosenthal and Jacobson's work. She was forced to conclude that 'it is unfortunate that the methodological criticisms of a study with such important practical implications appear to be justified. ... The basic weakness lies in the difficulty in attempting to alter teachers' expectations for the children in their classes.'

However, when evaluating the findings from many other investigations, Pilling is able to state that:

'Taken as a whole, a considerable amount of evidence that teachers' expectations do influence their behaviour and the pupils' actual achievements is accumulating. ... The exact way in which teacher behaviour is affected, though, needs further investigation in studies in actual classroom situations. The extent to which teachers' behaviour is differentiated may well be affected by the social class composition of the school population, by school organisation and by the philosophy and attitudes of both the school and the individual teacher. This too requires investigation.'

Pilling concludes that:

'The implications of this research for educational policy cannot be doubted. Teachers must be made aware of the non-intellectual factors which may bias their judgements of a child; of possible differences in their behaviour towards those for whom they have different expectations; and of their power to influence children's attainments.'

Conclusion

In a time of uncertainty when not only authority and the establishment are under attack but when moral and social values are also being questioned, it is inevitable that the role of education and of teachers should similarly be subjected to criticisms. Doubts and dissatisfaction in the face of an economic crisis are liable to lead to a search for scapegoats. A public service which affects every member of the public in one way or another is particularly vulnerable when there is no agreement on what its aims should be. Nor is such agreement likely between those who wish education to maintain the *status quo*; those who see it as an agent for social change; and those who believe education to be mainly concerned with the fullest development of each child's emotional, social, creative and intellectual potential.

The present renewed search for better quality, higher standards and nationally accepted methods for assessing them do not necessarily conflict with those three broad aims. However, the danger is an over-emphasis of what can be measured just because it is measurable, i.e. levels of attainments rather than personal maturity.

Moreover, comparisons with standards of even only twenty or thirty years ago are not valid for a number of reasons. Chief among them are that, as assessment techniques have become more sophisticated, a direct comparison is not possible when different tests and measurements are now being used; that greater demands are being made on schools because society has become more complex technologically; and that expectations of what the schools can achieve have by now grown unrealistically high.

There is always room for improvement – a truism with which most teachers would agree. But it is perhaps reassuring that a British national survey in 1974 of school-leavers – the first group who had to remain at school till the age of sixteen – found that the great majority (and their parents) were satisfied with the education they had received (*Britain's Sixteen-Year-Olds*, ed. K. Fogelman, 1976).

Disadvantage and intervention

In the following pages I comment, in the light of Pilling's review of the

21

literature on aspects of disadvantage, with specific reference to the 'nature and nurture' controversy, cultural and linguistic disadvantage, and the possibility of successful intervention.

There is no generally accepted definition of 'disadvantage'. Like the concept of 'poverty', it is relative and thus changes with changing economic and social conditions. In the National Childrens Bureau's study *Born to Fail*? (P. Wedge and H. Prosser, 1973), four factors were chosen as being of fundamental relevance to social disadvantage: family size, i.e. five or more children; only one parent figure; low income; and poor housing. Applying these four criteria together, one child in sixteen, or 6 per cent of all children in Britain were found to be socially disadvantaged in 1969. Common sense would lead one to expect, and research evidence confirms, that children growing up in disadvantaged homes thus defined are much more likely than those from ordinary families to have developmental, including educational, difficulties. In fact over half of them were backward in reading and a very similar proportion were behind in arithmetic. However about a third had average attainment in these subjects and a small minority – just under 10 per cent – were doing better than that.

From the point of view of intervention, and particularly early prevention, it would be invaluable if it were possible to predict which children are likely to fall behind; then scarce resources could be concentrated on them. So far no one has isolated the relevant predictors. Until this becomes possible, one must regard all children from socially disadvantaged homes as being potentially 'at risk' of becoming educationally backward; the same is true for first-generation immigrant children, for those growing up in institutional care, and for children who have been abused.

The debate continues between those who argue that everyone must be given an equal educational opportunity and those who advocate that special attention ought to be devoted to the abler child. The former advocate positive discrimination in favour of the disadvantaged child; whereas the latter argue that a country's survival in a scientific and technological age depends on the fostering of excellence.

The conflict is more apparent than real. It springs from the mistaken belief that all men are equal despite their enormous differences in physical and intellectual potential. Every child has a right to equality of opportunity. To expect equal capacity to make use of it runs counter to common sense and experience, and has harmful consequences because such expectation is likely to engender a sense of failure.

Instead we must act as if all children were equal and then respect, as well as accept and cater for, their differences. This means giving recognition to and developing all the different abilities and talents a child may have, which must include positive discrimination in favour of the handicapped and the disadvantaged. Within such a framework, it is legitimate both to provide a democracy of opportunity while at the same time to strive for excellence so as to ensure an aristocracy of achievement.

Intellectual and educational disadvantage

The relative contribution made to intellectual development by the genes and the environment respectively has for long been debated, with greater or lesser heat. It has once again become a topical controversy. However, it differs in two ways from that which raged in the 1930s. On the one hand, no one any longer denies that environment plays a part in shaping a child's intelligence, even if it is believed that heredity has the much greater influence. On the other hand, the pure environmentalist has been discredited too. More explicit racial overtones have now been added to the previous political implications. This has increased the bitterness of the argument since it polarises political divisions and consequent educational and social planning.

Although a belief in the interaction of heredity and environment is the generally accepted standpoint, available research findings allow a wide range of possible interpretations. The debate about measuring the relative influence of the two is likely to remain rather sterile, since it is doubtful whether conclusive evidence will ever be provided. The situation is only too familiar to the farmer: to obtain a good crop of wheat, he needs not only good seed but also good soil and appropriate moisture, temperature and fertiliser, to nourish its growth. All these can be controlled and varied in experimental ways which are at present not acceptable in relation to human beings.

A related issue concerns the reliability and usefulness of intelligence tests. The credibility of most educational testing – whether of aptitude, attainment or intelligence – depends largely on a tautology. The validity of the tests is demonstrated by their ability to predict performance at school; yet such performance amounts to an ability to perform well on tasks similar to those in the tests. This has led to the false assumption that doing well in tests necessarily means a greater competence in coping with life in general.

The solution is not – as some would have it – simply to abandon testing; if for no other reason than that subjective judgements are considerably less reliable. Three changes are required: first, the search for innate factors such as intelligence should be abandoned, to be replaced by measuring instead improvement resulting from new experiences and from deliberate teaching. Second, currently used items, consisting of artificial word and number games, should be replaced by issues and problems occurring in everyday social and occupational life. Third, rate of progress over time should become the yardstick for learning potential instead of the static concept of the IQ.

Genetic-environmental interaction starts in utero and hence 'pure' inborn abilities and characteristics can never be assessed. For example, the development of the nervous system in the foetus and newborn is affected during pregnancy and parturition by adverse conditions, e.g. malnutrition, drugs, exposure to certain diseases, heavy manual work or extreme anxiety. Thus a child may be born with a brain which is incapable of normal development, not because of defective genes but because of pre-natal conditions or birth injury. On the other hand, inborn temperamental differences inevitably affect the environment; for example, a hypersensitive, irritable baby is more likely than a placid one to call out irritability in his mother which in turn only serves to increase his own irritability.

Human capacity to learn is such that the newborn child can adapt to widely different environments. Since to begin with he has a rather limited range of innate behavioural mechanisms, this very limited capacity makes him entirely dependent on his environment; having only the potential for becoming human, he must needs have a human environment to do so. Hence for the purpose of social action and policy, the environment is of over-riding importance. All available evidence confirms that, from a practical viewpoint, the most important element in shaping behaviour and development is the environment in general and other people in particular. So this is where intervention — whether preventive or remedial — should be concentrated.

Cultural and linguistic disadvantage

It has been known for at least forty years that children growing up in unstimulating and deprived environments — whether these be their own homes or institutions — often have limited language skills. The most recent evidence from the National Child Development Study, which is being carried out in Britain by the National Children's Bureau, demonstrates that some handicapping effects begin before birth and affect subsequent physical, psychological and educational development. To start with, there is a relationship between family size and over-crowding: the larger the former, the worse the incidence of the latter is likely to be. The disadvantages of belonging to a large, low-income family are further magnified by the consequences of suffering from other associated shortcomings. Housing, play space, parental interest shown in the child's scholastic progress and the parents' own education — all these and many other circumstances are more frequently unfavourable in such homes.

The overall effect of social disadvantage, and hence readiness to respond to educational expectations, is already clearly evident at an early age. For example, after only two years of schooling, the chance of a seven year old being unable to read was found to be fifteen times greater for a child from an unskilled working-class home than from a professional home background; and the proportion of children from the former who would − in the opinion of their teachers − benefit from attending a special school was forty-five times larger than those from a professional home.

In relation to linguistic disadvantage, probably the single and in the long run most crucial factor which promotes intellectual growth is the quality of the child's speech environment, in particular how relevant, distinctive and rich the conversation is. The most essential element is the reciprocity of speech between child and adult, the latter initiating or responding to conversation. Hence the mere presence of adults or just listening to conversation (on TV, for example) is insufficient.

The sixties saw the birth of a new hypothesis, that language shapes not only thought but also (via various other processes) social class. The different language modes, characteristically used by middle and working-class people are held to initiate and then reinforce different patterns of behaviour and personality and hence to perpetuate the structure of society itself.

Research findings point to three conclusions. First, many children growing up in large families whose income is low are beset by multiple, interrelated and interacting disadvantages which have a detrimental effect on their physical, social and educational development. Second, these effects usually work in combination and are cumulative; hence, as the child grows older the gap widens between the most advantaged and most disadvantaged. Third, equality of opportunity cannot be brought about through changes in secondary or higher education. It is during the pre-school and early school years that ways must be sought to overcome or compensate for the consequences of environmental disadvantages on children's development. Limiting the initial gap is likely to be the most effective way.

Intervention

Pilling's review of recently reported intervention programmes reflects a cautious but not narrow view of intervention and she emphasises that much further experimentation and evaluation seem necessary. Nevertheless, she argues:

'It appears unlikely that even an optimal educational intervention programme can, on its own, be sufficient for the most disadvantaged children. ... Without attack also on the social inequalities that give rise to disadvantages throughout the children's school careers the effect on their lives is likely, in most cases, to be limited.'

25

In my view, while one must act in practice as if it were never too late to intervene, there can be little doubt of the validity of the popular saw 'prevention is better than cure'. Just as the foundation of a house is disproportionately more important because it is the foundation, so early experiences provide the vital basis for what follows. There is only too much evidence to show the relative ineffectiveness of later intervention to alter the consequences of early damaging experiences. Schools for the maladjusted, approved schools (now renamed community homes with education on the premises), borstals and the like, all have a dismally low rate of success.

In contrast, most early intervention programmes, both in the USA and the UK, resulted in children showing substantial developmental improvement. However, these then faded with the passage of time. The disenchantment which this has produced is as widespread as it is unreasonable. It is rather like expecting that a starved child who gains weight when temporarily provided with an enriched diet would not lose weight again when returned to the starvation diet. Similarly, the effects of early intervention programmes disappeared because they were discontinued after relatively short periods.

What is needed for disadvantaged, deprived and rejected children is a programme of early, comprehensive and continuing intervention; it must either involve their parents or, where they are no longer in the picture, then the provision and involvement of a substitute family. In the UK there have as yet been only three comparatively major programmes: the Educational Priority Areas, the Community Development Programme and the Inner Areas Study, all of which were primarily concerned with school-age children and adults.

Because attempts to reverse the effects of a deprived early environment have so far met with only limited success, policy makers and practitioners alike seem to have become afflicted by a mood of pessimism. This is both unjustified and premature. In the light of recent understanding of the nature of emotional, social and intellectual development it is unrealistic to expect that formal education could itself bring about the desired changes. Intervention programmes devised so far have been too short-term; and have had too narrow a framework, too late a start, too limited a methodology and insufficient theoretical knowledge about early learning. Most of them failed to involve the parents, whereas there is now some evidence that maternal participation can lead to substantial improvement.

Nevertheless, there are grounds for optimism regarding the possibility of recovery from and reversing the effects of even severe and early deprivation. Work with mentally subnormal patients over the past fifteen years has shown that some degree of recovery can be achieved even in adulthood. The second source of evidence comes from studies of children

26

who have suffered prolonged and extremely severe social isolation in early life. These suggest that considerable improvement, if not complete recovery, is possible, provided they undergo a carefully devised and prolonged programme of rehabilitation.

A third source for greater optimism lies in the adoption of more realistic expectations. The early US programmes on the whole were launched with too high hopes and are now being dismissed with similarly unwarranted disappointment. It was unrealistic to expect that providing some extra hours of schooling for a year or two could tip the scales against such powerful factors as poverty, ignorance, disease and despair, to which the children had been exposed for years and in which they continued to live. A real breakthrough will require a multi-pronged and sustained approach, including parental support and involvement.

Conclusion

Rarely, if ever, are either learning difficulties or problem behaviour due to one single circumstance. Since there are usually a multiplicity of unfavourable interrelated and interacting factors, simple or quick interventions are unlikely to succeed. It had been thought that rising standards of health and material prosperity would reduce the incidence of backwardness, maladjustment and delinquency. Now it has become evident that intellectual, linguistic and educational malfunctioning will not be solved by improvements in health and in standards of living alone. These make satisfactory family and community life more likely but they do not ensure it.

No one would question that it should be possible to bring about vast improvements in children's physical health and educational achievements. In relation to intelligence there is less agreement while in relation to social and emotional aspects outright scepticism still prevails. One reason for these doubts may be that much more is known about deficiencies and failure than about optimal or even normal growth. For example, there have been many studies of poor readers or of pupils who are generally backward. However, detailed understanding of how intellectual, language and reading skills are acquired is still very limited. Perhaps even more important, there is as yet little knowledge about what enables a child to develop normally despite an adverse cultural, emotional or social environment. Does the evidence that a substantial proportion succeed in overcoming unfavourable circumstances provide a signpost to future strategy?

This might have three strands. The first would be to promote studies which aim to discover what factors enable some children but not others to overcome complex and continuing patterns of disadvantage; second, to apply this knowledge to all children 'at risk'; and, third, to act

27

meanwhile on the reasonable assumption that intervention is likely to be more effective and less costly – in terms of personnel, time and techniques – not merely during the earliest years but the earliest weeks and months of life.

Reasons for omitting other controversial issues

When work on this literature review commenced, it soon became apparent that it would not be possible for it to cover all the areas and topics which *The Needs of Children* had dealt with. Therefore we decided to concentrate on those major issues of current concern which have considerable theoretical and methodological implications. They are important too from a policy and practice point of view yet the evidence available so far is by no means clear cut or unequivocal; also the research strategies employed are in many cases too 'laboratory-bound' and not sufficiently multi-dimensional to unravel the complexity of the questions under investigation. Some would argue that there is still a lack of sufficiently sophisticated or subtle research methodologies.

It might be thought that many other issues, not only similarly controversial but also major areas of current concern with important implications for policy and practice, should or could have been chosen. Chief among them are the following: children who have physical or mental handicaps; those who are seriously neglected or physically abused by their parents; children growing up in one-parent families; those who are living apart from their biological families in institutions or foster homes, or who are adopted; and the whole question of preparation for parenthood. Why were none of these included?

Constraints of time were one reason. But there were others. In the report *Living with Handicap* prepared and published by the National Children's Bureau in Britain in 1970, a very comprehensive look was taken at the needs of handicapped children and their families from birth to adulthood, by a working party composed of practising teachers, doctors and social workers, some of whom were also a parent of a handicapped child. The conclusions and recommendations contained in this book are as valid today as when they were first published some six years ago. Some of them have already been translated into reality. In addition, since 1968, the Bureau has carried out reviews of the literature relating to handicap which have so far resulted in some ten books; a further review to bring the early work up-to-date is due to start early in 1977.

The literature and current professional practice in relation to non-accidental injury both in Britain and the USA was also recently reviewed by the Bureau and published under the title of *The Abused Child* in 1976. Also, I have discussed policy issues, especially possible preventive measures, in recent articles (*Municipal Review*, No 563, November 1976; *Community Care*, 13 October 1976 and 9 November 1977).

One-parent families were the subject of a major UK government enquiry (the Finer Report) which published its findings in 1974. Two years later the Bureau produced the results of its own study of such families in two books entitled *Growing up in a One-Parent Family* and *Coping Alone*. The first is a major study of a national sample of children who have been brought up by single parents; the second, a comparative study, describes the experience of being a single mother or father. Taken together, these enquiries give an up-to-date picture of present problems and put forward practical policies which would go some way towards solving them.

With regard to substitute family care, the Bureau launched a series of research reviews which were published in three *Facts and Fallacies* books in 1966 and 1967. The first, on adoption, was brought up-to-date in 1973; the second, on residential care, was up-dated and published in 1976; and the third, on foster care, should be ready for publication in 1978. Now that the 1975 Children's Act is gradually being implemented in the UK, the long-term position of children living in institutional and foster home care is likely to change; it is to be hoped that the effects of these changes will be monitored from the start. In the United States, the Children's Bureau of the Department of Health, Education and Welfare has sponsored the preparation of the Model Act for freeing children for permanent placement; it has been widely distributed for consultation prior to introducing legislation.

Whether preparation for parenthood is necessary, for whom, and at what stage, is still a matter for debate. Meanwhile, most practical schemes are still in their infancy and they are few and far between. It is doubtful whether they have been running for a sufficiently long time and on a sufficiently large scale to make monitoring and evaluation a tenable proposition. Hence it is premature to consider including this topic in a literature review.

In the preceding sections I placed the five issues chosen for review in their wider setting of contemporary life. Then I commented on each of them in the light of the research review presented in this book, giving my own conclusions.

Perhaps it should be stressed that much of the research evidence on these issues is inconclusive and that differing policy implications can be drawn from it. This is particularly the case for evidence on the type of care – whether full-time care by the mother or shared care – that is preferable for the pre-school child. Long-term evaluations of the effects of different types of care arrangements, entered into at different ages, are almost entirely lacking. The interpretations, and even more the policy conclusion drawn in this Overview from the research evidence are entirely mine; the first author's views can be found in the individual reviews.

References

(Bold type at the end of an entry indicates the page number on which an annotation appears.)

ADVISORY COMMITTEE ON CHILD DEVELOPMENT. 1976. *Toward a National Policy for Children and Families*, National Academy of Sciences, Washington.

BENNETT, M. 1976. *Teaching Styles and Pupil Progress*, Open Books, London.

BERNSTEIN, B. 1961a. 'Aspects of language and learning in the genesis of the social process', *Journal of Child Psychology and Psychiatry* 1, 4, 313–24.

BERNSTEIN, B. 1961b. 'Social structure, language and learning', *Educational Research* 3, 2, 163–76.

DAVIE, R., BUTLER, N. R. and GOLDSTEIN, H. 1972. *From Birth to Seven*, Longman, London; Humanities Press, Atlantic Highlands, N.J. **p. 312**

FERRI, E. 1976. *Growing-up in a One-Parent Family*, NFER, Slough, 196 pp; Humanities Press, Atlantic Highlands, N.J. **p. 221**

FERRI, E. and ROBINSON, H. 1976. *Coping Alone*, NFER, Slough.

FOGELMAN, K. (ed) 1976. *Britain's Sixteen-Year-Olds*, National Children's Bureau, London.

GROTBERG, E. H. (ed) 1976. *200 Years of Children*, US Department of Health, Education and Welfare, Washington.

JACKA, A. 1973. *Adoption in Brief. An Annotated Bibliography*, NFER, Slough.

JOBLING, M. 1976. *The Abused Child. An Annotated Bibliography*, National Children's Bureau, London.

PRINGLE, M. KELLMER. 1974. *The Needs of Children*, Hutchinson, London; Schocken Books, New York.

PRINGLE, M. KELLMER. 1975. *Early Child Care in Britain*, Gordon and Breach, London; New York; Paris.

ROBINSON, H. B., *et al.* 1973. *Early Child Care in the United States of America*, Gordon and Breach, London; New York; Paris.

ROSENTHAL, R. and JACOBSON, I. 1968. *Pygmalion in the Classroom*, Holt, Rinehart and Winston, New York, 240 pp. **p. 239**

WEDGE, P. and PROSSER, H. 1973. *Born to Fail?* Arrow Books, London, 64 pp. **p. 368**

The reviews of the literature
by Doria Pilling

The form of the reviews

Some explanation about the form taken by the five reviews in this volume is needed. As will be obvious to the reader, the five subjects under review have not been dealt with in a uniform manner. When the project was in its early stages it was decided that we should try to find a form of presentation which would provide the reader with the clearest view possible of the 'state of the game' in each of the topics – of the main issues involved, of any conclusions which could be reached with reasonable certainty, and of the remaining areas of controversy, unresolved or unlooked at problems. It soon became obvious that there was no single form of treatment which would be equally suitable for all five of the reviews.

The simplest form of review, perhaps, consists, for each aspect of the topic, of an overview of research findings followed by annotations of all, or the most important, of the studies made over the period to be covered. This appeared to fit admirably the material on several of the topics included here. It was particularly suitable for the first subject, *The impact of very early life experiences on development*, where there has been an increasing flood of studies since the late 1960s investigating a fairly narrow range of questions which can be categorised relatively easily.

To adopt this mode of presentation for the reviews of *The father's role in the family* or *Shared care* appeared to be far less satisfactory. Here findings had to be unearthed from a mass of material dealing with different questions, some of it not centrally concerned with the subject under review. Hence in these parts only the one major study (in the former case) or a few of the more important studies (in the latter case) have been selected for annotation; other relevant findings from a wide variety of sources have been summarised in a way which, it is hoped, will quickly reveal what evidence there is, how far there is agreement and disagreement, and which issues are unexplored. In deciding to use the method of presentation best adapted to the material available, uniformity had to be sacrificed. It is hoped that our choice is justified by the usefulness of the reviews.

For those interested, some explanation follows of the reasons for choosing the particular mode of presentation in each of the five reviews:

I. The impact of very early life experience on development

Since the late 1960s there has been an upsurge of interest in the child's early experiences. Often several studies are available investigating similar or closely related questions. It was relatively easy to group findings under three main themes: (A) Influences on the child's early relationship with his care-taker (usually his mother). How the mother's personal and social characteristics, her experiences during pregnancy, around the time of birth, and after, affect the mother-child relationship. The extent to which the infant's own characteristics shape the mother-child relationship; (B) The course of development of social attachments among infants living with their own families, differences in the manner in which infants relate to their mothers (or other main preferred persons), and the relationship between attachment and other aspects of behaviour; (C) The extent to which the variety, timing, appropriateness and specific types of stimulation provided in the home, as well as the quantity, influence cognitive and social development in the early years. To what extent do environmental influences of the first few years have consequences for later development?

II. Shared care

This review examines the question of whether shared care – between the mother and other adults – affects, either beneficially or detrimentally, the child's emotional, social and cognitive development. It is evident that the child has very different needs at different stages in his development and that shared care is unlikely to affect him similarly at different ages. The evidence on the effects of shared care also comes from a wide variety of sources, which are somewhat different for the different age groups. For these reasons, the review is divided into three sections, each dealing with a particular age group: (A) infancy (0–3 years); (B) the pre-school years (3–5 years); (C) the school years (5–16 + years), but with particular emphasis on the primary school child.

In the infancy period, studies concerned with the development of social attachments, with children who have experienced daily substitute care, with kibbutz upbringing, with day care, and with children of working mothers, all provide findings on the effects of shared care on the development of the young child. In the pre-school period, evidence comes from studies of children who have experienced daily substitute care, of nursery school children, of children of working mothers, and of pre-school intervention programmes for socially disadvantaged children. In the school-age group, the main source of evidence is from studies investigating the effects of maternal employment on the child.

For each of the age groups, findings are summarised so that evidence of the effects on the child's (1) emotional and social adjustment, and (2) intellectual development, are presented separately according to the type of study from which they were obtained. Following the summary of findings is a discussion which draws together the evidence from the various sources for the age group, showing the similarities and conflicts, and considers policy implications. It is hoped that this approach has enabled relevant findings from a wide variety of rather disparate material to be brought concisely to bear on the issues under discussion without losing sight of the type of study (and therefore of limitations in the applicability of the findings) from which they came.

III. The father's role in the family

This review examines the extent to which the father directly influences the child's development, apart from his role as economic support for the family. The sources from which the findings come can be grouped into two main types. Increasingly frequent in the last decade are studies, with a few important exceptions small in scale, which investigate the effect of the father not living at home on some aspect of the child's intellectual functioning or adjustment. There are also a number of studies which provide findings suggesting an association between some characteristic or behaviour of the father living at home with his family, and the child's development.

The most useful type of review here appeared to be a summary of findings on the father's influence teased out from a quite extensive but scattered literature. In the case of investigations studying the effects of father absence, an attempt has been made, as far as the material allows, to distil the effects of lack of (or decrease in) interaction with the father in the family from those of other consequences of his departure, often economic adversity, an initial crisis, or a change in community attitudes to the family. However, these findings can only provide pointers to some areas of the father's influence for they tend to under-estimate his importance when present, others fortunately, taking over aspects of his role when he is not available. It was felt that a comparative evaluation of the father absence studies, aiming to unravel the effect of the father himself being absent from the family, and showing the factors which modify such effects, could also usefully be presented in the form of a concise summary of findings.

The review then is divided into three main sections concerned with: (A) the child's cognitive development; (B) sex-role development; and (C) social and emotional adjustment, findings from the father absence studies and those of the father's influence in the intact family being summarised separately in each section. An introduction deals with methodological

33

problems in the studies reviewed, while findings are drawn together and implications discussed in a concluding section.

IV. Teacher expectations and pupil performance

This review is rather different from the others in that it centres around one particular study and the controversy generated by it. Rosenthal and Jacobson claimed to have shown in their 1968 study *Pygmalion in the Classroom* that teachers' expectations of pupil performance (even when bearing no relation to actual ability) affect actual attainments. Their study has been the subject of intense criticism and inspired not only a whole body of research but also exerted influence on researchers working in fields quite other than education.

In (A), an examination is made of the study itself and the literature arising from it and there is an attempt to reach some overall conclusions on the effects of teacher expectations on pupil achievement; (B) deals with the study itself and provides a long summary of this as well as shorter annotations of the criticisms made of it. The following sections are concerned with the literature arising from the study, grouped according to the main subject of investigation: (C) replications; (D) other experimental attempts to alter teacher expectations; (E) effects of naturally occurring teacher expectations; (F) the mechanisms through which teachers' expectations may influence their pupils' performance; (G) the influences shaping teachers' expectations. In each section, brief comments on the research material included are followed by annotations of virtually all the relevant studies. The relatively limited nature of the material made comprehensive annotation possible in this review. It is hoped that the method of presentation adopted allows an objective assessment of the evidence to be made while providing the reader with some of the flavour of the controversy.

V. Disadvantage and intervention

This review returns to the form of the first − each of the five sections, which are relatively self-contained, consists of an overview of research findings followed by annotations. This method seemed particularly appropriate for certain sections of the review where there are a number of recent studies investigating specific topics.

Section A, Intellectual disadvantage, brings together studies investigating whether social class differences in intelligence test scores can be accounted for by such factors as the 'middle-class' content of the tests, differences in test taking motivation, or in the case of black children, the presence of a white examiner; whether 'racial' differences in scores remain when environmental similarity increases; whether Jensen's hypothesis of social class differences in conceptual but not in associative ability holds up; whether there are social class differences in performance on Piagetian tasks. Section B, Language disadvantage, brings together studies examining whether there are social class differences in the understanding or use of complex syntactic structures, not accounted for by dialect differences, and whether there are social class differences in the purposes for which language is used. Section E, Intervention, evaluates findings of recently published British educational intervention studies.

In Section C, Health disadvantage, the position is rather different. While the possible contribution made by health problems to educational disadvantage could not be ignored, the material available is very uneven. There is a considerable amount of material on the effects of prematurity and other perinatal complications known to occur more frequently among the socially disadvantaged, much published in the early 1960s, but little on later illness, though the incidence is known to be greater. To cover the older material extensive use was made of existing research reviews, but findings from pertinent recent research have been introduced where possible.

Section D, Social and cultural disadvantage, deals with the contribution made by material adversities to educational disadvantage; the extent to which the level of literacy in the home, parental expectations, interest and knowledge of the educational system, influence ability and attainment; and whether differences in early environmental experiences of more and less advantaged children are likely to result in differences in readiness for the intellectual tasks required at school. Much of the research in this section is likely to be more familiar to the reader than that found elsewhere in the review. The policy here was to annotate the most recent studies, but some slightly older ones which have particular relevance to the questions under discussion have also been included.

Period covered by the review

The aim of the review was to bring the most recent research evidence to bear on the issues under discussion. Most emphasis has been placed on studies published from 1970 onwards – until the time of writing (summer 1976). However, where earlier evidence is of continuing relevance to these issues, it has also been included.

Part I
The impact of very early life experiences on development

A. Influences on the child's relationship with his care-taker

There is ample evidence that sensitivity to the infant's signals by his care-taker and the provision of a high level and variety of social stimulation in the first years of life fosters his development. These qualities in the interaction between the baby and his care-taker in the first years appear to facilitate the development of a close attachment between the child and his care-taker (Ainsworth and Bell, 1969; Ainsworth *et al.*, 1971; S. M. Bell, 1970; Clarke-Stewart, 1973; Schaffer and Emerson, 1964). Cognitive development, even in the first eighteen months of life, appears to be influenced by the amount and variety of social stimulation and the extent to which it is geared to the baby's needs (Beckwith, 1971; Clarke-Stewart, 1973; Lewis and Goldberg, 1969; Yarrow *et al.*, 1972). There is some evidence that experiences in the first three years of life, even in the first six months, may affect intellectual and social development in the later primary school years (Honzik, 1967; Moore, 1968; Yarrow *et al.*, 1974), although much will depend of course, on later circumstances. The implications for future development of the quality of a child's attachment relationships and of the kinds of stimulation provided in the home in the first three years of life will be discussed in more detail in the second and third sections of this review. In this section, the emphasis will be placed on the factors which influence the child's interaction with his care-taker in the first years, and on some possible consequences of the interaction in early development. Most of the discussion will be focussed on the mother-child relationship, not because interaction with others, particularly the father, is unimportant, but because there is practically no research concerned with these other relationships.

It is generally accepted now that the mother-child relationship in the early years develops as an interaction between the contribution of the mother and the contribution of the infant (R. Q. Bell, 1971; Clarke-Stewart, 1973; Lewis and Lee-Painter, 1974; Schaffer, 1974; L. J. Yarrow, 1963). It has been shown that the same mother's sensitivity to a child's needs and provision of stimulation for him may be quite different for different children (L. J. Yarrow, 1963). The infant's contribution, though, by no means consists only of his genetically determined characteristics (R. Q. Bell, 1971). Not only are the characteristics the infant brings to the mother-child relationship affected by prenatal and perinatal influences, but even a few days after birth his behaviour may already be modified by the interaction with his care-takers. In one study (Richards and Bernal, 1971 and 1972) it was concluded that the eighth day of life may well have been too late to assess infants relatively independently of their post-natal experiences, for findings showed that breast- and bottle-fed babies were already differing in rates of non-nutritive sucking. Nevertheless, even though the infant's behaviour may be a product of his experiences with others almost from the beginning of life, it will still affect his mother's behaviour and contribute to the mother-child interaction.

The mother's contribution to the mother-child interaction

A few studies have indicated that the mother's attitudes, measured before the child's birth, can affect the mother-child interaction. Positive attitudes towards infants have been found to be related to maternal responsiveness to the baby's crying (Moss, 1967) and to his social behaviour (mutual regard) (Moss and Robson, 1968) in the early months of life. Interest in children and adaptation to each stage of pregnancy with relatively little anxiety have been found to be related to various aspects of the mother-infant interaction in the first six months — the mother's responsiveness to the infant and her ability to relate sensitively to his capacities and individual characteristics (Shereshefsky et al., 1973). In an earlier study (Davids et al., 1963) mothers who had been rated as highly anxious during pregnancy were evaluated (without knowledge of the psychological assessment during pregnancy) as having a less satisfactory interaction with their babies at eight months than mothers who had been rated low in anxiety. Another study, (Hubert, 1974) found that whether the baby was intended or not was related to the decision on whether to breast-feed. These findings suggest, then, that the mother's attitudes during, or even before, pregnancy, may have some consequences for the mother-child interaction. Breast-fed infants, it seems, are fed for longer periods than bottle-fed babies during the first ten days of life, they spend less time in the cot and cry more (Richards and Bernal, 1972), all of which may have possible consequences for subsequent mother-child interaction and the child's development. Maternal responsiveness to the child's signals appears to be established as a crucial influence on the child's development in the first two years, affecting his attachment to the mother (Ainsworth et al., 1971; Clarke-Stewart, 1973; Schaffer and Emerson, 1964) and his cognitive development (Lewis and Goldberg, 1969; Yarrow et al., 1972).

However, although maternal attitudes before the child's birth probably do have some effects that are measurable in the early months of the child's life, these should not be over-emphasised. Unintended babies may become fully wanted (Miller, 1974), attitudes tending to change favourably during pregnancy (Hubert, 1974). Also, it is not simply prior maternal attitudes that determine the mother's behaviour with her child. The actual experiences with the child may also lead to more positive attitudes later (Clarke-Stewart, 1973).

Social class might be expected to affect the mother's behaviour with her child, through its influence both on attitudes and life-style. Findings show no social class differences in the extent of care-taking provided for the infant from two weeks to four years old, in the amount of time spent in close proximity to him or in physical contact with him (Kilbride *et al.*, 1971, cited by Streissguth and Bee, 1972; Lawson and Ingleby, 1974; Tulkin and Kagan, 1972), although working-class mothers perhaps provide more physical stimulation in the first few months (Lewis and Wilson, 1972). The main social class differences found are undoubtedly in verbal behaviour (Cohen and Beckwith, 1976; Kilbride *et al.*, 1971, cited by Streissguth and Bee, 1972; Lewis and Wilson, 1972; Tulkin and Kagan, 1972). Middle-class mothers also appear to give their infants more opportunities to explore and manipulate a variety of toys and objects, and are more involved in their infants' play with these things (Collard, 1971; Kilbride *et al.*, 1971, cited by Streissguth and Bee, 1972; Tulkin and Kagan, 1972).

When the child is three months old the difference in maternal verbal behaviour may lie not so much in the frequency of the mother's vocalisations but in their use (Lewis and Wilson, 1972). Findings of this study indicate that middle-class mothers were likely to respond to infant vocalisation with a vocalisation of their own, while working-class mothers were more likely to touch the infant in response. Other studies have found that middle-class mothers do vocalise more frequently than working-class mothers to infants aged between two weeks and ten months (Kilbride *et al.*, 1971, cited by Streissguth and Bee, 1972; Cohen and Beckwith, 1976; Tulkin and Kagan, 1972). Working-class infants were found to be as likely, (Tulkin and Kagan, 1972) or even more likely, (Lewis and Wilson, 1972) to vocalise spontaneously than middle-class infants so it seems improbable that the class difference in the behaviour of the mothers can be attributed to initial infant differences. As there is evidence that verbal stimulation by the mother is strongly related to competence, particularly language ability in the first half of the second year of life (Clarke-Stewart, 1973; Wachs *et al.*, 1971), these class differences may have particular significance for later development. The child's speech quotient at eighteen months has actually been found to have predictive value for language and intellectual ability at five and eight years, at least for girls (Moore, 1967).

The social class differences in play experiences may also be of significance. The variety of inanimate objects available to the child has been found to be related to the development of cognitive skills (exploratory behaviour, problem solving, development of the concept of object permanence) in the first six months of life (Yarrow *et al.*, 1975). By the second year, though, the complexity of the child's play with objects seems to be related to the extent to which the mother is involved in his play rather than to the mere variety of objects available to him. The feature distinguishing the experiences of children who appear to be developing outstanding intellectual competence at the age of three from those of children developing less well is the amount of time spent by the mother (and other adults) in 'intellectually stimulating' activities with the child from the second year onwards (White and Watts, 1973; Watts *et al.*, 1974).

Most of the studies making social class comparisons of maternal behaviour have confined themselves to the investigation of the mother's relationship with first- or second-born infants (Lawson and Ingleby, 1974; Tulkin and Kagan, 1972) and with infants who are full-term (Kilbride *et al.*, 1971, cited by Streissguth and Bee, 1972; Tulkin and Kagan, 1972). Working-class mothers are likely to have more children than middle-class mothers, and their children are at greater risk of being premature or of low birth-weight. These are all factors which may possibly influence the mother-child interaction and increase the differences that have been found between the social classes.

There is evidence that parity may affect the mother's behaviour. Differences have been found between mothers of first- and later-born infants in their behaviour during the feeding of the newborn baby (between sixteen and seventy-two hours old) which appear to be independent of the method of feeding (Thoman *et al.*, 1970; 1971; 1972). Mothers of first-borns, whether bottle- or breast-feeding, devoted a greater length of time to the feeding process, showed more changes of activity during feeding, were generally less effective in feeding and dominated the feeding process more than mothers of later-borns. These findings suggest perhaps that mothers of first-borns tend to be more stimulating but less responsive. There is, in fact, some evidence that mothers of first-borns, at least those who are breast-feeding, are less responsive to the baby's crying than mothers of second-borns (Bernal, 1972). Most of these differences could be transient, of course, disappearing as soon as the mothers of the first-borns gain experience. Thoman *et al.*, though, suggest that they are more permanent. According to these researchers, similar patterns of feeding have been found for four- to twenty-four-weeks-old infants (Brody, 1956, cited by Thoman *et al.*, 1970), and similar features are found in the mother-child relationship for older first-borns.

Mothers of first-borns do face considerable difficulties in present-day society. A study of the experiences of working-class south London women during and after their first pregnancy graphically portrays this (Hubert, 1974). The relative isolation of families and close spacing of births means that many girls have no contact at all with a baby before the birth of their own. Despite the attempts of ante-natal clinics to prepare the women for the care of their infants, few had any realisation of the needs of a young baby. Overwhelmed by the work involved, and subject to fits of panic about the child's health, most women went to stay with their mothers if this was possible. An American study (Shereshefsky *et al.*, 1973) found a similar picture of physical exhaustion and anxieties about the baby amongst middle-class mothers of first-borns in their first weeks of caring for the infant at home.

In these circumstances it may be difficult for the mother to establish the sensitive interaction with the child which appears to be of such importance for later development. Of course, the position generally improves after the first six weeks or so. It has been shown, for a sample of American mothers of first-borns (Moss, 1967) that the mother displays considerably more affection for the infant and is socially more responsive to him when he is three months old rather than three weeks. This, it is suggested, is largely due to the maturation of the infant, but also partly to the mother's increased confidence and increased familiarity with the baby. Nevertheless, it may be that difficulties of the initial period do sometimes have lasting effects on the mother-child interaction. This question needs further investigation. Hubert's work suggests that there is a greater need for sympathetic professional advice and reassurance on the anxieties of caring for a baby for the first time, including the initial difficulties of breast-feeding where this is attempted, than is often offered at present. Practical help with washing, and other household tasks, may also sometimes be necessary for not all women can turn to their own mothers or other relatives.

Although mothers of later-borns are more experienced, they too may have problems, especially where there are several children under school-age. Several studies have found that later-born children receive less care-taking from their mothers and less attention than first-borns (Jacobs and Moss, 1976; Kilbride *et al.*, 1971, cited by Streissguth and Bee, 1972; Lawson and Ingleby, 1974; Roberts and Rowley, 1972). The shorter time spent in care-taking may be due to the greater efficiency of the mother rather than to a lack of time or interest or the demands made on her by the other children. The amount of care-taking the child receives does not, in any case, appear to be related to competence in the second year of life (Clarke-Stewart, 1973). However, mothers' verbal communications, as well as their social interactions, have been found to be less frequent with later-born children than with first-borns in the first three years of life (Cohen and Beckwith, 1976; Ling and Ling, 1974). This could have important consequences for later development.

Is there a sensitive period for the development of maternal attachment to the infant?

It has been suggested in the preceding discussion that the experiences of the mother after the child's birth may affect her behaviour, and may sometimes have more lasting effects on the mother-child relationship. There has been speculation by some researchers that the period immediately following the child's birth may be, as in certain animal species, a sensitive period for the development of the mother's attachment to the child (Klaus *et al.*, 1972) and that temporary separation from the baby at this time (as occurs when a premature baby is placed in an intensive care unit) has deleterious effects on later mothering (Leifer *et al.*, 1972). It is suggested that the hormonal condition of the mother soon after birth may facilitate acceptance of the child and that contact through all sensory modes also elicits attachment behaviour in the mother. These speculations were apparently confirmed by findings that mothers who had a lesser or greater amount of contact with their babies in the first days and weeks after birth showed some differences in later maternal behaviour (Klaus *et al.*, 1972; Kennell *et al.*, 1974; Leifer *et al.*, 1972). However, an examination of the findings of these two teams of researchers shows that the similarities in the mothering behaviour of the mothers with lesser and greater contact far outweigh the differences and cast doubt on these conclusions.

One group of researchers compared the behaviour of mothers of full-term infants who had experienced in the days after birth only the routine contact with their babies that is traditional in American hospitals and mothers who were allowed extra contact in the first three days (Klaus *et al.*, 1972; Kennell *et al.*, 1974). As the investigators point out, one year after the child's birth, the extra-contact mothers did appear to be more attentive to the infants and more responsive to their crying during a physical examination of the infants (Kennell *et al.*, 1974). Nevertheless, the findings show that the mother-infant interaction of the two groups was not significantly different in four other situations which were observed, including a free-play session.

The other team compared the behaviour of mothers of full-term babies, and two groups of mothers of premature babies, those only allowed visual contact with the baby after his placement in the intensive care unit, as is customary, and an experimental group who were allowed to participate in care-taking as far as was practicable (Leifer *et al.*, 1972; Seashore *et al.*, 1973). While mothers of the full-term babies did maintain more close contact between themselves and their babies, and did smile more at the infants than mothers of the prematures one month after the baby's discharge from hospital, no differences were found between mothers of the full-term and premature babies in many other attachment behaviours (holding, affectionate touching, looking at, talking to, laughing or singing to the baby) or the time devoted to interaction with him outside care-taking. The two groups of mothers of prematures showed no differences at all in maternal behaviour, although the group who had experienced most separation were still somewhat less confident about their care-taking skills (Seashore et al., 1973). Similarly, a more recent study (Powell, 1974) failed to find differences in maternal behaviour one, four or six months after the birth between mothers allowed and not allowed to handle their premature babies in the hospital.

Nevertheless, Leifer et al., (1972) cite as evidence of behaviour disturbance amongst the mothers in their study who had experienced the most separation a higher incidence of relinquishing the baby and of divorce than in the other two groups. While relinquishing of the baby might possibly be connected with the separation from the infant (although Leifer et al., themselves say that, due to various difficulties, there were only minimal differences in the amount of separation actually experienced by the two groups of mothers of prematures) it is hard to see how the higher incidence of divorce can be attributed to the separation experience of the mother.

There is then little evidence of a sensitive period for the development of attachment in the human mother. This does not mean, though, that the experiences of the mother immediately after the child's birth, and the condition of the child, will not have some influence on the shape of the mother-child relationship.

The infant's contribution to the mother-infant interaction

As has already been discussed, there can be little doubt that the infant's behaviour contributes significantly to the infant's interaction with his mother or other care-takers. Illustrative evidence of this is provided by a widely quoted study (Moss, 1967). Changes in maternal behaviour over a period from the third week to the third month of the infant's life, although partly attributable to the mother's growing self-confidence, appeared to be largely responses to maturational changes in the infant. Compared with his behaviour at three weeks, the infant cried less and was awake more at three months; he also spent more time smiling, vocalising and looking at the mother's face. The mother decreased the amount of close physical contact but spent more time near the infant, increased affectionate behaviour, provided more stimulation and was more socially responsive to him.

However, to take this as evidence that it is the infant who largely determines the mother-child interaction would be a gross over-simplification. The behaviour shown by the child at three weeks is probably already quite considerably influenced by the interaction with the mother. Differential maternal treatment probably produces effects on infant behaviour even earlier than this. For example, the difference in rates of non-nutritive sucking and response to removal of the teat found on the eighth day of life between bottle- and breast-fed infants (Richards and Bernal, 1971 and 1972) were most probably due to the differential treatment received. Nevertheless, as a number of investigations have shown, there are considerable individual differences in the behaviour of babies only two to three days old, and these are very unlikely to be due to differences in post-natal experiences (Korner, 1974). Some of these differences in newborn behaviour – in frequency and duration of crying, duration of waking activity, restlessness, sensory responsiveness, and consolability – could very well influence the interaction with the care-taker, as Korner suggests.

Although it does seem likely that some, at least, of these infant characteristics do affect the mother-child interaction, actual evidence is scanty. Much infant behaviour has little stability over days or even hours (R. Q. Bell et al., 1971) so its effects on the mother-child interaction may be very limited. This appears to be the case with crying. Initial differences in infant crying, it seems, do not persist to any significant extent throughout the first year (S. M. Bell and Ainsworth, 1972). The analysis presented by these authors suggests that, in this instance, it is largely maternal behaviour which affects infant behaviour, mothers who are unresponsive to infant crying early in the first year having babies who cry more frequently and persistently later in the year.

On the other hand, there is evidence that even transient infant behaviour may have some influence on the mother-child interaction, at least in the short-term. Maternal medication during labour affects behaviour of the newborn infant (Aleksandrowicz, 1974; Aleksandrowicz and Aleksandrowicz, 1974), and there are indications that the infant may be treated differently in the first ten days of life by the mother (and the father) according to the type and amount of medication received (Parke et al., 1972; Richards and Bernal, 1971, 1972). Differences in behaviour during the feeding process between mothers of first- and later-born infants could perhaps be partly attributable to the effect of drugs on the first-borns (J. V. Brown et al., 1975). In this study, the behaviour of the first-borns tended to be more depressed than that of later-borns, and their mothers had also received significantly more drugs during labour. Richards and Bernal suggest that the altered mode of interaction may continue and have developmental consequences for the infant even when the direct effects of drugs on the infant's behaviour have disappeared. It seems that there is an association, though, between the amount of medication received during labour and delivery and anxiety in the mother during pregnancy and it is possible that the continuing anxiousness of the mother is one of the influences on the mother-child

43

interaction (Yang *et al.*, 1976). Longitudinal investigations are needed to determine whether, and to what extent, particular characteristics of the infant do affect the subsequent mother-child interaction.

There is little doubt that one characteristic of the infant that does affect his interaction with the care-taker is the child's sex. There are clear indications of differences in maternal behaviour towards boys and girls during the first year of life. Differential treatment of the sexes has been found at six months (Goldberg and Lewis, 1969) and at three months (Lewis, 1972; Moss, 1967) and even possibly by the second or third day of life (J. V. Brown *et al.*, 1975; Thoman *et al.*, 1972; Parke *et al.*, 1972). The evidence is, on the whole, remarkably consistent. Mothers appear to provide girls with more distal stimulation (vocalising, looking, smiling) (Lewis, 1972; Moss, 1967; Thoman *et al.*, 1972). This trend apparently persists throughout the first two years (Lewis, 1972). Boys, on the other hand, are provided with more proximal stimulation (touching and holding) from the second day of life (Parke *et al.*, 1972) to the third month (Lewis, 1972; Moss, 1967) at least. There seems to be a reversal in this trend, though, so that by six months of age it is the girls who are being held and touched more (Goldberg and Lewis, 1969; Lewis, 1972).

Can the differential treatment by parents be explained by innate sex differences in infant behaviour or is it entirely due to cultural expectations? At three months of age there appear to be sex differences in infant behaviour only among first-borns, boys being more irritable (S. M. Bell and Ainsworth, 1972; Moss, 1967), sleeping less, and possibly being more difficult to soothe (Moss, 1967). Even here, differences are found in maternal behaviour beyond those that can be accounted for by the behaviour differences in the infants (Moss, 1967). In samples not confined to first-borns there appear to be no sex differences in crying (S. M. Bell and Ainsworth, 1972; Lewis 1972) or other behaviour (Lewis, 1972). Nor have sex differences been found in the neonatal period for irritability or consolability (Korner, 1974; Osofsky and Danzger, 1974). However, the suggestion has been put forward by Korner (1974) that there may be subtle sex differences in the newborn infant which do influence parental behaviour. From a review of her own and others' research, she concludes that newborn females may possibly be more receptive to certain kinds of stimuli and that males may have greater strength and vigour, although in most other areas no differences are found (Korner, 1974). The mother's tendency to provide boys with more tactile stimulation could be, she suggests, an unconscious compensatory response for his lesser cutaneous sensitivity, or his muscular strength and sturdiness could make her less hesitant to handle him. While these hypotheses cannot be ruled out completely, it does appear that most of the evidence for innate sex differences in behaviour comes from single uncorroborated studies and that any differences are far outweighed by similarities in behaviour (R. Q. Bell *et al.*, 1971; Birns, 1976; Korner, 1974; Osofsky and Danzger, 1974; Shepard and Peterson, 1973). An infant's sex is an important influence on the mother-child interaction, but primarily because cultural expectations result in different treatment (Birns, 1976; Will *et al.*, 1976).

It appears, then, from a review of the literature that little is known as yet about the influence of innate infant characteristics on the mother-child interaction. However, the infant's behaviour, whatever its actual origin, will influence the mother-child relationship. One study provides substantial evidence for this (Clarke-Stewart, 1973). The child's social responses to his mother at eleven months, whatever had contributed to their development, were found to influence the mother's affection for and attachment to the child and her responsiveness to his signals of distress when he was seventeen months old.

The infant's relationship with his father and other adults

Not only do infants differ very much in the experiences they have with mothers, but the amount and quality of interaction with other people also differs greatly. Findings of one study (Escalona and Corman, 1971) have shown that the infant's experiences, when apart from his mother, may influence both the mother-child interaction and the child's development, cognitive and social. The contrasting development of two infants is described, both with loving and attentive mothers to whom they had formed strong ties by the end of the first year. One infant, though, generally looked after by a less stimulating and responsive grandmother in her mother's absence, diminished in social behaviour and non-social activity when apart from her mother. She developed an intense and ambivalent tie with her mother and was average in cognitive development. The other child, whose main care-taker apart from the mother was a fond and attentive father, increased slightly in social behaviour and non-social acitivty in his mother's absence. He was able to accept separation from the mother in everyday situations with little protest, and was well above average in cognitive development.

The extent to which the father contributes to the child's development in the early years should not be under-estimated. Although many fathers are able to spend little time with their children in the first year or so there is evidence that most do interact with the child when available. In their study of child-rearing, the Newsons (1963) found that virtually all the fathers of the 700 one-year-olds in their Nottingham sample were willing to play with the child at least sometimes, and that over half could be rated as 'highly participant' in care-taking duties. There is also an increasing body of evidence showing that most infants are attached to their fathers as well as their mothers, although often less strongly, by the time they are eighteen months old (Schaffer and Emerson, 1964) and probably before the end of the first year (Ban and Lewis, 1974; Cohen and Campos, 1974; Pedersen and Robson, 1969; Spelke *et al.*, 1973).

There are some indications, at least, that frequent interactions with the father may be associated with advanced cognitive development in the first fifteen months of life (Spelke *et al.*, 1973; Wachs *et al.*, 1971). A close relationship with the father in the second year of life has been found to be associated with high IQ scores in later childhood, for girls at any rate (Honzik, 1967).

There has been very little study of the father-child interaction as yet, but the scanty evidence available suggests that fathers and mothers possibly behave rather differently to the sexes (Rebelsky and Hanks, 1971) and to more and less active infants (Parke *et al.*, 1972). It seems likely that children whose variety of experience is greater because of frequent interactions with the father benefit at least in intellectual development (Spelke *et al.*, 1973).

Available findings are meagre and somewhat contradictory on the effect on the very young child of social experiences with people other than the parents. In one study, with middle-class infants as subjects, IQ scores (Catell) of seven- to eleven-months old infants appeared to be higher when they had more experiences of being played with and looked after by visitors, and of being taken shopping and on visits to other people's homes (Beckwith, 1971). In contrast, fifteen- to eighteen-months old infants, half from slum- and half from middle-class backgrounds, had lower scores on a test of psychological development (scale modelled on Piagetian concepts) when neighbours visited or the mother and child went to visit neighbours almost every day (Wachs *et al.*, 1971). Possibly, experiences with a variety of people and circumstances are beneficial to the child but too great a variety is over-whelming.

Conclusions

The research reviewed emphasises that the infant's relationship with his care-taker begins to be shaped very early, possibly in the first few days of life. Although the child's congenital characteristics (whether determined genetically or by pre- or peri-natal circumstances) affect the interaction they appear to do so to a large extent through the care-taker's reaction to the infant's behaviour and characteristics (S. M. Bell and Ainsworth, 1972; Birns, 1976; Yang and Halverson, 1976). In one study (R. Q. Bell *et al.*, 1971) it was found that some links between neonatal behaviour, relatively unmodified by post-natal environmental circumstances, and behaviour at two and a half years did exist, but they were much fewer than had been expected.

Realisation that the mother's behaviour does not have the same effect on all babies, and that she will not, in fact, behave in the same way to all her children should not result in the mother's contribution to the child's development being underrated. It does mean that measures must be taken to ensure, as far as is possible in the present state of knowledge, that the mother is able to attain a satisfactory relationship with the child. The consensus of research findings is that this involves sensitive responsiveness by the mother to the child's signals. Greater support in the weeks immediately after the child's birth for mothers of first-borns, and help at home both for them and for those with several young children would free these mothers from worry and over-work, and give them more time to get to know and enjoy the baby.

A high proportion (over 40 per cent) of working-class mothers with young children, including those with two children under the age of three, have been found to suffer from depression (G. W. Brown *et al.*, 1975; Richman, 1974) making it difficult for them to respond to the demands of a small child (Richman, 1976). Material problems, particularly housing difficulties, appear to be implicated in the onset, and perhaps even more, the continuation, of depression. Provision of adequate financial support and housing for all mothers caring for young children is likely to result in an increased number of satisfying mother-child relationships. The third section of this review will examine further the effects of various aspects of the mother-child relationship on the child's later development.

Annotations

BECKWITH, L. 1971. 'Relationships between attributes of mothers and their infants' IQ scores', *Child Development* 42, 4, 1083–97.

Infants who had been adopted in the first days of life were observed on two visits to their homes (at the ages of eight and ten months on average) in interaction with their middle-class adoptive mothers. Standardised tests of infant intellectual and motor development were also administered on each visit. Natural mothers' socio-economic status was found to be directly related to both Cattell IQ scores and Gesell gross motor scores – this could be due to genetic factors or it might be the result of pre-natal nutrition. The adoptive mothers' socio-economic level did not affect the infants' intellectual and gross motor scores, but these were affected by specific maternal behaviours. Low maternal verbal and physical contact when combined with high maternal restrictiveness of exploration significantly lowered the intelligence test scores. In these adequate middle-class homes it appears that experiences in several areas had to be curtailed for IQ scores to be influenced. Social experiences with people other than parents were found to enhance IQ scores. Performance on the Cattell Infant Scale did not correlate with level of gross motor development in this sample of well cared for babies.

BELL, R. Q. 1971. 'Stimulus control of parent or caretaker behavior by offspring', *Developmental Psychology* 4, 1, 63–72.

The child's contribution to the parent-child relationship has been equated with the operation of genetic or congenital factors, and so has been ignored by socialisation theorists reacting against instinct theories, and theories of innate differences between social classes and national groups. However, it is not necessary to suppose that the child's contribution to interaction must be biological – it may be a product of his experiences in the previous period. Although there is a paucity of published data, there is sufficient evidence to show that it is the infant who initiates many of the interactional sequences between mother and child.

BELL, R. Q., WELLER, G. M. and WALDROP, M. F. 1971. 'Newborn and pre-schooler: organisation of behavior and relations between periods', *Monographs of the Society for Research in Child Development*, Serial no. 142, 36, 1–2. 145pp.

In this study an attempt was made to identify the contribution of the infant to the parent-child relationship and to later behaviour. For this purpose, infants were investigated in the third and fourth days of life when their behaviour was relatively untouched by the parents. Observations and experimental procedures were carried out on seventy-five second- and later-born infants, who had experienced no complications during pregnancy or delivery, for two three-and-a-half hour periods between feeds. Only twelve out of thirty-one behaviour measures showed sufficient stability of individual differences to be used in a longitudinal study:
(a) (from sleep) the highest count for mouth and closed-eye movements, respiration rates, and tactile sensitivity;
(b) (from the waking period) prone head reaction, measures of nutritive and non-nutritive sucking.

Generally, there was a lack of difference due to sex or type of feeding, although males showed a higher lift of chin than females. Subsequently, seventy-three children aged twenty-seven to thirty-three months, including fifty-five of the newborns studied earlier, attended a research nursery school for four weeks in groups of five. Their behaviour in free play and experimental situations was observed, mechanically recorded, filmed and rated. Over seventy stable measures were obtained and these were assigned for each sex into seven independent classes consisting of intercorrelated and internally consistent behaviours. In contrast to the newborn period there were many sex differences in important classes of behaviour. Generally more relationships were found than expected by chance between the newborn and pre-school periods, particularly for males, but the number of links found was not large compared with the number of behaviours investigated. Findings indicated that any analysis which had been confined to logical equivalents between periods would have been fruitless. The one generalisation possible from a number of findings was that intensity appeared to be inversely related in the newborn and pre-school period. Newborns whose responses were slow were likely to be insensitive to touch and would not react quickly nor cry when their sucking was interrupted. In the pre-school period these children were likely to show assertive, active and co-ordinated behaviour, to be advanced in speech development and communication, and to be active and interested in the teachers' games. Newborns with intense reactions displayed opposite pre-school behaviour. Some measures of newborn behaviour did show a continuity in intensity between periods but the link was statistically more tenuous. Overall, the findings indicate that though there may be some congenital determinants of later behaviour these are less extensive that had been expected.

BELL, S. M. and AINSWORTH, M. D. S. 1972. 'Infant crying and maternal responsiveness', *Child Development* 43, 4, 1171–90.

Findings of this study suggest that infant crying by the end of the first year is influenced by maternal responsiveness to crying earlier in the first year. Contrary to popular belief, prompt response to crying decreases the frequency and duration of crying. In the fourth quarter of the first year infants who cried little were found to use a variety of other modes of communication with the mother, such as facial expressions and vocalisations, while babies who cried a great deal lacked other modes of communications. Subjects were twenty-six middle-class mother-infant pairs; observations were carried out in home visits throughout the first year.

BERNAL, J. 1972. 'Crying during the first ten days of life and maternal responses', *Developmental Medicine and Child Neurology* 14, 3, 362–72.

Data for this study was obtained from a diary kept by the subjects, twenty mothers of first-borns and fifty-seven mothers of second-born children, and from observations of selected feeds. Crying 'in the cot' was higher for first-borns than second-borns because their mothers responded less quickly, were less likely to respond by feeding and more likely not to respond at all than mothers of second-borns. Among mothers of second-borns breast-feeding was associated with an earlier response to crying. Some questions are raised on whether quickness of response to crying can be equated with maternal sensitivity.

DAVIDS, A., HOLDEN, R. H. and GRAY, G. B. 1963. 'Maternal

anxiety during pregnancy and adequacy of mother and child adjustment eight months following childbirth', *Child Development* 34, 4, 993–1002.

Mothers rated high and low in anxiety (Taylor Manifest Anxiety Scale) during pregnancy were found to differ in their child-rearing attitudes and maternal behaviour when the infant was eight months old. The mothers who had been rated high in anxiety were more controlling and authoritarian (Parental Attitudes Research Instrument) and their interaction with the child was evaluated as being less favourable. Children whose mothers had been rated low in anxiety had higher scores on the Bayley Infant Mental and Motor Scales, and their behaviour during the examination was assessed more favourably. All measures administered when the child was eight months old were scored without knowledge of the psychological findings during pregnancy.

HUBERT, J. 1974. 'Belief and reality: social factors in pregnancy and childbirth', in M. P. M. Richards (ed) *The Integration of a Child into a Social World*, Cambridge University Press, London. 37–51.

A study investigating the experiences of fifty-four working-class women living in South London during their first pregnancy, at the birth and in the immediate period afterwards, found that there was a great ignorance about the reproductive process, and that two-thirds of the pregnancies even among the married women were unintended, resulting from the use of ineffective methods of contraception. Although medical ante-natal care was of a high standard, and some attempts were made to prepare the women for labour and the care of the baby, a lack of rapport with the clinic staff meant that many women had little clear idea of what was happening to them. Most of the women were ill-prepared for labour, finding it much more lonely and painful than they had anticipated, and this often resulted in an initial indifference to the baby. The emphasis on pregnancy and the confinement made it difficult for many women to think beyond this. The relative isolation of the nuclear family also meant that few women had ever seen anyone care for a newborn baby. Faced with a quantity of work they had never anticipated, and subject to fits of panic about the baby's health, most women went to stay with their mothers where this was possible. This gave them both moral support and practical help. Even though attitudes to an unintended baby often changed favourably during pregnancy, the original intention appeared to retain some influence on the mother's behaviour, at least on the decision whether to breast-feed. Only a small proportion of the mothers did try to breast-feed and a majority of these gave up because they were exhausted by the amount of time taken breast-feeding – they did not know how much milk was being taken and so tended to go on and on feeding. These

50

problems appeared to arise from a lack of adequate preparation for motherhood and of sympathetic help at the time.

KENNELL, J. H. *et al.*, 1974. 'Maternal behaviour one year after early and extended post-partum contact', *Developmental Medicine and Child Neurology* 16, 172–9.

A follow-up of the Klaus *et al.*, (1972) study in which the maternal behaviour of mothers who were allowed extended contact with the newborn infants (sixteen extra hours) and of mothers allowed only the contacts that are routine in American hospitals was found to differ one month after the child's birth (see above). One year after the birth, the mothers were interviewed and mother-child interactions were observed in seven different situations. Mothers in the extended-contact groups were significantly different in their answers to an interview question (they were more preoccupied with the baby when away from him) and in their behaviour during the physical examination of the baby (they spent more time assisting the doctor, and more time soothing the baby). Mother-infant interactions in the two groups did not differ, though, during developmental testing of the child, in a free-play situation, during picture-taking of the mother and baby or at the interview. Findings suggest that an important factor affecting attachment is the time the mother spends in close contact with the baby in the first hours and days of life.

KLAUS, M. H. and KENNELL, J. H. 1970. 'Mothers separated from their newborn infants', *Pediatric Clinics of North America* 17, 4, 1015–37.

Studies of a large number of animal species and preliminary studies of human mothers suggest that what happens in the period immediately after the child's birth may be critical for later mothering. Separation of the mother and child, such as occurs generally when the baby is premature, may impair the development of maternal affection for the child. Further research on the effects of separation on mothering capacity is necessary, though, before any widespread changes in hospital practices can be advocated.

KLAUS, M. H., KENNELL, J. H., PLUMB, N. and ZUEHLKE, S. 1970. 'Human maternal behavior at the first contact with her young', *Pediatrics* 46, 2, 187–92.

Mothers of full-term infants were found to follow an orderly and predictable pattern of behaviour on first contact with their babies. Findings were not affected by the mother's parity or by whether she was married or unmarried. It is speculated by the authors that the immediate post-natal period may be especially sensitive for the development of emotional ties between the mother and child.

KLAUS, M. H. *et al.*, 1972. 'Maternal attachment: importance of the first post-partum days', *New England Journal of Medicine* 286, 9, 460–3.

Mothers who had extended contact with their newborn infants (one hour with the infant three hours after birth and five hours for the next three afternoons in addition to routine contact) showed differences in mothering behaviour one month after the birth from mothers who had only routine contact with their infants (glimpses after birth and at six and twelve hours, and visits for feeding every four hours). The extended-contact mothers were more reluctant to leave their babies, more often watched or soothed them during a physical examination and spent more time in eye-to-eye contact and fondling during feeding. All the babies were first-born, and mothers in both groups came from a lower socio-economic background. The authors suggest that it is remarkable that sixteen hours of extra contact with the baby in the first three days after birth has effects that persist over thirty days when there are so many other influences on maternal behaviour. However, before any practical recommendations can be made on the hospital regime, research is necessary to find out for how long the differences in maternal behaviour endure and whether they would occur at other socio-economic levels.

KORNER, A. F. 1974. 'The effect of the infant's state, level of arousal, sex and ontogenetic stage on the caregiver' in M. Lewis and L. A. Rosenblum (eds) *The Effect of the Infant on its Caregiver*, Wiley, New York. 105–21.

Recent research has indicated that the infant's characteristics influence the mother-child relationship from the beginning. Evidence from the author's own and others' research indicates that babies show considerable differences in their behaviour and that the infant's characteristics affect the mother's behaviour. Infants have been found to differ in their irritability, level of arousal and soothability and the infant's characteristics are likely to affect their care-givers. A number of studies have shown that males and females are treated differently from a very early age. While sex role expectations are probably the primary reason for the differential treatment, a few studies indicate that there may be sex differences in newborns. There is, for example, some evidence that the female may be more receptive to certain kinds of stimuli while the male may have more physical strength and muscular vigour. Babies at different stages of development have also been found to elicit different feelings and behaviour from their care-givers.

LEIFER, A. D., LEIDERMAN, P. H., BARNETT, C. R. and WILLIAMS, J. A. 1972. 'Effects of mother-infant separation on maternal attachment behavior', *Child Development* 43, 4, 1203–18.

Work with infra-human mammals and other animals indicates that a temporary separation from the mother in the immediate post-partum period or reduction in sensory modes of contact between the mother and infant may impair or even eliminate maternal behaviour. The present study investigated whether maternal behaviour in the human mother is also deleteriously affected by temporary separation. Three groups of mothers – mothers of full-term babies, mothers of premature babies separated from them for three to twelve weeks while the baby was in an incubator in an intensive care unit, and only allowed visual contact (the 'separation group'), and mothers of premature babies who were allowed to handle the babies to some extent, and possibly undertake some caretaking duties (the 'contact group') – were observed while carrying out caretaking activities before the child was discharged from hospital and one week and one month after discharge. Full-term mothers maintained significantly more close contact between themselves and their infants and smiled more at them than mothers of premature babies. The three groups did not differ, though, in other attachment behaviours involving either proximal or distal contact, or in the amount of mother-infant interaction, excluding care-taking. No significant differences were found between the behaviour of the two groups of mothers of premature infants. However, the only two instances of a mother relinquishing custody of her child and five of the six divorces occurred among mothers in the 'separated' group. It is suggested that this may be evidence of disruption of normal maternal behaviour in the 'separation group'. Differences between the mothers of full-term and premature infants may be due to the differences in the amount of separation experienced or to other differences in experiences of the groups.

LEWIS, M. 1972. 'State as an infant-environment interaction: an analysis of mother-infant interaction as a function of sex', *Merill-Palmer Quarterly* 18, 2, 95–121.

Findings of this study show that there are large differences in environmental response to the same infant behaviour. Subjects were thirty-two three-months-old infants observed at home with their mothers for a two hour session. Differences could often be accounted for by the sex of the infant. While no sex differences were found in the frequency with which different types of infant behaviour occurred, maternal behaviour did appear to be determined by the sex of the child. Mothers of boys generally showed more proximal behaviour (holding, touching) and mothers of girls more distal behaviour (looking, vocalising). These differences were also found in most of the interactive analyses which examined mother and infant behaviours within ten-second units. For example, mothers of boys responded more to their infant's vocalisations than mothers of girls but they were less likely to vocalise in response.

LEWIS, M. and LEE-PAINTER, S. 1974. 'An interactional approach to the mother-infant dyad', in M. Lewis and L. A. Rosenblum (eds), *The Effect of the Infant on its Caregiver*, Wiley, New York. 21–48.

Mother-child interaction data, obtained from observation of fifty-three three-months-old infants in their own homes, were analysed at a number of different levels:
(1) frequency distribution – amount of infant and maternal behaviour that occurred;
(2) simultaneous behaviour in ten-second units – number of ten-second units in which simultaneous behaviour from both the mother and child occurred;
(3) directional interactive analyses – determination of the flow of interaction between the mother and child;
(4) sequential analyses – construction of a matrix of transitional probabilities. This reveals for an individual infant the way in which the current state of the mother-infant interaction system influences the conditional probability of the next state.

Findings suggest that the types of results obtained are highly specific to the type of measurement. For example, there may be no differences in the frequency of behaviour, but significant differences in directed interaction (see Lewis and Wilson, 1972, for such differences as a function of social class). It is argued that each type of measurement contributes to a full understanding of the dyadic relationship. Both the infant and the care-giver actively and significantly influence one another. It is as mistaken to look only at the effects of the infant on the care-giver as it is only to study the effects of the care-giver on the infant (see Lewis, 1972, for earlier findings from this study).

LEWIS, M. and WILSON, C. D. 1972. 'Infant development in lower-class American families', *Human Development* 15, 112–7.

The effects of social class on the behaviour of the mother and her twelve-weeks-old infant were studied by observing thirty-two mother-infant pairs in their homes. Maternal behaviours of touch, hold, smile, look and play were more frequent among lower socio-economic group mothers than among middle-class mothers, only mothers' frequency of vocalisations showing no difference. There was a relatively strong relationship between infant and maternal behaviour, e.g. mothers who vocalised and smiled a great deal had infants who vocalised and smiled a great deal. There was a higher frequency of interaction between the lower-class infants and their mothers (i.e. a higher number of ten-second observational units in which both maternal and infant behaviour occurred). Middle- and lower-class mothers differed in their style of responses, e.g. middle-class mothers were more likely to vocalise when the infant vocalised, but lower-class mothers were more likely to touch. At twelve weeks, the lower-class infants tended to be superior in cognitive functioning to the middle-class infants, although there is considerable evidence that middle-class children have a superior performance from three years of age onwards. Later differences between the children are not explicable in terms of differences between lower- and middle-class mothers in attachment promoting behaviour, stimulation of the infant, or contingency of responses to the infant. Possibly the difference in the mothers' styles of response may provide the explanation.

LING, D. and LING, A. H. 1974. 'Communication development in the first three years of life', *Journal of Speech and Hearing Research* 17, 1, 146–59.

An observational study of the non-verbal and verbal communication between forty-eight middle-class mothers and their infants, aged one month to three years. Mothers communicated significantly more often with first- than with last-born children, and with younger children than with older children but the frequency of communication was not influenced by the child's sex. There were no significant differences in the frequency of child to mother communications with respect to age, sex or ordinal position. Mothers' verbal communications were significantly more frequent to first-born children, but they talked as often to young babies as to older children, and to boys as girls. Neither the quality nor the type of mothers' speech varied with the child's age. What they said was often related to the immediate situation, particularly with older children.

MINTON, C., KAGAN, J. and LEVINE, J. A. 1971. 'Maternal control and obedience in the two year old', *Child Development* 42, 6, 1873–94.

Each of ninety (forty-nine boys, forty-one girls) first-born, twenty-seven-months-old children were observed at home on two separate visits in order to obtain data on socialisation routines. In general, an event involving a maternal prohibition or command or a child request occurred once every three minutes. Children were generally obedient and non-aggressive, their misbehaviour being trivial, and the mothers were obliging and nurturant. Educational level was an important determinant of maternal behaviour. Mothers who were less educated (not more than high school) prohibited twice as frequently, used mild negatives and distraction less often and physical punishment more frequently than better-educated (some college education at least) mothers. Commands of the less-educated mothers were more often in the imperative than the request mode and their children disobeyed more often. Children of the less-educated mothers were also less likely to request their mothers to play with them. The mother's tendency to punish or explain was found to be relatively independent of the child's obedience. Attributes of the infants assessed in laboratory tests at earlier ages generally showed little relationship to maternal practices at two years. The exception was, for girls only, correlations between smiling and fixation times to human forms and faces at four to thirteen months and mother's tendency to explain her reprimands to the daughter. A possible explanation is that the mother who explains prohibitions is likely to interact in other ways with the infant that would promote attentiveness to faces and forms; alternatively, the mother might interpret the child's attentiveness as a sign of her potential for understanding explanations.

MOSS, H. A. 1967. 'Sex, age and state as determinants of mother-infant interaction', *Merrill-Palmer Quarterly* 13, 19–36.

Thirty first-born children and their mothers were observed in their homes during the first month of life and at about three months. A wide range of individual differences in both maternal and infant variables was found for both observation periods. There were marked shifts in both infant and maternal behaviour from three weeks to three months. For the maternal variables moderate correlations were obtained only for those concerning affectionate-social responses. Possibly these are more sensitive indicators of maternal attitudes than such activities as feeding or physical contact. The infant variables showing some stability were those concerning the state of the organism (cry, fuss, awake active, awake passive, sleep) and .vocalisation. Findings show that in general much more was happening to boys than girls, particularly at the three weeks observation. They slept less, cried more and this probably contributed to the more extensive and stimulating interaction they experienced with their mothers. When state was controlled there were no longer statistically significant sex differences, except that boys still received more maternal stimulation while girls were imitated more (repeating of vocalisations). Males had substantially higher scores both for irritability and maternal contact, but by three months mothers tended to spend more time with girls who were irritable and less time with boys who were irritable. This is probably because mothers were positively reinforced for responding to girls (they were quieted by maternal handling) but negatively reinforced for responding to boys. There is evidence from other research that boys are more subject to inconsolable states. Mothers' responsiveness to infants' crying, though, was also related to maternal attitudes – mothers who accepted the nurturant role (prior to the infant's birth) were more responsive. Findings of this study indicate then that both maternal attitudes and infant state are determinants of maternal behaviour.

MOSS, H. A. and ROBSON, K. S. 1968. 'Maternal influences in early social visual behavior', *Child Development* 39, 2, 401–8.

Positive attitudes towards infants, assessed in pregnancy in fifty-four primiparous mothers, were found to be related to the frequency with which the mother and infant, of both sexes, looked at each other simultaneously in the home situation at the end of the first month of life; at three months of age, though, maternal attitudes were related to mutual visual regard in the girls only. Also, for girls only, mutual visual regard was strongly related to visual attentiveness to social stimuli (a series of three faces) presented to the infant in a laboratory situation when three months old. Visual attentiveness in girls was related to the mother's attitudes during pregnancy. Factors which could interact with maternal attitudes during pregnancy to determine visual interaction with boys are discussed.

MOSS, H. A., ROBSON, K. S. and PEDERSEN, F. 1969. 'Determinants of maternal stimulation of infants and consequences of treatment for later reactions to strangers', *Developmental Psychology* 1, 3, 239–46.

Maternal characteristics were found in this study to influence the type and amount of stimulation the mother provided for the baby in the early months of life. Mothers whose speech had been assessed as animated at an interview during pregnancy provided more soothing stimulation (talking, kissing, rocking) for male infants at one month and more auditory and visual stimulation (through the use of inanimate objects such as a radio, rattle) for girls at three months than mothers whose speech had been rated low in animation. Less well-educated mothers provided more physical stimulation for the infants, especially girls, at both one and three months. It is suggested that the sex differences found may be related to the earlier development of girls. It was also found that the stimulation the infant received from the mother in the first three months of life was related to his later readiness to interact with a stranger. The greater the stimulation received by the infant, the less he feared strangers or averted his gaze from them at eight to nine-and-a-half months. A possible explanation is that the child who is accustomed to experiencing novel auditory and visual stimuli is better able to cope with 'strangeness'.

OSOFSKY, J. D. and DANZGER, B. 1974. 'Relationships between neonatal characteristics and mother-child interaction', *Developmental Psychology* 10, 1, 124–30.

In this study, it was found that maternal attentiveness and sensitivity to the baby during feeding were related to the neo-natal infant's visual, auditory and tactile responsivity. Consistencies were also found between the infant's state and behaviour during feeding and on the Brazelton Neonatal Behavioural Assessment Scale. No sex differences were found in infant behaviour either on the Brazelton Scale or during feeding, with the exception that males were more responsive to auditory stimulation in the interaction situation.

PARKE, R. D., O'LEARY, S. E. and WEST, S. 1972. 'Mother-father-newborn interaction: effects of maternal medication, labor and sex of infant', *Proceedings of the 80th Annual Convention of the American Psychological Association*. 85–6.

In this observational study of parent-infant interactions, six to forty-eight hours after the delivery of the baby, fathers were found to be as actively involved with the infants as were mothers. The fathers were more likely to hold the baby, than the mother, equally likely to look at, touch and vocalise to him, but less likely to smile at him. Medication had a differential impact on maternal and paternal behaviour. Maternal interaction with the infant increased as medication increased, paternal interaction decreased. Possibly fathers prefer an active awake infant, or mothers may be anxious about a highly medicated infant and may stimulate him more in an attempt to arouse his responsiveness. Subjects were nineteen well-educated white parents and their first-born babies.

RICHARDS, M. P. M. and BERNAL, J. F. 1971. 'Social interaction in the first days of life', in H. R. Schaffer (ed) *The Origins of Human Social Relations*. Academic Press, London. 3–13.

Preliminary report of a study aiming to describe the infant's development as a function of his individual characteristics as seen at birth and his interaction with the mother. Breast- and bottle-fed babies showed differences in a test of non-nutritive sucking on the eighth day of life. This could possibly be accounted for by differences in the infants at birth (bottle- and breast-feeding mothers differ in social class) or in the maternal-infant interaction during the first days of life (the breast-fed infants were fed for longer, touched, talked to and smiled at more frequently). Infants whose mothers were given the drug Pethilorfan during labour also differed in non-nutritive sucking from infants whose mothers were not given the drug. It is suggested that even if the direct effects of the drug disappear soon after birth, they may affect the mode of interaction with the mother and so have developmental consequences for the baby.

ROBSON, K. S., PEDERSEN, F. A. and MOSS, H. A. 1969. 'Developmental observations of diadic gazing in relation to the fear of strangers and social approach behavior', *Child Development* 40, 2, 619–27.

The extent to which an eight-and-a-half to nine-and-a-half-months old infant looks at a stranger was found to be negatively related to his fear of the stranger and, for boys, positively related to his social approaches to the stranger. The frequency of mother-infant mutual regard in the first three months of life was related to looking at, and social approaches to, the stranger later in the year, primarily for males. Also, for boys, positive maternal attitudes during pregnancy were related to looking at and social responsiveness to strangers. The findings of the study suggest that mutual visual regard in the early months has important developmental consequences, although whether it is the mother's gaze itself, or the smiling and talking that usually take place simultaneously that is influential is not clear at present. The contribution of infant differences both to early mutual visual regard and later social responses should not, though, be ignored. Sex differences found in the present study may be due to the earlier onset and course of fear of strangers in the girl. Subjects were the mother-infant pairs still available from an earlier study of mutual visual regard between mother and child (see Moss and Robson, 1968).

SANDER, L. W., STECHLER, G., BURNS, P. and JULIA, H. 1970. 'Early mother-infant interaction and 24-hour patterns of activity and sleep', *Journal of the American Academy of Child Psychiatry* 9, 103–23.

Interaction between infant activity (crying, movement) and care-taking activities was monitored, using automatic recording devices, twenty-four hours a day for the first month of life, in three groups of infants; sleeping-waking patterns were also observed. Differences in crying and sleep patterns and in synchrony of infant activity and care-taking interventions were found between the three groups, which appeared to be influenced by the extent to which the infant had experienced care-taking sensitive to his individual behaviour. In one group, the infants were cared for entirely by their own mothers, in the second infants were cared for individually by one or two surrogate mothers differing somewhat in their sensitivity to individual differences between infants, while a third group was cared for in a group nursery for the first ten days of life, and afterwards individually by one of the surrogate mothers.

SEASHORE, M. J., LEIFER, A. D., BARNETT, C. R. and LEIDERMAN, P. H. 1973. 'The effects of denial of early mother-infant interaction on maternal self-confidence', *Journal of Personality and Social Psychology* 3, 369–78.

Mothers of premature first-born children who were only allowed to view them through a nursery window (the separation group) were less self-confident in both social tasks and instrumental tasks (feeding, bathing and changing nappies) than mothers allowed to help in care-taking (the extended contact group). One month after discharge from hospital, primiparous mothers in the separation group were still somewhat less self-confident in instrumental tasks although their self-confidence in social tasks had risen to a level similar to that of mothers in the contact group. Differences in self-confidence could not be explained by differences in actual care-taking skills between the groups. Separation from their premature babies did not lower the self-confidence of the multiparous mothers. Mothers initially (twenty-four to forty-eight hours after birth) low in self-confidence, though, whether they were primiparous or multiparous, were more likely to have gained in self-confidence by the time their babies were discharged if they had been in the contact group.

SHEPARD, W. and PETERSEN, J. 1973. 'Are there sex differences in infancy?' *Catalog of Selected Documents in Psychology* 3, 121.

It is concluded from a review of research that the evidence is against there being sex differences in neonatal responsiveness, perceptual processes and social emotional behaviour.

THOMAN, E. B., LEIDERMAN, P. H. and OLSON, J. P. 1972. 'Neonate mother interaction during breast-feeding', *Developmental Psychology* 6, 1, 110–8.

A number of studies have found that mothers differ in their relationship with first- and later-born children. The findings of the present study suggest that many of these characteristics – inconsistency, greater attentiveness and persistence, greater stimulation and talking, greater interference – may be already apparent in the earliest mother-infant interactions. Forty-eight hours after the child's birth, primiparous mothers were found to spend more time than multiparous mothers in feeding the baby, especially boys, to change activities more frequently during feeding, and to provide more stimulation and talk more to the infant, especially girls. Primiparous mothers bottle-feeding their babies, were similarly found in an earlier study (Thoman *et al.*, 1970) to devote longer to the feeding process and to change activities more often. The inexperience of the primiparous breast-feeding mothers was shown in that the babies spent less time sucking at the breast, compared with babies of multiparous mothers, even though the primiparous mothers spent more time in stimulating them to suck. It is suggested that the primiparous mothers were less capable of responding to the babies' cues. For primiparous mothers only, talking to the baby during breast-feeding was found to be related to the total number of weeks the mother spent in breast-feeding.

THOMAN, E. B., TURNER, A. M., LEIDERMAN, P. H. and BARNETT, C. R. 1970. 'Neonate mother interaction: effects of parity on feeding behavior', *Child Development* 41, 4, 1103–11.

In this study it was found that middle-class mothers of first-born children, compared with mothers of later-born children, devoted significantly longer to bottle-feeding the two-day-old infant but with much less success (as indicated by the lower amount of formula consumed and lower rate of consumption). The prolonged efforts of the mother appeared to partially compensate for the lower rate of intake. It is suggested that some aspects of the mother-child relationship as seen in this study resemble those found in later childhood between mothers and their first-borns.

TULKIN, S. R. 1972. 'Social class differences in infants' reactions to mother's and stranger's voices', *Developmental Psychology* 8, 1, 137.

Middle-class ten-months-old infants showed greater differential responding to the mother's and a stranger's voices than working-class infants. This is probably because the middle-class children receive more verbal stimulation from their mothers.

TULKIN, S. R. and COHLER, B. J. 1973. 'Childrearing attitudes and mother-child interaction in the first year of life', *Merrill-Palmer Quarterly* 19, 2, 95–107.

Although it is believed that child-rearing attitudes are associated with the way in which the mother relates to her young child, previous research has had inconclusive findings. In contrast to previous research, which concentrated primarily on the issue of authoritarian control, the present study focussed on child care issues appropriate to the ages of the children being studied. Results of this study suggest that maternal attitudes (measured on the Maternal Attitudes Scale) were related to the mothers' observed interactions with their children. Maternal attitudes which reflected the encouragement of reciprocity (attitude that the infant can communicate with the mother, and the mother can understand and respond), were involved in most of the significant associations with aspects of behaviour (response to and imitations of the infant's vocalisations, giving the infant objects to play with, response to infant's frets), especially in middle-class mothers. It is suggested that working-class mothers whose attitudes endorse the acceptance of reciprocity may be less likely to act on their beliefs because mothers in this social class tend to feel that they can have little influence over the child's development. Subjects – thirty middle-class and twenty-six working-class mothers – were observed at home interacting with their ten-months-old first-born girls for two hours on two separate visits.

TULKIN, S. R. and KAGAN, J. 1972. 'Mother-child interaction in the first year of life', *Child Development* 43, 1, 31–41.

In this investigation of the experiences of infants from two social class backgrounds, thirty middle-class and twenty-six working-class mothers were observed at home for two hours a day on two separate days with first-born ten-months-old baby girls. Some differences in the environments of the two groups of children were found. The working-class infants lived in more crowded homes, had more interaction with adults other than the mother, and spent more time in front of television sets. They also had fewer opportunities to explore and manipulate the environment. Non-verbal maternal behaviour (proximity to infant, physical contact, response to non-verbal initiation of contact by infant) and prohibitions showed no class differences. In contrast, maternal vocalisations were much more frequent in the middle-class although middle-class infants showed no tendency to vocalise spontaneously more often. Middle-class mothers also entertained their infants more frequently, responded to a higher proportion of their frets, and responded more rapidly. When interaction of all adults, not just the mother, with the infant was taken into account, social class differences remained similar to those described above. Large within, as well as between, class differences were found. It is concluded that working-class mothers care for their infants as extensively as middle-class mothers, but there are class differences in maternal stimulation of cognitive development. Suggested explanations for the differences are:

(1) Some working-class mothers did not believe that their infants possessed the ability to communicate.

(2) Many working-class mothers thought that their children were born with particular abilities which they could do little to influence.

B. Social attachments in infancy: implications for development

Much recent research on the child's early development has been concerned with his 'attachment', particularly to the mother, but increasingly to the father as well. The debate generated by Bowlby's (1951) report to the World Health Organisation, over the 'maternal deprivation' theory, focused attention on the possible importance for future development of the child's first interpersonal relationships. Research relevant to this debate suggested that lack of opportunity for the child to form, in the first years of life, a specific relationship with a care-taker or other adult may have been responsible for the later difficulties in personal relationships experienced by children who had spent their early years in the older type of institutional care; also, this lack of specific tie may have – in addition to the deficiency of environmental stimulation – contributed to the retarded intellectual and educational development found in many of these children (Ainsworth, 1962; Dinnage and Pringle, 1967; Pringle, 1971). Controversy over what actually constitutes 'maternal deprivation' drew attention to the fact that practically nothing was known about the child's early social relationships.

The term 'attachment' was actually coined by Bowlby (1958) to denote his theoretical conception of the child's emotional tie to the mother. According to this conception (Bowlby, 1969), the infant is genetically biased to behave in ways that promote proximity and contact with adults. Through a process of discriminative learning, the various kinds of behaviour which promote attachment such as crying, smiling and – later, when mobility allows – following, become focused specifically on the mother, and perhaps on a few other familiar individuals, rather than on any person who is in the immediate vicinity. These separate kinds of behaviour eventually become linked together so that they can be used more or less interchangeable to achieve a 'set-goal' of proximity to the mother. The actual distance that is maintained from her will depend on various circumstances, including the familiarity of the environment and whether the child is tired, hungry or alarmed. The infant is equipped with these genetic biases, according to Bowlby's theory, because they were of survival value in the environment in which man evolved, proximity to the mother giving the child protection from predators. Much of the recent work on attachment has been carried out by Ainsworth and her colleagues who are in broad agreement with Bowlby's theoretical viewpoint.

A rather different formulation is offered by Schaffer and Emerson (1964). They suggest that the infant's primary need is not for proximity to other people, but for stimulation. At first, the infant seeks optimal arousal from all aspects of the environment. In time, he learns, though, that

63

THE IMPACT OF VERY EARLY LIFE EXPERIENCES

humans are a particularly satisfying source of stimulation and that they are also often sources of non-social stimulation. A need for proximity to other people develops when the infant has learned about their particular characteristics. Eventually, a narrowing down occurs and attachments are formed to specific people.

Among others who have adopted the term 'attachment' are some social learning theorists (particularly Bijou and Baer, 1973; Gewirtz, 1961; 1972). They hold that it is not necessary to propose that an infant is born with a 'need' for social contact. According to their view, it is the mother's function to provide the child with positive reinforcing stimuli (i.e. stimuli such as food, water and many others, including possibly skin contact, warmth and imitation, which follow upon and strengthen a response of the infant). General characteristics of the mother, such as her attention, her affection and her proximity to the infant, which often precede or are presented at the same time as the reinforcing stimuli acquire positive reinforcing value. A child is only attached to his mother, though, when her unique characteristics, both physical and behavioural, function as general reinforcing stimuli over a wide area of his behaviour, including his orientation, approach and following responses. Although it is not necessary from this viewpoint to suppose that the baby is equipped with instinctual responses which promote proximity, Gewirtz (1961), at least, considers that their existence would not be incompatible with social learning theory; these responses could become conditioned by the reinforcing stimuli provided by the mother and would result in her characteristics acquiring reinforcing value.

Although much of the research on attachment has been guided by these various theoretical viewpoints, the term now appears to be in general usage to describe the child's first specific interpersonal ties.

Despite the theoretical interest and the upsurge of research into these first interpersonal relationships, much remains unclear as yet. The research available so far gives some indication of the usual course of development of attachment, of the conditions necessary for the formation of attachments, of the varying ways in which children organise their attachment behaviour, and of the relationship between attachment and other aspects of behaviour. The findings provide some indirect indications of how these first interpersonal relationships may influence later development. However, no research so far has attempted to directly link differences either in patterns of attachment relationships or in characteristics of the child's attachment behaviour to later outcome.

Development of attachment

If a clear-cut attachment to the mother (or other particular person) is defined as an active preference for her, whether this is measured by separation protest or positive behaviour towards her, most infants become attached in the third quarter of the first year (Ainsworth, 1963; 1967; Schaffer and Emerson, 1964; Tennes and Lampl, 1964; 1966; Yarrow, 1967). However, discrimination and preference for the mother have been found much earlier, there being some evidence that a few infants even show selective attention towards the mother and signs of pleasure in contact with her by the end of the first month (Tennes and Lampl, 1966; Yarrow, 1967). The point in time at which an 'attachment' to a specific person can be said to be established will depend very much on the particular criteria used. However, most researchers would agree that the baby cannot be 'attached' to anyone before he has reached the stage of cognitive development at which he can conceive of another person as existing independently when outside his perception (Ainsworth, 1973; Schaffer and Emerson, 1964; Tennes and Lampl, 1966; Yarrow, 1972).

Evidence that infants form their first social attachment in the third quarter of the first year is also provided by studies which have investigated definitive separations (i.e. long-lasting or permanent, rather than brief everyday separations). These studies (Schaffer, 1958; Schaffer and Callender, 1959; Yarrow, 1967) found distinct differences in infant's reactions to separation in the first half of the year and afterwards. In Yarrow's study, all children permanently separated from their (foster) mothers at eight months showed marked disturbance, while only 20 per cent of those separated at five months displayed strong reactions. In Schaffer's study, infants younger than seven months showed little reaction in the first few days after entry into hospital. In contrast, infants aged seven months and over showed frequent crying after visits from the mother, and little responsiveness to toys or the observer. Reactions on return home were also different; the younger children showing an extreme preoccupation with the environment and the older ones, for a much longer period on average, over-dependence on the mother, physically clinging to her and protesting if she left the room.

Most children living with their families develop a clear-cut attachment to a specific person in the third quarter of the first year. The main environmental condition for the development of an attachment appears to be sufficient interaction with a particular person (Ainsworth, 1963, 1967; Schaffer and Emerson, 1964). At what age, though, do the experiences of the infant become relevant to the formation of attachments? Evidence reviewed in the previous section showed that mother-infant interaction even in the earliest days may have some influence on the later relationship and will probably affect the attachment bond. Findings from another study by Schaffer (1963), however, indicate that a sufficient level of social stimulation is the essential pre-condition for the development of attachments. Infants who returned home from

65

hospital in the third and fourth quarters of the first year, after a prolonged stay in hospital (seventeen to eighteen weeks) which began before they had formed any clear-cut attachments, differed in the time they took to develop attachments according to their experiences during separation. Those who had received a high level of social stimulation (indiscriminately, from a number of nurses), although allowed no contact with their mothers, formed their first specific attachment (usually to the mother) in a relatively short time after the return home (19.7 days). Infants who received a low level of stimulation during the separation, even though they maintained some contact with their mothers (visits, mainly once a week) took much longer to form their first specific attachments on their return (fifty-five days).

Findings of the Schaffer (1963) study also indicate that infants can form their first attachments somewhat later than usual — at the end of the first year — if this is when they first have the opportunity for sufficient interaction with a particular person. How long an infant can remain in a depriving institution and still be able to form a first attachment when given the opportunity remains uncertain. Earlier research (Ainsworth, 1962; 1973; Rutter, 1972) suggested that this is difficult after the first three years or so and perhaps earlier, but the findings need clarification. In any case, fortunately, residential care has much improved in recent years and infants usually live in small groups and are provided with plentiful stimulation. Even though they are cared for by multiple care-takers, many children are able to form social attachments in this kind of residential care (Stevens, 1971; Tizard and Tizard, 1971), especially where one nurse pays particular attention to a child, however briefly. These attachments appear to be rather 'shallow' and 'insecure' compared with those of children living at home (Tizard and Tizard, 1971). However, children who have formed some kind of attachment appear to be able to develop a 'deep' attachment to adoptive parents even when they have remained in residential care until the age of four (Tizard and Rees, 1975). Whether children who have received a high level of social stimulation without the opportunity to form specific attachments could still establish them at the age of four remains uncertain.

These findings raise the question of whether residential care for infants and young children should be organised so that they have the opportunity to establish close relationships with particular adults. Apparently, in most nurseries close relationships with nurses involved in care-taking are discouraged (although a 'special nurse' system, whereby a nurse not involved in the child's care-taking gives him special attention in her off-duty time, may operate) (Tizard and Tizard, 1971). The grounds for this are that the child would be very upset if the nurse to whom he was attached left, and that having had a close relationship with one person, the child would find it difficult to establish a later relationship with someone else, his own mother, or a foster or adoptive mother, if he himself later left the nursery. The issue then is whether separation from the main attachment object is in itself harmful, and whether the child can form a new attachment when his main tie has been permanently broken.

The most direct evidence comes from a recently published study (Yarrow et al., 1974). Ten-year-old children who had been separated from their foster mothers after the age at which they are likely to have formed attachments to them (six months) to go to adoptive homes differed from children whose attachments had not been disrupted (they went to adoptive homes soon after birth) in their capacity to establish different levels of relationship with people, but not in overall adaptation. The degree of trauma experienced by the infant at separation was not related to intellectual ability or personality characteristics of the child at ten years of age. The findings indicate that one separation, involving no deprivation of stimulation or 'mothering', has only very slightly disadvantageous effects.

In contrast, those children in the Tizard and Tizard (1971) study who were still in residential care at the age of four-and-a-half tended by then 'not to care deeply for anyone' although they might be attention-seeking and clinging. Similarly, this type of superficial over-friendliness was found in a considerable proportion (about 40 per cent) of institutional children who had been admitted to care under the age of two, but was very rare in children admitted after this age (Wolkind, 1974). The evidence remains sketchy but it seems it would be preferable for children in residential care to be given the opportunity to form close relationships with the staff. This would probably lead to a more favourable outcome if they had to remain in residential care and would not prevent the formation of new relationships on leaving. Encouragement of two or three 'deep' relationships, if possible, would give some insurance against one of the staff leaving. After all, it is quite usual in ordinary families for children to have more than one 'deep' attachment, as will be discussed below.

It has been widely accepted that temporary, as opposed to permanent separation, from the main attachment figure(s), such as occurs when a child is admitted to hospital in the early years, has no long-term ill-effects on behaviour, though it may cause considerable upset and distress in the immediate period after the return home. Two recent studies (Douglas, 1975; Quinton and Rutter, 1975) have re-opened the question, both finding a link between behaviour disturbance in later childhood or adolescence and repeated hospital admissions, of which at least one occurred when the child was below the age of five. Hospital admissions of a week or less were not associated with any long-term effects in either study, and Quinton and Rutter failed to replicate Douglas' findings that single admissions of four weeks or more did make adverse effects more

67

likely. The long-term ill-effects associated with long single admissions (of four weeks at least) in Douglas' study can be explained by the greater disadvantages of the families in which these admissions tend to occur but the effects of repeated hospital admissions cannot be accounted for in the same way. Thus it is possible that repeated temporary separations from those to whom he is attached may adversely affect a child. It is also possible, though, that the repeated separations are serving as an indicator of some other aspect of family circumstances, and that this is the casual factor (Clarke and Clarke, 1976). In any case, less than a third of the children with repeated admissions to hospital showed any evidence of later emotional or behavioural disturbance, and the main risks seemed to be for children who were already somewhat insecure in their family relationships.

Patterns of attachment relationships

Sufficient interaction with a person is necessary for a child to develop an attachment to a particular individual, but the mere carrying out of routine care-taking duties may not constitute sufficient interaction (Schaffer and Emerson, 1964). On the other hand, an attachment can be formed to a mother who shares care-taking with others (Ainsworth, 1963) or even to a person who takes no part at all in the routine care-taking, provided there is sufficient interaction with the child (Schaffer and Emerson, 1964).

It appears that a child will become most attached to those in his environment who are most responsive to his signals of distress and who themselves initiate interaction with him (Schaffer and Emmerson, 1964). Mostly, his mother will be the child's first and main attachment object, but not invariably so, even when she is the principal care-taker. Sometimes the father may be the first attachment object and sometimes the main tie is with him (Ainsworth, 1963, 1967; Cohen and Campos, 1974; Schaffer and Emerson, 1964). Most children appear to form an attachment to their father as well as their mother (Ban and Lewis, 1974; Cohen and Campos, 1974; Kotelchuck et al., 1975; Lamb, 1975; Lester et al., 1974; Schaffer and Emerson, 1964; Ross et al., 1975; Spelke et al., 1973; Willemsen et al., 1974), probably before the end of the first year, though it may be less deep than the tie with the mother.

That other attachments follow soon after the formation of the first clear-cut attachment, is undisputed (Ainsworth, 1963, 1964, 1967; Schaffer and Emerson, 1964). There is some conflict, though, on whether a child usually has one main attachment, mostly to the mother, and other subsidiary attachments or whether he is quite likely to be more or less equally attached to two or three people, often the father and the mother (Schaffer and Emerson, 1964). Despite their high research output,

Ainsworth and her colleagues have not systematically investigated the child's attachments to people other than the mother. On the other hand, Schaffer and Emerson used separation protest in everyday situations as their sole criterion of attachment. While this was probably adequate (based as it was on data obtained from the mother at regular intervals over a period often as long as fourteen months) to determine the pattern of an individual child's attachments, the findings need to be substantiated by further research, using additional criteria. Separation protest in the home environment may often express 'insecurity' rather than 'depth' of attachment (Stayton and Ainsworth, 1973).

The more recent findings are somewhat equivocal. Separation protest in an unfamiliar environment fails to indicate any preference for mother rather than father in twelve to twenty-one-months-old infants, but may not be a reliable measure of 'depth' of attachment to the departing parent (Cohen and Campos, 1974; Kotelchuck et al., 1975). The strength of the protest appears to be related to a number of factors including whether the infant is left with a familiar or an unfamiliar person, his previous experience and cognitive understanding of the situation (Kotelchuck et al., 1975; Spelke et al., 1973) as well as the cumulative stress he has undergone (Cohen and Campos, 1974). There is some evidence that one-year-olds in relatively stress-free unfamiliar situations show a preference towards the mother when measures such as proximity seeking (Ban and Lewis, 1974) or the amount of playing in the parent's presence (Feldman and Ingham, 1975) are used as criteria of attachment, though other studies using these measures have failed to find any difference in preference (Lamb, 1976; Willemsen et al., 1974). In more stressful situations, given a choice between the parent, there seems to be a preference for the mother (Cohen and Campos, 1974; Lamb, 1976). By the time infants are two years old, evidence is consistent that there is little or no preference for interaction with either parent in relatively stress free situations (Feldman and Ingham, 1975; Lewis, Weinraub and Ban, 1972, Lamb, 1974, cited by Lamb, 1975), but findings are so far unavailable on whether the preference for the mother in more stressful situations is retained by infants at this age. The question of whether the primary attachment tie remains somewhat different from other ties that are formed is so far unresolved.

The issue of whether a child has one main attachment, the others being subsidiary or whether he can be more or less equally attached to two people has practical implications, as was seen above. It is also relevant to the question of how the attachments of young children are likely to be affected by the mother's working. It might well be advantageous for the child to be equally attached to his substitute care-taker and his mother, for example, while difficulties could arise if the main tie was with the substitute care-taker, the attachment to the mother being subsidiary.

Is it generally advantageous or detrimental for a child to have two or three 'deep' attachments rather than one main attachment? There is some rather tenuous evidence that infants with a 'deep' attachment to both father and mother may be cognitively advanced (Escalona and Corman, 1971; Spelke et al., 1973). In the latter study, infants who had frequent interactions with their fathers were found to be more advanced in cognitive development than those who had little interaction with their fathers. The other study presents findings on only two infants but they were studied intensively over the first two years of life. The infant whose main attachment appeared to be with the mother had an intense and ambivalent relationship with her, and lost in social responsiveness and interest in the environment when with other care-takers. The other child, also 'deeply' attached to his mother, differed little in his social behaviour when he was with her or his other main care-taker, an attentive father to whom he was also presumably 'deeply' attached. This second child was considerably more advanced in cognitive development.

Whether or not one tie is usually of more importance than the others, it does appear that most children living with their families have more than one attachment (Schaffer and Emerson, 1964; Tizard and Tizard, 1971) and that ties to people other than the mother increase as the child grows older (Schaffer and Emerson, 1964). In the Tizards' study, two-year-old working-class London children were likely to have four attachments on average. At a minimum, this is likely to be advantageous if the mother has to leave the child with someone else for a while. Recent research shows that infants are much less distressed by an unfamiliar environment if they are with their fathers than if alone or with an acquaintance or a stranger (Feldman and Ingham, 1975; Lester et al., 1974; Willemsen et al., 1974). Earlier work also indicated that people other than the mother to whom the child was attached could reduce the stress of a strange situation (Rutter, 1972). It is likely that care by someone to whom he had already formed an attachment would be less distressing for a child in the mother's absence than care by an unfamiliar person (Rutter, 1972). However, it does seem that children need one or more 'deep' attachments for favourable development, and that very many less deep attachments cannot be substituted. The residential nursery children discussed above, who at two-and-a-half showed intense attachment behaviour to anyone they knew well and at four-and-a-half appeared, on the whole, not to care much for anyone, provide evidence of this (Tizard and Tizard, 1971).

The nature of the attachment relationship: strength and security of attachment

The findings on the attachment behaviour of the residential nursery children mentioned above imply that a child can display intensive attachment behaviour to someone without being 'deeply' attached to them. This may appear somewhat contradictory but there is evidence that intensive attachment behaviour often indicates the insecurity rather than the strength of the relationship (Ainsworth *et al.*, 1971; Stayton and Ainsworth, 1973).

Ainsworth and her colleagues (Ainsworth, 1973; Ainsworth *et al.*, 1971) have stressed the difficulties in trying to measure the 'strength' of attachment. Pain, illness, tiredness, alarm, absence of the attachment object, reunion, and unfamiliarity of the environment may all heighten attachment behaviour (Ainsworth, 1963; Schaffer and Emerson, 1964). Although the child shows stronger attachment behaviour under these circumstances, it does not seem very sensible to interpret this as showing that the relationship with the preferred person has grown 'stronger'. Ainsworth and her colleagues (1971) have also pointed out that the use of different criteria would result in very different rankings of strength of attachment. In a study carried out in surroundings which were unfamiliar to the child, it was found that proximity and contact-seeking taken as criteria of attachment would have resulted in one set of children being rated as 'strongly' attached, while other sets of children would have been judged as strongly attached if distress during separation from the mother or search for her were used as criteria; behaviour in the home environment would have produced another set of rankings.

A number of studies have shown, in fact, that the various kinds of behaviour which indicate attachment — behaviour that is directed differentially towards the mother or other preferred person, at least when stress is heightened as in an unfamiliar environment — do not all correlate positively. Studies of intercorrelations between kinds of attachment behaviour in ten, fourteen, and eighteen-months-old infants (Coates *et al.*, 1972a) and two, two-and-a-half, and three-year-old children (Maccoby and Feldman, 1972) have found a number of correlations but these are usually only of a moderate magnitude, and some kinds of attachment behaviour do not correlate at all.

When the child is alone with his mother in unfamiliar surroundings, proximity-seeking and touching her are positively correlated (the relationship is inflated because touching necessarily involves proximity) (Coates *et al.*, 1972a) but there is little association between proximity-seeking and the more distal kinds of attachment behaviour (smiling, talking to, and showing objects to the mother) (Coates *et al.*, 1972a; Maccoby and Feldman, 1972). Nor is there much evidence for a relationship between the positive and negative indicators of attachment. Proximity-seeking and touching the mother were related to crying during separation only in fourteen-months-old infants, not for the ten- and eighteen-months-old infants in the Coates *et al.* study. In other studies of infants aged about eight months to two years (Tennes and Lampl, 1966) or two to three years (Maccoby and Feldman, 1972), no relationship was found between proximity-seeking and separation protest. A positive relationship (increasing with age) was found between separation protest and proximity-seeking after reunion with the mother in the Coates *et al.* study. However, in the familiar home environment the relationship found was the opposite, crying on separation from the mother being negatively correlated with positive greetings on her return in nine- to twelve-months-old infants (Stayton and Ainsworth, 1973).

Unless 'attachment' is viewed as a unitary trait, as some researchers (e.g. Blurton Jones and Leach, 1972; Coates *et al.*, 1972a) appear to regard it, these findings do not weaken the concept. They do imply, though, that no one attachment behaviour can be used as an index of the strength of attachment. Does this mean then that there is no way in which differences in the manner in which different children relate to their mothers (or other preferred persons) can be categorised? Studies by Ainsworth and her colleagues, confirmed to some extent at least by others (Blurton Jones and Leach, 1972; Clarke-Stewart, 1973), suggest that the different ways in which children organise their attachment behaviour can be meaningfully categorised. The differences appear to arise from differences in the prior mother-child (or person-child) interaction, and they are likely to affect both other aspects of behaviour and future relationships of the child.

Some of these points can be illustrated by findings from Ainsworth *et al.*'s study of a sample of middle-class American infants over the first year of life (Ainsworth and Bell, 1970; Ainsworth and Wittig, 1969; Ainsworth *et al.*, 1971). When they were nearly one year old, the infants were tested in a 'strange situation' in a laboratory using a standard procedure (the infant was placed with his mother in a free play situation in an unfamiliar room, and his responses to the entry of a stranger, separation from the mother and reunion with her were observed). In the pre-separation episodes, infants tended not to touch the mother or even approach her, and there was little crying. The infants used the mother as a secure base to explore the strange situation. During the mother's absence, exploratory behaviour declined, crying increased and many infants searched for the mother. Proximity-seeking and contact-maintaining behaviour was much higher on reunion with the mother than before, crying did not immediately subside in many children and exploratory behaviour never recovered to its initial level. Ambivalent behaviour (both wanting and resisting contact) was not found prior to separation but occurred in about a third of the sample on the first reunion with the mother, and in about half of the infants on the second reunion. About half of the infants also showed proximity-avoiding behaviour in the reunion episodes, although this kind of behaviour did not occur before separation.

Similar changes in behaviour in infants who experience separation from their mothers in a strange situation have been found in a number of studies (Coates *et al.*, 1972a; Cox and Campbell, 1968; Feldman and Ingham, 1975; Lester *et al.*, 1974; Rheingold, 1969). However, none of these other studies has attempted to classify the infants into groups, differing in the way in which attachment behaviour was affected by the strange situation procedure and in the balance shown between attachment and exploratory behaviour. The classification by Ainsworth and her colleagues was primarily, though not entirely, made on the behaviour shown in the reunion episodes, in which the children's behaviour was differentially heightened.

Babies displaying one extreme of behaviour showed acute distress during separation and/or relatively strong proximity-seeking and contact-maintaining behaviour even in the low-stress period before separation from the mother. They were unable to use the mother as a secure base for exploration even in the pre-separation period, before stress had been heightened; some did explore, but unenthusiastically. On reunion, these infants displayed ambivalent behaviour, both wanting contact and resisting it. They may be characterised as 'mal-attached'.

At the other extreme were children who generally showed only very weak attachment behaviour – little or no separation distress and relatively weak proximity-seeking even in the reunion episodes – although they did search strongly for the mother when separated from her. These children were able to maintain exploratory behaviour throughout the strange situation procedure, but signs of disturbance were seen in their tendency to avoid proximity with the mother, this behaviour sometimes being mingled with proximity-seeking in the reunion episodes.

The largest group, whose behaviour approximated to the common behavioural trends for the sample as a whole, are designated 'secure' attached by Ainsworth (1973). They explored in the pre-separation episode, their attachment behaviour was clearly heightened by separation, though some avoided crying, at least until the second separation, and they showed little or no contact resisting or proximity-avoiding behaviour in the reunion episodes.

Ainsworth *et al.* (1971) conclude from their observations that the infants in each group (or sub-group, for they were actually further divided) were attached to the mother in their own fashion, the qualitative character of the attachment relationship overriding the significance of the concept of 'strength of attachment'. In one study, though, in which the Ainsworth type strange situation procedure was used, a measure of intensity of attachment was obtained by totalling up all the proximity-and-attention seeking behaviour displayed by an infant throughout the

73

entire session (Clarke-Stewart, 1973). As might be expected, infants with moderate scores were highly likely to be placed in the 'secure' attached group, those with the highest scores were likely to be in the 'mal-attached' group and those with the lowest in the proximity-avoiding category. This suggests that some quantification of the attachment relationship might be possible, using this type of standardised procedure and taking into account all the attachment behaviour shown. Extreme scores would represent some disturbance in the attachment relationship. However, the particular constellation of kinds of attachment behaviour shown by the child, and the way in which this differs from normative trends, in a particular set of circumstances is likely to give information about the relationship − and its effect on other aspects of behaviour − beyond that which would be provided by a quantitative measure. While the details of the Ainsworth *et al.* categorisation cannot be accepted unreservedly without further replication, the method used appears to be a promising one for investigation of the nature of attachment relationships.

Unless the variations of attachment behaviour observed in the 'strange situation', though, bear a consistent relationship to behaviour in everyday life and unless they have some stability over time, they are unlikely to be of developmental consequence. Some evidence for congruence between 'strange situation' and home behaviour was supplied in the Ainsworth *et al.* (1971) study. Infants who at home used the mother as a secure base for exploration accepting contact with the mother positively and occasionally initiating contact, and who showed little separation distress were all placed in the 'secure' category on the basis of their 'strange situation' behaviour. The other infants mainly showed some disturbance in their relationship with the mother at home which resembled that shown in the 'strange situation', though in a few instances aspects of the relationship were heightened which were not particularly prominent in the home environment. These infants generally tended to show more separation distress at home than the 'secure' attached children.

The developmental changes occurring in the frequencies with which the various kinds of attachment behaviour are shown, makes the assessment of individual consistency over time difficult. After the child is eighteen months old, there is evidence, in an unfamiliar environment at least, of a decline in separation protest and in proximity-seeking, when the situation is relatively stress-free; distal forms of attachment behaviour such as speaking to, smiling at and showing things to the mother increase (Cox and Campbell, 1968; Maccoby and Feldman, 1972). Nevertheless there is some evidence for individual consistency in proximity-seeking over the period from ten to eighteen months (Coates *et al.*, 1972b) and over the age period from two to three years, at least in presence of a stranger (Maccoby and Feldman, 1972). There is also some individual consistency in crying when the mother departs, particularly when the child is left with a stranger, over the two- to three-year period (Maccoby and Feldman, 1972). However a more satisfactory method of investigating consistency might be to categorise children at different age levels in relation to the frequency norms for the age. Of course, some changes in the nature of the child's attachment relationships to his mother and others are to be expected.

Antecedents of attachment relationships

Evidence indicates that the mother's behaviour is related to the characteristics of the infant's attachment behaviour towards her. Sensitivity of the mother in perceiving and responding promptly and appropriately to the child's signals appears to be the key determinant of a 'secure' attachment. Initiation of interaction with the child, expression of affection for him, acceptance, accessibility and non-interference also appear to be associated with a 'secure' attachment. Most of the evidence comes from the studies of Ainsworth and her colleagues, but there is corroborating evidence from other researchers on the relationship between various aspects of maternal behaviour and the child's attachment behaviour.

Mothers who are sensitive to their children's needs have infants who are classified as 'secure' attached in a strange situation (Ainsworth and Bell, 1969; Ainsworth et al., 1971; Clarke-Stewart, 1973). At home, their infants also show 'security' in their attachment behaviour to the mother, displaying little separation protest (Stayton and Ainsworth, 1973). Insensitive mothers have infants who show their insecurity either by being particularly upset by the 'strange situation' or who use proximity-avoiding behaviour as a defence against a disharmonious relationship with the mother (Ainsworth et al., 1971; Clarke-Stewart, 1973). At home their behaviour also suggests insecurity – frequently crying in general as well as on separation and being put down (Stayton and Ainsworth, 1973).

While mothers who are sensitive also appear to be accepting, accessible to the baby, and non-interfering in the baby's activities, mothers who are negative in one of these characteristics are not necessarily negative in all the others (Ainsworth et al., 1971). Ainsworth and her colleagues found a complex relationship between characteristics of the mother and the child's attachment behaviour. Mothers who are the most rejecting have infants who show proximity-avoiding behaviour and little separation protest in a 'strange situation' (Ainsworth et al., 1971). There is some confirmation of this from earlier work (Tennes and Lampl,

1966) in which the mothers who were the most (and also least) hostile were found to have infants who showed little or no distress on separation in a laboratory situation. It is the mothers who are moderately rejecting whose infants appear to be most upset by the 'strange situation' and show most separation protest (Ainsworth *et al.*, 1971; Tennes and Lampl, 1966). There is also some confirmation for Ainsworth *et al.*'s findings that mothers who are both rejecting and interfering have babies who tend to ignore them at home (Beckwith, 1972).

It is perhaps somewhat surprising that mothers who provided their infants with an excessive amount of physical contact had infants who showed 'mal-attachment' in an Ainsworth-type of 'strange situation' in one study (Clarke-Stewart, 1973). However, findings from the Ainsworth *et al.* study are in partial agreement, mothers of children who were most vulnerable to the stresses of the strange situation all interacted playfully and affectionately with their children at times, one at least to an excessive extent, but their behaviour was always geared to their own desires rather than the baby's needs.

On the other hand, the provision of a high amount of social stimulation for the baby (looking, smiling, coming near him, talking to him, imitating him, replying to his vocalisations) appears to be related to 'secure' attachment (Clarke-Stewart, 1973). Provision of greater stimulation for the baby, by taking him on outings more often, has also been found to be related to 'secure' attachment (S. M. Bell, 1970).

There are findings, though, from one carefully carried out study which appear to contradict all the evidence associating maternal sensitivity and responsiveness with 'secure' attachment behaviour in the child. It was found (Schaffer and Emerson, 1964) that mothers who were most responsive to their infant's crying and who initiated most interaction with them had infants who displayed not the least separation protest at home, as in the Stayton and Ainsworth study, but the most. However, an examination of the method by which data was collected suggests that in this particular investigation, separation protest in everyday situations may not have been measuring 'insecurity' of attachment. The main source of data was the mother's recollections of instances of protest over the previous month, and she is particularly likely to have noticed occasions on which protest was intense, especially if a sensitive mother. Also, only those separations were taken into account in which the child was prevented from following and this should have greatly increased the rate of protest (following was negatively related to crying on separation in the Stayton and Ainsworth 1973 study) even in the 'secure' child. Additionally, intensity of separation protest was rated when the infants were seventeen to eighteen months old, a period at which it appears to be near its peak (Lester *et al.*, 1974; Tennes and Lampl, 1964). When these points are taken into consideration, the Schaffer and Emerson findings probably do not contradict the association between maternal sensitivity and 'secure' attachment.

Attachment and cognitive development

There is some evidence that maternal behaviour may provide a link between the quality of a child's attachment to his mother and his level of cognitive development. Infants who showed more 'secure' attachment in the 'strange situation' were also found in one study (S. M. Bell, 1970) to have reached a more advanced stage in the concept of persons (and also of objects) as permanent (i.e. existing outside the infant's perception) than those who showed proximity-avoiding behaviour or 'mal-attachment'. Infants classified as 'secure' attached on the basis of their 'strange situation' behaviour have also been found to be the most advanced in mental development in another study (Clarke-Stewart, 1973). The explanation appears to be that the same kinds of maternal behaviour which promote the formation of a 'secure' attachment – sensitivity and appropriate responsiveness to the child's signals and provision of a high amount of social stimulation – also promote mental development (Clarke-Stewart, 1973; Lewis and Goldberg, 1969; L. J. Yarrow, 1963). Institutionalised infants whose relationships with staff were such that they were unable to form attachments to anyone have been found to be extremely retarded in the stage of object permanence reached (and even more so in person permanence) compared with home-reared infants who had established attachments with their mothers (Lamb, 1973).

However, it would be greatly over-simplifying to suggest that either the child's cognitive development or even the quality of his attachment to the mother is affected only by the prior maternal-child interaction. There is evidence that the amount of social stimulation received by the child in the early months, whatever the source, is the determinant of an infant's readiness to form specific attachments (Schaffer, 1963). Also, as the Escalona and Corman (1971) study, discussed above, shows, the nature of the child's relationship to his mother may be affected by influences outside that relationship itself. Once the child has formed specific attachments, it seems likely that the quality of these will influence other aspects of his development, including possibly cognitive development, while cognitive development certainly appears to influence some aspects of attachment behaviour (Lester et al., 1974; Schaffer, 1971; Spelke et al., 1973).

Recent research findings have shown that young children living in residential nurseries which provide good physical care and a high level of staff-child interaction, are not retarded in intellectual or linguistic development even though close ties with particular staff members are discouraged (Tizard *et al.*, 1972). These findings have been interpreted as showing (Rutter, 1972) that a sufficient level of stimulation, including verbal stimulation, is what matters for cognitive growth, and that the formation of attachments is unimportant in relation to this (though not to emotional and social development).

Two recent sources of evidence throw doubt on these conclusions. The first is a study (Saltz, 1973) in which it was found that young institutionalised children who were given the opportunity to form attachments (to foster grandparents) made better intellectual progress than children not given this opportunity, even though both groups were provided with excellent physical care and much social stimulation. The second source of evidence comes from home-based intervention programmes for young disadvantaged children. It was found (Bronfenbrenner, 1974) that these programmes were more effective when the mother, rather than a tutor, was the agent of intervention. Bronfenbrenner suggests that this was partly because the interaction between mother and child necessary to carry out the programme strengthened the child's attachment, and increased his motivation to attend to the mother; also the interaction shaped the mother's behaviour, encouraging appropriate responsiveness to the child's acts. It should also be noted that most of the residential nursery children in the Tizard *et al.* (1972) study were not without attachments to the staff, although these appeared to be 'shallow' and 'insecure' in relation to the attachments of the home-reared children (Tizard and Rees, 1975; Tizard and Tizard, 1971; 1974).

Attachment and other aspects of behaviour

One way in which a child's attachment relationships may affect his cognitive development is through their influence on his exploratory behaviour. Evidence that most children use their mothers as a secure base for exploration when in unfamiliar surroundings is found in a number of studies. Children between the ages of ten months and three years are able to explore a strange situation in the mother's presence but exploratory behaviour diminishes, particularly in infants under the age of eighteen months, when the mother departs and the child is left alone (Ainsworth and Bell, 1970; Cox and Campbell, 1968; Maccoby and Feldman, 1972; Rheingold, 1969) or with a stranger (Ainsworth and Bell, 1970; Lester *et al.*, 1974). The father's presence also can support exploration in an unfamiliar environment (Lester *et al.*, 1974; Willemsen *et al.*, 1974).

When a ten-months-old infant is placed alone in strange surroundings, he explores less and cries more than a child whose mother has been with him first and then departed (Rheingold, 1969). The presence of a person to whom the infant is attached transmutes strangeness into novelty (Rheingold, 1969). An infant of this age will himself, however, leave the mother to explore interesting toys (Eckerman and Rheingold, 1974; Rheingold and Eckerman, 1969) or even an empty room (Rheingold and Eckerman, 1969). Similarly, an infant will delay following his mother into an adjoining room if he finds an attractive toy on the way (Corter et al., 1972) even though his mother is out of sight. Nevertheless, the evidence indicates that the infant is still using his mother as a secure base for there seems to be a limit to the time he will spend away from her; he may follow or return to her and then go back again to play with the interesting toy (Corter et al., 1972). An enforced separation from the accompanying parent, even though very brief, may make an unfamiliar environment insecure enough for the one- to two-year-old infant to be inhibited in his exploration of it a week later (Smith, 1975). Eight- to thirteen-months-old infants in institutional care were found in one study to have fewer patterns of exploratory behaviour than working-class, home-reared children (Collard, 1971). Both the fewer opportunities for exploration of the institutional infants and the difference in quality of their attachments (home-reared children looked and smiled at their mothers twice as often as did the institutional children at their nurses) may be influences on their exploratory behaviour.

The mother or other preferred person may also be used as a secure base for the exploration of people. It is clear from the literature that most children show wariness of strangers on occasion, and that the incidence of this increases in the second half of the first year (Morgan and Ricciuti, 1969; Tennes and Lampl, 1964; Yarrow, 1967). The presence of the mother (Bronson, 1972; Morgan and Ricciuti, 1969), or to a lesser extent, of a familiar care-giver (Ricciuti, 1974) reduces wariness. Recent studies, measuring heart rate responses of infants, have confirmed the change in wariness with age (Campos et al., 1975; Waters et al., 1975) and the attenuation of wariness produced by the mother's presence (Campos et al., 1975). The use of the child's attachment object as a secure base for exploration of people is seen in one study (Cohen and Campos, 1974) which found that eye contact with a stranger in ten- to sixteen-months-old infants was significantly greater when they were near to the mother or father than when they were on their own. It has also been found (Maccoby and Feldman, 1972) that children aged two to two-and-a-half years look more towards and interact to a greater extent with a stranger in the mother's presence than when she is absent.

It has sometimes been suggested that 'fear of strangers' is simply an expression of the child's attachment to his mother. There is little evidence to support this view. Actual fear (crying, distressed look, moving away) as opposed to wariness, appears to be relatively rare (Yarrow, 1967) and positive responses are also quite common (Rheingold and Eckerman, 1973). In two experimental studies (Greenberg *et al.*, 1973; Morgan and Ricciuti, 1969) fear was found, when at its height, in a third or less of the infants. Its occurrence appears to depend a great deal on the behaviour of the stranger (Morgan and Ricciuti, 1969), and the rather odd behaviour adopted by the stranger in the experimental studies is likely to have maximised its incidence. Longitudinal research (started when the infants were a few weeks old and carried on until they were eighteen months) indicates that about 30 to 50 per cent of children who show fear on one occasion never show it again (Schaffer, 1966). Evidence suggests that it is 'insecurity' as shown by vulnerability in a 'strange situation' (Ainsworth *et al.*, 1971; Tennes and Lampl, 1964), not 'depth' of attachment (Yarrow, 1967) that is related to 'fear of strangers'. At least a partial explanation for the greater wariness of a strange adult found in residential nursery two-year-olds, compared with children living at home (Tizard and Tizard, 1971), may be that their 'insecure' relationship with the familiar nurse prevented them from using her as a secure base for exploration of the stranger.

Conclusions

The infant becomes attached from about the third quarter of the first year to people who interact sufficiently with him, and he is likely to become 'deeply' attached to those (usually including his mother) who are most sensitive to his signals and who provide the most social stimulation for him. He is likely to experience more heightened emotions, make a greater variety of social responses and engage in more complex social interactions in his mother's presence than in her absence, when his closest tie is with her (Escalona and Corman, 1971). He is motivated to attend to and learn from the person to whom he has an enduring emotional attachment (Bronfenbrenner, 1974). However, it is not just the child who is affected by the relationship. The more responsive the child is to his mother, the more affectionate and attached to the child she becomes, and the more responsive she is to his signals (Clarke-Stewart, 1973). Thus she is likely to become more appropriately responsive to his needs. This is also the kind of maternal behaviour that appears to promote mental development in the first and second years of life (Clarke-Stewart, 1973; Lewis and Goldberg, 1969; Schaffer, 1971).

It is not just the interaction with the person to whom he is attached that appears likely to have developmental consequences for the child. 'Paradoxically, it is one of the principal functions of mothering to free the child from the mother' (Schaffer, 1971). It is the child's social attachments which provide him with the security from which he can explore the world, both inanimate and social. Young children, especially between the ages of ten and eighteen months tend to be inhibited or distressed by a strange environment and wary of strange people, but the presence of the mother (or other person to whom the child is attached) changes the strange into the interesting.

Virtually all infants living in ordinary families have sufficient interaction with their mothers to become attached to them. However, it seems that the quality of the mother-child interaction influences the characteristics of the relationship (Ainsworth et al., 1971; Clarke-Stewart, 1973). Infants whose mothers are insensitive appear to develop attachment behaviour differing in various ways from the normative behaviour of children of similar age. They may be ambivalent in relation to the mother, some are unable to use her as a secure base for exploration of the unfamiliar, and others tend to spend much of their time in activities independent of the mother, presumably engaging less in reciprocal interactions with her. Only a beginning has been made in classifying children according to differences in their attachment to the mother, and practically no attempt has been made to investigate developmental outcomes. However, even less is known about the nature of attachments to people other than the mother. A close relationship with both parents rather than the mother alone seems likely to be beneficial for a child but the research findings available so far are very scanty. They are non-existent on the outcomes of different patterns of attachments. Research has established the potential importance for the child of forming close ties with others in the early years, but the links with later development have not yet been put together.

Annotations

AINSWORTH, M. D. S. 1963. 'The development of infant-mother interaction among the Ganda', in B. M. Foss (ed) *Determinants of Infant Behaviour. II*, Methuen, London. 67–112.

Subjects of this study were twenty-six Ganda mothers and their twenty-eight infants, aged up to twenty-four months, visited by the investigator at approximately two-weekly intervals over a period averaging seven months. Twenty-three babies developed a clear-cut attachment to the mother (discriminated the mother from others and responded differentially to her) while five did not.

Judgement that the infant had formed an attachment to the mother was made not on a single criterion but on a variety of behaviour patterns (differential crying, smiling, vocalising, looking, separation protest, following, scrambling, burying face, use of mother as a secure base for exploration, clinging, lifting arms or clapping hands in greeting). The developmental sequence of attachment responses during the first year is

81

described: In the second quarter of the first year the babies observed all showed differential response to the mother; some cried when she left the room, especially if they were left alone or with strangers, a few followed after her, and those who showed neither behaviour gave joyous greetings on her return. In the third quarter, attachment to the mother grew stronger, following became more consistent, though not invariable, and greeting responses became more conspicuous. In the fourth quarter, babies were more likely to follow and less likely to cry than previously. Following and greeting extended to other familiar figures as well as the mother. Infants tended to fear strangers although they had not been afraid earlier.

Sixteen children were judged to be secure-attached (showed typical signs of attachment for their stage of development and cried little), seven insecure attached (cried even when held by the mother, and unable to use her as a secure base for exploration) and five non-attached (or not yet attached) (showed none of the patterns of attachment to the mother, nor to anyone else). The security of attachment to the mother was related to the amount of care she gave the infant, her excellence as an informant (reflecting her involvement with the child) and her enjoyment of breast-feeding. A child could be securely attached to his mother even if he had multiple-care-takers, but the mother invariably gave the most care to the child. Children who had formed an attachment to the mother were then able to form attachments to other care-takers, and also to those who played with them but took no part in routine care. Several infants formed their strongest attachment to the father, even though the mother gave most care. However, no instance of the child becoming attached to someone other than the mother, and not to the mother, was found.

AINSWORTH, M. D. S. 1967. *Infancy in Uganda: Infant Care and Growth of Love*, Johns Hopkins, Baltimore (chapters 20–23, pp 331–400).

Later, and expanded, report of development of attachment to the mother among Ganda infants, containing much additional illustrative material (see Ainsworth, 1963).

AINSWORTH, M. D. S. and BELL, S. M. 1969. 'Some contemporary patterns of mother-infant interaction in the feeding situation', in A. Ambrose (ed) *Stimulation in Early Infancy*, Academic Press, London and New York. 133–63.

In this study, it was found that relatively little crying in babies during the first three months of life was related to feeding patterns in which the mothers were relatively sensitive to the babies' signals and communications (whether labelled 'schedule' or 'demand' feeding by the mother). Mothers sensitive to the baby's state and wishes in feeding tended also to be sensitive in their other social interactions with the baby. Findings do not necessarily imply that it is the mother's behaviour which influences the child, for constitutional characteristics of some babies may make it easier for the mother to interact harmoniously with them. It is suggested that the mother's contribution and the baby's contribution to interaction become caught in an interaction spiral. It is also suggested that active participation by a baby in timing and pacing of feeding helps in establishing regular rhythms. Additionally, obtaining a favourable feedback from his signals and actions may build up a baby's confidence in his ability to influence what happens to him. A strong relationship was found in the present study between mother-infant interaction in the first three months and the baby's attachment to his mother at the end of the year. Babies whose mothers were relatively sensitive in the feeding interaction all showed clear-cut evidence of attachment to the mother on reunion after a brief separation. Babies whose mothers were less sensitive in feeding tended to show ambivalence in their attachment on reunion. It seems that the kinds of mother-child interaction established, although not necessarily the feeding interaction itself, have a significant effect on later development. Subjects were twenty-six infants from a middle-class background, subjects of a longitudinal study by the senior author.

AINSWORTH, M. D. S. and WITTIG, B. A. 1969. 'Attachment and exploratory behaviour of one-year-olds in a strange situation', in B. M. Foss (ed) *Determinants of Infant Behaviour, IV*, Methuen, London. 111–36.

The behaviour of fourteen middle-class infants in an unfamiliar room (the strange situation) was observed throughout a sequence of eight episodes in which the baby was left with his mother, with a stranger and on his own. Separation from the mother resulted in decreased exploration and increased crying but attempts to regain the mother and crying were much stronger in the second separation than in the first. Also babies generally only approached the mother on reunion after the first separation but clung to her after the second. Findings suggest that distress on minor separations cannot be used as the sole criterion of attachment for some babies who protested strongly appeared to be strongly attached to the mother while others showed ambivalence. Few babies were distressed by a stranger in their mother's presence and even in her absence most tended not to withdraw from the stranger. It appears that there is no simple relationship between stranger anxiety and attachment. The babies showed more exploratory behaviour when alone with the mother than in any other episode, and it is suggested that an important function of attachment is use of the mother as a secure base.

Although all the babies in the study were attached to their mothers, the quality of attachment differed. Impressionistic evidence suggests some relationship between the quality of attachment and the nature of the mother-infant interaction (see also Ainsworth *et al.*, 1971).

AINSWORTH, M. D. S., BELL, S. M. and STAYTON, D. J. 1971. 'Individual differences in strange-situation behaviour of one-year-olds', in H. R. Schaffer (ed) *The Origins of Human Social Relations*, Academic Press, London and New York. 17–51.

Findings of this study suggest that there is a relationship between maternal behaviour and the quality of the infant's attachment to his mother. Where the mother is sensitive to the baby's signals, accessible, co-operative and accepting, babies tend to use their mothers at home as a secure base for exploration. However, when subjected to a series of stresses in the strange environment (being left alone with stranger and then entirely alone) exploratory behaviour is reduced, the babies show a clear-cut desire for proximity and contact with the mother on reunion with her and most, but not all, show distress on separation particularly on the second separation when left alone. This pattern of behaviour was considered to be normal and healthy and it was found in about one-third of the babies in the sample.

Several other patterns deviating from the normative were found. Where the mother was rejecting, babies responded to stresses of the strange situation with defensive, proximity-avoiding behaviour – they continued independent play throughout the experimental situation, ignored, avoided or showed ambivalent response to the mother on reunion but nevertheless showed heightened attachment behaviour during separation. Where the mother was insensitive or ignoring but not rejecting, babies failed to use the mother as a secure base for exploration in the unfamiliar environment, reacted with great distress to the separation episodes and were highly ambivalent on reunion with the mother. The findings of the study illustrate the difficulty in trying to estimate the strength of attachment – different criteria such as proximity-seeking, or separation distress or search during separation would indicate that different sub-groups of children were strongly attached. Rather, it appears that infants in each sub-group were attached to the mother in their own fashion. The main sample consisted of twenty-three middle-class infants, including fourteen whose strange situation behaviour was reported earlier (see Ainsworth and Wittig, 1969).

AINSWORTH, M. D. S., BELL, S. M. and STAYTON, D. J. 1972. 'Individual differences in the development of some attachment behaviors', *Merrill-Palmer Quarterly* 18, 2, 123–43.

In a sample of twenty-six middle-class infants, observed over the first year of life, there was little evidence of anxiety in brief everyday separations from the mother. The mean incidence of crying in the third and fourth quarters of the year never exceeded 28 per cent of the times that their mothers left the room. By thirty-nine weeks, babies followed the mother, when free to do so, more often than crying when she left the room. At forty-eight weeks the average baby followed 58 per cent of the time when free to do so. Babies who responded positively to physical contact in the fourth quarter tended to have experienced a tender, careful quality of holding by the mother in the first quarter of the year and had not experienced frequent abrupt picking up. The findings suggest that mother-infant interaction affects attachment behaviours and the quality of the attachment relationship. Although it appears that the quality of the attachment relationship can be characterised by a security-insecurity dimension, not all attachment behaviours can be fitted into this. Following the mother, for example, may denote insecurity or a positive response.

AINSWORTH, M. D. S., BELL, S. M. and STAYTON, D. J. 1974. 'Infant-mother attachment and social development: socialisation as a product of reciprocal responsiveness to signals', in M. P. M. Richards (ed) *The Integration of a Child into a Social World*, Cambridge University Press, London. 99–135.

Exposition of the authors' views of attachments which are derived from Bowlby's formulations but also considerably influenced by their own research work. It is hypothesised that the infant is genetically biased towards interaction with people. The infant's signalling behaviours are genetically programmed and adults are generally biased to respond to these signals. Acceptance of the infant as he is and sensitive response to his signals tends to facilitate the kinds of behaviour commonly believed to be desirable in infancy. Specifically, maternal responsiveness to infant crying tends to reduce its frequency and duration, and maternal acceptance, co-operation and sensitivity to signals tends to be related to compliance with maternal commands and beginnings of 'internalisation' of prohibitions.

BAN, P. L. and LEWIS, M. 1974. 'Mothers and fathers, girls and boys: attachment behavior in the one year old', *Merrill-Palmer Quarterly* 20, 3, 195–204.

Ten male and ten female one-year-old infants were observed in a low stress, free-play situation on two visits to the laboratory, in one visit accompanied by their mothers and in the other by their fathers. Generally, the children were found to be more proximally attached (touching, proximity-seeking) to their mothers than their fathers. Girls looked equally at both parents, though, and boys looked more at their fathers. Boys' behaviour showed a high level of integration. Boys who were high touchers also tended to be high in proximity-seeking, looking and vocalising. Boys who were strongly attached to one parent were likely to be strongly attached to the other. Girls showed little overall behaviour integration. Evidence from other studies suggests that in a more stressful situation, differential attachment to mother and father might be lessened. Also, other studies have reported sex differences in behaviour to the mother, while relatively few differences were found in the present research. This is possibly explained by the high socio-economic level of the sample, parents perhaps using less sex-related socialisation than those from other strata.

BELL, S. M. 1970. 'The development of the concept of object as related to infant-mother attachment', *Child Development* 41, 2, 291–311.

In this study, twenty-three out of thirty-three eight-and-a-half- to eleven-and-a-half-months old babies were found to be more advanced in the concept of persons as permanent than in the concept of inanimate objects as permanent (i.e. existing outside the infant, even when not present to his perception). Seven babies tended to be more advanced in the concept of inanimate objects than in the concept of persons as permanent. By thirteen months, the babies who had been advanced in person permanence reached higher levels on a scale of object permanence than those who had been more advanced in the concept of inanimate objects as permanent. Babies who tended to be more advanced in person permanence also all had an unambivalent attachment to their mothers. In contrast, babies who were more advanced in the concept of permanence of inanimate objects showed ambivalence in attachment to the mother. There is evidence from other studies that maternal sensitivity is associated with the development of unambivalent attachment and it is likely that harmonious mother-child interaction also influences the development of the concept of object. Two studies (Golden and Birns, 1968; Wachs *et al.*, 1971) have had equivocal findings on whether environmental factors influence the concept of object but have ignored the quality of the baby's interaction with his mother.

BROOKS, J. and LEWIS, M. 1974. 'Attachment behavior in thirteen month old, opposite-sex twins', *Child Development* 45, 1, 243–7.

Thirteen- to fourteen-months-old girl twins, in the presence of their mothers in a playroom situation, showed significant differences in attachment behaviours towards the mother, compared with boy twins. The girls looked at, vocalised to and maintained proximity to the mother longer than the boys. Boy twins who had experienced a period of separation from the mother before the free-play session (cared for by a research assistant while the mother was in the playroom with the girl twin) touched and maintained proximity to the mother significantly more than boys who were seen in the playroom first, before separation. Girls' behaviour, in contrast, was not significantly affected by order. No sex differences were found in the number of toy changes, number of toys played with, total amount of time playing or in activity level.

COATES, B., ANDERSON, E. P. and HARTUP, W. W. 1972a. 'Interactions in the attachment behavior of human infants', *Developmental Psychology* 6, 2, 218–30.

An investigation of the attachment behaviours of ten, fourteen- and eighteen-months-old infants in the presence of their mothers and before, during and after a brief separation in an unfamiliar situation. Infants cried more during the separation period than before, and attempted to follow the mother. On reunion with the mother, visual regard of the mother, touching and remaining close to her were significantly more frequent than before separation, as was crying (although this occurred less frequently than during separation). These behaviours were little influenced by the child's age or sex, or by the order of the experimental sessions. Support for the concept of attachment was provided by the numerous significant correlations among the behaviours investigated, though these were generally of moderate size and some of the attachment measures were not correlated. In the mother's presence visual regard, touching and staying close to the mother were significantly correlated. During separation, crying, looking at the door and attempts at following were significantly correlated. Touching and proximity to the mother before separation were related to crying during separation only at fourteen months, when walking was a recently acquired skill for most of the infants. Size of the correlation between crying and touching and proximity to the mother after reunion increased with age, as the child became more skilful at walking.

COATES, B., ANDERSON, E. P. and HARTUP, W. W. 1972b. 'The stability of attachment behaviors in the human infant', *Developmental Psychology*, 6, 2, 231–7.

Findings of this study suggest that some attachment behaviours are more stable than others. Behaviours having the greatest short-term stability are also those having the greatest long-term stability. Proximity-seeking was found to be the most stable behaviour, and it became more stable with increase in the child's age. Touching also showed moderate stability. Visual regard and vocalisations generally possessed little stability. The two groups of subjects were aged ten and fourteen months on the initial testing, a second testing taking place four months later. At both the testing periods each infant was observed during the experimental sessions which took place on consecutive days: during one the infant was observed in an unfamiliar environment in his mother's presence, while in the other he was observed before, during and after a brief separation from the mother.

COHEN, L. J. and CAMPOS, J. J. 1974. 'Father, mother, and stranger as elicitors of attachment behaviors in infancy', *Developmental Psychology* 10, 1, 146–54.

In an unfamiliar environment, sixty ten, thirteen, and sixteen-months-old infants were found to show attachment behaviour towards the father as well as towards the mother, but usually less strongly. Infants showed overwhelmingly greater proximity-seeking towards the father than towards a stranger, but when both parents were present more time was spent in proximity to the mother than the father. Also, when one parent was present with two strangers, the infant travelled significantly faster towards the mother than the father, and spent significantly more time in proximity to her. Infants showed greater eye contact with a stranger when near one of the parents rather than when on their own, but eye contact with the stranger was greater when the infant was in proximity to the mother than when in proximity to the father. Separation protest, though, failed to differentiate between the parents. A minority of infants (6 per cent) showed consistent preference for the father rather than the mother. This confirms findings of Schaffer and Emerson (1964) and Ainsworth (1967) that some infants are more attached to their fathers than their mothers. However, in contrast to findings of Schaffer and Emerson that attachment to the father increases with age, in the present study about 90 per cent of infants at all three age levels showed attachment to the father as well as to the mother. Possibly separation protest in everyday situations, the sole criterion of attachment used by Schaffer and Emerson, fails to pick up attachment to the father at the younger ages. Alternatively, differences in child-rearing practices in the Scottish sample of the Schaffer and Emerson study and the American sample of the present study may be responsible for the difference in findings.

CORTER, C. M. 1973. 'A comparison of the mother's and a stranger's control over the behavior of infants', *Child Development* 44, 4, 705–13.

Ten-months-old infants were placed in a room with a toy, and the mother and a stranger walked away, each going into a different adjoining room – for one group the mother shut the door and only the stranger was available; for a second group both the doors were open and both the mother and stranger were accessible. Most infants followed the mother, both when she was the only person available and when she and the stranger were accessible. When only the stranger was available, most infants did not follow. Infants usually played with the toy, looked at accessible adult(s) and smiled before following the mother. The findings indicate that following is an attachment behaviour, i.e. it is directed selectively at the mother and increases the infant's proximity to her. Presence of the stranger delayed the infant's following of the mother. This is probably because she evoked exploratory behaviour – looking and some smiling. The mother's presence delayed the onset of crying, and tended to encourage more play and more responses to the stranger.

CORTER, C. M., RHEINGOLD, H. L. and ECKERMAN, C. C. 1972. 'Toys delay the infant's following of his mother', *Developmental Psychology* 6, 1, 138–45.

In the first experiment, ten-months-old infants left alone by the mother in an unfamiliar room followed her into an adjoining room with little delay, but those left with an attractive toy took almost ten times as long to follow even though the mother was out of sight. In a second trial, in which both groups of infants were left with the same toy, those to whom the toy was novel delayed longer in following the mother, and cried less, than those to whom the toy was now familiar.

In the second experiment, availability of six toys in an unfamiliar room did not reliably delay following more than did one toy. Infants in the six-toy group, though, returned to the start room more and touched the toys longer than those in the one-toy group. Possibly there is a limit to the time an infant will spend away from his mother, and he may not always have exhausted the stimulation in the environment before he goes to her. Findings of the study clearly show that the characteristics of the environment affect the infant's response to the mother's departure.

COX, F. N. and CAMPBELL, D. 1968. 'Young children in a new situation with and without their mothers', *Child Development* 39, 1, 123–31.

In this study, the behaviour of young children was observed when they played in a strange environment for twelve minutes. Half of the children had their mothers present throughout the period and half were left alone for the middle four minutes. Absence of the mother produced decrements in speech, movement and play measures, and an increase in crying. Decrease in play, movement and speech was significantly less in the group of subjects aged twenty-four to thirty-seven months than in those aged thirteen to fifteen months, and there was little crying in the older group. After the return of the mother, the younger children showed a partial recovery of activity and the performance of the older children returned to its original level.

ECKERMAN, C. O. and RHEINGOLD, H. L. 1974. 'Infants' exploratory responses to toys and people', *Developmental Psychology* 10, 2, 255–9.

Ten-months-old infants in an unfamiliar situation with their mothers were found quickly to approach and contact a novel toy, and to maintain prolonged contact with it. In contrast, infants looked and smiled from a distance at an unfamiliar person, and the few who approached did so after considerable delay and for a brief period only. Smiling was more frequent when the unfamiliar person was responsive. Infants showed no sign of distress on being exposed to an unfamiliar person. The authors suggest that infants at ten months explore new people as well as toys but do so in different ways. Possibly infants find from an early age that responses can be evoked from people just by looking and smiling, while objects do not change usually unless they are contacted and manipulated.

ESCALONA, S. K. and CORMAN, H. H. 1971. 'The impact of mother's presence upon behavior: the first year', *Human Development* 14, 2–15.

Detailed observations in everyday situations of two infants from birth until their first birthday give some indication of differences in the patterns of their experiences which led to their developing relationships with the mother that were very different in quality, though close in both cases. Both infants were first-borns, looked after primarily by their own mothers. The parents of both infants were loving and attentive and both families were near the poverty level.

However, the parents of Subject 1, the white girl, were culturally somewhat impoverished and conservative in outlook. In contrast, the parents of Subject 2, a black boy, were highly educated and liberal in their views. Subject 1 discriminated the mother much earlier than Subject 2. By nine months of age, Subject 1 had developed an intense and ambivalent relationship with her mother, crying when she left and screaming angrily on her return, obeying prohibitions but under protest. Subject 2 spent much time in exploration with his mother but was content to play with toys on his own as long as he knew she was accessible, was rarely thwarted and obeyed prohibitions cheerfully after some initial ignoring. Subject 2 was advanced in all aspects of cognitive development, while Subject 1 was in the average range.

In the mother's absence, Subject 1 was cared for mainly by a less accommodating and attentive grandmother, while Subject 2 had as his main subsidiary care-taker an attentive and indulgent father. Generally, the mother's absence made more difference to Subject 1 than to Subject 2. Subject 1 experienced much more pleasure in the mother's presence than in her absence, and her social responsiveness and interest in the environment were greater. Both babies, though, experienced stronger feelings in the mother's presence than in her absence, and displayed a greater variety of and more complex social behaviour when with her. It is suggested that this partly accounts for the development of the close tie between mother and child in both cases. The earlier discrimination of the mother and establishment of a sense of separateness from her by Subject 1 probably results from the greater contrast of experience in the mother's presence and in her absence for this child. Findings of the study indicate that the development of the mother-child relationship is not determined exclusively by the mother and her direct experiences with the child but also by what happens to the child at other times.

FLEENER, D. E. and CAIRNS, R. B. 1970. 'Attachment behaviors in human infants: discriminative vocalisation on maternal separation', *Developmental Psychology* 2, 2, 215–23.

While there is evidence from a number of studies that infants cry on separation from the mother, none has unambiguously shown that crying is specific to maternal rather than non-maternal departures. This study was designed to show whether there is discriminative crying on separation from the mother. Each of the sixty-four three- to nineteen-months-old infants was placed in a crib in an unfamiliar room with the mother and a research assistant present. Then successive departures and returns to the room of the mother and the assistant took place so that each person left the room twice. Findings confirmed that infants do cry more frequently on the departure of the mother than on the departure of another person, but a significant difference was found only for infants between the ages of twelve and seventeen months. Neither total crying nor discriminative crying on separation from the mother was related to the child's sex, or to the mother's responsiveness to the child's crying.

GOLDBERG, S. and LEWIS, M. 1969. 'Play behavior in the year old infant: early sex differences', *Child Development* 40, 1, 21–31.

Thirty-two boys and thirty-two girls, aged thirteen months, and their mothers, were observed in a free-play situation. Sex differences were found in attachment behaviours (girls returned more to their mothers, touched them more, vocalised more to them and stayed nearer) and in play behaviour (girls, unlike boys, chose toys which involved fine rather than gross motor co-ordination, and were less active and vigorous in play). Sex differences were also found in a frustration situation (mesh barrier placed between children and mother), the girls crying and motioning more for help, while the boys made more active attempts to get round the barrier. Some relationships were found between the children's behaviour at thirteen months and the mothers' behaviour at six months. The mothers of girls touched their infants more often, vocalised to them more, and breast-fed them more than the mothers of boys. The more a mother touched a boy at six months the more he touched mother at thirteen months, but for girls the relationship appeared to be curvilinear.

GREENBERG, D. J., HILLMAN, D. and GRICE, D. 1973. 'Infant and stranger variables related to stranger anxiety in the first year of life', *Developmental Psychology* 9, 2, 207–12.

Stranger anxiety was found in this study to occur more frequently in older infants (in twelve-month-old rather than eight-month-old infants) and to adult rather than child strangers. Only nineteen of the ninety-six infants, though, showed a clear negative or avoidance reaction to the stranger. However, stranger anxiety was more frequent than in Rheingold and Eckerman's (1973) study in which it was virtually absent. In both studies the child was placed with his mother in an unfamiliar room, but there were marked differences in procedure which probably account for the contrast in the findings. Rheingold and Eckerman's experimental period resembled a play session in which the child was given ample time to get used to a friendly stranger. In the present experiment, the child had only a short period of adjustment to the unfamiliar environment before a sombre-looking stranger entered, knelt down and shook the child's hand.

JACKLIN, C. N., MACCOBY, E. E. and DICK, A. E. 1973. 'Barrier behavior and toy preference: sex differences (and their absence) in the year old child, *Child Development* 44, 1, 196–200.

In a previous study (Goldberg and Lewis, 1969), sex differences were found in the behaviour of thirteen-months-old children placed behind a barrier which separated them from the mother and toys. The behaviour of thirteen- to fourteen-months-old infants was observed in the present study as part of a larger experiment. Goldberg and Lewis' findings that girls are more likely to remain at the centre of the barrier while boys went to the ends, attempting to get around them, were not replicated. Boys did manipulate the barrier more than the girls but not significantly more. Barrier behaviour was found to depend more on experiences in previous phases of the experiment than on sex.

The previous phases consisted of a play session in the presence of the mother (phase I) followed by a fear stimulus (a loud angry male voice played over the loud-speaker) (phase II) and a play session with the mother (phase III). Half of the children were originally placed near the mother at the onset of phases I and II while the remainder were placed further from her. Among the children who had been placed near to the mother originally girls cried more at the barrier than boys (thus replicating the Goldberg and Lewis findings) but among those who had been placed further away from the mother, no sex differences were found.

Findings suggest that boys derive more comfort from proximity to the mother than girls. Sex differences in toy preferences were found in the first two phases of the study, boys preferring robots to cuddly and activity toys. This preference was not accounted for by the mother's behaviour in the play session.

LAMB, M. E. 1973. 'The effects of maternal deprivation on the development of the concepts of object and person', *Journal of Behavioral Science* 1, 5, 355–64.

In a previous study (Bell, 1970, see above) it had been found that infants who were securely attached to their mothers were usually more advanced in the concept of the person as permanent than in the concept of an inanimate object as permanent; those with an insecure attachment to the mother were generally more advanced in the concept of an inanimate object as permanent than in person permanence. Also babies in the first group were as advanced even in the concept of object permanence with respect to inanimate things as babies in the second group at the ages of eight-and-a-half and eleven months. In the present study of seven-and-a-half- to twelve-months-old institutionalised infants, they were found to be more advanced in inanimate object than in person permanence. They showed no evidence of attachments to institution staff and were intellectually retarded compared with a home-reared control group.

LESTER, B. M., KOTELCHUCK, M., SPELKE, E., SELLERS, M. J. and KLEIN, R. E. 1974. 'Separation protest in Guatemalan infants: cross cultural and cognitive findings', *Developmental Psychology* 10, 1, 79–85.

Subjects of this study were forty-two lower-class Guatemalan infants at four age levels: nine, twelve, eighteen and twenty-four months. Infant behaviour in an unfamiliar room was examined as a function of the presence and absence of the mother, father and a stranger. Infants were found to show separation protest – decrease in play, increase in crying – when either the mother or the father departed, leaving the child alone with the stranger. When the child was alone with either parent he maintained the same high level of play. The peak in separation protest occurred at twelve and eighteen months. The infants were also tested on object permanence. It was found that nine- and twelve-months-old infants who were above the third stage (able to search for an object after it disappears according to Piaget's conception) showed more separation protest than those who were at the third stage. This gives tentative support to Schaffer's (1971) hypothesis that separation protest begins when the infant's attempts to recover the missing parent are frustrated. The pattern of separation protest in the Guatemalan infants was similar to that found in US infants in a previous study (Kotelchuck, unpublished). However, the US infants showed greater protest at separation from the father, possibly because American fathers spend more time with their children. Also, separation protest showed earlier onset in the Guatemalan children, and was stronger at twelve months of age. This may be because separation is more unusual for a Guatemalan infant, most families living in a one-room *rancho*.

LITTENBERG, R., TULKIN, S. R. and KAGAN, J. 1971. 'Cognitive components of separation anxiety', *Developmental Psychology* 4, 3, 387–8.

Findings of this study support the authors' hypothesis that cognitive factors are relevant to separation anxiety. As predicted, a higher incidence of crying, staring and crawling to the exit was found among eleven-months-old infants when the mother left a room in her home by a door she rarely used than when she left by a familiar exit. This is consistent with the hypothesis that the child shows separation anxiety when the sight of the mother leaving the room is a discrepant event which he cannot assimilate, prevent or avoid. If the distress was due only to a threat to the security of the mother-child relationship whether the mother left the room by a familiar or unfamiliar exit should make no difference.

MESSER, S. B. and LEWIS, M. 1972. 'Social class and sex differences in the attachment and play behavior of the year old infant', *Merrill-Palmer Quarterly* 18, 295–306.

Thirty-three lower-class infants (sixteen boys, seventeen girls) and their mothers were observed in a free-play situation, and their behaviour was compared to that of sixty-four infants observed in a previous study (Goldberg and Lewis, 1969, see above). The lower-class infants vocalised to their mothers significantly less than the middle-class infants, but did not differ from them in other attachment behaviours (proximity towards and looking at mother). The middle-class infants were more mobile than the working-class infants and had somewhat different toy preferences. Sex differences in the lower-class sample were in the same direction as those in the middle-class sample, girls showing stronger attachment behaviours, but the differences were less marked. In other studies (Ainsworth and Wittig, 1969; Rheingold and Eckerman, 1969), no sex differences have been found in attachment behaviours. The difference may have been due to the shorter observational period in these studies (attachment behaviours were stronger at the beginning of the play period in the Goldberg and Lewis study) or to the more stressful experimental situations, which possibly reduced individual differences.

MORGAN, G. A. and RICCIUTI, H. N. 1969. 'Infants' responses to strangers during the first year', in B. M. Foss (ed) *Determinants of Infant Behaviour, IV*, Methuen, London. 253–72.

Infants placed with their mothers in an unfamiliar environment reacted very positively to a stranger at four-and-a-half months. Although the positive responses declined with increasing age, negative responses predominated only for infants aged twelve-and-a-half months. Four-and-a-half- to six-and-a-half-months old babies reacted just as positively when separated from the mother by four feet as when sitting on her lap, but older infants reacted more negatively when separated from the mother. The behaviour of the stranger was an important determinant of the infant's reaction. Younger infants became more positive when the stranger approached and touched them than when the stranger was at the opposite side of the room. Older infants were likely to become more negative when the stranger approached. However, when the stranger smiled, talked and moved the head, as if playing 'peek-a-boo', even ten-and-a-half- to twelve-and-a-half-months-old infants reacted in a mildly positive manner.

No correlation was found between previous experiences with strangers and the infant's reaction in the experimental situation but the relative homogeneity of the subjects may have obscured any relationship that exists. Possible explanations for the negative reactions of the older children in terms of fear of separation from the mother, and in terms of stranger behaviour which may have appeared inappropriate to the infant are discussed. The subjects were eighty middle-class infants, in five age groups from four to thirteen months.

PEDERSEN, F. A. and ROBSON, K. S. 1969. 'Father participation in infancy', *American Journal of Orthopsychiatry* 39, 3, 466–72.

Intensity of attachment to the father (measured by greeting behaviour) in nine-and-a-half-months-old boys was related to several aspects of the father's behaviour (positively to the amount of care-taking, emotional investment in the child and stimulation level of play with the child but

95

negatively to irritability); attachment in girls was related negatively to the father's apprehension over the child's well-being. Generally, a high level of involvement with the child was found in this sample of forty-five middle-class fathers of first-borns, but there was a high degree of variability.

RHEINGOLD, H. L. 1969. 'The effect of a strange environment on the behavior of infants', in B. M. Foss (ed) *Determinants of Infant Behaviour, IV*, Methuen, London. 137–66.

Four experiments were conducted with ten-months-old infants who could crawl to determine the effects of a strange environment on their behaviour. Overall, it was found that the strange environment – a large unfurnished room – produced crying and inhibition of locomotion whether it was empty or whether it contained toys or an unfamiliar person. Practically no manipulation of toys occurred when these were present. However, when the mother was present the infants vocalised instead of crying and explored freely. When the infants who had previously been exposed to one of the three strange environments were subsequently re-introduced to the large room, but this time with the mother present, their behaviour differed from that of infants whose mother was present on their first exposure to the strange environment. About two-thirds of the infants who had prior experience of the strange environment without the mother went to her faster when she appeared and stayed with her longer but the others cried and did not move towards her. All subjects were children who easily accepted separation from the mother, allowing the experimenter to take them from the mother without signs of stress. It is concluded that a strange environment has a distressing and inhibiting effect on children of this age but that the presence of a familiar social object converts strangeness into novelty.

RHEINGOLD, H. L. and ECKERMAN, C. O. 1969. 'The infant's free entry into a new environment', *Journal of Experimental Child Psychology* 8, 271–83.

An investigation of some properties of the environment that would lead a ten-months-old infant away from his mother. Each infant was placed with his mother in a small empty room and allowed access to a larger room. The first experiment tested the effect of a toy in the larger room compared with no toy. All infants entered the larger room irrespective of the presence of a toy. Where a toy was present all infants played with it, and contact with the mother was reduced but all infants returned at least once to the starting room. The second experiment tested the effect of previous experience with a toy or no toy, and the effect of the number of toys. Infants who had experienced a toy in the larger room for the first time entered the room sooner, touched the toy earlier and played with it longer than infants who had no previous experience of the toy. Three toys spaced across the larger room increased the time the infant spent there, the distance travelled and the time playing with toys. Nevertheless all infants returned to the starting room at least once, and often several times, although not all made physical contact with the mother. Many infants looked back and vocalised to the mother when they entered the larger room, especially when a toy was present, but none fussed. Entry into the larger room when empty is probably exploratory behaviour, for although unfurnished it was brighter and contained many visual stimuli – curtains, lines and angles.

Findings are in contrast to a previous experiment (Rheingold, 1969) in which infants placed alone in the same larger room showed marked distress and an almost complete inhibition of locomotion.

SALTZ, R. 1973. 'Effects of part-time "mothering" on IQ and SQ of young institutionalized children', *Child Development* 44, 1, 166–70.

Findings of this study suggest that it is not merely a deficiency in the quantity of stimulation but also the lack of opportunity for formation of attachment to an adult that causes intellectual and social retardation in young long-term institutionalised children. A comparison was made of the intellectual development of two groups of children, aged sixteen months to six years, both living in good quality institutions which provided extensive physical, social and intellectual stimulation.

The experimental group differed only in that the children received 'mothering' five days a week, four hours a day from foster grand-parents. The children who had taken part in the foster grandparent programme were found to have significantly higher IQs (Cattel or Stanford-Binet) than the controls, the difference between the groups being greatest for long-stay (twenty-five to sixty months) children. One year after the introduction of the foster grandparent programme, thirteen of the experimental children were found to have made significantly better progress in intellectual development than thirteen controls, matched for initial IQ, age at initial testing and length of institutionalisation prior to the introduction of the foster grandparent programme. The children exposed to the foster grandparents also made normal progress in social competence (Vineland Scale), even when institutionalised for considerable time.

SCHAFFER, H. R. and EMERSON, P. E. 1964. 'The development of social attachments in infancy', *Monographs of the Society for Research in Child Development*, serial no. 94, 29, 3, 77pp.

Subjects of this study were sixty normal Scottish infants mainly from a skilled working-class background. The mother had primary responsibility for child care in all the families. Protest at separation in everyday situations was used as the criterion of the child's attachment to the mother and to other individuals. Intensity of attachment was measured by the intensity of protest. Data was obtained from interviews with the mothers held during visits at regular intervals from early in the first year until the infant was eighteen months of age; observational checks on data accuracy were also carried out. Fear of strangers was measured by an experiment involving the infant's reponses to the interviewer at the beginning of each visit.

The majority of infants formed specific attachments in the third quarter of the first year, but there were considerable individual differences. Fear of strangers usually followed in time the development of attachments but sometimes preceded it. It is suggested that one phenomenon is not merely the reverse of the other but both may be part of a more general developmental trend. Intensity of separation protest varied considerably in the individual child, generally being minimised by environmental stimulation and heightened by pain, illness, fear and fatigue. Variations also took place over time. Most infants formed an initial attachment with one person, and then the number of their attachments increased rapidly. However, over a quarter of the infants formed attachments to several people from the onset of the attachment phase. The mother was the first attachment object for most, but not all, of the children. The children had a hierarchy of attachment objects, the mother generally being the principal attachment object. With increasing age there was a tendency for others, particularly the father, to become joint principal attachment objects with the mother. The infant with an intense attachment to the principal object was more, not less, likely to have other attachments as well, while weakly attached infants tended to focus on one person. Intensity of attachment to the mother at eighteen months was not related to her mere availability. Maternal responsiveness to the child's crying and the amount of interaction with the child initiated by the mother were significantly related to the intensity of attachment. The type of stimulation provided by the mother, though, was not related to the intensity of attachment. Similarly, infants chose as their other objects of attachment not people who were necessarily the most available to them but those who were most responsive to the infants's crying and provided them with most stimulation. Breadth of attachment was determined by the opportunities the child had for meeting people who interacted with him.

SPELKE, E., ZELAZO, P., KAGAN, J. and KOTELCHUCK, M. 1973.

'Father interaction and separation protest', *Developmental Psychology* 9, 1, 83–90.

Twelve-months-old infants tended to show separation protest when either the mother or the father left them alone in an unfamiliar room with a stranger. However, the view that crying on separation is a measure of the intensity of attachment was not supported. Children cried as much when father left them with a stranger as when the mother did. Also, children who experienced frequent interaction with the father at home, and who should have been the most strongly attached to him, cried least when the father left the room. Those whose fathers interacted with them least at home, who should have been the most weakly attached, cried most at their father's departure. Children who cried least at separation also appeared to be the most cognitively advanced (on a test designed to measure attentiveness to an unexpected visual discrepancy).

The hypothesis is advanced that separation protest occurs towards the end of the first year, when the infant is mature enough to perceive his parent's departure as a discrepant event and to generate a hypothesis about the location of his attachment object, but not mature enough to resolve the question. Cognitively advanced children were not only able to generate hypotheses but also able to explain the experience of being left alone with a stranger. Children who have frequent interactions with both parents have a greater variety of experiences and so they may be cognitively advanced, and show little separation protest. Alternatively, the child who has frequent interaction with his father may be more accustomed to his mother's departure, and so less anxious about it. A temperamental trait may also contribute to variance in separation protest.

STAYTON, D. J. and AINSWORTH, M. D. S. 1973. 'Individual differences in infant responses to brief, everyday separations as related to other infant and maternal behaviors', *Developmental Psychology* 9, 2, 226–35.

Findings of this study indicate that by the fourth quarter of the first year, different infants have organised their attachment behaviour towards the mother in different ways. Infants who are 'secure' in their attachment to the mother protest only infrequently on separation from her in the home surroundings, greet her happily on reunion, welcome physical contact but also accept being put down and cry little in general. Infants 'insecure' in their attachment to the mother cry frequently on separation from her, protest on reunion, on cessation of physical contact, and generally cry often. The 'secure' attached infants, it is suggested, have confidence in their mother's accessibility and responsiveness, while the 'insecure' attached infants are anxious about the mother's accessibility and whereabouts. Crying when the mother leaves the room was positively and significantly related to the frequency and duration of maternal ignoring of crying.

It was found in an earlier study (S. M. Bell and Ainsworth, 1972) that maternal ignoring of crying in the early part of the first year was related to more frequent crying by infants later in the year. It seems that the infant's confidence in his mother's accessibility and responsiveness is built up in the course of the first year largely on the basis of her consistency and promptness in responding to his signals. The findings do not confirm those of Schaffer and Emerson (1964) that frequency and intensity of the child's separation protest in everyday situations is positively associated with maternal responsiveness to crying. The discrepancy may be due to the different measures of maternal behaviour used in the two studies, Schaffer and Emerson's being based mainly on interview with the mothers, who are probably not able to give dependable accounts of their responsiveness to the baby. In the present study, kinds of attachment behaviour did not all co-vary positively, but were correlated in a complex intelligible matrix. Attachment cannot be regarded as a unitary trait or a generalised drive. Various kinds of attachment behaviour may be viewed as alternative means to a common end, some kinds being incompatible with others in a particular situation, and different individuals using some kinds of attachment behaviour more frequently than other infants. Subjects (as in the Stayton *et al.*, 1973, study) were twenty-six mother-infant pairs from a middle-class background who were observed during three-weekly visits to the home throughout the first year of life.

STAYTON, D. J., AINSWORTH, M. D. S. and MAIN, M. B. 1973. 'Development of separation behavior in the first year of life: protest, following and greeting', *Developmental Psychology* 9, 2, 213–25.

Responses to a person leaving the room and to the person's return were observed in twenty-six infants at three-weekly visits to their homes when they were between the ages of fifteen and fifty-four weeks. Positive greeting was the earliest behaviour related to separation to appear (at about four months), while separation crying appeared at five months and following was the last separation behaviour to appear. Crying and most positive greeting behaviours (apart from smiling) were differential (evoked more frequently) by the mother from onset. However, although the occurrence of discrimination and preference is a necessary pre-condition for attachment, it is unlikely that an infant can be attached until he has a rudimentary conception of object permanence, which is acquired at about eight months. Findings from the present study indicate that distress is not the typical response to separation from the mother in the familiar home environment, as most investigators have assumed. Infants were more likely to greet the mother with pleasure on her return than to cry when she left, and following was twice as frequent as protest in infants capable of locomotion.

TENNES, K. H. and LAMPL, E. E. 1966. 'Some aspects of mother-child relationship pertaining to infantile separation anxiety', *Journal of Nervous and Mental Disease* 143, 5, 426–37.

Twenty-seven infants were observed over the first two years of life both in their own homes and in a laboratory. All infants showed differential proximity-seeking towards the mother (libidinal attachment) before the age of a year, the majority before seven months; a few infants preferentially sought contact with the mother even before they were three months old. The child's contact-seeking behaviour increased gradually during the first two years. Half of the sample showed separation anxiety by eight months of age, and almost all by the end of the first year. Separation anxiety was greatest in children whose mothers were moderately hostile towards them and who were intolerant of the expression of aggression in the child. Separation anxiety did not occur in the absence of the child showing positive evidence of attachment towards the mother, but intensity of contact-seeking by the child was not related to the intensity of separation anxiety shown by him. A few infants (nine) showed very little separation anxiety. All these children had mothers who were low in inhibition of the child's aggression. In some cases, the relationship appeared to be disturbed, the child showing hostility towards the mother and having little pleasure in contact with her; in others, though, the relationship appeared to be ideal, affording continuous pleasurable exchanges to both mother and child.

TIZARD, J. and TIZARD, B. 1971. 'The social development of two-year-old children in residential nurseries', in H. R. Schaffer (ed) *The Origins of Human Social Relations*, Academic Press, London. 147–64.

A comparison of the social behaviour of thirty normal two-year-old children, who had entered a long-stay residential nursery before the age of four months, with that of thirty children from London working-class families in which the mother was not working full-time. The children living at home were found to be significantly more friendly with a stranger than the nursery children. The mean number of attachments of the home child was 4.13, the mother being the most frequent attachment object. Attachment was usually expressed at this age by following around the house, distress at separation having waned. The nursery child was attached to 'anyone he knew well'. The principal object of attachment, though, was the child's mother, if she visited frequently, or the 'special nurse' (a nurse who took no part in routine care but who paid particular attention to the child in her free time). The intensity of attachment, both to the preferred person and the rest of the staff was much greater in the nursery than the home children, crying on separation from a familiar person, rushing to be picked up and clinging being much more common. The social characteristics of the nursery children can be characterised as immature. Some organisational features of the residential nurseries which may account for this are discussed.

TIZARD, J. and TIZARD, B. 1974. 'The institution as an environment for development' (section on 'Institutions and the development of personality') in M. P. M. Richards (ed) *The Integration of a Child into a Social World*, Cambridge University Press, London. 146–9.

At their second birthday children brought up in an institution since they were four months old showed different patterns of attachment from children living at home. The institutional children tended to be attached to anyone they knew well while the home children were strongly attached to their mothers. The deviance in attachment was found to be reversible if the children were restored to their parents or adopted after the age of two. Children who remained in the nursery, though, tended not to care for anyone or to follow anyone, at four-and-a-half years. Nursery care usually involved not just many care-takers but also changes in care-takers and impersonality in care-taking. The dilemma for institutions is that if care-taking is organised so that close attachments are allowed to develop, the almost inevitable departures of staff are likely to result in prolonged and marked grief for the child.

TULKIN, S. R. 1973. 'Social class differences in attachment behaviors of ten months old infants', *Child Development* 44, 171–4.

This study indicates that mother-infant attachment is a complex problem which cannot be assessed simply by separation distress. No differences were found between mother-infant attachment for middle-class and working-class infants, except that the average period before the infant cries after the mother had left the room was longer for working-class mothers (probably because working-class infants were more used to being restricted in play-pens and high-chairs). Infants of working-class mothers who were employed showed much less separation distress than infants of non-employed working-class mothers, although they showed attachment to their mothers in a play session (indicating that lack of distress was due to their previous experiences of the mother leaving them).

C. Early environmental experiences and development

The necessity of a sufficient quantity of stimulation for normal development has indisputably been established by studies of infants in the older type of institutional care: infants receiving a low level of stimulation showed both mental and social retardation while those who were provided with extra stimulation through various 'environmental enrichment programmes' made developmental gains (Dinnage and Pringle, 1967; Schaffer, 1971; Starr, 1971). Nevertheless, although it is accepted that a certain level of stimulation is needed for normal functioning, doubts have been expressed on whether environmental stimulation above this level can have beneficial effects on development (Jensen, 1969). Also, the question of whether quantity of stimulation, or other parameters such as variety, timing and appropriateness are more important for infant development remains. Recent findings on these issues will be reviewed in this section.

Stimulation and early development

There is accumulating evidence from recent research that for the infant at home, as well as the infant in institutional care, cognitive and social development in the first two years or so of life are related to the amount of stimulation provided by the mother and others (Clarke-Stewart, 1973; Lewis and Goldberg, 1969; Rubenstein, 1967; L. J. Yarrow, 1963; Yarrow et al. 1972; 1975). Recent findings also show that the variety (Yarrow et al. 1972; 1975), appropriateness (Clarke-Stewart, 1973; L. J. Yarrow, 1963) and timing (Clarke-Stewart, 1973; Lewis and Goldberg, 1969; Yarrow et al. 1972; 1975) may be as, if not more, important than sheer quantity of stimulation for some aspects of development; also both social stimulation (provided by people) and non-social stimulation (provided by inanimate objects) appear to be necessary from optimal early development (Yarrow et al., 1972; 1975).

It should be noted that in most of the studies that are to be discussed, attempts have been made to measure the influence of environmental stimulation on those central processes and abilities that are the foundations of later intellectual functioning. Instead of, or in conjunction with, standardised tests of infant intelligence, several studies have used scales based on Piaget's model of intellectual development (Clarke-Stewart, 1973; Wachs et al., 1971; Wachs, 1976), measures of cognitive-motivational behaviour based on tests of exploratory behaviour (Rubenstein, 1967; Yarrow et al., 1972; 1975) or the infant's response to a redundant signal, which appears to be related to his cognitive processing (Lewis and Goldberg, 1969). Scores on standardised infant tests, at least before the age of eighteen months, have been found to bear

103

little relationship to later intelligence test scores (Birns and Golden, 1972; Golden and Birns, 1971). This is possibly because the single scores derived from them conceal variations in particular categories of ability (Wachs et al, 1971) rather than because intellectual functioning in early infancy has no relevance for later development. Additionally, it has been found that even on standardised infant tests retarded development at eight months is seven times more likely to predict intellectual retardation at four years of age in infants from a low socio-economic background than in infants from a high socio-economic background (Willerman et al., 1970). Differences found in early infant functioning may well, then, have some significance for later development.

In the first few months of life, both social (variety and level of) stimulation and non-social sensory stimulation appear to influence many aspects of infant development (Yarrow et al., 1972; 1975). Not only, though, does stimulation in general appear to affect most aspects of development but one type of stimulation may be more effective than another in promoting a particular area. In one study (Brossard and Décarie, 1971), fifteen minutes of extra stimulation a day, whether solely social (singing, talking to, caressing and playing with the baby) or solely perceptual (a mobile attached to the cot; tape-recorded everyday sounds, excluding the human voice) over a ten-week period was sufficient to bring mentally retarded, two- to three-months-old institutionalised infants into the normal range at four to five months. Although both social and inanimate stimulation favourably modified development generally, there was a suggestion from the data that social stimulation had more influence on the development of social responsiveness than perceptual stimulation. Findings of Yarrow and his colleagues suggest that in the first six months of life inanimate stimulation is related to several aspects of cognitive and motivational development but not to language or social development. On the other hand, social stimulation is related to social responsiveness and language development as well as to measures of cognitive and motivational functioning, but not to any great extent with exploratory behaviour.

Yarrow's findings also showed that different types of social stimulation differ in the generality of their effects. Kinaesthetic stimulation (picking up, rocking, carrying, moving the baby) had a particularly widespread influence on development. Visual and auditory stimulation, in contrast, were related only to social responsivity, and in the case of auditory stimulation, to the beginnings of language development. Touching and patting had little relationship to measures of infant development, perhaps because most home-reared infants receive adequate tactile stimulation. Both the level (the intensity and frequency of the mother's interactions with the infant) and the variety (the richness and diversity of the experiences she provided) of social stimulation appeared to be important for the infant's development but the influence of variety was found to be particularly widespread.

Both the variety of the toys and objects available to the child in the early months of life and their responsiveness were related to many aspects of cognitive and motivational functioning in Yarrow's study, with variety again having a wide-ranging influence. Responsiveness, the visual and auditory feedback obtainable from play materials within the infant's reach, was most strongly related to measures concerned with the infant's motivation to act on the environment. Findings of an experiment (Watson, 1971) suggest that even very young infants can learn that they have no control over a stimulus change and cease to make further efforts to master it. Three groups of two-months-old infants were presented with a mobile for ten minutes a day in their homes. A special system enabled the mobile provided for one group of infants to be turned by head movements. The mobile given to the second group remained static, while that provided for the third group turned periodically but could not be controlled by the infant. Those infants given the opportunity learned to control their mobile (Watson and Ramey, 1972). When all three groups of infants were presented in a laboratory with a mobile which could be controlled by the infant, only the third group, with experience of a noncontingent mobile, were unsuccessful in learning to do so. Six weeks later the infants were re-tested without any further experience of mobiles and the results remained the same. The importance of auditory/ visual feedback provided by toys does not diminish for the older infant, Wachs (1976) finding it related to mental development in the twelve- to twenty-four-months-old infant more consistently than any other aspect of the inanimate environment.

The variety of toys and objects available to the child also continues to be important for cognitive development in the second year of life (Wachs, 1976). Several studies (Clarke-Stewart, 1973; Wachs, 1976; White and Watts, 1973) have found that infants who are developing competently at this stage have mothers who use fewer physical restrictions, thus presumably allowing them to provide themselves with a variety of environmental experiences. By the second year at least, though, the extent to which the mother or others play with toys and objects with the child appears to be more important for his mental development than the mere variety of toys and objects available to him (Clarke-Stewart, 1973; Collard, 1971). White and Watts' findings suggest that one- to two-year-olds who are developing competently intellectually and socially are distinguished from those developing less well primarily by the kind of interaction they have with their mothers (and other adults). Only about 25 to 30 per cent of an infant's time is spent in interaction with his mother (Clarke-Stewart, 1973; White and Watts, 1973), but within that time the mother of the child who is developing competently is more likely

105

to suggest things for him to do, help him when he is in difficulties, supply necessary materials, directly participate in his activities, admire his achievements, and (although this occupies only a very small proportion of total interaction time) engage in actual teaching. Thus the intellectual stimulation the child derives from his environment appears to a large extent to depend on how it is mediated to him through the adults in his life. It is possible that the differences in mother-infant interaction found are reflections of social class differences rather than having any casual significance, for all the less competent children were found to come from a working-class background while about two thirds of the competent were from middle-class families. Against this interpretation is the evidence that all competent children, regardless of the social class from which they came, had mothers who behaved similarly.

The appropriateness of the stimulation provided by the mother for the baby's individual needs and stage of development may be more important for his mental development at least (perhaps not for his social development) than the amount of stimulation provided (Clarke-Stewart, 1973; L. J. Yarrow, 1963). Stimuli that are too discrepant from the infant's level of functioning may be detrimental to his development (Wachs et al., 1971). In one study, institutionalised infants in the second month of life were provided with extra environmental enrichment, including a complex mobile attached to the cot and other visual stimuli (White, 1967). Not only did this appear to delay rather than accelerate the development of hand regard and visual exploratory behaviour in the experimental infants but they were more irritable than the controls. Perhaps similarly, it was found in another study (Wachs et al., 1971) that infants living in surroundings in which there was a high level of background noise, or who experienced a great variety of circumstances, were hampered in their mental development. A high intensity of stimulation which is not meaningfully related to things that are happening to the infant may be disadvantageous to him.

The importance of contingent responsiveness by the mother has been much stressed in recent research. A number of laboratory studies showed that smiling (Brackbill, 1958; Brossard and Décarie, 1968) and vocalisation (Haugan and McIntire, 1972; Rheingold et al., 1959; Todd and Palmer, 1968; Weisberg, 1963) can be increased by social stimulation which immediately follows the infant behaviour, but not by randomly administered social stimulation (Weisberg, 1963). These findings were confirmed in Yarrow et al.'s (1972; 1975) observational study of five- to six-months-old babies, the baby's quantity of vocalisations to an interesting toy in a test situation being significantly related to the mother's contingent responsiveness to the baby's vocalisations at home. Interestingly, the mother's spontaneous vocalisations, rather than her contingent responsiveness to the baby's behaviour, were not related to his vocal output in the test situation.

It has been suggested, though, that contingent responsiveness does more than strengthen a specific response. Lewis and Goldberg (1969) propose that contingent responsiveness by the mother to any behaviour of the baby helps him to learn that he can have an effect on the environment, and promotes his general cognitive development. These authors found that contingent responsiveness to both vocalisations and crying in three-months-old infants was related to cognitive development. Findings were confirmed, at least for contingent responsiveness to crying, in Yarrow *et al.*'s study of five to six months old infants. By the second year of life, though, it appears to be contingent responsiveness to the baby's positive behaviour, rather than to crying, which is related to mental development (Clarke-Stewart, 1973). Maternal responsiveness was found in this study to be as highly related to mental development as the amount of stimulation provided.

In the first months of life, the amount of physical stimulation experienced by the infant is related to his mental development (Lewis and Goldberg, 1969; L. J. Yarrow, 1963). By the middle of the second year, the amount of physical contact with the mother appears to be unrelated to cognitive development (Clarke-Stewart, 1973). Many aspects of maternal care are related to the infant's overall competence—social stimulation, the mother's responsiveness to the infant's signals, the number and variety of objects she provides and the extent to which she is involved in his play. From fifteen months or so, though, verbal stimulation (Wachs *et al.*, 1971), particularly responsive verbal stimulation (Clarke-Stewart, 1973) appears to be the main influence on the infant's mental development.

Language ability in the second year seems to be related to the total amount and variety of maternal speech with the child, including non-responsive speech (Clarke-Stewart, 1973). At this early age, children's language appears to depend primarily on the quantity of verbal stimulation received. In a study of language development in residential nurseries in which there was a high quantity of staff talk, the only children who were retarded in language comprehension were the youngest, the two- to two-and-a-half-year-olds, who were spoken to significantly less than the other children (Tizard *et al.*, 1972). However, this does not mean that the quality of verbal stimulation is unimportant. Children in nurseries in which there was a higher level of active interaction between the staff and children, in which staff more often read, played with, conversed with and responded affectionately to the children, had higher language comprehension scores than those in nurseries with less staff-child involvement. These findings appear to provide substantial evidence that environmental enrichment above a certain level of adequacy can benefit development.

Overall, the research findings suggest that level and variety of stimulation are important for development, but that optimal development also requires that stimulation be adjusted to the child's individual needs. They also give some insight into the importance of at least one aspect of mothering – a person who has an enduring affectionate relationship with a child is most likely to be sensitively aware of his developmental stage and needs at a particular time. Mothers who provide stimulating and enriching care also tend to be those who are warm, loving and non-rejecting (Clarke-Stewart, 1973; Yarrow *et al.*, 1972).

Early environmental influences and later development

Findings from a number of studies which show that the level, variety, appropriateness and timing of stimulation provided for the infant in the first two years or so of life are correlated with later intellectual and social functioning are perhaps even more convincing evidence of the importance of early experiences for later development (Elardo *et al.*, 1975; Moore, 1968; Yarrow *et al.*, 1974). In two of these studies (Elardo *et al.*, 1975; Moore, 1968), environmental stimulation was actually found to be less closely related to concurrent than to later intellectual functioning. In the former study, home environment variables measured when the infant was six months old, such as the provision of a variety of stimulation, appropriate play materials, and maternal involvement with the child, bore no relationship to the infant's intellectual performance at six months, as measured by the Bayley Mental Development Scale but were related significantly to intelligence test scores at the age of three; similarly, home environment variables at twelve and twenty-four months were less closely related to intelligence scores at these ages than at three years. In Moore's (1968) study, variables related to the stimulation provided when the child was two-and-a-half, such as toys, books and experiences, and the example and encouragement he was given to speak, were only slightly related to ability at three but were significantly predictive of ability at eight years.

In the third study (Yarrow *et al.*, 1974) moderate correlations were found for boys at least, between variables relating to the stimulation and affection provided by the mother at six months and intellectual and social functioning when the child was ten years old. It is not surprising that these variables were more closely related to concurrent infant functioning rather than later development in this particular study for a number of infants were living in foster homes rather than in their permanent adoptive homes at six months of age.

Environment versus heredity

It is possible to argue, of course, that environmental experiences provided by the home, at least above a certain level of adequacy, only appear to influence development because parents of genetically well-endowed children are also those likely to provide a stimulating home environment. Findings of the study cited above (Yarrow *et al.*, 1974), in which moderate correlations were found between the environment provided by foster and adoptive parents, rather than the child's own parents, and later development are of evidence against this argument. The home environment of adoptive parents, at least, was likely to be very different from that which would have been provided by the child's natural parents, for the adoptive parents were markedly higher in socio-economic status.

Evidence of the influence of environmental circumstances, uncontaminated by genetic factors, is provided by the study which investigated the relationship between differences in verbal environment in a number of residential nurseries and the children's linguistic development (Tizard *et al.*, 1972). Language comprehension scores were related to entirely environmental experiences, the quality of the talk between staff and children. Differences in this quality between the nurseries were related to differences in organisation, and in no way to the innate abilities of the children, who were placed quite unselectively.

Another study (Paraskevopoulos and Hunt, 1971) gives some indication of environmental influences on the concept of object permanence, a central aspect of intellectual development in infancy. Two orphanages in Athens, to which infants were assigned a few days after birth on a chance basis, had very difference infant-caretaker ratios. Infants in the orphanage with a 3:1 infant-caretaker ratio achieved the various levels of object permanence about a year earlier than children at the orphanage with a ratio of 10:1, and much less individual attention for the children. Home-reared children from working-class families of roughly the same status as those of the orphanage children reached the levels of object permanence earlier than either group of institutionalised children.

The greater similarity between the intelligence test scores of identical (monozygotic) compared with fraternal (dizygotic) twins is often used to substantiate the argument that it is genetic factors which are the main influence on the child's development. Much of the evidence, though, is capable of interpretation in more than one way. Even the high concordance found between the scores of identical twins reared apart is by no means unequivocal support for the view that genetic influences are of overwhelming importance – these twins not only experienced a common pre-natal environment, but usually remained for a few months at least in the same home before being split up, and were mostly brought up in environments that were not too dissimilar.

Recent evidence from a study of mental development in eight-months-old twins suggest that genetic factors play only a relatively small role –

109

when retarded twins were removed from the sample correlations between the scores of identical twin pairs were no higher than those between the scores of fraternal twins (Nichols and Broman, 1974). Also, concordance in the test scores of fraternal twin pairs within the first two years of life is much higher than within pairs of ordinary siblings, though the degree of genetic overlap is precisely the same (Wilson, 1972). The most likely explanation is that twins share environmental circumstances to a much greater extent than ordinary siblings in a family (McCall, 1972; Wachs, 1972). At a minimum, twin studies provide no basis for the view that genetic factors are overwhelmingly more important than environmental factors in infant mental development (Wilson, 1972). The issue of the relative importance of genetic and environmental factors on intelligence at older ages is discussed in Part V: Disadvantage and Intervention (see pp. 291–6).

Are early experiences decisive for later development?

The environment provided for the infant at six months was found in one of the studies discussed above (Yarrow *et al.*, 1974) to have some impact, at least for boys, on later development even though a number of infants changed their environmental circumstances, moving to adoptive families. Where children live in their own families, quite high correlations have been found between the stimulation provided by the environment in the first two-and-a-half years and later intellectual development (Elardo *et al.*, 1975; Moore, 1968). However, the same environmental circumstances are likely to persist in most families and their influence on the child is not only during infancy.

This can also be seen in the classic study which provides the most dramatic evidence of the influence of early life experiences on later development (Skeels, 1966). Infants with retarded mental development who were moved from an unstimulating orphanage to an environment in which they received a great deal of attention and generally formed attachments to a specific person, were found twenty years later to be living normal adult lives; originally similar children who remained in the unstimulating orphanage had unsuccessful lives as adults, being either in low status jobs or still institutionalised, and generally remaining unmarried. These two groups of infants differed not only in their experiences in infancy but in their later experiences as well. The experimental infants not only received stimulating and affectionate care in infancy but were afterwards adopted and continued to experience a favourable environment. The control children remained in unstimulating institutional care. The later development of both of these groups of children depended not only on their experiences in infancy but also on those in childhood. It is significant that the only control child to be successful in adult life had been transferred after infancy to a residential school for the deaf (he had a partial hearing loss) where he was given special attention by the matron. Even extremely depriving circumstances in infancy may be overcome to a very great extent if the child is transferred to more favourable conditions in early childhood.

Dennis's (1973) findings also suggest that the experiences both of infancy and later childhood affect intellectual development. Children in his study had lived from a few days after birth in an extremely depriving institution, in which there was no responsiveness to their individual needs, little social – including verbal – stimulation, and very few toys or objects with which to play. When tested between the ages of one and six, the average IQ scores of these children was only slightly above 50, for both sexes. After the age of six, the experiences of the girls and boys diverged, the girls being transferred to another 'custodial' type of institution while the boys were sent to an institution which was more like a boarding school. In adolescence the average IQ score of the girls remained around 50 while that of the boys rose to an average of about 80. These findings are clear evidence of the beneficial effect of a more favourable environment after the pre-school years in counteracting the effects of an adverse infancy.

Children adopted after the age of two (when this became legalised in the Lebanon) also reached a much higher level of intellectual development than those who had remained in a depriving institution, developing at a normal rate after adoption though not overcoming their initial retardation. Children adopted before the age of two did manage to achieve a normal level of intellectual development. Differences in the intellectual status of children adopted before and after the age of two do not appear to be explicable by a selective adoption policy. Findings suggest then that an extremely depriving infancy may place limitations on what a later favourable family environment can achieve, although this can offset the adverse effects of the early experiences to a considerable extent. It is possible, though, that the children adopted after the age of two had not reached the full limits of their intellectual development when last tested. Few were beyond the age of sixteen, and previous work (Clarke and Clarke, 1976) has show that mildly retarded adolescents and young adults who have experienced extremely adverse home circumstances in early childhood may make large IQ increments, which sometimes bring them to intellectual normality.

Three recently reported case histories (Clarke and Clarke, 1976), suggest that children who are severely retarded after early extreme and prolonged social isolation (from eighteen months or earlier) can reach normality if they receive skilled and intensive education and sympathetic care from the age of seven or so. It should be noted, though, that these children did have the opportunity to form an emotional relationship with someone during their period of severe deprivation; one girl with a deaf-mute mother (with whom she could communicate to some extent by means of gestures) and twins with each other. These studies do not of course show that the early adverse experiences were without any retarding effect for it is impossible to know how the child might otherwise have developed. They leave open the age at which recovery from severe deprivation can occur. They do show that an extremely favourable environment in late childhood can do much to overcome severely depriving experiences in the early years.

Most children, though, continue to experience similar environmental circumstances in infancy and in childhood. The infant from a lower socio-economic background who receives little verbal stimulation from his mother at ten months (Tulkin and Kagan, 1972) is also the child whose mother uses language to instruct him, rather than to explore the meaning of a situation with him, at three years (Tough, 1973). Infancy is by no means decisive for later development. However, the child is much more likely to reach his optimum level if the foundations for his development are laid through his experiences during infancy than if deficits arise which have to be remedied in later childhood.

Conclusions

Research indicates that for optimal development, infants require an adequate level and variety of both social and inanimate stimulation which is geared to their individual needs. Although the infant spends much time exploring the physical environment on his own, at least from the second year, the intellectual benefits he derives from this exploration appear to be much enhanced by the extent to which his mother or other adults he knows well are on hand to encourage, suggest, help and explain (White and Watts, 1973). The findings imply that the child is most likely to develop to a maximal level if he has an enduring relationship with at least one person who is sensitive to his individual needs and stage of development. They do not imply that this person necessarily has to be the mother, though it is likely to be of course, nor that more than one person cannot satisfactorily share this role. This issue is discussed in detail in Part II of the review. An insufficiency of stimulation and responsiveness to the child's individual characteristics and developmental level do not necessarily have effects on later development that are irreversible but they make the attainment of optimal development much more difficult.

Annotations

BIRNS, B. and GOLDEN, M. 1972. 'Prediction of intellectual

performance at three years from infant tests and personality measures', *Merrill-Palmer Quarterly* 18, 1, 53–8.

Generally, low correlations are found between performance on infant tests which largely tap perceptual-motor skills, and later measures of intelligence which depend more on language. Findings of the present study confirm the authors' hypothesis that there may be personality traits which, when used in combination with infant tests, substantially increase our ability to predict later intelligence. Infant intelligence scores (Cattell; Piaget Object Scale) at eighteen months failed to correlate significantly with Stanford Binet intelligence scores at three years, although the twenty-four-month scores did correlate significantly with the three-year scores. However, the amount of pleasure that the infant showed in the task both at eighteen and twenty-four months was correlated significantly with the Stanford Binet at three years. Differences in pleasure at the task at twenty-four months still predicted Stanford Binet IQs at three years even when the subjects were equated statistically in terms of their intelligence. This suggests that pleasure in problem-solving facilitates cognitive development rather than merely being a reaction to it. Subjects in the study were the black children from three socio-economic levels tested at eighteen and twenty-four months in an earlier study (see Golden and Birns, 1968).

BROSSARD, M. and DECARIE, T. G. 1971. 'The effects of three kinds of perceptual-social stimulation on the development of institutionalized infants', *Early Child Development and Care* 1, 1, 111–30.

In this study it was found that two- to two-and-a-half-months-old institutionalised infants appeared to benefit equally from perceptual stimulation (mobile attached to cot, exposure to recorded sounds, but no human intervention) and social stimulation (singing, talking to, smiling at, playing with and holding baby by one of the researchers, but no toys). Infants received the programme of stimulation for fifteen minutes per day for ten weeks. Progress of the experimental groups was compared with that of a control group on the Griffiths Mental Development Scale. A third 'mixed' experimental group, receiving perceptual stimulation for half the programme and social stimulation for the remainder, did not differ significanctly from the controls although some benefits were seen on pre-language development and hand-eye co-ordination.

Findings suggest that stimulation *per se* is more important than the type of stimulation but that a certain minimum duration of stimulation is necessary for it to be beneficial. However, although stimulation per se may be sufficient for normal development in the first few months of life, it would not provide the child with the experiences necessary for the development of an attachment to an adult later in the first year − a relationship that appears to be an essential of human socialisation.

CLARKE-STEWART, K. A. 1973. 'Interactions between mothers and their young children: characteristics and consequences', *Monographs of the Society for Research in Child Development*, serial no. 153, 38, 6−7, pp. 109.

An investigation of the relationship between the behaviour of mothers and that of their young children. The subjects were thirty-six normal first-born infants and their mothers from the lowest socio-economic level. Repeated home observations were carried out when the infants were between nine and eighteen months of age, and behaviour of the infants and their mothers was also observed in various structured experimental situations.

The main finding from the research was of a strong association between infant competence and maternal care. Measures of competence in the infant − in the areas of cognitive, language and social development − were highly intercorrelated. Similarly, measures of maternal competence − expression of affection for the child, social stimulation and stimulation with appropriate materials, contingent responsiveness to the infant's social behaviour and signs of distress − were highly intercorrelated. Specific relationships were found between the infant's language ability and verbal stimulation from the mother, the child's skill with objects and the amount of stimulation he received from the mother with play materials and between the infant's and the mother's positive social responses to each other.

Some support was obtained for the Lewis and Goldberg (1969) thesis that contingent responsiveness creates in the child a generalised expectation that he will be competent to affect the environment. Maternal responsiveness to the infant's social behaviour was correlated more highly with infant competence than with the frequency of social behaviours to which the response was made. On the other hand, maternal responsiveness to distress was correlated only with the infant's attachment to his mother, and negatively to fretfulness. Infants who showed a secure attachment to the mother, using her as a secure base for exploration in an unfamiliar environment (see Ainsworth and Wittig, 1969), had mothers who were socially stimulating, responsive and affectionate, but who were not excessive in physical contact. The infant's mental development (Bayley Scale) was more closely related to the mother's responsiveness to her infant's social behaviours and to the appropriateness of her behaviour than to the sheer amount of stimulation she provided. In contrast, language ability and involvement with the mother were more highly related to the amount of stimulation.

Analysis of correlations across time indicated that it is maternal stimulation, responsiveness and affectionate behaviour that affects the child's competence rather than the influence being in the opposite direction. However, at least over the time period investigated, it was the infant's social behaviour which affected the mother's affection for and attachment to the child and her responsiveness to his signs of distress.

COLLARD, R. R. 1971. 'Exploration and play behaviors of infants reared in an institution and in lower- and middle-class homes', *Child Development* 42, 4, 1003–15.

Institutionalised infants (eight to thirteen months old) showed less variety of exploratory responses (such as looking at, transferring, extending, turning) to a test toy than home-reared infants of similar age; they also made a lower number of exploratory responses (such as handing or showing the toy to the nurse (mother) or experimenter) than the home children. Home-reared, lower-class children made less variety of exploratory responses, fewer responses requiring fine co-ordination and fewer social responses than the middle-class children but did not differ from them in the number of exploratory responses made.

The three groups were similar in the number of play responses (including banging, waving, dropping and casting the toy) but the institutionalised infants made many more repetitive responses. It is suggested that the differences in the amount and variety of exploratory behaviour depend on the child's opportunities for exploration and manipulation, on the variety of objects available, and on the opportunities for playing with toys with other people. On the Gesell Cubes sub-test the institutionalised infants, who had played with blocks, did as well as the lower-class infants most of whom had not played with blocks; middle-class infants, though, did better than either of these groups. On the Gesell Cup and Cubes sub-test, institutionalised infants, one of whom had played with containers, did significantly less well than the home infants, all of whom had played with containers. The social class differences found in this study, in contrast to most previous research, may have resulted from the extremes in social background of the two home groups – one coming from a ghetto area and the other group consisting of children of college professors.

ELARDO, R., BRADLEY, R. and CALDWELL, B. M. 1975. 'The relation of infants' home environments to mental test performance from six to thirty-six months: a longitudinal analysis', *Child Development* 46, 1, 71–6.

Home environment scores (Caldwell Inventory of Home Stimulation) at six, twelve and twenty-four months were correlated quite highly with IQ

(Stanford Binet) at three years. The scales concerned with the organisation of the physical and temporal environment and opportunities for variety in daily stimulation were the aspects of the home environment at six months which had the highest correlations with later development. From twelve months the provision of appropriate play materials and maternal involvement with the child showed the strongest relationships with later development. Subjects were seventy-seven children and their mothers from a wide social class range.

GOLDEN, M. and BIRNS, B. 1968. 'Social class and cognitive development in infancy', *Merrill-Palmer Quarterly* 4, 2, 139–49.

No differences were found in cognitive development at twelve, eighteen or twenty-four months (measured on Piaget Object Scale and Cattell Infant Intelligence Scale) of three groups of children – from fatherless welfare families, stable low-income and middle-income black families, when every effort was made to overcome motivational factors which might interfere with test performance. Welfare children showed resistance to testing but by giving them more trials, taking more time and using special techniques, it was possible to get them to perform at the same intellectual level as the other two groups. It is possible that the home environment of children from socially disorganised slum families is adequate for the development of sensorimotor intelligence and concrete thinking, but not for the development of language and abstract thinking. However, by not taking the difficulties in testing into consideration, the social class differences in behaviours important for later learning may have been washed out.

GOLDEN, M. and BIRNS, B. 1971. 'Social class, intelligence and cognitive style in infancy', *Child Development* 42, 6, 2114–6.

Substantial social class differences were found in the Stanford Binet intelligence test scores of black three-year-olds although no social class differences had been found in performances of the same children on Cattell or Piaget Object Scales at eighteen and twenty-four months (Golden and Birns, 1968). However, children from the lowest socio-economic level had proved difficult to test at the earlier ages and had been given more time, and various inducements to perform at their best. It is suggested that the use of such non-standard conditions may have resulted in social class differences either in intellectual ability or cognitive style related to intellectual ability being concealed.

To test this hypothesis, eighteen- and twenty-four-months-old children from three socio-economic levels (black welfare families; black higher educational achievement families; white higher educational achievement families) were tested on the Cattell and Object Scales under both standard and optimum conditions. Contrary to expectations, no social class differences were found under either standard or optimal conditions, nor were there significant social class differences in improvement of performance from the standard to the optimal conditions. The intellectual performances of the black and white children did not differ significantly. It is concluded that social class differences emerge only between eighteen and thirty-six months of age, when language enters the picture.

JONES, S. J. and MOSS, H. A. 1971. 'Age, state, and maternal behavior associated with infant vocalizations', *Child Development* 42, 4, 1039–51.

Twenty-eight first-born infants were observed in their homes when they were about two weeks old, and again at about three months. When the infant was in the passive awake state, he vocalised the same amounts in his mother's presence and absence; in the active awake state, however, the infant vocalised less in the mother's presence. In the early period the amount mothers talked directly to their infants was related to the infants' vocalisations in the active awake state. For older infants, contingent maternal speech (assessed as maternal speech following the infant's vocalisations within a two-second period) was related to the amount of vocalisations. For the younger children, mothers who talked most were those whose infants spent least time in the active awake state. The study shows that one interesting social object – the mother – does not always elicit the most overt responses from the infant. This may be because the infant spends time 'taking in' the object, or the home-reared infant may have so much contact with his mother that her mere presence is not interesting. Possibly the first interpretation is valid for the highly active mother, and the second for the passive mother.

KAGAN, J. 1969. 'Continuity in cognitive development during the first year', *Merrill-Palmer Quarterly* 15, 1, 101–19.

Findings from the present study suggest that vocalisation during the first year is related to attentiveness in girls but not boys. There is supporting evidence from other research of a link between early vocalisation and indices of level of cognitive development in girls. Findings that well-educated mothers engage in more distinctive face-to-face vocalisations with daughters but not sons, compared to less-educated mothers, support an environmentalist interpretation. However, the possibility cannot be ruled out that there may be basic sex differences in neuromotor organisation.

LEWIS, M. and GOLDBERG, S. 1969. 'Perceptual-cognitive development in infancy: a generalised expectancy model as a function of the mother-infant interaction', *Merrill-Palmer Quarterly* 15, 1, 81–100.

Greater maternal stimulation (touching, looking at, holding and smiling) of the infant, more frequent responses to his crying and vocalisations and more rapid maternal responses were all related to more advanced cognitive development (as assessed by response decrement to repeated signals) in three-months-old infants. It is argued that maternal reinforcement of infant behaviour not only reinforces that specific behaviour but also creates a generalised expectation in the infant about his competence to affect the environment. Given this expectancy, the infant is motivated to produce behaviours and skills not reinforced by his experiences. Each of the twenty mother-infant pairs taking part in this study was observed while left alone in a controlled naturalistic setting.

McCALL, R. B. 1972. 'Similarity in developmental profile among related pairs of human infants', *Science*, 178, 1004–5.

A re-interpretation of findings from Wilson's (1972) study (see below) of infant mental development in twins. It is possible that the high concordance of mental development found for the dizygotic (fraternal) twin pairs in this study may derive from common non-genetic as well as genetic circumstances, as Wilson proposes. In fact, as the genetic correlation averages .50 for dizygotic twins, correlations substantially higher than this, as found in Wilson's study, must reflect common environmental circumstances, or assortative mating, or both. Correlations of the test scores and developmental profiles of the dizygotic twins were two to six times as high as in sibling pairs from the Fels study, despite the degree of genetic overlap being the same for the dizygotic twins as for the sibling pairs. Twins may be more similar than siblings because they share environmental circumstances to a greater extent. A comparison of three groups of children from the Fels sample: (1) 142 pairs of siblings; (2) unrelated pairs matched for year of birth, sex and parent's education; (3) unrelated pairs matched for year of birth and sex only, found that while siblings were more similar on test scores at six, twelve, eighteen and twenty-four months than the other pairs, no differences in within-pair similarity between the three groups for development profile were found.

MOORE, T. 1968. 'Language and intelligence: a longitudinal study of the first eight years. Part II. Environmental correlates of mental growth', *Human Development* 11, 1–24.

Seventy-six children, fairly representative of the London population, were tested on measures of intelligence and language (Griffiths Scale of Infant Development, Stanford Binet and other language measures) at the age of six months, eighteen months, three, five and eight years. Significant correlations were found between intelligence and language scores and a number of environmental variables – social class, mother's vocabulary, ordinal position, and home environment in the early years. With social class held constant, the variables most closely associated with later ability were the home environment variables (toys, books and experiences; example and encouragement to speak; emotional atmosphere – assessed when the child was two-and-a-half years old). These ratings of home environment were only slightly related to ability scores at three years but they predicted the eight-year assessments of ability to a significant degree. Ordinal position also correlated with ability when social class was held constant, but the relationship between the ability scores and maternal vocabulary almost disappeared.

NICHOLS, P. L. and BROMAN, S. H. 1974. 'Familial resemblance in infant mental development', *Developmental Psychology* 10, 3, 442–6.

Correlations between scores on the Bayley Scale of mental development of eight-months-old twins were high (.84 monozygotic (identical) and .55 for dizygotic (fraternal) twins), suggesting a large genetic influence. However, average correlation between scores of other siblings was low (.22) and inconsistent with high heritability. Higher correlations between scores of dizygotic twins and other sibling pairs may have resulted from greater environmental similarities. When retarded twins were removed from the sample, correlations between the scores of monozygotic twins and between those of dizygotic twins became identical, indicating that genetic factors have only a small influence on infant mental development in the normal population.

PARASKEVOPOULOS, J. and HUNT, J. McV. 1971. 'Object construction and imitation under differing conditions of rearing', *Journal of Genetic Psychology* 119, 301–21.

Although there is evidence that orphanage rearing is associated with low developmental quotients on standardised tests of infant abilities the importance of these findings for later intellectual development has been questioned. Part of the criticism arises from the failure of these tests to predict later IQ. To overcome this problem, an attempt was made in the present study to assess the effect of environmental circumstances on the ages at which infants achieved certain levels in two basic domains of intellectual development first described by Piaget – object permanence and imitation. The subjects were 233 Greek children, aged five months to five years, living in three conditions of rearing:
(a) a Municipal Orphanage, with an infant-caretaker ratio of 10:1, resulting in some children receiving much more attention than the others;

(b) the Metera Centre, an orphanage with an infant-caretaker ratio of 3:1, in which all the children received very similar care;
(c) working-class families, very similar to those from which the orphanage children came.

The home-reared children achieved the various levels of object permanence earlier than either group of orphanage children but only the difference from the Municipal Orphanage group was statistically significant. Also the standard deviations of the ages at which the children achieved the higher levels of object construction were larger for the home-reared children than for the children in both the other groups. This indicates that the conditions which foster the development of object permanence vary more among working-class families than in the Municipal Orphanage, where the children differ very much in the amounts of attention received. The home-reared children also attained the various levels on the scales of vocal and gestural imitations earlier than either of the orphanage groups, although differences were non-significant for the latter. Findings show then that environmental circumstances do affect the ages at which children achieve the concept of object permanence and imitation, both of which appear to be basic for the development of language and thought. Also, the findings offer no support for Jensen's (1969) hypothesis that the environment must operate with respect to intelligence in a threshold fashion, i.e. while a highly inadequate environment can stunt growth, once the minimum requirements are available further environmental improvements add little. Rather, it appears that the specific factors in the environment which influence object permanence and imitation do so continuously.

REPUCCI, N. D. 1971. 'Parental education, sex differences, and performance on cognitive tasks among two year old children', *Developmental Psychology* 4, 2, 248–53.

The performance of twenty-seven-months-old girls on three different types of cognitive tasks (two vocabulary tasks, an embedded figures task, and a two-choice discrimination task) was related to parental educational level, but the boys' performance was unrelated to their parents' education. The father's educational level had a greater influence on the girls' performance than the mother's. Consistent with these findings, there is some research evidence that educational level influences the way parents treat their young sons. The study also draws attention to the need for further investigation of the influence of father-child interaction on children's cognitive development.

RUBENSTEIN, J. 1967. 'Maternal attentiveness and subsequent exploratory behavior in the infant', *Child Development* 38, 4, 1089–1100.

In this study, maternal attentiveness in the infant's fifth month was found to be related to exploratory behaviour in the six-months-old infant. Infants whose mothers were highly attentive to them (measured by the number of times during an observation period the mother looked at, touched, held and talked to the baby while going about her normal activities), looked at, manipulated and vocalised to a novel stimulus presented by itself more than infants in the low attentiveness group. Mothers who were highly attentive offered their babies a significantly larger variety of toys and more play opportunities than mothers who were medium or low in attentiveness. Subjects were forty-four infants living in intact nuclear families. The three groups of infants were comparable on father's occupation, mother's age and birth-weight.

TIZARD, B., COOPERMAN, O., JOSEPH, A. and TIZARD, J. 1972. 'Environmental effects on language development: a study of young children in long-stay residential nurseries', *Child Development* 43, 337–58.

No retardation, either verbal (Reynell Developmental Language Scales) or non-verbal (Minnesota Pre-school Scale) was found in this study in eighty-five two- to five-year-old children living in eleven British residential nurseries. All the nurseries investigated provided a high level of verbal stimulation (staff talked to the children in half of the periods observed) as well as excellent physical care and as much variety of social experiences as possible. The importance of a sufficient quantity of verbal stimulation is indicated by the finding that the children who were talked to least by the staff, the youngest, also had language comprehension scores significantly lower than those of the older children. While all the nurseries provided a sufficient quantity of verbal stimulation to promote average language development, the developmental level reached by the children in different nurseries was related to the quality of the staff talk. Language comprehension scores of the children were significantly and positively related to the frequency of 'informative' staff talk (reading to, explaining to, informing the children), of staff 'social' activity (playing, reading to, conversing with, teaching, responding affectionately to the children), to the frequency with which the staff answered the children's remarks, and to the amount of play in which the children were actively rather than passively involved. Differences in the quality of staff talk were related to differences in the social organisation of the nurseries, particularly the amount of autonomy allowed to the staff in charge of the nursery group, and in no way to the abilities of the children, who were placed unselectively. Findings of the study provide evidence, uncontaminated by genetic influences, that the verbal environment experienced by the child affects his language development.

121

TODD, G. A. and PALMER, B. 1968. 'Social reinforcement of infant babbling', *Child Development* 39, 2, 591–6.

Previous research (Rheingold *et al.*, 1959; Weisberg, 1963, see below) has shown that the frequency of vocalisations in the three-months-old human infant can be increased by reinforcement consisting of visual (smile), tactile (light touch) and auditory ('tsk' or 'yeah' sounds) stimulation but that the human presence alone (Weisberg, 1963) does not increase vocalisations. In the present study, reinforcement of vocalisations by a tape-recorded human voice increased the frequency of vocalisations. However, the presence of an adult, in addition to the tape-recorded human voice, produced a greater increase in the frequency of vocalisations. Findings suggest that human presence enhances the effect of the human voice, although ineffective by itself.

WACHS, T. D. 1972. 'Similarity in developmental profile among related pairs of human infants', *Science* 178, 1005–6.

A critique of Wilson's (1972 – see below) study of infant mental development in twins. Wilson's data indicates a high within-pair concordance for overall intellectual development of dizygotic (fraternal) twins. Differences within twin pairs were relatively small compared with differences between twin pairs. Wilson presents findings showing that socio-economic levels contain a great diversity of environmental circumstances, so that they can give little indication of the relationship between environment and early intelligence. The maximum expected genetic correlation between dizygotic twins should be .50 but correlations were actually above this level in Wilson's data indicating the operation of non-genetic factors on their mental development. There is, in fact, evidence that specific proximal experiences of the child, such as linguistic stimulation or over-stimulation do influence performance on a Piaget-based scale of infant development (see Wachs *et al.*, 1971). This argument does not deny the importance of genetic factors in the development of intelligence, but it does suggest that they may not have the overwhelming importance proposed by Wilson.

WACHS, T. D., UZGIRI, L. C. and HUNT, J. McV. 1971. 'Cognitive development in infants of different age levels and from different environmental backgrounds: an explanatory investigation', *Merrill-Palmer Quarterly* 17, 4, 283–317.

An investigation of the relationship between home environment and psychological development. Fifty-one infants from a slum area of a city in the United States were tested on the Infant Psychological Development Scale, which is based on Piaget's model of intellectual development, in either the seventh, eleventh, fifteenth, eighteenth or twenty-second month of life. Fifty-one middle-class infants, matched with the disadvantaged children for date of birth and sex, were tested at the same ages. Differences in favour of the middle-class children were found on several of the scales at various age levels, and no difference favoured the disadvantaged children. It is suggested that the failure in previous studies to find social class differences in the cognitive development of infants may have been due to the lumping together of separate categories of ability. Two kinds of home circumstances (items from Caldwell's Inventory of Home Stimulation) were found to be most consistently related to psychological development. High intensity of auditory stimulation from which the infant could not escape and involuntary exposure to an excessive variety of circumstances were negatively related to several aspects of psychological development at all the age levels. The second group of items consistently related to psychological development from the age of fifteen months and involved vocal and verbal stimulation of the infant by the parents. These findings are consistent with other evidence indicating the importance of linguistic stimulation for early infant development.

WAHLER, R. G. 1967. 'Infant social attachments: a reinforcement theory interpretation and investigation', *Child Development* 38, 4, 1079–88.

The frequency of smiling in three-months-old home-reared infants was reliably increased when smiles were immediately followed by social reinforcement from the mother (consisting of 'Hi' followed by the infant's name, a smile and a light touch of the chest). Identical social reinforcement of smiling by a stranger, though, did not reliably increase the frequency of infant smiling. Results indicate that the infant's social attachment to the mother has undergone significant development by the time he has reached three months.

WEISBERG, P. 1963. 'Social and nonsocial conditioning of infant vocalizations', *Child Development* 34, 377–88.

Contingent social stimulation (smile, rubbing infant's chin and 'yeah' sound presented after each vocalisation) was found to reliably increase the frequency of vocalisations in three-months-old institutionalised infants. The presence of an unresponding adult, non-contingent social stimulation (as above, but presented at random), and contingent non-social stimulation (door chimes sounded immediately after each infant vocalisation) all failed to produce reliable increases in the frequency of infant vocalisations.

WHITE, B. L. 1967. 'An experimental approach to the effects of experience on early human behavior', in Hill, J. P. (ed) *Minnesota Symposia on Child Psychology*, Vol. I. University of Minnesota Press, Minneapolis. 201–26.

Description of a number of studies by the author and his colleagues, first tracing the evolution of fundamental sensorimotor abilities from birth and, secondly, investigating whether development can be accelerated by environmental enrichment. Subjects were physically normal institutionalised children. In the first experiment, modification consisted of twenty minutes extra handling per day from days six to thirty-six. No changes were found in any developmental process except that the handled group were more visually attentive than the controls.

The second experiment was designed to enrich the environment in as many respects as possible:
(1) extra handling as in the first experiment;
(b) increased motility – infants placed in prone position for fifteen minutes a day after three feeds from thirty-seventh to 124th day;
(c) enriched visual surroundings – multicoloured objects suspended over the crib.

Hand regard and swiping were delayed compared with the controls but top-level-reaching was significantly advanced. Visual exploratory behaviour was decreased for the first five weeks of the test period but once top-level-reaching occurred visual attention increased sharply. In the first five weeks, the babies ignored the multicoloured objects but they began swiping at them at about seventy-two days and in less than a month completed the integration of grasp and approaching movements. This transition took three months in the controls (see also White, 1969).

In the third experiment paced modification of the environment took place:
(a) extra handling as in previous experiments;
(b) the only modification from thirty-seven to sixty-eight days was the placing of two pacifiers on crib rails, positioned to elicit maximum attention from an infant of this age;
(c) from sixty-eight to 124 days, multicoloured objects were placed over cot.

Hand regard was no longer delayed, top-level-reaching was achieved earlier than in the previous experiment, and this experimental group was more consistently attentive than the others. The study shows that certain aspects, at least, of visual-motor functioning are remarkably plastic. It is not possible to say whether the accelerated development has long-term significance, but it could have important implications for optimal development of human potential.

WHITE, B. L. 1969. 'The initial co-ordination of sensorimotor schemas in human infants – Piaget's ideas and the role of experience', in D. Elkind, and J. H. Flavell, (eds) *Studies in Cognitive Development*, Oxford University Press, London. 237–56.

According to Piaget, the one-month-old infant can grasp a rattle if it is pressed into his palm, suck it if brought to his mouth, look at it if placed in his visual field. However, these schemas exist in isolation, a one-month-old baby will not look at something he is grasping, not grasp something he is sucking and so on. During the next few months, these schemas become co-ordinated until at between four and five months the hand grasps the seen object for the first time, and at five to six months, true reaching occurs. In this study it was found that rearing conditions can accelerate the co-ordination of schemas. Institutionalised infants (all physically normal) who had experienced an experimental enrichment programme designed to optimise learning conditions for acquisition of visual control over the hand were significantly more advanced than control infants (see also White, 1967).

WILSON, R. S. 1972. 'Twins: early mental development', *Science* 175, 914–7.

Correlations between IQ scores (Bayley Scales) of pairs of monozygotic (identical) twins at ages three, six, nine, twelve, eighteen and twenty-four months were significantly higher than those between pairs of dizygotic (fraternal) twins. The pattern of mental development across ages was also closer in the monozygotic twins, lags and spurts in their development being more closely aligned. These results suggest that there is a significant genetic influence on infant mental development. The findings also show a relatively high degree of concordance for overall developmental level in dizygotic twin pairs – differences within twin pairs are relatively small compared with differences between twin pairs. At the ages tested, there was only a weak relationship between socio-economic level and test scores. It is suggested that for the majority of children life circumstances are sufficient to permit the genetic blueprint to control the course of infant development, although the development of one or both twins may sometimes be suppressed by serious prematurity or an impoverished environment.

YARROW, L. J. 1963. 'Research in dimensions of early maternal care', *Merrill-Palmer Quarterly* 9, 2, 101–14.

This study examines the relationship between infant psychological development at six months and three classes of environmental variables (concerned with physical care, stimulation and affection). The environmental variables which showed consistently high association with many aspects of infant behaviour (IQ, handling stress, exploratory and manipulative behaviour and social inititative) were those concerned with maternal stimulation. IQ was related to both the amount and appropriateness of the stimulation, but only moderately to the variables concerned with physical care and an affectional relationship. On the other hand, the infant's capacity to handle stress was highly related to all three kinds of variables. Findings show then some fairly direct relationships between aspects of maternal behaviour and infant characteristics. It is an over-simplification, though, to look at this relationship in terms of the mother's effect on the child and ignore the influence of the infant's behaviour on the mother. Several examples are found in the present study of foster mothers and foster children of how the mother may provide quite different environments for infants with different characteristics.

YARROW, L. J., GOODWIN, M. S., MANHEIMER, H. and MILOWE, I. D. 1974. 'Infancy experiences and cognitive and personality development at ten years', in L. J. Stone, H. T. Smith and L. Murphy (eds) *The Competent Infant*, Tavistock, London; Basic Books, New York.

IQ scores (Wechsler Intelligence Scale for Children) at ten years of age were related to several aspects of the maternal care given to the child when six months old (amount of physical contact given the child, appropriateness of stimulation for his developmental level, responsiveness to the infant's cues, degree to which the infant is seen as a unique person, involvement with and affection for the baby); correlations, though were significant only for boys.

Boys' capacity to contribute constructively to a social situation and to relate to other people on a meaningful level at ten years of age was also related to maternal behaviour when the child was six months old (responsiveness to infant's cues, ability to express warmth for him, extent to which the mother was sensitive to his special characteristics and to which her behaviour was adapted to his needs). Social dominance in boys at ten years of age was related to the social stimulation provided by the mother at six months and extent to which she overtly expressed warmth for him.

Children who had been separated from foster mothers to go to adoptive homes before they were six months old did not differ from controls in intellectual ability or social adjustment at ten years of age. However, children who were separated from their foster mothers to go to adoptive homes after they were six months of age were lower in their capacity to establish different levels of relationship with people than the children in the other two groups. The three groups did not differ significantly in overall adaptation or intellectual ability. Severity of distress on separation was not related to later intellectual or social functioning.

Correlations between early experiences and later development, although mainly significant for boys, were not generally very high. The findings do not indicate that early experiences are decisive for later development but that they are variables, along with many others, which do have some influence on it.

YARROW, L. J., RUBENSTEIN, J. L., PEDERSEN, F. A. and JANKOWSKI, J. J. 1972. 'Dimensions of early stimulation and their different effects on infant development', *Merrill-Palmer Quarterly* 18, 3, 205–18.

In this study both inanimate and social stimulation were found to be important for the development of the five-months-old infant. Social responsiveness of the infant was related to the level and variety of social stimulation and to positive effect but to only one of the inanimate stimulation variables. Infant vocalisations were related to the contingency of the mother's response to infant vocalisations (although not to total vocalisations) and to variety of social stimulation but to none of the inanimate stimulation variables. On the other hand, exploratory behaviour was quite strongly related to level, variety and responsiveness of inanimate stimulation but only slightly to social stimulation. Cognitive motivational variables (goal-directed behaviours such as reaching persistently for an object, attempting to elicit a response from an object) were particularly strongly related to environmental variables, both social and inanimate.

It is suggested that the infant's orientation to objects and people may become, at a very early stage, part of a feed-back system with the environment, and a more significant characteristic than any particular cognitive skill. That these motivational behaviours are amenable to environmental influences may be of importance for intervention programmes, as well as for developmental theory. The subjects of the study – forty-one black infants and their mothers, mainly from a lower-class background – were observed for six hours in their homes; the infants were also administered the Bayley Scales of Infant Development and a test measuring exploratory behaviour and preference for novelty.

References

(When a title has been annotated, this is indicated at the end of the entry by the relevant page number printed in bold type.)

AINSWORTH, M. D. S. 1962. 'The effects of maternal deprivation: a review of findings and controversy in the context of research', in *Deprivation of Maternal Care: A Reassessment of its Effects*, World Health Organisation, Geneva.

AINSWORTH, M. D. S. 1963. 'The development of infant-mother interaction among the Ganda', in B. M. Foss (ed) *Determinants of Infant Behaviour, II*, Methuen, London. 67–112. **p. 81**

AINSWORTH, M. D. S. 1964. 'Patterns of attachment behavior shown by the infant in interaction with his mother', *Merrill-Palmer Quarterly* 10, 51–8.

AINSWORTH, M. D. S. 1967. *Infancy in Uganda: Infant Care and the Growth of Love*, Johns Hopkins, Baltimore (chapters 20–23, pp 331–400) **p. 82**

AINSWORTH, M. D. S. 1973. 'The development of infant-mother attachment' in B. M. Caldwell and H. N. Ricciuti (eds) *Review of Child Development Research, Vol. 3*, University of Chicago Press, Chicago. 1–94.

AINSWORTH, M. D. S. and BELL, S. M. 1969. 'Some contemporary patterns of mother-infant interaction in the feeding situation', in A. Ambrose (ed) *Stimulation in Early Infancy*, Academic Press, London and New York. 133–63. **p. 82**

AINSWORTH, M. D. S. and BELL, S. M. 1970. 'Attachment, exploration and separation: illustrated by the behavior of one-year-olds in a strange situation', *Child Development* 41, 1, 49–67.

AINSWORTH, M. D. S. and WITTIG, B. A. 1969. 'Attachment and exploratory behavior of one year olds in a strange situation', in B. M. Foss (ed) *Determinants of Infant Behaviour, IV*, Methuen, London. 111–36. **p. 83**

AINSWORTH, M. D. S., BELL, S. M. and STAYTON, D. J. 1971. 'Individual differences in strange-situation behavior of one year olds', in H. R. Schaffer (ed) *The Origins of Human Social Relations*, Academic Press, London. 17–52. **p. 84**

AINSWORTH, M. D. S., BELL, S. M. and STAYTON, D. J. 1972. 'Individual differences in the development of some attachment behaviors', *Merrill-Palmer Quarterly* 18, 2, 123–43. **p. 84**

AINSWORTH, M. D. S., BELL, S. M. and STAYTON, D. J. 1974. 'Infant-mother attachment and social development: socialisation as a product of reciprocal responsiveness to signals', in M. P. M. Richards (ed) *The Integration of a Child into a Social World*, Cambridge University Press, London. 99–135. **p. 85**

ALEKSANDROWICZ, M. K. 1974. 'The effect of pain-relieving drugs administered during labor and delivery on the behavior of the newborn: a review', *Merrill-Palmer Quarterly* 20, 2, 121–41.

ALEKSANDROWICZ, M. K. and ALEKSANDROWICZ, D. R. 1974. 'Obstetrical pain-relieving drugs as predictors of infant behavior variability', *Child Development* 45, 4, 935–45.

BAN, P. L. and LEWIS, M. 1974. 'Mothers and fathers, girls and boys: attachment behavior in the one year old', *Merrill-Palmer Quarterly* 20, 3, 195–204. **p. 85**

BECKWITH, L. 1971. 'Relationships between attributes of mothers and their infants' IQ scores', *Child Development* 42, 4, 1083–97. **p. 47**

BECKWITH, L. 1972. 'Relationships between infants' social behavior and their mothers' behavior', *Child Development* 43, 2, 397–411.

BELL, R. Q. 1971. 'Stimulus control of parent or caretaker behavior by offspring', *Developmental Psychology* 4, 1, 63–72. **p. 48**

BELL, R. Q., WELLER, G. M. and WALDROP, M. F. 1971. 'Newborn and preschooler: organization of behavior and relations between periods', *Monographs of the Society for Research in Child Development*, Serial no. 142, 36, 1–2. 145 pp. **p. 48**

BELL, S. M. 1970. 'The development of the concept of object as related to infant-mother attachment', *Child Development* 41, 2, 291–311. **p. 86**

BELL, S. M. and AINSWORTH, M. D. S. 1972. 'Infant crying and maternal responsiveness', *Child Development* 43, 4, 1171–90. **p. 49**

BERNAL, J. 1972. 'Crying during the first ten days of life, and maternal responses', *Developmental Medicine and Child Neurology* 14, 3, 362–72. **p. 49**

BIJOU, S. W. and BAER, D. M. 1973. 'A social learning model of attachment', in S. J. Hutt and C. Hutt (eds) *Early Human Development*, Oxford University Press, London. 214–23.

BIRNS, B. 1976. 'The emergence and socialisation of sex differences in the earliest years', *Merrill-Palmer Quarterly* 22, 3, 229–54.

BIRNS B. and GOLDEN, M. 1972. 'Prediction of intellectual performance at three years from infant tests and personality measures', *Merrill-Palmer Quarterly* 18, 1, 53–8. **p. 112**

BLURTON JONES, N. and LEACH, G. M.. 1972. 'Behaviour of children and their mothers at separation and greeting', in N. Blurton Jones (ed) *Ethological Studies of Child Behaviour*, Cambridge University Press, London. 217–48.

BOWLBY, J. 1951. *Maternal Care and Mental Health*, World Health Organisation, Geneva.

BOWLBY, J. 1958. 'The nature of the child's tie to his mother', *International Journal of Psycho-Analysis* 39, 350–73.

BOWLBY, J. 1969. *Attachment and Loss, I*, Hogarth, London; Basic Books, New York.

BRACKBILL, Y. 1958. 'Extinction of the smiling response in infants as a function of reinforcement schedule', *Child Development* 29, 1, 115–24.

BRONFENBRENNER, U. 1974. *A Report on Longitudinal Evaluations of Preschool Programs, Vol. II. Is Early Intervention Effective?* DHEW Publication No (OHD) 74–25, US Department of Health, Education and Welfare, 60 pp.

BRONSON, G. W. 1972. 'Infants' reactions to unfamiliar persons and novel objects', *Monographs of the Society for Research in Child Development*, Serial no. 148, 37, 3. 46 pp.

BROOKS, J. and LEWIS, M. 1974. 'Attachment behavior in thirteen months old, opposite-sex twins', *Child Development* 45, 1, 243–7. **p. 86**

BROSSARD, L. M. and DECARIE, T. G. 1968. 'Comparative reinforcing effect of eight stimulations on the smiling response of infants', *Journal of Child Psychology and Psychiatry* 9, 1, 51–60.

BROSSARD, M. and DECARIE, T. G. 1971. 'The effects of three kinds of perceptual-social stimulation on the development of institutionalized infants', *Early Child Development and Care* 1, 1, 111–30. **p. 113**

BROWN, G. W., BHROLCHAIN, M. N. and HARRIS, T. 1975. 'Social class and psychiatric disturbance among women in an urban population', *Sociology* 9, 2, 225–54.

BROWN, J. V. *et al.* 1975. 'Interactions of black inner-city mothers with their newborn infants', *Child Development* 46, 3, 677–86.

CAMPOS, J. J., EMDE, R. N., GAENSBAUER, T. and HENDERSON, C. 1975. 'Cardiac and behavioral interrelationships in the reactions of infants to strangers', *Developmental Psychology* 11, 5, 589–601.

CLARKE, A. M. and CLARKE, A. D. B. 1976. *Early Experience: Myth and Evidence*, Open Books, London. 314 pp. Free Press, New York, NY

CLARKE-STEWART, K. A. 1973. 'Interactions between mothers and their young children: characteristics and consequences', *Monographs of the Society for Research in Child Development*, Serial no. 153, 38, 607. 109 pp. **p. 114**

COATES, B., ANDERSON, E. P. and HARTUP, W. W. 1972a. 'Interrelations in the attachment behavior of human infants', *Developmental Psychology* 6, 2, 218–30. **p. 87**

COATES, B., ANDERSON, E. P. and HARTUP, W. W. 1972b. 'The stability of attachment behaviors in the human infant', *Developmental Psychology* 6, 2, 231–7. **p. 87**

COHEN, L. J. and CAMPOS, J. J. 1974. 'Father, mother and stranger as elicitors of attachment behaviors in infancy', *Developmental Psychology* 10, 1, 146–54. **p. 88**

COHEN, S. E. and BECKWITH, L. 1976. 'Maternal language in infancy', *Developmental Psychology* 12, 4, 371–2.

COLLARD, R. R. 1971. 'Exploratory and play behaviors of infants reared in an institution and in lower- and middle-class homes', *Child Development* 42, 4, 1003–15. **p. 115**

CORTER, C. M. 1973. 'A comparison of the mother's and a stranger's control over the behavior of infants', *Child Development* 44, 4, 705–13. **p. 89**

CORTER, C. M., RHEINGOLD, H. L. and ECKERMAN, C. O. 1972. 'Toys delay the infant's following of his mother', *Developmental Psychology* 6, 1, 138–45. **p. 88**

COX, F. N. and CAMPBELL, D. 1968. 'Young children in a new situation with and without their mothers', *Child Development* 39, 1, 123–31. **p. 89**

DAVIDS, A., HOLDEN, R. H. and GRAY, G. B. 1963. 'Maternal anxiety during pregnancy and adequacy of mother and child adjustment eight months following childbirth', *Child Development* 34, 4, 993–1002. **p. 49**

DENNIS, W. 1973. *Children of the Crèche*, Appleton Crofts, New York. 120 pp.

DINNAGE, R. and PRINGLE, M. L. K. 1967. *Residential Child Care – Facts and Fallacies*, Longman in association with National Bureau for Co-operation in Child Care (now National Children's Bureau), London; Humanities Press, Atlantic Highlands, NJ. 344 pp.

DOUGLAS, J. W. B. 1975. 'Early hospital admissions and later disturbances of behaviour and learning', *Developmental Medicine and Child Neurology* 17, 4, 456–80.

ECKERMAN, C. O. and RHEINGOLD, H. L. 1974. 'Infants' exploratory responses to toys and people', *Developmental Psychology* 10, 2, 255–9. **p. 90**

ELARDO, R., BRADLEY, R. and CALDWELL, B. M. 1975. 'The relation of infants' home environments to mental test performance from six to thirty-six months: a longitudinal analysis', *Child Development* 46, 1, 71–6. **p. 115**

ESCALONA, S. K. and CORMAN, H. H. 1971. 'The impact of mother's presence upon behavior: the first year', *Human Development* 14, 2–15. **p. 90**

FELDMAN, S. S. and INGHAM, M. E. 1975. 'Attachment behavior: a validation study in two age groups', *Child Development* 46, 2, 319–30.

FLEENER, D. E. and CAIRNS, R. B. 1970. 'Attachment behaviors in human infants: discriminative vocalization on maternal separation', *Developmental Psychology* 2, 2, 215–23. **p. 91**

GEWIRTZ, J. L. 1961. 'A learning analysis of the effects of normal stimulation, privation and deprivation on the acquisition of social motivation and attachment', in B. M. Foss (ed) *Determinants of Infant Behaviour*, Methuen, London. 213–90.

GEWIRTZ, J. L. 1972. 'Attachment, dependence, and a distinction in terms of stimulus control', in J. L. Gewirtz (ed) *Attachment and Dependency*, Halstead Press, 139–77.

GOLDBERG, S. and LEWIS, M. 1969. 'Play behavior in the year old infant: early sex differences', *Child Development* 40, 1, 21–31. **p. 91**

GOLDEN, M. and BIRNS, B. 1968. 'Social class and cognitive development in infancy', *Merrill-Palmer Quarterly* 14, 2, 139–49. **p. 116**

GOLDEN, M. and BIRNS, B. 1971. 'Social class, intelligence and cognitive style in infancy', *Child Development* 42, 6, 2114–6. **p. 116**

GREENBERG, D. J., HILLMAN, D. and GRICE, D. 1973. 'Infant and stranger anxiety in the first year of life', *Developmental Psychology* 9, 2, 207–12. **p. 92**

HAUGAN, G. M. and McINTIRE, R. W. 1972. 'Comparison of vocal imitation, tactile stimulation, and food as reinforcers for infant vocalizations', *Developmental Psychology* 6, 2, 201–9.

HONZIK, M. P. 1967. 'Environmental correlates of mental growth', *Child Development* 38, 2, 337–64.

HUBERT, J. 1974. 'Belief and reality: social factors in pregnancy and childbirth', in M. P. M. Richards (ed) *The Integration of a Child into a Social World*, Cambridge University Press, London. 37–51. **p. 50**

JACKLIN, C. N., MACCOBY, E. E. and DICK, A. E. 1973. 'Barrier behavior and toy preference: sex differences (and their absence) in the year old child', *Child Development* 44, 1, 196–200. **p. 92**

JACOBS, B. S. and MOSS, H. A. 1976. 'Birth order and sex of siblings as determinants of mother-infant interaction', *Child Development* 47, 2, 315–22.

JENSEN, A. R. 1969. 'How much can we boost IQ and scholastic achievement?' *Harvard Educational Review* 39, 1, 1–123.

JONES, S. J. and MOSS, H. A. 1971. 'Age, state, and maternal behavior associated with infant vocalizations', *Child Development* 42, 4, 1039–51. **p. 117**

KAGAN, J. 1969. 'Continuity in cognitive development during the first year', *Merrill-Palmer Quarterly* 15, 1, 101–19. **p. 117**

KENNELL, J. H. *et al.* 1974. 'Maternal behavior one year after early and extended post-partum contact', *Developmental Medicine and Child Neurology* 16, 172–9. **p. 52**

KLAUS, M. H. and KENNELL, J. H. 1970. 'Mothers separated from their newborn infants', *Pediatric Clinics of North America* 17, 4, 1015–37. **p. 51**

KLAUS, M. H., KENNELL, J. H., PLUMB, N. and ZUEHLKE, S. 1970. 'Human maternal behavior at the first contact with her young', *Pediatrics* 46, 2, 187–92. **p. 51**

KLAUS, M. H. *et al.* 1972. 'Maternal attachment: importance of the first post-partum days', *New England Journal of Medicine* 286, 9, 460–3. **p. 51**

KORNER, A. F. 1974. 'The effect of the infant's state, level of arousal, sex and ontogenetic stage on the caregiver', in M. Lewis and L. A. Rosenblum (eds) *The Effect of the Infant on its Caregiver*, Wiley, New York. 105–21. **p. 52**

KOTELCHUCK, M., ZELAZO, P., KAGAN, J. and SPELKE, E. 1975. 'Infant reaction to parental separations when left with familiar and unfamiliar adults', *Journal of Genetic Psychology* 126, 255–62.

LAMB, M. E. 1973. 'The effects of maternal deprivation on the development of the concepts of object and person', *Journal of Behavioral Science* 1, 5, 355–64. **p. 93**

LAMB, M. E. 1975. 'The sociability of two year olds with their mothers and fathers', *Child Psychiatry and Human Development* 5, 3, 182–8.

LAMB, M. E. 1976. 'Twelve month olds and their parents: interaction in a laboratory playroom', *Developmental Psychology* 12, 3, 237–44.

LAWSON, A. and INGLEBY, J. D. 1974. 'Daily routines of pre-school children: effects of age, birth order, sex and social class, and developmental correlates', *Psychological Medicine* 4, 399–415.

LEIFER, A. D., LEIDERMAN, P. H., BARNETT, C. R. and WILLIAMS, J. A. 1972. 'Effects of mother-infant separation on maternal attachment behavior', *Child Development* 43, 4, 1203–18. **p. 53**

LESTER, B. M., KOTELCHUCK, M., SPELKE, E., SELLERS, M. J. and KLEIN, R. E. 1974. 'Separation protest in Guatemalan infants: cross-cultural and cognitive findings', *Developmental Psychology* 10, 1, 79–85. **p. 93**

LEWIS, M. 1972. 'State as an infant-environment interaction: an analysis of mother-infant interaction as a function of sex', *Merrill-Palmer Quarterly* 18, 2, 95–121. **p. 53**

LEWIS, M. and GOLDBERG, S. 1969. 'Perceptual-cognitive development in infancy: a generalised expectancy model as a function of the mother-infant interaction', *Merrill-Palmer Quarterly* 15, 1, 81–100. **p. 117**

LEWIS, M. and LEE-PAINTER, S. 1974. 'An interactional approach to the mother-infant dyad', in M. Lewis and L. A. Rosenblum (eds) *The Effect of the Infant on its Caregiver*, Wiley, New York. 21–48. **p. 54**

LEWIS, M. and WILSON, C. D. 1972. 'Infant development in lower-class American families', *Human Development* 15, 112–7. **p. 54**

LING, D. and LING, A. H. 1974. 'Communication development in the first three years of life', *Journal of Speech and Hearing Research* 17, 1, 146–59. **p. 55**

LITTENBERG, R., TULKIN, S. R. and KAGAN, J. 1971. 'Cognitive components of separation anxiety', *Developmental Psychology* 4, 3, 387–8. **p. 94**

McCALL, R. B. 1972. 'Similarity in developmental profile among related pairs of human infants', *Science* 178, 1004–5. **p. 118**

MACCOBY, E. E. and FELDMAN, S. S. 1972. 'Mother-attachment and stranger-reactions in the third year of life', *Monographs of the Society for Research in Child Development*, Serial no. 146, 37, 1. 85 pp.

MESSER, S. B. and LEWIS, M. 1972. 'Social class and sex differences in the attachment and play behavior of the year old infant', *Merrill-Palmer Quarterly* 18, 295–306. **p. 94**

MILLER, W. B. 1974. 'Relationships between the intendedness of conception and the wantedness of pregnancy', *Journal of Nervous and Mental Disease* 159, 6, 396–406.

MINTON, C., KAGAN, J. and LEVINE, J. A. 1971. 'Maternal control and obedience in the two year old', *Child Development* 42, 6, 1873–94. **p. 55**

MOORE, T. 1967. 'Language and intelligence: a longitudinal study of the first eight years. Part I. Patterns of development in boys and girls', *Human Development* 10, 88–106.

MOORE, T. 1968. 'Language and intelligence: a longitudinal study of the first eight years. Part II. Environmental correlates of mental growth', *Human Development* 11, 1–24. **p. 118**

MORGAN, G. A. and RICCIUTI, H. N. 1969. 'Infants' responses to strangers during the first year', in B. M. Foss (ed) *Determinants of Infant Behaviour, IV*, Methuen, London. 253–72. **p. 95**

MOSS, H. A. 1967. 'Sex, age and state as determinants of mother-infant interaction', *Merrill-Palmer Quarterly* 13, 19–36. **p. 56**

MOSS, H. A. and ROBSON, K. S. 1968. 'Maternal influences in early social visual behavior', *Child Development* 39, 2, 401–8. **p. 57**

MOSS, H. A., ROBSON, K. S. and PEDERSEN, F. 1969. 'Determinants of maternal stimulation of infants and consequences of treatment for later reactions to strangers', *Developmental Psychology* 1, 3, 239–46. **p. 57**

NEWSON, J. and NEWSON, E. 1963. *Infant Care in an Urban Community*, George Allen & Unwin, London; Aldine Publishing Co., Chicago. 268 pp.

NICHOLS, P. L. and BROMAN, S. H. 1974. 'Familial resemblance in infant mental development', *Developmental Psychology* 10, 3, 442–6. **p. 119**

OSOFSKY, J. D. and DANZGER, B. 1974. 'Relationships between neonatal characteristics and mother-child interaction', *Developmental Psychology* 10, 1, 124–30. **p. 58**

PARASKEVOPOULOS, J. and HUNT, J. McV. 1971. 'Object construction and imitation under differing conditions of rearing', *Journal of Genetic Psychology* 119, 301–21. **p. 119**

PARKE, R. D., O'LEARY, S. E. and WEST, S. 1972. 'Mother-father-newborn interaction: effects of maternal medication, labor and sex of infant', *Proceedings of the 80th Annual Convention of the American Psychological Association.* 85–6. **p. 58**

PEDERSEN, F. A. and ROBSON, K. S. 1969. 'Father participation in infancy', *American Journal of Orthopsychiatry* 39, 3, 466–72. **p. 95**

POWELL, L. F. 1974. 'The effect of extra stimulation and maternal involvement on the development of low birth-weight infants and on maternal behavior', *Child Development* 45, 1, 106–13.

PRINGLE, M. L. K. 1971. *Deprivation and Education* (2nd ed), Longman in association with National Bureau for Co-operation in Child Care (now National Children's Bureau), London. 305 pp; Humanities Press, Atlantic Highlands, NJ.

QUINTON, D. and RUTTER, M. 1975. 'Early hospital admissions and later disturbances of behaviour: an attempted replication of Douglas' findings', Unpublished paper. *Department of Child and Adolescent Psychiatry, Institute of Psychiatry.*

REBELSKY, F. and HANKS, C. 1971. 'Fathers' verbal interaction with infants in the first three months of life', *Child Development* 42, 63–8.

REPUCCI, N. D. 1971. 'Parental education, sex differences, and performance on cognitive tasks among two year old children', *Developmental Psychology* 4, 2, 248–53. **p. 120**

RHEINGOLD, H. L. 1969. 'The effect of a strange environment on the behavior of infants', in B. M. Fodd (ed) *Determinants of Infant Behaviour, IV*, Methuen, London. 137–66. **p. 96**

RHEINGOLD, H. L. and ECKERMAN, C. O. 1969. 'The infant's free entry into a new environment', *Journal of Experimental Child Psychology* 8, 271–83. **p. 96**

RHEINGOLD, H. L. and ECKERMAN, C. O. 1973. 'Fear of stranger: a critical examination', in H. W. Reese (ed) *Advances in Child Development and Behavior*, Academic Press, New York. 185–222.

RHEINGOLD, H. L., GEWIRTZ, J. L. and ROSS, H. W. 1959. 'Social conditioning of vocalizations in the infant', *Journal of Comparative Physiological Psychology* 52, 68–73.

RICCUITI, H. N. 1974. 'Fear and the development of social attachments in the first year of life', in M. Lewis and L. A. Rosenblum (eds) *The Origins of Fear*, Wiley, New York. 73–106. **p. 187**

RICHARDS, M. P. M. and BERNAL, J. F. 1971. 'Social interaction in the first days of life', in H. R. Schaffer (ed) *The Origins of Human Social Relations*, Academic Press, London. 3–13. **p. 58**

RICHARDS, M. P. M. and BERNAL, J. F. 1972. 'An observational study of mother-infant interaction', in N. Blurton Jones (ed) *Ethological Studies of Child Behaviour*. Cambridge University Press, London. 175–98.

RICHMAN, N. 1974. 'The effects of housing on pre-school children and their mothers', *Developmental Medicine and Child Neurology* 16, 1, 53–8.

RICHMAN, N. 1976. 'Depression in mothers of pre-school children', *Journal of Child Psychology and Psychiatry* 17, 1, 75–8.

ROBERTS, C. J. and ROWLEY, J. R. 1972. 'A study of the association between quality of maternal care and infant development', *Psychological Medicine* 2, 42–9.

ROBSON, K. S., PEDERSEN, F. A. and MOSS, H. A. 1969. 'Developmental observations of diadic gazing in relation to the fear of strangers and social approach behavior', *Child Development* 40, 2, 619–27. **p. 59**

ROSS, G., KAGAN, J., ZELAZO, P. and KOTELCHUCK, M. 1975. 'Separation

135

protest in infants in home and laboratory', *Developmental Psychology* 11, 2, 256–7.

RUBENSTEIN, J. 1967. 'Maternal attentiveness and subsequent exploratory behavior in the infant', *Child Development* 38, 4, 1089–1100. **p. 120**

RUTTER, M. 1972. *Maternal Deprivation Reassessed*, Penguin. 175 pp.

SALTZ, R. 1973. 'Effects of part-time "mothering" on IQ and SQ of young institutionalized children', *Child Development* 44, 1, 166–70. **p. 97**

SANDER, L. W., STECHLER, G., BURNS, P. and JULIA, H. 1970. 'Early mother-infant interaction and 24-hour patterns of activity and sleep', *Journal of the American Academy of Child Psychiatry* 9, 103–23. **p. 59**

SCHAFFER, H. R. 1958. 'Objective observations of personality development in early infancy', *British Journal of Medical Psychology* 31, 174–83.

SCHAFFER, H. R. 1963. 'Some issues for research in the study of attachment behaviour', in B. M. Foss (ed) *Determinants of Infant Behaviour, II*, Methuen, London. 179–96.

SCHAFFER, H. R. 1966. 'The onset of fear of strangers and the incongruity hypothesis', *Journal of Child Psychology and Psychiatry* 7, 2, 95–106.

SCHAFFER, H. R. 1971. *The Growth of Sociability*, Penguin. 199 pp.

SCHAFFER, H. R. 1974. 'Early social behaviour and the study of reciprocity', *Bulletin of the British Psychological Society* 27, 209–16.

SCHAFFER, H. R. and CALLENDER, W. M. 1959. 'Psychologic effects of hospitalization in infancy', *Pediatrics* 24, 528–39.

SCHAFFER, H. R. and EMERSON, P. E. 1964. 'The development of social attachments in infancy', *Monographs of the Society for Research in Child Development*, Serial no. 94, 29, 3. 77 pp. **p. 97**

SEASHORE, M. J., LEIFER, A. D., BARNETT, C. R. and LEIDERMAN, P. H. 1973. 'The effects of denial of early mother-infant interaction on maternal self-confidence', *Journal of Personality and Social Psychology* 3, 369–78. **p. 60**

SHEPARD, W. and PETERSON, J. 1973. 'Are there sex differences in infancy?', *Catalog of Selected Documents in Psychology* 3, 121. **p. 60**

SHERESHEFSKY, P. M., LIEBENBERG, B. and LOCKMAN, R. F. 1973. 'Maternal adaptation', in P. M. Shereshefsky and L. J. Yarrow (eds) *Psychological Aspects of a First Pregnancy and Early Postnatal Adaptation*, Raven Press, New York. 165–180.

SKEELS, H. M. 1966. 'Adult status of children with contrasting early life experiences: a follow-up study', *Monographs of the Society for Research in Child Development*, Serial no. 105, 31, 3. 65 pp.

SMITH, L. 1975. 'Effects of brief separation from parent on young children', *Journal of Child Psychology and Psychiatry* 16, 3, 245–54.

SPELKE, E., ZELAZO, P., KAGAN, J. and KOTELCHUCK, M. 1973. 'Father interaction and separation protest', *Developmental Psychology* 9, 1, 83–90. **p. 98**

STARR, R. H. 1971. 'Cognitive development in infancy: assessment, acceleration and actualization', *Merrill-Palmer Quarterly* 17, 2, 153–86.

STAYTON, D. J. and AINSWORTH, M. D. S. 1973. 'Individual differences in infant responses to brief, everyday separations as related to other infant and maternal behaviors', *Developmental Psychology* 9, 2, 226–35. **p. 99**

STAYTON, D. J., AINSWORTH, M. D. S. and MAIN, M. B. 1973. 'Development of separation behavior in the first year of life: protest, following and greeting', *Developmental Psychology* 9, 2, 213–25. **p. 100**

STEVENS, A. G. 1971. 'Attachment behavior, separation anxiety and stranger anxiety in polymatrically reared infants', in H. R. Schaffer (ed) *The Origins of Human Social Relations*, Academic Press, London. 137–44.

STREISSGUTH, A.P. and BEE, H. L. 1972. 'Mother-child interactions and cognitive development in children', in W. W. Hartup (ed) *The Young Child: Reviews of Research, II*. National Association for Education of Young Children, Washington. 158–83.

TENNES, K. H. and LAMPL, E. E. 1964. 'Stranger and separation anxiety in infancy', *Journal of Nervous and Mental Disease* 139, 247–54.

TENNES, K. H. and LAMPL, E. E. 1966. 'Some aspects of mother-child relationship pertaining to infantile separation anxiety', *Journal of Nervous and Mental Disease* 143, 5, 426–37. **p. 101**

THOMAN, E. B., BARNETT, C. R. and LEIDERMAN, P. H. 1971. 'Feeding behaviors of newborn infants as a function of parity of the mother', *Child Development* 42, 5, 1471–83.

THOMAN, E. B., LEIDERMAN, P. H. and OLSON, J. P. 1972. 'Neonate-mother interaction during breast-feeding', *Developmental Psychology* 6, 1, 110–18. **p. 60**

THOMAN, E. B., TURNER, A. M., LEIDERMAN, P. H. and BARNETT, C. R. 1970. 'Neonate-mother interaction: effects of parity on feeding behavior', *Child Development* 41, 4, 1103–11. **p. 61**

TIZARD, B. and REES, J. 1975. 'The effect of early institutional rearing on the behaviour problems and affectional relationships of four-year-old children', *Journal of Child Psychology and Psychiatry* 16, 1, 61–73. **p. 322**

TIZARD, B., COOPERMAN, O., JOSEPH, A. and TIZARD, J. 1972. 'Environmental effects on language development: a study of young children in long-stay residential nurseries', *Child Development* 43, 337–58. **p. 121**

TIZARD, J. and TIZARD, B. 1971. 'The social development of two-year-old children in residential nurseries', in H. R. Schaffer (ed) *The Origins of Human Social Relations*, Academic Press, London. 147–64. **p. 101**

TIZARD, J. and TIZARD, B. 1974. 'The institution as an environment for development', (section on 'Institutions and the development of personality'), in

137

M. P. M. Richards (ed) *The Integration of a Child into a Social World*, Cambridge University Press, London. 146–9. **p. 102**

TODD, G. A. and PALMER, B. 1968. 'Social reinforcement of infant babbling', *Child Development* 39, 2, 591–6. **p. 122**

TOUGH, J. 1973. 'The language of young children: the implications for the education of the young disadvantaged child', in M. Chazan (ed) *Education in the Early Years*, Faculty of Education, University College of Swansea. 60–76. **p. 346**

TULKIN, S. R. 1972. 'Social class differences in infants' reactions to mother's and stranger's voices', *Developmental Psychology* 8, 1, 137. **p. 61**

TULKIN, S. R. 1973. 'Social class differences in attachment behaviors of ten month old infants', *Child Development* 44, 171–4. **p. 102**

TULKIN, S. R. and COHLER, B. J. 1973. 'Childrearing attitudes and mother-child interaction in the first year of life', *Merrill-Palmer Quarterly* 19, 2, 95–107. **p. 61**

TULKIN, S.R. and KAGAN, J. 1972. 'Mother-child interaction in the first year of life', *Child Development* 43, 1, 31–4. **p. 62**

WACHS, T. D. 1972. 'Similarity in developmental profile among related pairs of human infants', *Science* 178, 1005–6. **p. 122**

WACHS, T. D. 1976. 'Utilization of a Piagetian approach in the investigation of early experience effects: a research strategy and some illustrative data', *Merrill-Palmer Quarterly* 22, 1, 11–30.

WACHS, T. D., UZGIRIS, I. C. and HUNT, J. McV. 1971. 'Cognitive development in infants of different age levels and from different environmental backgrounds: an explanatory investigation', *Merrill-Palmer Quarterly* 17, 4, 283–317. **p. 122**

WAHLER, R. G. 1967. 'Infant social attachments: a reinforcement theory interpretation and investigation', *Child Development* 38, 4, 1079–88. **p. 123**

WATERS, E., MATAS, L. and SROUFE, L. A. 1975. 'Infants' reactions to an approaching stranger: description, validation and functional significance of wariness', *Child Development* 46, 2, 348–56.

WATSON, J. S. 1971. 'Cognitive-perceptual development in infancy: setting for the seventies', *Merrill-Palmer Quarterly* 17, 2, 139–52.

WATSON, J. S. and RAMEY, C. T. 1972. 'Reactions to response-contingent stimulation in early infancy', *Merrill-Palmer Quarterly* 18, 3, 219–27.

WATTS, J. C., HALFAR, C. and CHAN, I. 1974. 'Environment, experience and intellectual development of young children in home care', *American Journal of Orthopsychiatry* 44, 5, 773–81.

WEISBERG, P. 1963. 'Social and nonsocial conditioning of infant vocalisations', *Child Development* 34, 377–88. **p. 123**

WHITE, B. L. 1967. 'An experimental approach to the effects of experience on early human behaviour', in J. P. Hill (ed) *Minnesota Symposia on Child Psychology, I.*, University of Minnesota Press, Minneapolis. 201–26. **p. 123**

WHITE, B. L. 1969. 'The initial coordination of sensorimotor schemas in human infants – Piaget's ideas and the role of experience', in D. Elkind and J. H. Flavell (eds) *Studies in Cognitive Development*, Oxford University Press, London. 237–56. **p. 125**

WHITE, B. L. and WATTS, J. C. 1973. *Experiences and Environment: Major Influences on the Development of the Young Child*, Prentice-Hall Inc, Englewood Cliffs, NJ. 552 pp.

WILL, J. A., SELF, P. A. and DATAN, N. 1976. 'Maternal behavior and perceived sex of infant', *American Journal of Orthopsychiatry* 46, 1, 135–9.

WILLEMSEN, E., FLAHERTY, D., HEATON, C. and RITCHEY, G. 1974. 'Attachment behavior of one year olds as a function of mother *vs* father, sex of child, session, and toys', *Genetic Psychology Monographs* 90, 2nd half, 305–24.

WILLERMAN, L., BROMAN, S. H. and FIELDER, M. 1970. 'Infant development, preschool IQ, and social class', *Child Development* 41, 69–77.

WILSON, R. S. 1972. 'Twins: early mental development', *Science* 175, 914–7. **p. 125**

WOLKIND, S. N. 1974. 'The components of "affectionless psychopathy" in institutionalized children', *Journal of Child Psychology and Psychiatry* 15, 3, 215–20.

YANG, R. K. and HALVERSON, C. F. Jr. 1976. 'A study of the "inversion of intensity" between newborn and preschool-age behavior', *Child Development* 47, 2, 350–9.

YANG, R. K., ZWEIG, A. R., DOUTHITT, T. C. and FEDERMAN, E. J. 1976. 'Successive relationships between maternal attitudes during pregnancy, analgesic medication during labor and delivery, and newborn behavior', *Developmental Psychology* 12, 1, 6–14.

YARROW, L. J. 1963. 'Research in dimensions of early maternal care', *Merrill-Palmer Quarterly* 9, 2, 101–14. **p. 125**

YARROW, L. J. 1967. 'The development of focused relationships during infancy', in J. Hellmuth (ed) *Exceptional Infant, I*, Special Child Publications, Seattle. 429–42.

YARROW, L. J. 1972. 'Attachment and dependency: a developmental perspective', in J. L. Gewirtz (ed) *Attachment and Dependency*, Winston/Wiley. 81–137.

YARROW, L. J., GOODWIN, M. S., MANHEIMER, H. and MILOWE, I. D. 1974. 'Infancy experiences and cognitive and personality development at ten years', in L. J. Stone, H. T. Smith and L. Murphy (eds) *The Competent Infant*, Tavistock, London; Basic Books, New York. **p. 126**

YARROW, L. J., RUBENSTEIN, J. L., PEDERSEN, F. A. and JANKOWSKI, J. J. 1972. 'Dimensions of early stimulation and their different effects on infant development', *Merrill-Palmer Quarterly* 18, 3, 205–18. **p. 127**

YARROW, L. J., RUBENSTEIN, J. L. and PEDERSEN, F. A. 1975. *Infant and Environment: Early Cognitive and Motivational Development*, Hemisphere, Washington. 255 pp.

Part II
Shared care

A. Introduction

Despite continuing controversy on whether care of the child can be safely, or even beneficially, shared between the mother and other adults, there is a surprising lack of research evidence. This review gathers together the evidence that is available from a variety of sources – studies of maternal employment (unexpectedly rare for children under secondary school age), day-care centres, nursery schools, pre-schools, intervention programmes for socially disadvantaged children, and of children brought up in kibbutzim – on the question of how shared care affects the child's emotional, social and intellectual development. The review is divided into three sections dealing with the period of infancy (0-three years), the pre-school years (three-five years) and the school years (five-sixteen +), particularly the primary school years, because children's needs are very different at these stages, and the effects of shared care have to be considered separately.

In the section on infancy consideration is given to the question of how far the maternal deprivation theory is relevant to the shared caring which occurs when the mother of the young child is employed. This theory focussed attention on the possible importance of the child's social attachments in the first three years, especially of his main attachment (which is usually to his mother when she is his principal care-taker), for his future social relationships, and even, to some extent, his cognitive development. The review examines whether the usual pattern of attachments is altered by shared caring, particularly whether any weakening of the attachment to the mother occurs, and considers available evidence on whether any differences are likely to be detrimental or beneficial for the child's development. Other evidence on the infant's social and emotional adjustment from studies of the effects of substitute care, especially high quality day care, are examined to see if they justify fears of a detrimental effect from shared care in the first three years. The effect of shared care on intellectual development, and the question of how far combined day care and education can help to eliminate the educational disadvantage of children from a socially deprived background are also discussed.

By the time the child reaches three years old it is generally accepted that a few hours a day away from the mother is unlikely to be harmful, and that some forms of group care, particularly the richly stimulating environment provided by the nursery school, may positively benefit the child's social adjustment and intellectual development. The section on the three-to-five age group uses evidence from studies of maternal employment and substitute care in its consideration of how care by someone other than the mother for the full working day affects the child; it also looks at whether part-time substitute care, particularly at a nursery school is actually advantageous for a child. The question of whether pre-school education can prevent school failure in socially disadvantaged children is also examined. A more detailed discussion of this issue is presented in Part V of the review.

After the age of five, it is generally assumed that it is beneficial for the child to spend the greater part of the working day at school, away from the mother. What are the consequences, though, of care being provided for an hour or two each weekday night and for the full working day in the holidays by someone other than the mother? Does this cause too much strain on the child, especially the younger child, and does it have adverse effects on the mother's relationship with the child, or can it have positive benefits for the child and family? Is it only the child who is inadequately supervised or not supervised at all who suffers from maternal employment? The third section examines the research available to see how far these questions can be answered. There is also some consideration of how the mother's emotional state is affected by working, and of the effects of this on the child. Some of the findings are also applicable to mothers of younger children, though, of course, the difference in age and needs of the children will also affect the mother's attitudes and behaviour.

In each section, a summary of research evidence is presented first. This is followed by a discussion which draws together findings on the important issues for the age group, and considers the implications of the evidence. The emphasis is on recent research as far as possible but much of the work on maternal employment was carried out in the late 1950s and early 1960s, and this has been included.

B. Infancy (0-Three Years) – Summary of findings

1. The development of attachment in infancy – and how this is affected by shared caring

(For definitions of attachment and a discussion of the problems of measurement, see Part I, pp. 63–4 and 70–5)

Usual pattern of attachments of the child living with his family

a) When the child is brought up in his own family it is usual for him to become attached in the first year to several familiar people, not just to one person (Ainsworth, 1967; Schaffer and Emerson, 1964). While it is usual for the initial attachment (mostly occurring in the third quarter of the first year) to be formed to one person it is uncertain whether this is a necessary step (Ainsworth, 1967), or whether, in a minority of children, attachments can be straightway directed towards several people (Schaffer and Emerson, 1964). It is clear, though, that once a first attachment has formed, attachments to other people follow rapidly (Ainsworth, 1963, 1967; Schaffer and Emerson, 1964).

b) The child has a hierarchy of preferences among his attachments. Generally, the mother (who has chief responsibility for the child's care) is the child's principal object of attachment. Occasionally, the father may be the main attachment object, even though the mother is the main care-taker (Ainsworth, 1963, 1967; Cohen and Campos, 1974; Schaffer and Emerson, 1964). There is some evidence that other people, particularly the father, may increasingly become joint principal objects of attachment with the mother as the child gets older (Schaffer and Emerson, 1964). Other researchers (Ainsworth, 1973; Bowlby, 1969) suggest that one tie is usually primary and the others subsidiary. Schaffer and Emerson used as their criterion of attachment separation protest in everyday situations, which has been criticised as indicating insecurity as well as strength of attachment (Ainsworth and Wittig, 1969). However, in the way used by Schaffer and Emerson (mother's recollections and observations over a period often as long as fourteen months) separation protest probably gives a valid indication of the pattern of the child's attachments at least.

Findings of more recent studies, using various interaction measures as criteria of attachment, suggest that there tends to be some preference for the mother in one-year-olds (Ban and Lewis, 1974), particularly under conditions of stress (Cohen and Campos, 1974; Lamb, 1976). However, these studies also leave little doubt that most infants are attached to fathers as well as mothers and that in the mother's absence fathers are adequate sources of security in stressful situations (Feldman and Ingham, 1975; Willemsen et al., 1974). By the time the child is two, the difference in preference seems to have disappeared in stress-free situations (Lamb, 1975). Research is awaited on whether infants of this age still tend to prefer the mother in times of stress, given a choice between the parents.

c) A close relationship with the principal attachment object does not prevent the formation of attachments with others, but appears rather to foster the development of other attachments (Ainsworth, 1964, 1967; Schaffer and Emerson, 1964).

d) Somewhat limited availability of the mother and sharing of the care-taking role with others does not preclude the development of a close attachment to the mother (Ainsworth, 1963, 1967). Sensitivity to the

143

child's signals and initiation of interaction with him attuned to his needs have been found to be the variables most important for the development of a secure attachment (Ainsworth, 1967; Ainsworth and Wittig, 1969). Nevertheless there is probably a minimum amount of time which has to be spent with the child for the development of the sensitive and appropriate interaction which fosters secure attachment (Ainsworth, 1967).

The effects of shared care on attachment to the mother

a) *Day-care centres*
i) The evidence from studies of children entering day care very early (in the first year or so) conflicts with that from studies of children entering somewhat later (between the ages of two and three) on whether or not enrolment in day care affects attachment to the mother.

Very early care. Two-and-a-half-year-old, mainly disadvantaged children, who had entered high-quality day care (a high staff/infant ratio and carefully planned materials and activities to promote cognitive development) when they were about one year old were found to be as attached to their mothers as children brought up at home (Caldwell *et al.*, 1970). However, the measurements used in this study have been criticised (Ainsworth, 1973) as high scores on some of the items (e.g. intense separation protest in a familiar situation) may indicate insecurity rather than strength of attachment. Two other studies, though, also found no differences in attachment to their mothers between children entering day care during their first year and home-reared children (Brookhart and Hock, 1976; Saunders, 1972). The former study had middle-class subjects and used the Ainsworth and Wittig (see p. 83) 'strange situation' procedure to measure the quality of the attachment relationship but found no difference between the groups on any of the behaviour categories measured. The only difference so far found between infants entering day care in the first year and home-reared children, of greater negative reaction to strangers (Ricciuti, 1974), was contradictory to the findings of an earlier study (Saunders, 1972).

Entry to care between two and three years. In contrast to the findings on very early entry to day care, two studies of entrants aged two to three have found adverse effects on the quality of attachment to the mother, at least in the short-term (Blehar, 1974; Van Leeuwen and Tuma, 1972). In the former study, using the Ainsworth 'strange situation' procedure, day-care children, about five months after entry, were found to show more avoidance of the stranger. On reunion with the mother (thought by Ainsworth and Wittig to be the best indicator of the quality of attachment) two-year-olds were more likely to show signs of detachment and three-year-olds of anxious ambivalent attachment than home-reared children. In the latter study, three-year-olds were found to be more clinging and demanding in relation to the mother fifteen days after entry than they had been before, though this type of behaviour had declined (but not to pre-entry level) by the ninetieth day after entry. A third study (Doyle, 1975) found no evidence of insecure attachment in the reunion or any other type of behaviour of day-care children aged up to thirty months, with seven months experience of day care, observed during the 'strange situation' procedure.

Possible explanations for differences between the findings of the early and later entry studies are: (i) the care was of higher quality in the early entry studies. Two, at least (Caldwell, *et al.*, 1970; Saunders, 1972), of the day-care centres in the early entry studies were set up as research projects, and, so far as information is provided, they seem to have had higher staff/child ratios than the centres in the later entry studies; (ii) entry to day care may be more disturbing, at least temporarily, to the child who has grown used to an exclusive relationship with the mother. There is some evidence that children who experience group care for the first time at the age of three or so go through a temporary phase of timidity and emotional dependence, but regain their confidence in the fifth and sixth years (Moore, 1975).

ii) Mothers of day-care children appear to be as attached to their children as mothers whose children remain at home (Caldwell *et al.*, 1970).

b) *Kibbutz rearing*
Children brought up in an Israeli kibbutz — where the mother performs little care-taking after the first year of life but devotes several hours a day to playing activity with the child — appear to be as attached to their mothers (using as criterion the child's behaviour in unfamiliar situation — see a(i) above) as children brought up in American nuclear families with the mother as principal care-taker (Maccoby and Feldman, 1972).

c) *Working mothers*
There is only one study (Tulkin, 1973) which has directly investigated children's attachment to the mother when she is employed. Ten-months-old working-class infants whose mothers were employed showed as much attachment behaviour during a play session as infants whose mothers were not employed, but they failed to show separation distress in an unfamiliar situation (probably because they were used to their mothers leaving them).

Effect of shared care on attachments to people other than the mother

a) *Attachment to the substitute care-taker*
Findings of the only study to directly investigate this (Ricciuti, 1974)

indicate that the infant who enters high-quality day care from a very early age (in the second or third month) begins to develop an attachment towards his care-taker from about seven months, showing distress at parting from her and her presence ameliorating negative reactions to a stranger, though not as effectively as that of the mother.

b) *Attachment to people other than the mother*
Caldwell *et al.*'s (1970) study of day-care children is the only other to investigate this. The day-care children differed from the home controls on only one of the seven scales used to assess attachment, scoring slightly higher (borderline significance) on the 'dependency' scale. As interpreted by the authors this indicates proximity-seeking rather than help-seeking, and perhaps was evidence of enjoyment of interaction with others. However, they note that Bowlby suggested in a personal communication to them that this might indicate 'overanxious' attachment. Further research is needed.

2. Emotional and social adjustment

Effects of daily substitute care

a) *Very early care.* Evidence is inconclusive on whether children who experience very early substitute care (before the age of two) are somewhat more dependent, clinging and nervous than children who do not experience substitute care until later (after the age of three). The somewhat dependent and anxious behaviour found in six-year-old children who had experienced substitute care from a very early age (average age at commencement, one year approximately) in one study (Moore, 1969, 1975) is probably due, at least in part, to the instability of the care experienced by all but a very small number (four) of the children in the group (fifteen), see (b) below. Children in high-quality day care from an early age show little evidence of any excess of behaviour disturbance (see 'Effects of different types of shared care', below), but they may, at least in the pre-school years, be rather more active and aggressive and less co-operative with adults.

b) *Stable versus unstable care.* The only comparison comes from Moore's (1969) study, children who had experienced several changes of care-taker tending to be much more dependent, clinging and nervous than those who had experienced stable care. However, this group also tended to come from families with insecure relationships and to have suffered moderately long separations from the mother (in itself the latter was not found to be associated with problem behaviour where family relationships and care were stable). From these findings it is impossible to determine how far the children's behaviour problems were the effects of the unstable care *per se*.

c) There is some evidence (though only impressionistic) that mothers who work when their children are very young (one year plus) may fail to establish a close relationship with them (Moore, 1969, 1975). Mothers of three- and four-year-olds have also been found to become less involved with them after entry to nursery school (Van Leeuwen and Tuma, 1972). On the other hand, mothers of mainly disadvantaged two-and-a-half-year-olds who had experienced day care for about eighteen months on average were just as much attached to them as mothers whose children were at home (Caldwell *et al.*, 1970). Very early day care (from three months) appears to increase the involvement of severely disadvantaged mothers with their children (Ramey *et al.*, 1975).

Effects of different types of shared care

a) *Day-care centres* (American, with educational enrichment programmes)
i) Overall, early entry into care does not appear to be associated with a high incidence of emotional or social disturbance. Day-care children who enrolled in their first or second years were found to be as well adjusted (at age of four) as children who entered day care after their third birthday (Braun and Caldwell, 1973). Similarly, children who entered day care at a very early age (in the first seven months, or early in the second year) have been found to be at least as well adjusted (at about two years of age) as home-reared controls (on the limited number of items for which comparison was made), and at or above the standardisation norms of infant behaviour scales on most characteristics (Fowler, 1972). Exceptions were on traits of irritability and belligerence, where scores were below the norms, particularly those of the disadvantaged children, who also entered earlier (typically in the first seven months). Evaluation of findings is difficult in the absence of a home-reared control group in this part of the analysis, but they appear to be compatible with those on social adjustment of children entering day care early (see (ii) below).
ii) Day-care children, from both lower- and middle-class homes, who enter before they are three years old appear to differ in some aspects of social behaviour from children entering after they are three. Early day-care children have been found to be less co-operative with adults, more aggressive (physical and verbal aggression to adults and peers), and more inclined to run about than later entrants to day care (some of whom had had, though, experience of private substitute care) (Schwarz *et al.*, 1974). Differences are probably not due to the personality of the mother as those

147

in both groups eventually sought day care for their children. There is some corroborating evidence from other studies. Very early entrants to day care, especially those from disadvantaged backgrounds, showed a tendency towards increase in activity levels in relation to standardisation norms by the time they were two years old in Fowler's (1972) study. Also, substitute-care children have been found to be less co-operative with adults than children remaining at home (Raph *et al.*, 1963; Moore, 1969, 1975, see Section C).

iii) Day-care children who enter before they are three years old do not appear to differ from children who enter after they are three in ability to get along with peers (Schwarz *et al.*, 1974). Similarly children with and without nursery school experience have been found to differ little in their ability to get on with each other, but nursery school experience does seem to have some role in reducing negative interactions (Raph *et al.*, 1968, see Section C).

iv) Children entering day care before they are three adjust more easily to a new day-care setting than children without previous day-care experience (Schwarz *et al.*, 1973). This is in line with findings of easier school adjustment in children with nursery school experience (see Section C).

b) *Kibbutz rearing*

i) There is some evidence of retardation in personal and social development of kibbutz reared children in infancy, but this does not appear to persist into later childhood, kibbutz children being at least as well adjusted as those living in nuclear families at pre-adolescence (Rabin, 1958) and adolescence (See Section D). There appears to be no particular type of psychopathology that could be attributed to the method of child-rearing and rather less severe emotional pathology than among urban children (Kaffman, 1965).

ii) Pre-adolescent kibbutz children tend to have more positive attitudes to their families than village children reared in nuclear families (Rabin, 1959). Findings are similar for adolescents (see Section D).

Effect of maternal employment

Adolescents whose mothers were employed in the first three years of their lives have been found not to differ in selected personality characteristics or school and social adjustment from those whose mothers were not employed (Burchinal, 1963). However, as Burchinal points out, the effect of the mother's employment on the child will depend on a variety of circumstances. These include, most importantly for the under-three age group, the quality of substitute care, but also perhaps such variables as the mother's emotional state, and the family's social class, which appear to influence the effect on older children at least (see Section D).

3. Intellectual development

Effects of daily substitute care

i) Substitute care before the age of three does not necessarily hamper intellectual development. Some children in Moore's (1968, 1969) study who experienced substitute care (individual or day nursery) for most of their second and third years had ability increments up to the age of eight above the average for their sex. Much will obviously depend on the quality of care (see 'Effects of different types of shared care', below).

ii) Reading competence relative to mental age was below average in the early substitute care group in Moore's (1969, 1975) study. This is consistent with findings for children who experience substitute care in the three- to five-year-old period (see Section C).

Effects of different types of shared care

a) *Day care* (Polish)
Children in Polish day-care centres were found to be lower in psychomotor development (though within the limits of normal development) in the first two years of life than children brought up at home. The difference diminished in the third year, though, and was no longer statistically significant (Gornicki, 1964). The somewhat lower performance of the day-care children is not necessarily attributable to day care *per se*, more of the children attending coming from one-parent families, and from families with rather poorer housing conditions and child care. Additionally, at the time of the study, there was a shortage of qualified staff and of suitable premises and equipment.

b) *Day-care centres* (American – with educational enrichment programmes)
i) Children from all social backgrounds entering high-quality day care at an early age (sometimes as early as the first year) perform at least as well on tests of mental development as children remaining at home (Caldwell, 1973; Fowler, 1972; Robinson and Robinson, 1971).

ii) Children from disadvantaged backgrounds entering this type of high-quality day care, which has educational enrichment as one of its main aims, during the first year and a half of life, seem to avoid the drop in intellectual achievement that tends to occur in children from such backgrounds from eighteen months onwards (Caldwell *et al.*, 1970; Fowler, 1972; Robinson and Robinson, 1971).

iii) Disadvantaged children who enter this type of day care between the ages of two and four years may make dramatic advances, compared with controls who are not enrolled in such day-care programmes (Robinson and Robinson, 1971).

iv) Children from middle-class backgrounds still perform better than children from disadvantaged backgrounds, even though both groups are attending high-quality day-care centres (Fowler, 1972; Robinson and Robinson, 1971).

v) Middle-class children who enter day care between the ages of two and four may differ little in their intellectual attainments from control children who do not have this experience (Robinson and Robinson, 1971). There is some indication from Fowler's (1972) study that advantaged children benefit most from high-quality day care, compared with home reared controls, when they enter in the first year, but there is no corroborating evidence for this.

vi) There is some indication that the intellectual benefits of this type of educational enrichment programme for children from disadvantaged backgrounds are not retained to a great extent once the children leave the day-care centres. In the one study in which this question has been investigated the children entering day care before they were three years old showed a sharp drop in intellectual performance after leaving, although the day-care children did maintain a slight advantage over matched controls from the same class at the end of the first school year (Caldwell and Smith, 1970). These findings are consistent with the well-known pattern for slightly older (three- to four-year-old) children attending pre-school compensatory education classes – although they make a significantly greater gain on measures of intelligence than controls, this is followed by a decline after the end of the programmes (see Section C). A follow-up of children who experienced educational intervention from early in the first year is still awaited (Heber *et al.*, 1972; Garber and Heber, 1973).

c) *Kibbutz rearing*
Generally, children brought up in a kibbutz appear to be similar in intellectual development to those cared for at home. A representative sample of kibbutz infants (aged up to twenty-seven months) was found to be similar in mental development to those brought up in advantaged (one parent at least had completed high school) private homes (Kohen-Raz, 1968). While another study found kibbutz infants to be slightly retarded in overall development, this was largely accounted for by lower scores on the personal-social subscale of the measure used (Rabin, 1958). The same author found pre-adolescent kibbutz children to be superior in intelligence to village children living in nuclear families.

150

The effect of maternal employment

There is some evidence that infants (up to about two years in age), from advantaged backgrounds, perform at least as well on scales of intellectual development as those whose mothers do not work (Golden and Birns, 1968; Kohen-Raz, 1968). These findings cannot be generalised to all infants with working mothers as much is likely to depend on the substitute-care arrangements made, on the time left available for mother-child interaction, and on the mother's motivations.

Discussion

Is the theory of 'maternal deprivation' relevant to shared caring?

In his report to the World Health Organisation on the needs of homeless children, Bowlby (1951) put forward the thesis that ' ... what is believed to be essential for mental health is that the infant and young child should experience a warm, intimate and continuous relationship with his mother (or permanent mother substitute) in which both find satisfaction and enjoyment', and that the lack of such a relationship constituted 'maternal deprivation'. This thesis has been interpreted by many, including an Expert Committee of the World Health Organisation (1951) to mean that the mother must exclusively care for the child, and that day nurseries and other provisions which might allow mothers of young children to work should be discouraged. However, this is a leap unwarranted either by the research evidence presented by Bowlby to support his thesis or by the findings of subsequent research relevant to the 'maternal deprivation' theory.

What has been established by this research is that entry into the older type of institutional care at an early age (before the age of three, and especially in the first year) tends to have adverse effects on the child's subsequent emotional and intellectual, especially language development (Dinnage and Pringle, 1967; Pringle, 1971). Conditions in most institutions, particularly those of the older type – many care-takers, frequent changes in care-takers, impersonal care – generally deprive the child who enters during the first year of the opportunity to make a close attachment with an adult of the kind that a child at home usually makes with his mother at this stage; similarly these conditions prevent the child who enters after he has become attached from forming further attachments to other adults. This, of course, is not the only way in which an institutional environment of this kind is depriving. The infant is dependent on adults for the provision of both inanimate and social stimulation, including verbal stimulation, and this may be inadequate,

151

insufficiently varied or insufficiently adapted to the child's needs in an institutional setting.

Recent research suggests, in fact, that in good-quality institutions, where there is a high level of staff-child interaction and stimulation, intellectual retardation can be avoided even though a close attachment between a child and staff member is prevented by the somewhat impersonal care, by many adults looking after each child and by a policy of actively discouraging such relationships (Tizard and Tizard, 1971). Despite their satisfactory intellectual development, the institutional children in this study were showing, by the time they were four years old, difficulties in forming relationships, either not caring for anyone, or being indiscriminately friendly with everyone (Tizard and Tizard, 1971; Tizard and Rees, 1975). Similar behaviour has been found among children who entered institutional care before the age of two, but not in those entering after this, in another study (Wolkind, 1974).

Combined with findings from other studies (Dinnage and Pringle, 1967; Pringle, 1971) showing that institutional children are better adjusted when they have been able to maintain from an early age a stable relationship with an adult outside the institution, the evidence suggests that children who fail to establish a close relationship in the first three years or so may also experience difficulties in later social relationships. The consequences may be less severe, and of a somewhat different type, when children who have been able to form an initial attachment to their mothers (or other adults) are then separated from them during the first three years of life in circumstances which make the formation of other attachments unlikely (Rutter, 1972); here, too, though, the evidence indicates that there is a tendency towards some impairment in later personal relationships (Dinnage and Pringle, 1967).

While it is possible to infer from these findings that the establishment of a close attachment between a child and an adult in the early years is important for the child's future social relationships, and that the provision of appropriate stimulation is important for his intellectual development, it is over-simplifying the issue to conclude that these are entirely separate processes. Recently, research has shown that a secure relationship with the mother facilitates (though is not invariably necessary for) exploratory behaviour, and thus cognitive development, in the child (Ainsworth and Wittig, 1969; Ainsworth, 1973). Institutionalised infants with a close relationship to an adult (foster grandparents in this case) have been found in one study to be not only better adjusted than infants who were provided with social stimulation by people with whom they did not have a strong relationship (voluntary workers), but also tended to have better intellectual development (Saltz, 1973). Findings from home-based, pre-school intervention programmes for disadvantaged children under the age of three also indicate that these are most successful when the principal agent of intervention is the mother, rather than a teacher (Bronfenbrenner, 1974). The explanation is probably not only that the child has a greater motivation to attend to the person to whom he is emotionally attached but also that the adult who has a close relationship with him is more able to respond to his needs. Conversely, one study has found (at least among relatively disadvantaged children), that the higher the level of stimulation in the home, the more the child is attached to his mother (Caldwell *et al.*, 1970).

This literature suggests then that the quality and pattern of the child's social attachments in infancy may possibly have great importance for his future development. So far there have been no longitudinal studies attempting to link attachments in infancy to later behaviour. There is considerable current research interest, though, in the development of attachment – which has been defined as 'an affectional tie that one person forms to another specific person, binding them together in space and enduring over time' (Ainsworth, 1973) – in infancy (see Part I, section B, for a more detailed discussion). This research indicates that it is necessary for an individual to spend sufficient time in actual interaction with the child, rather than in routine care-taking, for an attachment to be formed. It is the opportunity for this interaction that is often missing in institutional environments. The sharing of care which occurs when the mother is employed cannot be equated with institutional care. The child retains a daily contact with a small number of people who are particularly interested in him, his mother and other members of his immediate family. He may also be cared for during the working day by one, or a small number of people, who have, or develop a close relationship with him. Nevertheless the situation is different from that of a child living at home and cared for mainly by his mother, and it is necessary to look at the research findings to see whether, and in what manner, this alters the pattern and quality of his attachments.

The research evidence on the formation of attachments indicates clearly that the child living at home with his family is usually attached to several people, not just his mother, even when she remains at home. The child is usually most strongly attached to his mother when she is his principal care-taker, but not invariably so. Someone (mostly the father) who spends less time with the child than the mother, but who is more responsive to him, may become the child's principal attachment object (Ainsworth, 1963; 1967; Cohen and Campos, 1974; Schaffer and Emerson, 1964).

The effect of shared care on the child's social attachments

These findings suggest then that shared care need not, in fact, fundamentally alter the pattern of attachments of the child living at home with his family. It appears to be possible for the mother to be the child's principal attachment object even if she is away from him for much of the day, provided that she is able to interact sufficiently with him in the time they have together. The child is also likely to develop an attachment to his substitute care-taker; most children have several attachments, though, so this is in no way a departure from the usual situation. The crucial question is whether, in fact, the mother will be capable of the sensitive interaction that appears to be necessary for the establishment of a secure attachment when she spends so much less time with the child, has less opportunity for getting to know the small details of his behaviour, and is likely to be tired or hurried in the time that is available. It is true that children in Israeli kibbutzim appear to be as attached to their mother as children living in American nuclear families whose mothers are at home full-time (Maccoby and Feldman, 1972). Here, though, the mother not only plays a major part in care-taking during the first year, but afterwards has several hours a day free from chores which can be devoted exclusively to the child. Fathers in our society are sometimes in a rather similar position – although they are away from the child for many hours a day, the time at home with the child may be unburdened by other tasks. Few full-time working mothers are likely to be in such a fortunate position – although husbands frequently 'help out' with the household tasks it is still quite rare for them actually to be shared (Hoffman, 1974).

There is some evidence of what actually happens to the child's attachment to his mother when she works, but it is inconclusive. Several studies have found that children whose mothers work when they are very young (ten months old – Tulkin, 1973) or who are placed in day-care centres during the first year (Brookhart and Hock, 1976; Saunders, 1972) differ little in attachment to their mothers from children remaining at home. Two-and-a-half-year-olds who had about eighteen months' experience of day care have also been found to be similar to home-reared children in their attachment behaviour (Caldwell *et al.*, 1970). However, there is some doubt about the measurement of attachment in this study (Ainsworth, 1973), high scores on some of the items perhaps indicating insecurity rather than strength of attachment. Studies of children entering day care rather later, between the ages of two and three, have found some evidence of disturbance in the quality of attachment to the mother, at least in the short-term (Blehar, 1974; Van Leeuwen and Tuma, 1972). The differences between the early and rather later entry studies could be due to the higher quality of the day care in the former studies, several of the centres having been set up as research projects (Caldwell *et al.*, 1970; Saunders, 1972). Possibly, too, older children, who have been used to exclusive care by their mothers, find entry to group care more disturbing at first.

There is some evidence that the rather anxious attachment found in children entering day care for the first time near the end of their third year (Blehar, 1974) may be temporary. Findings of the only study so far to follow up the effects of different types of care regimes on children at later ages found that children who entered group care for the first time at around three went through a temporary phase of timidity and emotional dependence but regained their confidence in their fifth and sixth years (Moore, 1975). Children who became more clinging and demanding towards the mother after entry to nursery school around the age of three (Van Leeuwen and Tuma, 1972) also appeared to be losing this behaviour three months later. Moore's (1975) findings suggest that it is early daily substitute care that is rather more likely to have longer lasting adverse effects. In this study the children who experienced substitute care before the age of two were more nervous and emotionally dependent on the mother at six than children who were placed in substitute care between the ages of three and four. However, all but four of the fifteen early daily substitute care children had experienced several changes of regime, which also tends to produce these characteristics. The four children in relatively stable care appeared to be similar but little information is given about the quality of the care they received, though it was with relatives, or about family circumstances. Obviously, generalisations cannot be made from so small a sample. The children who had been in high-quality, stable day care from an early age in Caldwell's study do not seem to show these characteristics of nervousness and emotional dependence at three to four years.

The evidence is also contradictory on the effect of employment on the mother's relationship to the child. The mothers of children who had been in day care since they were about one in Caldwell et al.'s (1970) study did not differ in attachment towards the child from mothers whose children remained at home. Mothers from severely disadvantaged backgrounds actually appeared to be more involved with their infants when they were in day care from an early age (Ramey et al., 1975). In contrast, impressionistic evidence from Moore's (1969, 1975) study suggests that mothers who leave their children in care from a very early age may be somewhat detached from them. Middle-class mothers were found to become somewhat less involved with their children after entry to nursery school in another study (Van Leeuwen and Tuma, 1972). Much probably depends on family circumstances and the mother's personality.

No firm conclusions are possible. It seems probable, though, that some children have a secure attachment with the mother even though she is working full-time, but that various circumstances associated with, or exacerbated by, the mother's working, may mean that other children are somewhat insecure in their relationship with the mother. Sometimes such difficulties, particularly in the case of older children, are probably only temporary. Much is also likely to depend on the quality of the substitute care available. However, there are two additional points that must be considered.

Current research emphasises the importance of sensitive interaction with the child for his optimal development. Although it is necessary to spend a sufficient amount of time with the child to achieve this, it cannot be assumed that the longer the time spent in his care the more responsive and sensitive the mother will become. It should not be forgotten that unrelieved care of a baby or small child can be exhausting both physically and mentally, and far from conducive to enjoyment of the child and sensitivity to his needs. There is no direct research evidence available here but it seems likely that a certain amount of time off to pursue her own interests will increase a mother's enjoyment in her child and enhance her responsiveness and sensitivity to him. There seems to be no reason why this should not be spent in part-time employment, at least after the first year, if high-quality care is available for a few hours a day. Secondly, mothers who work when the child is very young mainly do so out of economic necessity. The idealistic picture of mother and child taking 'mutual delight ... in their transactions with each other' (Ainsworth and Wittig, 1969) is hardly likely to occur if the home is over-crowded and squalid and the mother oppressed by financial worries. The material advantages gained from full-time work may enable mothers in such circumstances to enjoy their children more, even if they have little time to spend exclusively with them. The finding that mothers from severely disadvantaged backgrounds are more involved with the infant when day care provides them with some relief (Ramey *et al,*, 1975) substantiates this view.

So far, the effects of maternal employment and shared caring have been considered only in relation to the child's tie with the mother. Must the child's main attachment be to his mother? When children are institutionalised, a stable tie with an adult appears to benefit adjustment, and the identity of the person with whom the relationship is formed may be relatively unimportant. But the situation is not necessarily the same for the child living in a nuclear family. Possibly the child may develop his main tie to his substitute care-taker, particularly when he has been in her care from an early age, and he is her sole charge. There are indications from Moore's (1969) study of this situation arising on occasion, and sometimes creating tensions. The mother may find it difficult to accept that the child has a closer relationship with someone other than herself, particularly another woman. The other disadvantage of the main relationship being with the substitute care-taker rather than with the mother (or the father) is, of course, that this relationship is likely to be less enduring. Another possibility is that the father may become the child's principal object of attachment more frequently when the mother works, for he may then take a greater part in the child's care and will perhaps have more time free from other tasks than the mother. This is unlikely to matter, unless it causes family frictions. In general, it would appear advantageous for fathers to take a greater part in caring for the child from an early age than they usually do — there is evidence of the favourable influence of early father-child interactions on the child's cognitive development, at least (see Part III). However, as yet there is no research on the patterns of attachment of children experiencing shared care, and of the effects of different patterns on development.

While it is possible that difficulties may arise if the child becomes more attached to his substitute care-taker (or even perhaps his father in present society) than his mother, the development of several attachments, rather than an exclusive mother-child tie, is likely to be advantageous for the child. Enforced absence of the mother appears to be much less distressing if the child can be cared for by someone to whom he has already formed an attachment. Perhaps, as has been suggested (Mead, 1966), several attachments produce greater flexibility of personality, or at least facilitate the formation of new relationships. The greater variety of experiences they provide for the child is also likely to enhance the child's development (see Part I, p. 70). Shared care is likely to be beneficial then in that it gives the child — particularly the child whose family has few close relatives or friends living nearby — greater opportunity of making several attachments. So far there has been only one investigation comparing the attachment to people other than the mother of children in substitute care and those at home. Unfortunately, the findings are equivocal, the only difference being that the day-care children scored higher on a measure termed 'dependency', which can be interpreted as either greater enjoyment of interaction with adults, or else as somewhat over-anxious attachment to them (Caldwell *et al.*, 1970).

There is one remaining problem to consider in relation to attachment. Is it necessary for the child to form an attachment to his substitute care-taker? Where the child has stable care from one person, and where he is in good-quality day care with a high staff-child ratio (Ricciuti, 1974), he is likely to become attached to his care-taker. Where, however, he has frequent changes of care-taker, or where he is placed in poor-quality day care, with a low staff-child ratio and high staff turnover he may have difficulty in forming relationships with his substitute care-takers. In Moore's study of children experiencing various types of substitute care, the children who had unstable substitute care from an early age (early in the second year, on average) showed more signs of emotional disturbance at the age of six — dependent, clinging, attention-seeking behaviour — than either children who had been cared for entirely by their mothers or those who received stable substitute care. However, there was also considerable insecurity of family relationships of children in the unstable care group and at least part of their emotional insecurity may be attributable to this. It is not certain from present evidence that unstable substitute care would have the same effect on children from a more harmonious background.

Are children under three who experience shared care well adjusted?

Until there has been further investigation of these problems concerning the development of attachments and their consequences it cannot unreservedly be stated that maternal employment and substitute care for a long period each day, while the child is under three years old, will not have some adverse later consequences. Overall, though, the limited evidence that is available suggests that children who are in good-quality, stable substitute care are satisfactorily emotionally and socially adjusted. Evidence comes from American studies of children in high-quality day care, who entered from the beginning of the second year (Braun and Caldwell, 1973) or even earlier (Fowler, 1972), from both advantaged and disadvantaged backgrounds. In the latter study the day-care children were at or above the norms of standardised infant behaviour scales in most areas. The only exception was on items of belligerence and irritability, the disadvantaged and to a lesser extent, the advantaged (who were also later entrants) children having negative evaluations here. Perhaps similarly, early entrants to the day-care centre developed by Caldwell were found to be less co-operative with adults and more aggressive with both adults and peers than children who had individual care up to the age of three (Schwarz et al., 1974). There are somewhat similar findings for slightly older children (three years onwards), those, especially boys, with some experience of substitute care being more aggressive and less conforming to adult demands than children without such experience (Moore, 1969, 1975); also children who have attended nursery school longer tend to have more negative interactions with adults (but not peers) than children with shorter attendance (Raph et al., 1968). However, it would be wrong to interpret these differences at this early age as signs of maladjustment – it seems, rather, as Moore suggests, that substitute care and maternal care tend to encourage the development of certain different kinds of personality characteristics. Only studies of later outcome of children who have experienced early substitute care, will provide a definite answer.

Effects of shared care on intellectual attainments

The evidence on the effects of full-time substitute care on the child's intellectual development is almost entirely one-sided. The findings certainly do show that shared care is compatible with intellectual attainments as high or higher than those of children of similar background remaining at home. However, evidence comes from subjects who had the benefit of educationally oriented care, or of an exceptionally favourable home background. American day-care children (from both advantaged and disadvantaged backgrounds) who performed better than children remaining at home with their mothers were benefitting from a carefully devised educational enrichment programme (Caldwell, 1973; Fowler, 1972; Robinson and Robinson, 1971). The infants with working mothers who performed at least as well on scales of intellectual development as those with non-working mothers probably enjoyed a particularly stimulating home background, coming from highly educated, middle-class Israeli families (Kohen-Raz, 1968) or black American families who had managed to achieve middle-class status (Golden and Birns, 1968). Kibbutz children, who are at least equal to non-kibbutz children in intellectual attainments by middle childhood (Marcus, 1971; Rabin, 1958) enjoy both an educationally oriented environment, and parents with sufficient time and energy for stimulating interaction with them. In his study of substitute care, Moore (1968) found that five of the seven boys and two of the eight girls who had substitute care while under the age of three had ability increments above the average of their sex. These children, though, may have had exceptionally energetic mothers, for they managed to take part in a research scheme over an eight-year period despite working at least some of the time. Moore gives no information about the attainments of the other two boys and six girls. There can be little doubt that children in poor-quality day care, or in the charge of paid child-minders — untrained women, who may have up to sixteen children in their care, and little space or equipment for them to play with — do suffer intellectually (Jackson, 1974). At present, there is an almost complete absence of research findings on the attainments of children who have experienced child-minding.

Socially disadvantaged children undoubtedly benefit intellectually while they are attending educationally oriented day-care centres. It is unlikely that the setting up of such centres would, by itself, prevent the school failure that is experienced by many such children. In the only evaluation of later outcome findings were unfortunately in line with those already familiar from studies of the slightly older (three- to five-year-old) children who attended pre-school compensatory education classes — once the children left the day-care programme their intellectual performance declined (Caldwell and Smith, 1970). Evidence from the American pre-school intervention programmes suggests that parental involvement may have some sustaining effect on intellectual gains

(Bronfenbrenner, 1974 – see Part V, section on 'Intervention'). Parents have to be convinced that their own interaction with the child can have a crucial role in his development. The earlier this parental involvement is achieved the more effective it appears to be, but it is also essential for parental interest and support to be maintained into the school years. How can this parental involvement be achieved? The day-care centre can have an important role here. Day-care staff have unparalleled opportunities for informal contacts with parents. Individual discussion, group discussion and involvement of parents in the children's activities at the centre (insofar as parents have the time available) could all be used to convince parents of their own role in the child's development and help them to play it more effectively. Of course, no amount of encouragement by day-care staff is going to help the mother who is worn out by long hours of full-time work, household responsibilities, and problems of unsuitable housing to interact more effectively with her child. The mother (and the father) needs time and energy, as well as suitable living conditions for this. Local authority help with housing and adequate allowances for families with young children so that the mother does not need to work full-time (unless she wishes) nor the father an inordinate amount of overtime, are essential if a policy of parental involvement is to have any chance of success.

Shared caring: advantages and disadvantages

Overall, it seems very unlikely that care by someone other than the mother for a few hours a day will have adverse effects on the child under three. For the mother, it may provide considerable benefits of relief from child care and increased enjoyment of the child in the time spent with him. For the child, too, it offers the opportunity of increasing his breadth of attachments, and his enjoyment of interaction with people. Doubts do arise, though, about the effects of the child under the age of three spending most, rather than a few, of his waking hours with someone other than his mother (or his father). If the child is provided with stable, good-quality care and is able to develop secure attachments to one or two adults there are unlikely to be direct adverse effects on his development. As was pointed out by Yudkin and Holme (1963) some time ago, it may be the mother who misses most in this situation – she loses much of the pleasure that comes from involvement in the details of the child's development (as do so many fathers), and may find it difficult to establish a close relationship with him later on. If the child receives inadequate or unstable care, the position may be much more serious and will possibly result in poor intellectual development or emotional insecurity.

Should measures be taken then to discourage mothers with children under three from working full-time? Certainly no mother of a young child, including mothers in father-absent families, should be forced to work from economic necessity. But it hardly seems sensible to oppose the setting up of high-quality, day-care facilities on the grounds that these would encourage mothers to work. Some mothers of young children do feel they need to work, and if there are no day-care facilities available, they may be forced into using much less adequate types of care. Individual care by a relative or friend may sometimes be an ideal solution but it is essential that the mother is able to maintain a good relationship with the substitute care-taker if tensions are not to arise. Otherwise, day care which has been carefully designed to foster children's emotional and educational needs has many advantages. Preferably such care should be situated in the local community, and should cater for children from all social backgrounds of both working and non-working mothers, whether they need to stay all day or only for an hour or two. Staff in such day-care centres would be encouraged to see their role as supporting, not taking over from, parents.

C. The pre-school child (3–5 Years) – Summary of findings

1. Emotional and social adjustment

Effects of daily substitute care

a) Few consistent differences have been found between children who receive exclusive maternal care and those who experience substitute care for the full working day in the three- to five-year-old period. There is some evidence, though that the substitute-care children are generally more self-assertive, less conforming and more capable of looking after themselves (Hansson et al., 1967 cited by Sjølund, 1969; Moore, 1969, 1975). Children attending part-time nursery school show a similar pattern to the children having substitute care for the full day, but to a less marked degree (Stukat, 1966, cited by Sjølund, 1969).

b) The type of care experienced by the child in the pre-school period may have effects which persist into later childhood and even adolescence (Moore, 1969, 1972a and b, 1975). Only Moore, however, has carried out a long-term follow-up so far and his findings are based on a smallish (167) and selective (a quarter of the original sample dropped out), though socially fairly representative sample.

c) Sex differences. There is some indication that substitute care in the pre-school years may have rather different effects on boys and girls (Moore, 1969, 1972a and b, 1975). In Moore's study, boys who had experienced daily substitute care were found, in various assessments up to the age of fifteen, to be more outgoing, fearless, superficially self-confident and resistant to discipline, while boys who had experienced exclusive maternal care were more obedient, conforming to adult standards, timid and anxious. Differences were less clear-cut for girls, the substitute-care girls claiming attention from their mothers, and having an ambivalent attitude towards them, while their aggression was expressed in fantasy. Moore found that the regime had a greater effect than the mother's personality on the boys' behaviour but the girls' behaviour was more directly affected by the mother's personality in interaction with the regime.

Effects of different types of shared care

a) *Nursery school*
i) Generally, children attending nursery school, whether full- (Hansson *et al.*, 1967, cited by Sjølund, 1969) or part-time (Stukat, 1966, cited by Sjølund, 1969) are more outgoing, self-confident and spontaneous than children kept at home. The nursery-school children are at least as socially competent as children at home (Cohen and Bagshaw, 1973) and possibly more so (Stukat, cited by Sjølund, 1969; Widlake, 1973).

ii) Children who have attended nursery school for one or two years appear not to differ in frequency of interaction with peers from children without this experience but they tend to have fewer negative interactions with them. However, they have more negative interactions with teachers (Raph *et al.*, 1968). These findings partially confirm those in the previous section – children who entered day care early were less co-operative with adults but differed little in their ability to get along with peers, compared with children who entered day care at three to four years (Schwarz *et al.*, 1974).

iii) Generally children who have attended nursery school are better able to adjust to primary school than those without nursery school experience (Sjølund, 1969). However, teachers sometimes rate nursery-school children lower in general adjustment than non-nursery children of similar socio-economic background (Brown and Hunt, 1961), possibly because of their more outgoing or less co-operative behaviour (see (i) and (ii) above) or because children with problems enter nursery school more frequently.

b) *Different types of individual care*
Adjustment of children in daily substitute care was found in one study (Perry, 1961) to be unrelated to: the substitute care-taker's training, experience or attitude to work; the length of time per week and total time in substitute care; whether the child had been in the care of one or more

substitute mother; the number of children cared for by the substitute mother; whether the substitute care-taker and the child's mother agreed on child care practices. However, it should be noted that the arrangements made appeared to be relatively stable and mutually satisfactory.

c) *Nursery school versus individual substitute care*
Nursery-school children and those in individual substitute care appear to show similar patterns of self-assertion and non-conformity, although the nursery-school children have fewer fears, less guilt, are less tidy and rather more assertive (Moore, 1964, 1969, 1975). Moore (1975) found that children entering nursery school for the first time when they were about three years old went through a phase of timidity and emotional dependence but regained confidence in the fifth and sixth years. There are very similar findings from another study (Van Leeuwen and Tuma, 1972). Children entering nursery school between two years eleven months and three years two months increased in clinging and demanding types of behaviour towards the mother immediately after entry, but three months later this type of behaviour was showing signs of decline (see also section B, p. 145). No consistent changes in attachment to the mother were found after entry to nursery school in children above this age, although some (no indication of how large a proportion is given) showed a temporary decrease in exploration.

The effects of maternal employment

a) Whether the mother works or not in the pre-school years does not affect the child's emotional or social adjustment, either at this stage (Nye *et al.*, 1963) or subsequently, in the early primary years (at the age of seven – Davie *et al.*, 1972), at pre-adolescence or adolescence (Burchinal, 1963). Findings at the age of seven are from the National Child Development Study, having as its sample a representative group of British children, taking into account social class and family size. However, it cannot be ruled out that there are sub-groups of working mothers, as there appear to be with older children, e.g. those who enjoy their work and those who do not enjoy their work (Hoffman, 1963a and 1974), who have differing effects on the children's adjustment.

b) From the available evidence, mothers of pre-school children who are employed differ little in their child-rearing attitudes from non-employed mothers (Nye *et al.*, 1963; Powell, 1963). Employed mothers in the former study did not appear to 'over-compensate' for working. However, no indication was given of the class composition of the sample, and it may be that mothers of pre-school children from a middle-class background tend to feel guilty and over-compensate, as they appear to do with older children (Hoffman, 1963a).

2. Intellectual development

Effects of daily substitute care

a) From the only evidence available (Moore, 1968, 1969), it appears that there are no differences at the age of eight in intellectual or language development between children who have experienced only maternal care until school age and those who have experienced at least one year of substitute care for the full day (private, nursery school or day care). As Moore (1969) points out, though, the mothers who both worked and found energy to take part in the research over an eight-year period must be a selective group.

b) Sex differences. Boys who experienced substitute care tended to develop more rapidly between infancy and eight years than boys who had exclusive maternal care (borderline significance), but the opposite was found for girls (Moore, 1968, 1975).

c) Reading competence relative to intelligence of both boys and girls in the substitute care group was below that of children who had experienced only maternal care until school-age (Moore, 1968, 1975).

Although Moore's study is the only one which has investigated the effects of substitute care for the full day, his findings are broadly substantiated by those from studies of nursery school children (see 'Effects of local authority nursery schools' below), and working mothers (see 'Effects of maternal employment' below).

Effects of local authority nursery schools

a) Attendance for two-and-a-half hours a day at a British nursery school appears to result in children attaining greater improvement in language and conceptualisation than those who have not attended nursery school of similar socio-economic background. This applies to both working- and middle-class children (Cohen and Bagshaw, 1973). There is some evidence that the advantage of the nursery-school children on intellectual and educational attainment scores is retained for some time into the primary school years but it is gradually eroded (Douglas and Ross, 1964). Six- to seven-year-old socially disadvantaged children who had attended nursery school were not found to be superior on tests of linguistic achievement to those who had not attended nursery school, in one study (Widlake, 1973). It should be noted, though, that British nursery schools are in the main organised on the traditional free-play approach and that there is no specific language development programme (Widlake, 1973) (see 'Pre-school intervention programmes for socially disadvantaged children (a) and (b), below).

b) Primary school children who have attended local authority nursery schools for at least two hours a day may be somewhat lower in reading competence in relation to intelligence than children of similar social background who have not attended nursery school (Douglas and Ross, 1964), at least when the mother works (except for the child of above average ability) (Singh, 1971). This is in line with Moore's findings (see 'Effects of daily substitute care', above) that children who have experienced exclusive maternal care until school age have higher reading attainments than children with experience of substitute care.

Pre-school intervention programmes for socially disadvantaged children

a) *American*
i) Evaluation of the many American pre-school intervention projects has shown that disadvantaged children attending pre-school classes, whether full- or part-time, make substantial gains in intelligence test scores compared with children of similar socio-economic background who have not attended such classes. These gains are not, however, generally maintained after the intervention has ceased, the IQ of the experimental children beginning to drop after the special programme has ended and there usually being little difference from the controls by the time the children are eight years old (Bronfenbrenner, 1974).

ii) Children in the academic, more cognitively oriented programmes generally make more substantial gains on the intelligence tests and other cognitive measures than children receiving traditional nursery-school education (Di Lorenzo, 1969, and Karnes, 1969, cited by Bronfenbrenner, 1974). However, although such an approach may enable children to perform better on objective tests, there is also evidence that it is less effective in developing the ability to solve problems or in changing attitudes towards school (Bronfenbrenner, 1974).

b) *British*
Findings of the more limited British intervention programmes are similar to the American. The main British studies, the Educational Priority Area project and the National Foundation for Educational Research study have been concerned with evaluating the effectiveness of special programmes introduced for the most part into pre-existing nursery schools, classes or playgroups run generally on the traditional free-play lines. Although not designed to find out whether nursery-school

165

attendance as such is educationally more beneficial to the disadvantaged child than staying at home, findings nevertheless showed benefits of attendance in terms of gains in relation to national norms on standardised tests of language and intelligence. There was the usual pattern of decline against the norms in the infant school but the rate at which this occurred appeared to be influenced to some extent by the characteristics of the particular school. The special programmes in the British studies generally tended to produce short-term cognitive and linguistic advantages but these tended to decline after the programme had ended (see Part V, section on 'Intervention' for a detailed discussion of this research).

c) *Canadian*

Relatively disadvantaged (mainly from one-parent families) pre-school children attending day-care centres with educational enrichment programmes for the full day have been found not to differ in school readiness from advantaged children (middle-class in professional families) attending nursery school for only two hours a day (Bottrill, 1968). This study contained no follow-up to find out whether the performance of the relatively disadvantaged children held up at primary school level. It should also be noted that the sample was far from typical of disadvantaged children – the mothers apparently had mainly lower middle-class jobs or were trying to qualify themselves for such work by taking educational courses and probably had quite high educational aspirations for their children.

Effects of maternal employment

In a nationally representative sample of British children, those whose mothers worked before the children started primary school were, at the age of seven, slighty inferior in reading attainments (three months' progress) compared with children whose mothers had not worked, social class and family size having been taken into account. The children whose mothers had worked were also slightly behind in arithmetic attainments but the deficit was even smaller, equivalent to one month's progress (Davie *et al.*, 1972). Consistently with the substitute care and nursery school studies these findings suggest that full-time care by the mother before the child reaches school age tends to have a beneficial effect on reading abilities.

Discussion

Issues in the pre-school period

The situation is very different in the three- to five-year-old period from that in the first three years of the child's life. Probably there are few who would not agree that care by someone other than the mother for a few hours a day is unlikely to be harmful to the child. For this age group, the issues are, rather, whether care by someone else for the full day is likely to have adverse effects, and whether it is positively beneficial to the child to spend some time away from his mother.

Shared care versus maternal care in the pre-school period: effects on adjustment and personality

Overall, the evidence does justify the conclusion that stable substitute care in the three- to five-year-old period does not have any deleterious effects on social or emotional adjustment. Findings come both from the one study that has examined the effects of full-time substitute care in some detail (Moore, 1969) and from studies of working mothers (Burchinal, 1963; Davie et al., 1972; Nye et al., 1963). In two of these studies (Moore, 1969, 1975; Davie et al., 1972) there is a clear distinction between children whose mothers had worked full-time, and who must have experienced substitute care at some time, and those whose mothers had never worked, so the lack of difference cannot be attributed to overlap between the groups.

This does not mean that different types of care regimes in the pre-school years make no difference at all to the child's behaviour. It is rather, as Moore (1972b, 1975) suggests that substitute care and maternal care appear to encourage certain kinds of personality traits, not that one type of regime leads to maladjustment. Moore, in fact, found rather clear-cut differences between the groups, particularly in the case of boys. He found the substitute care boys to be more outgoing, superficially self-confident, and more resistant to discipline, while the maternal-care boys were more obedient and conforming, but also more timid and anxious. A similar picture is obtained from studies of children attending full-(Hansson, cited by Sjølund, 1969) and half-time (Stukat, cited by Sjølund, 1969) Swedish nursery schools. A number of studies in the 1930s in the United States compared children attending part-time nursery schools and non-nursery school children and again the findings are very similar (Sjølund, 1969).

Differences in personality of children experiencing maternal and substitute care could, however, be due not to the regimes themselves, but to the personality of the mothers who choose the regimes. Moore (1969, 1972b, 1975) found some differences in child-rearing attitudes between the two groups of mothers when the child was eight years old, those who had cared exclusively for the child being more dominant and favouring stricter discipline. In infancy and the pre-school years, though, the mothers in the two groups had differed little in basic attitudes towards their children, although mothers of the maternal-care boys were somewhat more anxious and more involved with them. It appears that the experience of the regime itself shapes the mother's attitudes to some extent, sometimes reinforcing her own inclinations, sometimes modifying them. Moore concluded from his analysis that the regime is of main importance for the boys' behaviour while the girls' behaviour is affected by the mother's personality in interaction with the regime. One of the nursery-school studies (Stukat, 1966, cited by Sjølund, 1969) attempted to control for parental attitudes by comparing children attending the half-day nursery school with those on the waiting list – differences were slight but the nursery-school children showed the tendencies already noted, being more outward going, self-confident, spontaneous and importunate, and having a significantly greater ability to look after themselves.

Moore concludes from his study that part-time substitute care may be the most satisfactory situation for children in the pre-school age group. In these circumstances, the mother is able to give the child some independence from her, and also maintain a close and warm relationship. He found individual instances of children with mothers working part-time who were confident, spontaneous and not too anxious, but who valued the approval of adults, although there were too few cases to establish a statistical relationship. Further studies comparing children who experience a few hours a day substitute care with those cared for exclusively by their mothers are needed to substantiate these views. Existing studies of children attending part-time nursery are of little help as they generally fail to exclude children in other types of substitute care from the control groups.

There is little evidence on whether individual substitute care and group care have different effects on the emotional and social adjustment of children in this age range. The similarity of findings on children's personality in Moore's substitute-care group (including private and nursery care) and of those for children attending nursery school in other studies (Sjølund, 1969) has already been pointed out. Moore also made a specific comparison of the individual substitute-care and nursery-school children in his study, and found unexpectedly few differences between them, though the nursery-school children did have fewer fears, were less guilty and tidy, and rather more assertive. Children entering group care for the first time at about three sometimes seem to go through a phase of timidity and emotional dependence but this appears to be only temporary (Moore, 1975 – see also section B, p. 155).

It is often assumed that group experience helps children to get on better together. Evidence from the earlier nursery school studies on this question is limited and inconclusive (Sjølund, 1969). More recent studies of day-care (compared with individual substitute or maternal care)

(Schwarz *et al.*, 1973) or nursery school children (Raph *et al.*, 1968) show that group care does not affect the frequency of interactions between children, but findings from the latter study suggest that it may reduce the frequency of negative interactions. Of course, at the very least, group care does give the relatively isolated child the opportunity of meeting others of his own age.

Shared care versus maternal care in the pre-school period: effects on intellectual attainments

So far, then, the evidence suggests that substitute care for the full working day is unlikely to be harmful to the child's emotional and social adjustment, and some hours away from the mother, whether she is working or not, may have positive benefits.

As far as intellectual attainments are concerned, the evidence generally indicates that substitute care for the full day does not have any adverse effects, but reading attainments relative to intelligence may be slightly lower than in children cared for exclusively by their mothers. Evidence comes from Moore's study of children in substitute care and from findings on working mothers in the National Child Development Study (Davie *et al.*, 1972). There are probably, though, differences between children in various types of substitute care. It seems likely that those in the care of paid childminders, who often provide little environmental stimulation, will have lower educational attainments (Jackson, 1974). On the other hand, it might be expected that children attending nursery schools, whether full- or part-time, will benefit intellectually from the wider experiences available there.

The evidence on attendance at part-time nursery schools indicates, in fact, that there is some intellectual advantage for children while they are actually at the nursery schools but that this advantage is probably not retained in the long-term. A large number of studies were carried out on nursery-school children in the United States in the 1930s. Some studies found that the nursery-school children made significantly greater gains in intelligence than matched controls, while none of the studies found adverse effects from nursery school attendance (Sjølund, 1969). Findings from two studies of local authority nursery schools in Britain (run presumably on the traditional play-based approach) indicate that the children attending, whether from working- or middle-class backgrounds, do make greater advances in intellectual development than children without this experience (Douglas and Ross, 1964; Cohen and Bagshaw, 1973). These gains are probably retained for some time into the primary-school period, although differences were found in one study (Douglas and Ross, 1964) to be insignificant by the time they were eleven. The recent Educational Priority Area project had similar findings on the

169

effects of nursery-school attendance (see Part V, section on 'Intervention', pp. 373–4). Moreover, although the nursery-school children made advances in intellectual development compared with children at home, reading attainments relative to intelligence were found to be slightly worse in the primary school years in the Douglas and Ross study. Although gains may not hold up in the long-term, findings suggest that nursery-school attendance is a worthwhile intellectual experience for children of all social classes. One of the main reasons for the expansion of the nursery-school system, though, is the conviction that this will help to prevent school failure in socially disadvantaged children. The findings indicate that by itself the traditional nursery school cannot overcome the educational disadvantage of children from a deprived background.

Can pre-school educational programmes benefit socially disadvantaged children?

This conclusion does not mean, of course, that pre-school education has no role to play in helping socially disadvantaged children to catch up, although the part-time nursery system as presently organised may not be the most suitable form. Research discussed in Part V of this review, on 'Intervention', suggests that the introduction of special programmes into nursery schools run on the traditional free-play child-centred lines may produce gains greater in cognitive development in the short-term. This is perhaps because such programmes provide teachers with objectives about cognitive and linguistic objectives that can be attained and guidance on the activities likely to produce them. The review also shows, though, that to expect gains to be retained without taking other sustaining measures is unrealistic. One such measure is parental involvement with the child in activities likely to promote his development, a feature which was common to most of the more successful American intervention programmes. There has been much discussion amongst British researchers (Tizard, 1975) of the best way to involve the parents of socially disadvantaged children. Informal contacts with nursery-school (or other forms of pre-school) staff may provide the best means of involving parents initially. Of course, as emphasised in the previous section of this review, such measures can only have an effect if parents and children live in suitable conditions for carrying them out – adequate housing and sufficient income for the family without the necessity of over-long hours of work for either parent are crucial here.

Part-time and full-time maternal employment and the pre-school child

Overall the findings suggest that a few hours away from the mother are likely to be of benefit both to her and to the child of pre-school age. Even those mothers who are most contented with staying at home are likely to find the constant demands of a small child wearisome if there is no break from them at all. The mother who has exclusive care of her child may also become over-protective, and find it difficult to let the child achieve the necessary independence from her. Some mothers are able to make informal arrangements with relatives or friends to provide relief for themselves and wider experiences for the child. It appears, though, that many mothers are unable to do this. There is evidence of a high rate of depression among mothers of children under five, particularly those from the working class (G. W. Brown *et al.*, 1975; Richman 1974, 1976). Provision of some form of pre-school education, which also provides mothers with opportunities for contacting other parents, and which encourages their involvement in and greater enjoyment of, the child's activities, appears to be needed. Part-time work appears to be quite compatible with the needs of children of this age. The difficulty is rather in finding such work, appropriate to the mother's skills, and finding high-quality substitute care for the child. The hours of such employment seldom coincide with those of the part-time nursery school, as presently organised.

What implications can be drawn about full-time maternal employment? There is no evidence that children in this age range suffer adverse consequences from substitute care for the full working day, apart from a very slight educational retardation. Obviously, there will be considerable differences in effects, according to the quality of the substitute care. The research on pre-school intervention programmes for socially disadvantaged children has emphasised the importance of parents' interaction with, and interest in, their children. It may be very difficult for a working mother to maintain this, particularly if she has a tiring job, and is then over-burdened with chores when she arrives home. The mother who is too exhausted to be involved with the details of her child's development also misses a life-enriching experience and is likely to have a less satisfactory relationship with the child. It is sad that fathers so often miss these experiences. There is little point, though, in trying to discourage full-time work by failing to provide high-quality facilities. This is only likely to result in less satisfactory substitute care being used. Even if the mother does stay at home through lack of good facilities, this is not necessarily to the child's advantage – research with primary-school age children has shown that mothers who are dissatisfied with being full-time housewives make the least adequate mothers (Yarrow *et al.*, 1962). Rather, three types of measures are needed: (i) provision of high-quality substitute care (probably a new type of service combining day care and education); (ii) encouragement of more effective and enjoyable interaction between parents and children (probably as one function of a new pre-school service); and (iii) policies which would enable working mothers (and fathers) to spend more time with their children (perhaps more flexibility in working hours, and more home help). In a few areas, there are plans to evaluate the needs of children under five and their families for services, and to set up comprehensive Children's Centres to meet these needs (Tizard, 1975; Pringle and Naidoo, 1975). Work on these lines is much needed.

D. The school-age child (5–16 + years) – Summary of findings

1. The effects of maternal employment on family life

Child-rearing practices

a) There is little difference between the child-rearing attitudes of employed and non-employed mothers. This applies whether the children are at the primary school (five to eleven plus) (Powell, 1963; Yarrow *et al.*, 1962) or secondary school stage (twelve to sixteen plus) (McCord *et al.*, 1963; Peterson, 1961; Powell, 1963); it also applies whether the mother is from a working-class background (McCord *et al.*, 1963; Peterson, 1961) or a middle-class background (Peterson, 1961; Powell, 1963; Yarrow *et al.*, 1962).

b) Working mothers cannot be distinguished as a group from non-working mothers in control over their children or strictness of discipline. Some working mothers appear to exercise less control (those who enjoy their work – Hoffman, 1963a; or those from stable working-class families – McCord *et al.*, 1963) than non-working mothers. Perhaps these mothers feel the need to compensate the child for working, or they may have higher morale (Hoffman, 1974). Other working mothers have been found to exercise more control (non-college educated middle-class mothers – Yarrow *et al.*, 1962).

c) Working mothers may encourage independence more than non-working mothers (Burchinal and Lovell, 1959, cited by Hoffman, 1974; Birnbaum, 1971; Yarrow *et al.*, 1962). Exceptions appear to be more highly educated mothers of primary-school age children (Hoffman, 1963a; Yarrow *et al.*, 1962) who possibly stress the nurturant role to compensate for working.

The child's perception of his parents

a) *The mother*

i) Both primary- (Hoffman, 1963a) and secondary-school (Franke, 1972; Nye, 1963a; Roy, 1963; Propper, 1972) children whose mothers are employed perceive them as being no less affectionate than do children whose mothers are not employed.

ii) In one-parent families, the mother who works may be seen as more affectionate than the mother who does not work (Nye, 1963a).

b) *The father*

i) Working-class boys whose mothers are working have been found in several North American studies to evaluate their fathers lower than boys whose mothers are not working (Kappell and Lambert, 1962, cited by Hoffman, 1974; McCord *et al.*, 1963; Propper, 1972). This possibly occurs where the father is viewed as an economic failure (Hoffman, 1974). In British working-class families the sons' attitudes are perhaps closer to the middle-class pattern (see (ii) below), for maternal employment seems to be accepted in the majority of cases and the father perhaps takes a larger share in child-care activities (Jephcott *et al.*, 1962; Yudkin and Holme, 1963). This needs further investigation (see 'Sharing the parental role' (a) below).

ii) Middle-class boys whose mothers work may regard their fathers as more nurturant (Vogel *et al.*, 1970), possibly because he takes more part in child-care (Hoffman, 1974). Middle-class boys do not evaluate the father lower when the mother works (Kappell and Lambert, 1972, cited by Hoffman, 1974).

Effect on the mother's emotional state

a) Satisfaction with working or non-working. The mother who is satisfied with her role, whether this is working or non-working is more adequate as a mother than the mother who is dissatisfied (Yarrow *et al.*, 1962). While the satisfied non-working mother may be slightly more adequate as a mother than the satisfied working mother, the least adequate mother is the dissatisfied non-working mother (Yarrow *et al.*, 1962).

b) Self-esteem. Working mothers, especially those who are professionally employed, generally have higher self-esteem than non-working mothers (Birnbaum, 1971; Nye, 1963c).

c) Anxiety and guilt. There is some evidence that working mothers, at least those from the middle classes, feel more anxiety about their role as a

173

mother than the non-working mother (Nye, 1963c; Yarrow *et al.*, 1962). Indications of guilt are found in a number of studies of middle-class working mothers (Birnbaum, 1971; Jones *et al.*, 1967). This may lead to attempts to compensate (Jones *et al.*, 1967) and sometimes over-compensate (Hoffman, 1963a) for working. Possibly anxiety and guilt are not found to the same extent among working-class employed mothers (Jephcott *et al.*, 1962) but this needs corroboration.

d) Role strain. Mothers from working classes (Jephcott *et al.*, 1962; Woods, 1972) to professional classes (Fogarty *et al.*, 1971) experience strain at carrying out two demanding roles. The amount of strain appears to be particularly related to the possibility of making adequate arrangements for the out-of-school supervision of the child (Jephcott *et al.*, 1962; Woods, 1972).

Sharing the parental role

a) A number of studies have found that the father takes more part in child-care activities when the mother is employed. This has been found for both middle-class (Fogarty *et al.*, 1971; Jones *et al.*, 1967; Yarrow *et al.*, 1962) and, at least in Britain, working-families (Jephcott *et al.*, 1962; Yudkin and Holme, 1963, 1969). However, recent findings from the National Child Development Study, having a representative sample of British eleven-year-olds are contradictory (Lambert and Hart, 1976). The relationship between greater father participation and maternal employment (part-time in two out of three cases) was found to disappear when social class and family size were taken into account. Further investigation is needed for children of different ages, particularly where the mother works full-time.

b) Relatives, particularly maternal grandmothers, and neighbours, are more likely to take some part in child-care activities when the mother is employed. Availability of a responsible person acts as a limiting factor on the mother's ability to work, at least when the child is still at the primary-school stage (Hoffman, 1974; Yudkin and Holme, 1963, 1969). Involvement of people other than the parents in child-care responsibilities may affect family relationships, and the child, but no direct investigation has been made for this age group.

2. Emotional and social adjustment

The effects of maternal employment

a) Primary-school-age children. Findings on the social and emotional adjustment of primary-school-age children whose mothers are employed are inconclusive, but give no indication of any marked maladjustment. Studies of Belgian six- to eight-year-old working-class boys (Dits and Cambier, 1966, cited by Etaugh, 1974) and of British six-year-olds from all social classes (Singh, 1970) suggest somewhat poorer emotional adjustment, but no differences were found between British primary-school working-class children with employed and non-employed mothers in an earlier study (Cartwright and Jefferys, 1958). The much more carefully controlled National Child Development Study (Davie *et al.*, 1972), taking both social class and family size into allowance, found that children's social adjustment in school at the age of seven was slightly worse when the mother started working after the child entered school but not when she was already working before this. This suggests that the problems may be due to temporary adjustment difficulties or to less adequate out-of-school supervision being provided for children whose mothers only started work after they entered school. Further carefully controlled research is necessary for more definite conclusions to be reached on the behaviour and adjustment at home of primary school age children with employed mothers.

b) Secondary-school-age children. The personal (Nelson, 1971; Nye, 1963a; Burchinal, 1963) and social adjustment (Burchinal, 1963; McCord *et al.*, 1963; Propper, 1972; Roy, 1963; Stott, 1965) of secondary-school-age children, from intact families, whose mothers are employed, differs little from that of children from a similar socio-economic background whose mothers are not employed.

c) Non-intact families. Children from father-absent families may be better adjusted when the mother is employed (Nye, 1963a). In the recent National Children's Bureau study of one-parent families (Ferri, 1976), though, the only group of father-absent children to be better adjusted when the mother was working were the illegitimate.

d) Delinquency. There is no evidence of an association between maternal employment and delinquency, when social class has been taken into account (Douglas *et al.*, 1968; Miller *et al.*, 1974; Nye, 1963a; West, 1969).

The effects of maternal employment — modifying factors

a) *Sex*

A number of studies have indicated that maternal employment may have differential sex effects (Hoffman, 1963a; Roy, 1963; Siegal *et al.*, 1959; Nelson, 1971). Trends are not consistent. However, a tendency towards

175

more dependent behaviour has been found among boys, but not girls, of kindergarten age (five to six in the United States) (Siegel *et al.*, 1959) and school age (nine to twelve years) (Hoffman, 1963a), especially where the mother dislikes her work and is less involved with the child. Also, ten-year-old black ghetto boys, but not girls, who were inadequately supervised out of school, were found to be less self-reliant than those who were adequately supervised (Woods, 1972). Possibly when maternal employment is associated with insecurity, it is perceived as rejection by the child (McCord *et al.*, 1963) and leads to more dependent behaviour. These authors found ten- to fifteen-year-old boys from unstable, but not from stable, working-class families to be more dependent when the mother was working. Any negative effect of maternal employment is perhaps counterbalanced for the girl by the more positive model presented by the working mother (Hoffman, 1963b).

b) *Social class*

No studies have made separate class analyses, apart from the Davie *et al.*, (1972) study, see 'The effects of maternal employment' (a), above. However, it is almost entirely in studies with working-class male subjects that any adverse effects of maternal employment have been found (Dits and Cambier, 1966; cited by Etaugh, 1973; Hoffman, 1963a; McCord *et al.*, 1963). In working-class families in some cultural backgrounds, maternal employment may lead sons to view their fathers as economic failures, and this may perhaps lead to sex-role anxiety (McCord *et al.*, 1963). However, in cultural backgrounds where the mother's economic contribution to family stability is accepted (e.g. black ghetto families) full-time maternal employment may be associated with better adjustment in the children (Woods, 1972). Satisfaction with work, feelings of guilt and anxiety, and role strain are all likely to differ with social class, and will influence the effect of the mother's employment on the child (see (c) below).

c) *The mother's emotional state*

i) Satisfaction with working. Where the mother is satisfied with working the effect on the child is more favourable than if she is dissatisfied (Kappell and Lambert, 1972, cited by Hoffman, 1974; Hoffman, 1963a; Woods, 1972). These findings appear to apply both within working and middle classes, but satisfaction with work is probably greater in the middle classes (Hoffman, 1963a; Nye, 1963b). However it should be noted that difference in adequacy of mothering was much greater between satisfied and dissatisfied non-working mothers than between satisfied and dissatisfied working mothers in one study (Yarrow *et al.*, 1962). Dissatisfied working mothers are working for family benefits, and they probably only feel frustrated when working is forced upon them by economic circumstances.

ii) Guilt. This is more likely in the middle class where the mother works for her own satisfaction rather than the family's economic advantage (Hoffman, 1963a; Yudkin and Holme, 1963, 1969). Guilt may induce, in highly educated mothers at least, attempts to compensate for working by setting aside time for activities with the child (Jones *et al.*, 1967; Yarrow *et al.*, 1962). However, it may also lead to overcompensation, with some adverse effects for the child.

iii) Role strain. Where full-time employment involves considerable role strain it may have a negative effect on the child (Kappel and Lambert, 1972, cited by Hoffman, 1974). Role strain is related to the adequacy of out of school supervision that can be arranged for the child (Jephcott *et al.*, 1962; Woods, 1972). Role strain occurs in all social classes, but not necessarily to the same extent.

d) *Adequacy of supervision*

i) The effect of adequacy of supervision in out-of-school hours has been investigated in only one study, of black American ten-year-old children (Woods, 1972). Girls who lacked adequate supervision were found to have more difficulty in school adjustment and boys to be less self-reliant than children with adequate supervision. This is a much neglected area, research being needed to investigate the effects of differences in amount, quality, type (neighbour, relatives, play centres) and stability of supervision for this age group.

ii) Adequacy of supervision may not only affect the child directly, but indirectly by its association with role conflict in the mother (Jephcott *et al.*, 1962; Woods, 1972).

e) *Age of child at onset and duration of maternal employment*

Very few studies have taken into account the child's age when the mother began working, or the length of time she has been working. In the study of a representative sample of British children (Davie *et al.*, 1972) school adjustment was found to be slightly worse at the age of seven than in children with non-employed mothers when the mother began work after the child had started school, but not when the mother was already employed before the child entered school. The adverse effect could be due to temporary adjustment difficulties, as Davie *et al.*, suggest. Nye (1963b) found that mothers' adjustment to children was worse in the first 15 months after beginning employment but then became better. The alternative explanation for the Davie *et al.*, findings is that less satisfactory arrangements were made for out-of-school supervision when the mother started work later.

177

f) *Part-time versus full-time employment*

This has been little investigated. Hoffman (1963b, 1974) suggests that part-time employment should have more favourable effects on the child as it involves less role conflict, less guilt and does not imply economic failure on the part of the father. However, in a study of British working-class primary-school-age children (Cartwright and Jefferys, 1958) no systematic differences were found between emotional adjustment in children with full- and part-time working mothers (the children with mothers in part-time employment tended to be more co-operative but also to have more 'nerves'). In contrast, in conditions where mother's employment is essential for family's economic survival, as in American black ghetto families, ten-year-olds were better adjusted when the mother worked full- rather than part-time (Woods, 1972). Findings from the few studies of secondary-school children which have investigated this question are also contradictory. Douvan (1963) found that girls, particularly those from the working-class, were better adjusted when the mother worked part- rather than full-time but middle-class boys were better adjusted in another study (Nelson, 1971) when the mother worked full-time. Probably greater contribution to the family's economic advantage and greater job satisfaction of full-time work act as counterbalancing factors against greater role strain involved – but further research is necessary.

The effects of kibbutz rearing

a) Early (Long *et al.*, 1973) and late (Antanovsky *et al.*, 1969, cited by Marcus, 1971; Jay and Birney, 1973) adolescents brought up in a kibbutz from birth are at least as well personally and socially adjusted as adolescents brought up in nuclear families. The latter study found no evidence that communal rearing results in excessive dependence on approval of the peer group (the kibbutz adolescents had significantly less need for approval, in fact, than those from a nearby agricultural village) or repression of individual expression and identity, as Bettleheim (1969) has suggested.

b) Kibbutz adolescents appeared to be no less identified with their parents than adolescents raised in traditional families (Long *et al.*, 1973).

3. Academic achievements

The effects of maternal employment

Overall, the evidence suggests that maternal employment makes relatively little difference to the child's educational attainments either at primary- or secondary-school level.

a) *Primary-school children*

i) Full-time maternal employment appears to have only negligible or very slight adverse effects on primary-school children from intact families, taking social class and family size into account (Davie *et al.*, 1972; Etaugh, 1974; Hoffman, 1963a). Findings from a representative sample of British children (Davie *et al.*, 1972) indicate that the very slight adverse effects of maternal employment found at the age of seven (three months in reading progress, one month in arithmetic progress) are mainly attributable to the mother having worked before the child reached school age. Findings of better educational performance in children with employed mothers in two British studies are possibly due to the high proportion of part-time employment amongst the mothers (see 'The effects of maternal employment – modifying factors' (c) below) but both studies had a number of methodological weaknesses, including a failure to take family size into account (families of working mothers tend to be smaller, and small families are associated with higher academic achievement (Douglas, 1964; Davie *et al.*, 1972) which probably caused the attainments of the children of the working mothers to be over-estimated.

ii) Non-intact families. Full-time maternal employment was found to be positively related to both reading and arithmetic attainment in illegitimate children or those living with their widowed mothers in the National Children's Bureau study of one-parent families (Ferri, 1976).

b) *Secondary-school children*

Both girls (Keidel, 1970; Nelson, 1969; Roy, 1963) and boys (Keidel, 1970; Nelson, 1969; Roy, 1963) of secondary-school age from intact families whose mothers are employed generally differ little in academic achievements from children of similar socio-economic backgrounds whose mothers are not employed. However, there is some indication that maternal employment may have some adverse effects on the academic achievements of boys from a middle-class background (Brown, 1970, cited by Etaugh; Banducci, 1967). Studies of secondary-school children may over-estimate achievements of children of working mothers, as family size was not controlled. This possibly accounts for finding higher achievement in one study among working-class boys with employed mothers (Banducci, 1967).

The effects of maternal employment – modifying factors

a) *Mother's occupational status*

Children whose mothers hold professional positions have higher academic achievements than children from the same socio-economic level whose mothers have non-professional occupations, or who do not work. This appears to be due to the mothers' higher education (Frankel, 1964; Jones *et al.*, 1967), to their conscious attempts to spend more time in activities with the child (it is not clear if this is associated with the mothers' occupational status or her educational level) (Jones *et al.*, 1967), and possibly to their greater satisfaction with work compared with non-professional women (Frankel, 1964).

b) *Adequacy of out-of-school supervision.*
Only one study (Woods, 1972) has examined this. Inadequate supervision was found to have deleterious effects on the cognitive development of black ten-year-old American girls, but not boys, attending school in a ghetto area. Perhaps the distinction between adequate and inadequate supervision is somewhat blurred in this neighbourhood, most boys spending out-of-school hours with their peer group, and having some informal contacts with adults. Studies are needed to examine the effects of the adequacy, quality and type of out-of-school supervision on the academic achievements of children from different social backgrounds.

c) *Part-time versus full-time employment*
There is some indication that part-time rather than full-time employment is slightly more favourable to reading achievements in the primary school-age child (Cartwright and Jeffery's 1958; Davie *et al.*, 1972). In the former study, children whose mothers were employed part-time were assessed by teachers as being higher in reading ability than children whose mothers were not working, but these findings do not take into account family size and it is difficult to interpret them. In contrast, black American ten-year-old ghetto children made better intellectual progress when the mother worked full- rather than part-time (Woods, 1972) – maternal employment is essential to family well-being in these families, and in such circumstances full-time employment appears to be more favourable for intellectual achievements. The one study (Nelson, 1969) which investigated the question of part-time maternal employment for children in the secondary-school-age group, found no differences in academic achievement between those whose mothers were employed full-, part-time or not at all, but further investigation is needed.

Discussion

Are there age differences in the effects of maternal employment?

When a child reaches five years of age, he starts going to school and his care is then necessarily shared between his parents and school-teachers. How important is it, though, for the child's mother to be available as soon as he comes home from school, and for her to be able to look after him herself in the holidays? Evidence is surprisingly scarce. It is true that there is an abundance of studies dealing with the question of the effects of maternal employment on the child. Most, though, have subjects who are older adolescents. While the need for parental interest and attention in this age group should not be under-estimated, there are obvious differences between the needs of a six-year-old and a fifteen-year-old, both for physical care and in the time that can be spent alone without adult supervision. The difference in the need for care of the two age groups is also likely to affect the mother's attitude to her employment – the mother of the young child is more likely to feel guilty about working and to be harassed by her dual role. Most of the studies with adolescents as subjects choose them on the basis of the mother's current working status, with little regard for her employment history during the child's primary school years. Even the few studies which have made a sharp demarcation, insisting that the criterion of the non-employed mother should be that she has never worked during the child's life, do not also insist that the employed mother should have been working in the earlier part of the child's school career (Nelson, 1969, 1971; Propper, 1972). Taken together, the findings of the studies with adolescents as subjects are consistent enough for it to be concluded, at least, that maternal employment has few, if any, adverse effects for most children in this age range. They can give very little indication, though, of the effects of maternal employment on children in the primary school age range.

Findings from the few studies which have been carried out on children at the primary school stage are mixed, some suggesting that there are no adverse effects of maternal employment on adjustment or attainments (Cartwright and Jefferys, 1958), and others suggesting that there may be such effects (Dits and Cambier, 1966, cited by Etaugh, 1974; Singh, 1970). Some clarification is possible from evidence of the National Child Development Study (Davie et al., 1972), which has as its subjects a representative sample of British children and which is the only study adequately to incorporate into its research design allowances for social class and family size effects. The evidence is clear here that educational attainments are not markedly affected by the mother working after the child enters school (although they are slightly affected by her working before this stage – see previous section); social adjustment in school, in contrast, is not adversely affected at all when the mother is already working before the child enters school but there are some slightly adverse effects when she starts working after the child begins school. Two possible explanations are suggested by the authors. The child whose mother was employed before he started school could already have adjusted to her working; or previous arrangements for substitute care could be more or less retained for the child whose mother worked before he was five, while arrangements for the child whose mother started working later could be less stable, or adequate, and sometimes, perhaps, even non-existent. The implication from this research is then that the mother's absence for an hour or two after school, and during the working day in the holidays need not have adverse effects, at least after a period of initial adjustment, provided that adequate care is given by someone else. Confirmation is needed, of course, from research which compares adequately and inadequately supervised children with those of non-employed mothers, and which examines home as well as school adjustment.

Adequate versus inadequate supervision

It is remarkable, when there is so much concern about the effect of maternal absence on the child, that only one study has in fact investigated whether adequately supervised children have better adjustment or attainments than inadequately supervised children (Woods, 1972) and even here no comparison was made with children whose mothers were not working. Findings confirmed that girls who were adequately supervised had better cognitive development and school relationships, though boys appeared to be little affected. Nevertheless, there was one interesting difference between the two groups of boys, those with inadequate supervision being less self-reliant. Possibly inadequate supervision gives the boy a feeling of insecurity, and perhaps makes him feel he is somewhat rejected by his mother. There is other evidence of boys (but not girls – there seem to be compensating factors for them – Hoffman 1963b) showing dependent behaviour where family relationships are insecure and maternal employment may be perceived by the child as evidence of rejection (McCord et al., 1963). Possibly the difference in adjustment between adequately and inadequately supervised children would be greater in other cultural backgrounds. The subjects of Woods' study were black American ten-year-olds from a ghetto area, and there is some indication that the distinction between adequate and inadequate supervision was somewhat blurred here (correlation between the children's and mothers' reports of adequacy of supervision was significant but low) – perhaps the children, particularly the boys, tended to spend their out of school hours with the peer group, whatever formal arrangements were made. Further studies are needed for children from different social groups which examine not only the effects of presence or absence of adult supervision, but also of the quality, stability and type of supervision.

Adequacy of supervision is important not only for the direct effects it may have on the child but also because it contributes to the amount of strain experienced by the mother in her dual role (Jephcott *et al.*, 1962; Woods, 1972). Problems of adequate supervision arrangements occur in all social classes and there is evidence of the care taken in making arrangements by mothers from both professional- (Fogarty *et al.*, 1971) and working-class backgrounds (Jephcott *et al.*, 1962). However, the problem is perhaps greater for working-class mothers who may have to work longer hours, and who do not have the paid domestic help still enjoyed by some middle-class women; some working-class mothers may be forced into work by economic circumstances even when dissatisfied with the arrangements available to them.

While out-of-school supervision is undoubtedly a major problem for working mothers, some arrangements may possibly have some positive benefits. The experience the child gains of other adults, and the reinforcement of relationships between families when out of school supervision is provided by relatives, neighbours or friends, may be advantageous to both child and family. However, no research evidence is available here.

The effects of maternal employment on family life

In quite a high proportion of families (Yudkin and Holme, 1963, 1969) it is the father who acts as child-minder in after school hours. In some circumstances, this cannot be regarded as an altogether satisfactory arrangement — for example, where the mother works an evening shift — for it means that the whole family will have very little time to spend together (Yudkin and Holme, 1963, 1969).

Evidence is conflicting on whether the father tends to take a greater part in child-care activities when the mother works. Greater involvement of the father has been reported in studies of British working-class families (Jephcott *et al.*, 1962; Yudkin and Holme, 1963, 1969) and of British (Fogarty *et al.*, 1971) and American (Jones *et al.*, 1967; Yarrow *et al.*, 1962) middle-class families, or at least in those in which the mother has higher education. Findings from the National Child Development Study, using a representative sample of British children, are contradictory (Lambert and Hart, 1976). For the age group in the study (eleven-year-olds) at least, the relationship between greater father participation and maternal employment (part-time in two out of three cases) disappeared when family size and social class were taken into account. The question needs further investigation for children of different ages, particularly where the mother is employed full-time. Where the father does take an increased part in child-care activities it is likely to be beneficial both to family life (Jephcott et al., 1962) and the child's development (see Part III).

Employed mothers do not necessarily spend any less time in attentive interaction with their children than non-employed mothers (Howell, 1973). Where the mother has higher education she may set aside time for planned activities with the child (Jones et al., 1967; Yarrow et al., 1962). It cannot be assumed, though, that all employed mothers will be able to spend as much time with the child, even if they recognise the child's need for interaction with the parents, rather than simply for good physical care. Full-time employment provides many working-class mothers with over-crowded timetables which leave little room for extra attention to the child (Jephcott et al., 1962). Of course, although attempts to spend more time with the child may be beneficial, there is also the danger that compensation may turn into over-compensation and over-protection. There is some evidence of such a pattern occurring among mothers, who are most likely to be middle-class (Hoffman, 1963a), working for their own self-fulfilment.

Provided that there is adequate out-of-school supervision, it seems that the primary-school child should not, in general, suffer adverse effects from maternal employment. There is some danger, though, of guilt leading to over-compensation, particularly among middle-class mothers; alternatively, and perhaps particularly among working-class mothers, there may be insufficient time to spend with the child, and possibly less involvement with him. On the other hand, there may be the positive benefits of the father taking more interest in child care, and of the family as a whole sharing more activities together. There is some evidence that the child does not benefit if a mother who would prefer to be working stays at home – dissatisfied housewives appear to be less adequate as mothers than either satisfied housewives or satisfied employed mothers (Yarrow et al., 1962). Working tends to enhance a mother's self-esteem (Birnbaum, 1971; Jephcott et al., 1962; Nye, 1963c) and this could also increase adequacy of mothering. This does not imply, of course, that all mothers should work. Children of employed mothers who would prefer not to work appear to be lower in adjustment (Woods, 1972) and self-esteem (Kappell and Lambert, 1972, cited by Hoffman, 1974) than children of working mothers who prefer to work; also the satisfied housewife made the most adequate mother of all in the Yarrow et al., (1962) study. No mother should be forced to work to obtain an adequate income for the family. However, provision of facilities for out-of-school supervision where satisfactory informal arrangements cannot be made, would not only be of direct benefit to the child but would help to remove some of the role strain and guilt experienced by working mothers who enjoy working.

Annotations

(In Part II of the review only a few studies of particular relevance to the issue of shared care have been selected for annotation. A number of other studies mentioned have been annotated in other parts of the review. The location of annotations is indicated in the reference list at the end of Part II, page 190).

BLEHAR, M. C. 1974. 'Anxious attachment and defensive reactions associated with day care', *Child Development* 45, 3, 683–92.

A study designed to investigate whether full-time day care affects the quality of a child's attachment to his mother. The behaviour of twenty middle-class, day-care children (ten three-year-olds and ten four-year-olds) and twenty home-reared children similar in social class and age was observed in an Ainsworth and Wittig (see Part I, p. 83) type of 'strange situation'. The child is subjected to being left alone with a stranger and then entirely alone in an unfamiliar environment. At the time of testing the day-care subjects had experienced group care for about four-and-a-half months on average. The ratio of care-takers to the younger children was 1:8 or 1:6, depending on the nursery. Compared with the home-reared children, day-care children cried more during separation from the mother and showed more avoidance of the stranger. The older day-care children sought more proximity to and contact with the mother upon reunion than their home-reared counterparts, though this was mixed with resistance and avoidance. The younger day-care children, compared with the home-care controls, showed more proximity and interaction-avoiding behaviour on reunion. It is suggested by the author that the brief separations involved in day care are responsible for the detachment on reunion with the mother found for the younger children and the anxious ambivalent behaviour of the older children. Differences could, though, have existed between the two groups in the quality of the attachment to the mother prior to the day-care experience. The mothers of the day- and home-care children were not distinguished by the stimulation they provided for their children or the empathy they showed, both of which appear to be necessary antecedents of 'secure' attachment but they may possibly have differed in more subtle dimensions of behaviour.

CALDWELL, B. M., WRIGHT, C. M., HONIG, A. S. and

TANNENBAUM, J. 1970. 'Infant day care and attachment', *American Journal of Orthopsychiatry* 40, 3, 397–412.

An investigation of whether there are any differences in attachment to the mother between children who have experienced day care from an early age and those who have been cared for at home. The forty-one subjects, mainly from lower-class families, were aged two-and-a-half at the time of the study; twenty-three had been cared for at home from birth and eighteen had entered day care when they were about one year old. The day-care centre was of very high quality, aiming to provide sufficient and appropriate stimulation for the child's level of development and a warm and enjoyable atmosphere. The care-taker/child ratio was approximately 1:4.

Children's attachment to their mothers was measured by rating their behaviour towards their mothers (as observed during interviews with the mothers at which the children were present and from maternal reports) on seven scales. High ratings on six of the scales – affiliation, nurturance, permissiveness, dependency, happiness and emotionality, and low ratings on the seventh, hostility – were interpreted as indicating strong attachment. The home- and day-care children were found not to differ on any of the ratings devised to test the child's relationship with his mother. The two groups were also rated on their relationship to other people and were found to differ only on the dependency scale, on which the day-care children had slightly higher ratings. Dependency on this scale connotes proximity-seeking rather than help-seeking and a possible interpretation of the findings is that the day-care children had greater enjoyment of interaction with people. Another possible interpretation (suggested to the authors by Bowlby), is that the greater dependency might be indicative of 'over-anxious' attachment. The two groups of mothers were rated on the same scales, the only difference found being that the day-care mothers were less permissive. There was also an association between a child's attachment to his mother and the level of stimulation provided by the home.

MOORE, T. W. 1975. 'Exclusive early mothering and its alternatives' *Scandanavian Journal of Psychology* 16, 255–72.

A longitudinal investigation comparing the effects on personality development of exclusive care by the mother throughout the pre-school years and of care that is diffused among several care-takers. The total sample consisted of 167 London children, reasonably respresentative of a socially mixed urban area. At various ages, up to fifteen, the children were tested by a psychologist, their behaviour was rated by their mothers, and the mothers were interviewed about their children; in the earlier years various aspects of the mothers' personalities and attitudes towards their children were rated by two psychologists and by means of an attitude questionnaire.

The exclusively mothered boys had a tendency towards sensitive, fastidious conformity, timidity and academic interests, which became more marked as they grew older. The diffusely mothered boys tended to be characterised by fearless, aggressive non-conformity and social and athletic interests, although they also showed some anxiety about parental approval. The differences between the two groups of girls were much less clear-cut. The outcomes could possibly be due to the personalities of the mothers who chose a particular type of regime rather than the regimes themselves. On investigation it was found that mothers of the exclusively mothered boys tended to be more anxious and ego-involved with their children but boys' behaviour characteristics correlated significantly with type of regime in the main rather than with personality characteristics of the mother. Nor can the difference in outcome be attributed to pre-existing characteristics in the children which might have influenced choice of regime for the two groups did not differ in behaviour in early infancy. Differences in behaviour began to emerge at about three when many children entered nursery schools. Although there was a marginally significant tendency for diffusely mothered boys and exclusively mothered girls to develop more rapidly in intelligence up to the age of eight, no differences were found in later years. The exclusively mothered children, though, particularly the boys, tended to read better, especially when mental age was held constant.

Sub-groups of the main sample give some indication of the effects of unstable substitute care, very early substitute care, and group versus individual substitute care, although the children were only followed up until they were six years old, due to sample loss. The fifteen children who had experienced three or more substitute care regimes compared with those who had only one or two were found to be more insecure and emotionally dependent at the age of six. The fifteen children placed in substitute care before they were two, compared with fifteen placed at three or four, also showed insecurity and emotional dependency, but all except four had also experienced a number of changes of regime. Some mothers who had placed their children very early in daily substitute care knew less about their development. Fifteen children who had attended nursery school were less fearful and more assertive than the children in individual substitute care. The nursery-school children had a temporary increase in fears of people and separation between the ages of three and four but they gained in confidence in their fifth and sixth years.

RICCIUTI, H. R. 1974. 'Fear and the development of social attachments in the first year of life', in M. Lewis and L. A. Rosenblum (eds) *The Origins of Fear*, Wiley, New York. 74–106.

An investigation of the effects of day-care experiences from as early as the second or third month of life on an infant's response in an unfamiliar setting to a brief separation from the mother, to a stranger, and to the familiar nursery care-giver. Monthly assessments using structured procedures of middle-class infants in half-day (about four hours), high-quality group care (one care-giver to two or three infants) showed that responses to both a stranger and the care-giver in the mother's presence were moderately positive up to eight months. Beginning at this age, responses to a stranger's approach became neutral or slightly negative, though only one or two children showed clearly negative responses while those to the care-taker generally continued to be positive. From seven months, infants showed increasing distress when left with a stranger on the mother's departure but responses on being left with the care-giver were neutral except at twelve months. Infants also showed distress when the the care-giver left them alone with a stranger. The care-giver's presence ameliorated reactions to a stranger but not to the same extent as the mother's presence. Findings of this longitudinal investigation then indicate that infants experiencing high-quality, half-day care begin to use the care-giver as an alternate attachment figure, though not equivalent to the mother, from seven months or so.

The second and third experiments, using an identical assessment procedure, showed that one-year-old, day-care (full- and part-time) and non-day care infants did not differ in their reactions to a stranger's approach in the mother's presence, though day-care infants were more negative in their reactions to the stranger after the mother's departure. In the fourth experiment which took place in a 'naturalistic' playroom setting, twelve- to nineteen-months-old infants with day-care experience were more willing than those without to move away from the mother towards a teacher and a small group of pre-school children and were less inclined to follow the mother when she moved momentarily out of sight into an adjoining space. Findings that the day-care children reacted with greater distress to the stranger's approach in the mother's absence are similar to those of Blehar (1974). Blehar's interpretation of her findings was that day care resulted in a more insecure or ambivalent attachment to the mother. An alternative explanation for the findings of the present study is that the experience was more incongruous for the day-care children. On arrival with their mothers at the usual site they were taken to a strange laboratory rather than their familiar nursery and were then left with a stranger rather than their familiar care-giver. The more positive approaches made by the day-care children to the strange adult and pre-school group in a more naturalistic setting support this explanation, but further investigation of this question is needed.

SCHWARZ, J. C., STRICKLAND, R. G. and KROLICK, G. 1974.

'Infant day care: behavioral effects at preschool age', *Developmental Psychology* 10, 4, 502–6.

A comparison of the social behaviour of two groups of three- to four-year-old infants attending a new day-care centre, one group with experience of day care from an early age (about nine months) and the other with no previous regular day-care experience (but some with experience of individual substitute care). The children were rated on nine traits by their teachers four months after entry and by independent observers eight months after entry. The early day-care group were rated less co-operative with adults, more physically and verbally aggressive with peers and adults and as more inclined to run about. There were no significant differences between the groups in ability to get along with peers, in spontaneity, or in problem solving success, ability to abstract and planfulness. It is unlikely that the differences which were found between the groups are due to pre-existing differences in maternal behaviour as both groups of mothers eventually selected day care for their children. The nineteen lower- and middle-class infants in each group were matched in pairs on sex, ethnic group, age, parents' occupation and education.

WOODS, M. B. 1972. 'The unsupervised child of the working mother', *Developmental Psychology* 6, 1, 14–25.

An investigation of whether or not maternal employment and the supervision arrangements made for the child in the mother's absence, have significant effects on the children's development. Subjects were 106 ten-year-olds, 95 per cent black, attending a black ghetto school in North Philadelphia. Psychological tests were administered to the children and other information about their development was obtained from teachers' ratings, and school, hospital and police records; thirty-eight of the mothers were also interviewed.

Unsupervised girls (during breakfast, lunch or after school, or during school holidays) had poorer intelligence test scores and school achievement than supervised girls. Supervised and unsupervised boys differed little in intelligence test scores, school achievement or personality adjustment but the unsupervised boys tended to be less self-reliant. Information obtained from the interviews with the mothers was used as the basis of a cluster analysis. Surprisingly, mothers who were employed full- rather than part-time, and who were absent from home before school, during lunch and after school had children whose school and social adjustment was the best and intelligence scores the highest. Children who had extensive household responsibilities also tended to do well at school. Mothers who enjoyed working had children with high personality adjustment scores. Mothers who had adequate substitutes available when they were absent from home felt little role conflict about working. The children's statements about the extent of adult supervision available had a low, though significant, correlation with the mothers' statements about the quality and quantity of supervision available.

Findings of this study suggest that the effects of maternal employment on the children will differ in middle- and lower-class families. Where maternal employment is essential for family survival and well-being, it will be viewed favourably by the husband, wife and children, and will have favourable effects on the children's development providing that adequate substitute care is available.

References

(When titles are annotated, this is indicated at the end of the entry by the relevant page number printed in bold type.)

AINSWORTH, M. D. S. 1963. 'The development of infant-mother interaction among the Ganda', in B. M. Foss (ed) *Determinants of Infant Behaviour II*, Methuen, London. 67–112. **p. 81**

AINSWORTH, M. D. S. 1964. 'Patterns of attachment behavior shown by the infant in interaction with the mother', *Merrill-Palmer Quarterly* 10, 51–8.

AINSWORTH, M. D. S. 1967. *Infancy in Uganda: Infant Care and the Growth of Love*, Johns Hopkins Press, Baltimore. 471 pp. **p. 82**

AINSWORTH, M. D. S. 1973. 'The development of infant-mother attachment', in B. M. Caldwell and H. N. Ricciuti (eds) *Review of Child Development Research. III*, University of Chicago Press, Chicago. 1–94.

AINSWORTH, M. D. S. and WITTIG, B. A. 1969. 'Attachment and exploratory behaviour of one year olds in a strange situation', in B. M. Foss (ed) *Determinants of Infant Behaviour, IV*, Methuen, London. 111–36. **p. 83**

BAN, P. L. and LEWIS, M. 1974. 'Mothers and fathers, girls and boys: attachment behavior in the one year old', *Merrill-Palmer Quarterly* 20, 3, 195–204. **p. 85**

BANDUCCI, R. 1967. 'The effect of mother's employment on the achievement, aspirations and expectations of the child', *Personnel and Guidance Journal* 46, 263–7.

BETTELHEIM, B. 1969. *The Children of the Dream*, Thames and Hudson, London; Avon Books, New York. 363 pp.

BLEHAR, M. C. 1974. 'Anxious attachment and defensive reactions associated with day care', *Child Development* 45, 3, 683–92. **p. 185**

BIRNBAUM, J. A. 1971. *Life Patterns, Personality Style and Self-esteem in*

Gifted Family Oriented and Career Committed Women. Unpublished doctoral dissertation, University of Michigan.

BOTTRILL, J. 1968. 'Effects of pre-school experience on school readiness level of privileged and under-privileged children', *Durham Research Review* 6, 21, 303–4.

BOWLBY, J. 1951, 1966. *Maternal Care and Mental Health*, Schocken, New York. 194 pp.

BOWLBY, J. 1969. *Attachment and Loss, I. Attachment*, Hogarth Press, London; Basic Books, New York. 428 pp.

BRAUN, S. J. and CALDWELL, B. M. 1973. 'Emotional adjustment of children in day care who enrolled prior to or after the age of three', *Early Child Development and Care* 2, 1, 13–21.

BRONFENBRENNER, U. 1974. *A Report on Longitudinal Evaluations of Preschool Programs, II. Is Early Intervention Effective?* DHEW Publication No. OHD 74–25, US Department of Health, Education and Welfare. 60 pp.

BROOKHART, J. and HOCK, E. 1976. 'The effects of experimental context and experiential background on infants' behavior towards their mothers and a stranger', *Child Development* 47, 2, 333–40.

BROWN, A. W. and HUNT, R. G. 1961. 'Relations between nursery school attendance and teachers' ratings of some aspects of children's adjustment in the kindergarten', *Child Development* 32, 585–96.

BROWN, G. W., BROLCHAIN, M. N. and HARRIS, T. 1975. 'Social class and psychiatric disturbance among women in an urban population', *Sociology* 9, 2, 225–54.

BURCHINAL, L. G. 1963. 'Personality characteristics of children', in F. I. Nye and L. W. Hoffman, (eds) *The Employed Mother in America*, Rand McNally, Chicago. 106–21.

CALDWELL, B. M. 1973. 'Can young children have a quality life in day care?', *Young Children* 28, 197–208.

CALDWELL, B. M. and SMITH, L. E. 1970. 'Day care for the very young – prime opportunity for primary prevention', *American Journal of Public Health* 60, 4, 690–7.

CALDWELL, B. M., WRIGHT, C. M., HONIG, A. S. and TANNENBAUM, J. 1970. 'Infant day care and attachment', *American Journal of Orthopsychiatry* 40, 3, 397–412. **pp. 185–6**

CARTWRIGHT, A. and JEFFREYS, M. 1958. 'Married women who work: their own and their children's health', *British Journal of Social and Preventive Medicine* 12, 4, 159–71.

COHEN, L. and BAGSHAW, D. 1973. 'A comparison of the achievements of nursery school and non-nursery school children', *Durham Research Review* 6, 30, 735–42. **p. 389**

191

COHEN, L. J. and CAMPOS, J. J. 1974. 'Father, mother and stranger as elicitors of attachment behaviors in infancy', *Developmental Psychology* 10, 1, 146–54. **p. 88**

DAVIE, R., BUTLER, N. and GOLDSTEIN, H. 1972. *From Birth to Seven*, Longman in association with National Children's Bureau, London; Humanities Press, Atlantic Highlands, NJ. 42–7. **p. 312**

DINNAGE, R. and PRINGLE, M. L. K. 1967. *Residential Child Care – Facts and Fallacies*, Longman in association with National Bureau for Co-operation in Child Care (now National Children's Bureau), London; Humanities Press, Atlantic Highlands, NJ. 344 pp.

DOUGLAS, J. W. B. 1964, 1967. *The Home and the School*, MacGibbon and Kee, London. 224 pp.

DOUGLAS, J. W. B. and ROSS, J. M. 1964. 'The later educational and emotional adjustment of children who went to nursery schools or classes', *Educational Research* 7, 1, 73–80.

DOUGLAS, J. W. B., ROSS, J. M. and SIMPSON, H. R. 1968, 1971. *All Our Future*, Peter Davies, London. 252 pp.

DOUVAN, E. 1963. 'Employment and the adolescent', in F. I. Nye and L. W. Hoffman (eds) *The Employed Mother in America*, Rand McNally, Chicago. 142–64.

DOYLE, A. 1975. 'Infant development in day care', *Developmental Psychology* 11, 5, 655–6.

ETAUGH, C. 1974. 'Effects of maternal employment on children: a review of recent research', *Merrill-Palmer Quarterly* 20, 2, 71–8.

EXPERT COMMITTEE ON MENTAL HEALTH, 1951. Report on the second session. Technical Report Series no 31. WHO Monograph, Geneva.

FELDMAN, S. S. and INGHAM, M. E. 1975. 'Attachment behavior: a validation study in two age groups', *Child Development* 46, 2, 319–30.

FERRI, E. 1976. *Growing up in a One-Parent Family*, NFER Pub. Co. Slough; Humanities Press, Atlantic Highlands, NJ. 196 pp. **p. 221**

FOGARTY, M. P., RAPOPORT, R. and RAPOPORT, R. N. 1971. *Sex, Career and Family*, Allen and Unwin for P. E. P., London; Sage Publications Inc., Beverly Hills, Calif. 581 pp.

FOWLER, W. 1972. 'A developmental learning approach to infant care in a group setting', *Merrill-Palmer Quarterly* 18, 2, 145–75.

FRANKE, H. B. 1972. 'A comparison of perceived parental behavior characteristics of eighth grade children of working and non-working mothers', *Dissertation Abstracts International* 32, 10–A, 5544–5.

FRANKEL, E. 1964. 'Characteristics of working and non-working mothers among intellectually gifted high and low achievers', *Personnel and Guidance Journal* 42, 8, 776–80.

192

GARBER, H. and HEBER, R. 1973. 'The Milwaukee Project: early intervention as a technique to prevent mental retardation', The University of Connecticut Technical Paper. National Leadership Institute. 11 pp.

GOLDEN, M. and BIRNS, B. 1968. 'Social class and cognitive development in infancy', *Merrill-Palmer Quarterly* 14, 2, 139–49.

GORNICKI, B. 1964. 'The development of children in the family and in day care centres in Poland', in World Health Organisation *Care of Children in Day Centres*, WHO, Geneva. 112–37.

HEBER, R., GARBER, H., HARINGTON, S., HOFFMAN, C. and FALENDER, C. 1972. *Rehabilitation of Families at Risk for Mental Retardation*, Rehabilitation Research and Training Center in Mental Retardation, University of Wisconsin, Madison. 247 pp.

HOFFMAN, L. W. 1963a. 'Mother's enjoyment of work and effects on the child', in F. I. Nye and L. W. Hoffman, *The Employed Mother in America*, Rand McNally, Chicago. 95–105.

HOFFMAN, L. W. 1963b. 'Effects on children: summary and discussion', in F. I. Nye and L. W. Hoffman, *The Employed Mother in America*, Rand McNally, Chicago. 190–212.

HOFFMAN, L. W. 1974. 'Effects of maternal employment on the child – a review of research', *Developmental Psychology* 10, 2, 204–28.

HOWELL, M. C. 1973. 'Employed mothers and their families (I)', *Pediatrics* 52, 2, 252–63.

JACKSON, S. 1974. *Educational Implications of Unsatisfactory Childminding*, Child Minding Research Unit, London. 7 pp.

JAY, J. and BIRNEY, R. C. 1971. 'Research findings on the kibbutz adolescent: a response to Bettelheim', *American Journal of Orthopsychiatry* 43, 3, 347–54.

JEPHCOTT, P. et al, 1962. *Married Women Working*, Allen and Unwin, London (Especially Chapter IX 'The children'). 208 pp.

JONES, J. B., LUNDSTEEN, S. W. and MICHAEL, W. B. 1967. 'The relationship of the professional employment status of mothers to reading achievement of sixth grade children', *California Journal of Educational Research* 18, 2, 102–8.

KAFFMAN, M. 1965. 'A comparison of psychopathology: Israeli children from kibbutz and from urban surroundings', *American Journal of Orthopsychiatry* 35, 3, 509–20.

KEIDEL, K. C. 1970. 'Maternal employment and ninth grade achievement in Bismarck, North Dakota', *Family Coordinator* 19, 95–7.

KOHEN-RAZ, R. 1968. 'Mental and motor development of kibbutz, institutionalised and home-reared infants in Israel', *Child Development* 39, 489–504.

LAMB, M. E. 1975. 'The sociability of two year olds with their mothers and fathers', *Child Psychiatry and Human Development* 5, 3, 182–8.

LAMB, M. E. 1976. 'Twelve month olds and their parents: interaction in a laboratory playroom', *Developmental Psychology* 12, 3, 237–44.

LAMBERT, L. and HART, S. 1976. 'Who needs a father?' *New Society* 37, 718, 80.

LONG, B. H., HENDERSON, E. H. and PLATT, L. 1973. 'Self-other orientations of Israeli adolescents reared in kibbutzim and moshavim', *Developmental Psychology* 8, 2, 300–8.

MACCOBY, E. E. and FELDMAN, S. S. 1972. 'Mother-attachment and stranger-reactions in the third year of life', *Monographs of the Society for Research in Child Development*, Serial no. 146, 37, 1, 86 pp.

McCORD, J., McCORD, W. and THURBER, E. 1963. 'Effects of maternal employment on lower-class boys', *Journal of Abnormal and Social Psychology* 67, 2, 177–82.

MARCUS, J. 1971. 'Early child development in kibbutz group care', *Early Child Development and Care* 1, 1, 67–98.

MEAD, M. 1966. 'A cultural anthropologist's approach to maternal deprivation', in M. D. Ainsworth *et al*, (eds) *Deprivation of Maternal Care: A Reassessment of its Effects*, Schocken, New York. 237–54.

MILLER, F. J. S., COURT, S. D. M., KNOX, E. G. and BRANDON, S. 1974. *The School Years in Newcastle upon Tyne, 1952–1962*, Oxford University Press, London. 362 pp.

MOORE, T. W. 1963, 1969. 'Effects on the children: (b) a report from the Child Study Centre', in S. Yudkin and A. Holme, *Working Mothers and Their Children*, Michael Joseph, London. 105–24.

MOORE, T. 1964. 'Children of full-time and part-time mothers', *International Journal of Social Psychiatry*, Special Congress Issue No. 2, 1–10.

MOORE, T. W. 1968. 'Language and intelligence: a longitudinal study of the first eight years, II: Environmental correlates of mental growth', *Human Development* 11, 1–24.

MOORE, T. W. 1972a. 'The later outcome of early care by the mother and substitute daily regimes', in F. J. Monks (ed) *Determinants of Behavioral Development*, Academic Press, New York. 401–10.

MOORE, T. W. 1972b. *Patterns of Early Care and Their Outcome to Adolescence*, paper given to psychological section of CIE meeting, London, February 1972.

MOORE, T. W. 1975. 'Exclusive early mothering and its alternatives: the outcome to adolescence', *Scandinavian Journal of Psychology* 16, 3, 255–72.
p. 186

194

NELSON, D. D. 1969. 'A study of school achievement among adolescent children with working and non-working mothers', *Journal of Educational Research* 62, 10, 456–8.

NELSON, D. D. 1971. 'A study of personality adjustment among adolescent children with working and non-working mothers', *Journal of Educational Research* 64, 328–30.

NYE, F. I. 1963a. 'The adjustment of adolescent children', in F. I. Nye and L. W. Hoffman, *The Employed Mother in America*, Rand McNally, Chicago, 133–41.

NYE, F. I. 1963b. 'Adjustment to children', in F. I. Nye and L. W. Hoffman, *The Employed Mother in America*, Rand McNally, Chicago. 353–62.

NYE, F. I. 1963c. 'Adjustment of the mother: summary and a frame of reference', *The Employed Mother in America*, Rand McNally, Chicago. 384–399.

NYE, F. I., PERRY, J. B. and OGLES, R. H. 1963. 'Anxiety and anti-social behavior in preschool children', in F. I. Nye and L. W. Hoffman, *The Employed Mother in America*, Rand McNally, Chicago. 82–94.

PERRY, J. B. Jnr. 1961. 'The mother substitutes of employed mothers: an exploratory inquiry', *Marriage and Family Living* 23, 362–7.

PETERSON, E. T. 1961. 'The impact of maternal employment on the mother-daughter relationship', *Marriage and Family Living* 23, 355–61.

POWELL, K. S. 1963. 'Personalities of children and child-rearing attitudes of mothers', in F. I. Nye and L. W. Hoffman, *The Employed Mother in America*, Rand McNally, Chicago. 125–32.

PRINGLE, M. L. K. 1971. *Deprivation and Education* (2nd ed.), Longman in association with National Bureau for Co-operation in Child Care (now National Children's Bureau), London; Humanities Press, Atlantic Highlands, NJ. 305 pp.

PRINGLE, M. L. K. and NAIDOO, S. 1975. *Early Child Care in Britain*, Gordon and Breach, London. 175 pp.

PROPPER, A. M. 1972. 'The relationship of maternal employment to adolescent roles, activities and parental relationships', *Journal of Marriage and the Family* 34, 417–21.

RABIN, A. I. 1958. 'Behavior research in collective settlements in Israel: 6. Infants and children under conditions of "intermittent" mothering in the kibbutz', *American Journal of Orthopsychiatry* 28, 3, 577–86.

RABIN, A. I. 1959. 'Attitudes of kibbutz children to family and parents', *American Journal of Orthopsychiatry* 29, 1, 172–9.

RAMEY, C. T., MILLS, P., CAMPBELL, F. A. and O'BRIEN, C. 1975. 'Infants' home environments: a comparison of high-risk families and families from the general population', *American Journal of Mental Deficiency* 80, 1, 40–2.

RAPH, J. B., THOMAS, A., CHESS, S. and KORN, S. J. 1968. 'The influence of nursery school on social interactions', *American Journal of Orthopsychiatry* 38, 144–52.

195

RICCIUTI, H. N. 1974. 'Fear and the development of social attachments in the first year of life', in M. Lewis and L. A. Rosenblum (eds) *The Origins of Fear*, Wiley, New York. 73–106. **p. 187**

RICHMAN, N. 1974. 'The effects of housing on pre-school children and their mothers', *Developmental Medicine and Child Neurology* 16, 1, 53–8.

RICHMAN, N. 1976. 'Depression in mothers of preschool children', *Journal of Child Psychology and Psychiatry* 17, 1, 75–8.

ROBINSON, H. B. and ROBINSON, N. M. 1971. 'Longitudinal development of very young children in a comprehensive day care program: the first two years', *Child Development* 42, 1673–83.

ROY, P. 1963. 'Adolescent roles: rural-urban differentials', in F. I. Nye and L. W. Hoffman, *The Employed Mother in America*, Rand McNally, Chicago. 165–81.

RUTTER, M. 1972. *Maternal Deprivation Reassessed*, Penguin, London. 175 pp.

SALTZ, R. 1973. 'Effects of part-time "mothering" on IQ and SQ of young institutionalized children', *Child Development* 44, 1, 166–70. **p. 97**

SAUNDERS, M. M. 1972. 'Some aspects of the effects of day care on infants' emotional and personality development', *Dissertation Abstracts International* 33, 4–b, 1805.

SCHAFFER, H. R. and EMERSON, P. E. 1964. 'The development of social attachments in infancy', *Monographs of the Society for Research in Child Development*, Serial no. 94, 29, 3, 77 pp. **p. 97**

SCHWARZ, J. C., KROLICK, G. and STRICKLAND, R. G. 1973. 'Effects of early day care on adjustment to a new environment', *American Journal of Orthopsychiatry* 43, 3, 340–6.

SCHWARZ, J. C., STRICKLAND, R. G. and KROLICK, G. 1974. 'Infant day care: behavioral effects at pre-school age', *Developmental Psychology* 10, 4, 502–6. **p. 188**

SIEGEL, A. E., STOLZ, L. M., HITCHCOCK, E. A. and ADAMSON, J. 1959. 'Dependence and independence in the children of working mothers', *Child Development* 30, 533–46.

SINGH, R. 1970. 'The health of children of working mothers', *Medical Officer* 123, 67–72.

SINGH, R. 1971. 'School performance of children of working mothers and housewives', *Medical Officer* 125, 4, 54–6.

SJØLUND, A. 1973. *Daycare Institutions and Children's Development*, Saxon House, Farnborough; Lexington Books, Lexington, Mass. 308 pp.

STOTT, D. H. 1965. 'Do working mothers' children suffer?' *New Society* 151, 8–9.

196

TIZARD, B. 1975. *Early Childhood Education. A Review and Discussion of Research in Britain*, NFER Pub. Co., Slough, 142 pp. Humanities Press, Atlantic Highlands, NJ.

TIZARD, B. and REES, J. 1975. 'The effect of early institutional rearing on the behaviour problems and affectional relationships of four year old children', *Journal of Child Psychology and Psychiatry* 16, 1, 61–73. **p. 322**

TIZARD, B., COOPERMAN, O., JOSEPH, A. and TIZARD, J. 1972. 'Environmental effects on language development: a study of young children in long-stay residential nurseries', *Child Development* 43, 337–58. **p. 121**

TIZARD, J. and TIZARD, B. 1971. 'The social development of two year old children in residential nurseries', in H. R. Schaffer (ed) *The Origins of Human Social Relations*, Academic Press, London. 147–63. **p. 101**

TIZARD, J. and TIZARD, B. 1974. 'The institution as an environment for development', in M. P. M. Richards (ed) *The Integration of a Child into a Social World*, Cambridge University Press, London. 137–152. **p. 102**

TULKIN, S. R. 1973. 'Social class differences in attachment behaviour of ten month old infants', *Child Development* 44, 171–4. **p. 102**

VAN LEEUWEN, K. and TUMA, J. M. 1972. 'Attachment and exploration: a systematic approach to the study of separation-adaptation phenomena in response to nursery school entry', *Journal of the American Academy of Child Psychiatry* 11, 2, 314–40.

VOGEL, S. R. et al, 1970. 'Maternal employment and perception of sex roles among college students', *Developmental Psychology* 3, 384–91.

WEST, D. J. 1969. *Present Conduct and Future Delinquency*, Heinemann, London, International Universities Press, New York. 207 pp.

WIDLAKE, P. 1973. 'Some effects of pre-school education', *Educational Review* 25, 2, 124–30.

WILLEMSEN, E., FLAHERTY, D., HEATON, C. and RITCHEY, G. 1974. 'Attachment behavior of one year olds as a function of mother versus father, sex of child, session, and toys', *Genetic Psychology Monographs* 90, 2nd half, 305–24.

WOLKIND, S. N. 1974. 'The components of "affectionateless psychopathy" in institutionalized children', *Journal of Child Psychology and Psychiatry* 15, 3, 215–20.

WOODS, M. B. 1972. 'The unsupervised child of the working mother', *Developmental Psychology* 6, 1, 14–25. **p. 189**

YARROW, M. R., SCOTT, P., DE LEEUW, L. and HEINIG, C. 1962. 'Child-rearing in families of working and non-working mothers', *Sociometry* 25, 122–40.

YUDKIN, S. and HOLME, A. 1963, 1969. *Working Mothers and Their Children*, Michael Joseph, London. 199 pp.

Part III
The father's role in the family

A. Introduction

There are an increasing number of studies in which the authors point out that the father's role in the child's development has been neglected, and then go on to include father-child relationships in their investigation of the familial antecedents of some aspect of the child's behaviour. Although there undoubtedly is a relative scarcity of research on the father's role in the child's development, compared to the research available on the mother's role, a diligent search through the literature does unearth a considerable amount of material that is concerned with the father. When an attempt is made to summarise this research, though, it proves difficult to answer questions about the father's influence in the child's development such as: which aspects of the father's behaviour and attitudes affect the child and which areas of the child's development do they affect; at which stage in the child's development do the father's attitudes and behaviour exert their influence on the child and when do the effects of this influence appear in the child's behaviour; does the father behave similarly to children of both sexes and are both sexes affected in the same way by the father-child relationship; how does the combination of maternal and paternal bahaviour affect the child? Nor is it easier to determine how the father's indirect influence in the family – through his emotional support or non-support of the mother – affects the child's development. The difficulties lie not so much in the quantity of research available as in the methodological and conceptual limitations of the research, limitations which are only beginning to be overcome in recent studies.

Methodological and conceptual considerations

i) Studies of the father's influence in the intact family

Until recently most studies investigating the father's role in the family obtained the data not through interview with the father or direct observations of father-child interactions, but by asking the mother or even the child himself for information on the father's behaviour. The distortions that arise when data about the father are obtained through the mother have been pointed out by M. R. Yarrow (1963). When data about the father are obtained from the child whose behaviour is being investigated, contamination is likely to be even greater. This technique has been used most often in studies of sex-role development. While the relationship between the child's sex-role behaviour and his perceptions of his father's behaviour are of interest, it is illegitimate to assume that the child's perceptions descibe the father's actual behaviour. It may well be that the child's sex-role behaviour determines his perceptions of the father's behaviour, rather than being influenced by it. Evidence on the father's behaviour from other sources is necessary then in interpreting these studies.

Another difficulty in interpretation of findings, again occurring predominantly in studies of the father's role in sex-role development, arises because the father's behaviour is rated in comparison with that of the mother. The difficulty occurs both where the information is obtained by interviewing the child and where it is obtained by the observation of the parents in an experimental situation. This technique means that two elements of the father's behaviour are combined – his interactions with the child in a particular area of family functioning and his influence over the mother in this area. It is thus impossible to determine from this type of study which element of the father's behaviour influences the child's development.

More recently, particularly when studying the father's influence on the child's intellectual achievements and achievement motivation, direct observational techniques have been used. These techniques raise their own problems, though, at least, they are not specific to the study of the father. The usual procedure is for the child to be given a number of tasks to perform while the parent is allowed to give as much help as he wishes. The artificiality of the situation and knowledge of being observed may well distort the parent-child interactions. There are also an increasing number of studies comparing the pattern of relationships (of father, mother and child) in families in which the child is emotionally disturbed (or poorly adjusted) with those in which the child is not disturbed (or well adjusted). The dilemma here has been discussed in a review of family interaction research (Haley, 1972): if the attempt is made to measure typical family behaviour this can only be subjectively interpreted by the observer; the more structured the interaction situation the less typical is the behaviour of the family members.

Studies using direct observational techniques in an experimental situation also raise particularly acutely a problem which besets studies of parent-child relationships. When the father's behaviour is studied at the same time as the child's it cannot be determined whether the parental behaviour is antecedent to the child's behaviour or simply a response to it. Longitudinal studies are the best solution here, but few are so far available which include investigation of father-child relationships. It may also be possible to determine whether the father's behaviour is likely to be simply a response to the child from internal evidence in studies where data for both is obtained concurrently (e.g. as in Solomon *et al.* 1971), and this should be attempted more often.

It has recently been pointed out (Osofsky, 1972), that methods used to obtain information on parent-child relationships will influence the kind of results obtained. Awareness of this on the part of researchers and the use of a combination of techniques should enable progress to be made in the study of father-child interactions and their influence on the child's development.

ii) Studies of father absence

There has been an increasing number of studies of prolonged and usually permanent father absence in the last decade. The complex changes that occur in the family when the father becomes absent (Biller, 1971; Sprey, 1970; Herzog and Sudia, 1971) are, though, only beginning to be taken into account by researchers. Father absence means far more than a lack (or decrease) of interaction between the father and child. The mother's behaviour towards the child is also likely to be affected by the absence (or decrease) of interaction with the father. The crisis occurring at the time of the father's departure in itself affects the family members. There are also changes in attitudes of the community towards the family and changes in the attitudes of the family members themselves. The type of crisis in the family, and the attitudes of the community to the family, will be affected by the reason for the father's absence. Until very recently the most usual type of research design has been to compare father-present families with father-absent families, regardless of the reason for father-absence. Such comparisons may well mean that differences between the groups are attributed to lack of interaction with the father, while actually being due to the impact of the crisis itself, or to changes in attitudes due to community pressures. Comparisons of groups of families father-absent for different reasons, a few of which are beginning to appear, are necessary to disentangle the effects due to the various causes.

The effects of lack of interaction with the father may well differ according to the age and sex of the child, the family's social class and ethnic group. The lack of interaction with the father may also be modified by the presence of a step-father, or male relative or friend of the family, by an older brother, or by the mother's own behaviour. While these modifying influences are being taken into account in a number of studies now appearing, grouping families together regardless of such factors has caused the effects of lack of interaction with the father to be minimised in the findings of many previous studies. The effect of the degree and quality of the contact with the father himself, where this is possible, has been ignored in most studies.

Additionally, there is the complex problem of adequately matching father-absent and father-present families for socio-economic level (Herzog and Sudia, 1971 and 1973). This necessitates taking into account the material circumstances of the father-absent families for otherwise the consequences of poverty may be attributed to lack of interaction with the father, or to the stresses of the family situation. However, it is not sufficient, as Herzog and Sudia appear to imply, to simply make comparisons between father-absent and father-present families equated as well as possible in their current material circumstances. The father-absent family is likely to retain much of the life-style of its former, and often higher, social status, particularly perhaps as far as the mother's attitudes and motivations are concerned. To determine the effects of the father's absence these influences on the child's development have also to be taken into account. These problems are particularly acute in studies investigating the effect of father absence on intellectual attainments, for these are known to be affected both by material circumstances and parental attitudes (Davie et al. 1972).

The only study which comes near to solving the problem of isolating the effects of the family situation itself on the child from those of the material adversities which often accompany the father's departure is the study of children living in one-parent families at the age of eleven, recently carried out by the National Children's Bureau (Ferri, 1976). The method used was an analysis of variance which enabled the effect of the family situation to be estimated after allowance had been made for other factors which may be associated with educational attainments or adjustment. These included the availability of household amenities, receipt of free school meals (to indicate income level), and the parents' educational aspirations for the child as well as social class and family situation. The family's former social status was taken into account by using the father's occupation at the time of the child's birth as the index of social class. Comparisons were also made between children fatherless because of marital breakdown, death and illegitimacy, thus enabling some estimate to be made of how far any effects found were due to lack of interaction with the father and how much to other difficulties in the family situation. The main problem in interpreting findings of this study is that the children had become fatherless at different ages, and the effects of the father's absence at particular stages in the child's development may have been obscured.

The complexities of research into father absence mean that studies so far carried out can be regarded only as pointers to areas in which lack of interaction is possibly of importance, to stages in the child's development at which the father's influence has most effect, and to whether this influence is the same for both sexes, for different social classes and ethnic groups.

201

Scope of the review

Research studies on the effects of father absence and of the father's influence in the intact family are summarised separately below under three main headings; cognitive abilities; sex-role development; emotional and social adjustment. Emphasis, as usual, is placed on recent research where possible, but relevant research findings from studies published since the mid–1950s are included.

B. Cognitive abilities – Summary of findings

1. The effects of father absence

a) Overall, the findings suggest that the family situation of father-absent children does tend to have adverse effects on their intellectual development, especially on numerical abilities, but these are relatively slight. The adverse effects are predominantly, although not entirely, due to stress in the family associated with the father leaving rather than to lack of interaction with the father himself, the mother and other significant persons in the child's environment often being able to compensate for this.

b) (i) Children whose fathers have been absent for a prolonged period tend to have lower scores on tests of intellectual (Lessing et al., 1970; Sutton–Smith et al., 1968) and academic attainments (Blanchard and Biller, 1971; Santrock, 1972) than father-present children matched broadly for socio-economic status, and these appear attributable at least partially to the family situation. The measures used to rate the socio-economic status of the families in two of these studies (Sutton–Smith et al., 1968; Blanchard and Biller, 1971) did include criteria* which enable the material disadvantages of the father-absent families to be taken into account to some extent at least, making it unlikely that the lower attainments of the father-absent children can be attributed entirely to their poorer economic circumstances. If the mother's occupation, rather than the father's, was used in rating the father-absent families (neither of these studies indicates which was used) the difference in scores could even underestimate the effects of the family situation. Rating on the mother's occupation would mean that the father-present and father-absent groups were fairly well matched on current material

---

*Sutton–Smith et al. used the Warner scale of socio-economic status (Warner, 1949) which rates on occupation, source of income, type of house and area of residence, and Biller and Blanchard used the Hollingshead index of social position (Hollingshead and Redlich, 1958), which rates on occupation, education and area of residence.

circumstances but the influence of the father-absent family's former, and probably higher, social status on life-style, motivations and child-rearing attitudes was not being taken into account.

(ii) Findings of the study of a nationally representative sample of children living in fatherless homes in this country, carried out by the National Children's Bureau, suggest, overall, that the family situation does have some effect on educational, particularly arithmetic, attainments, but that it is relatively slight compared with the influence of factors such as social class, family size and parental aspirations (Ferri, 1976). Children living with divorced or separated mothers had significantly lower arithmetic scores (and slightly lower reading scores) than children living in two–parent families even after allowance had been made for disadvantaging factors in their background. Study findings had shown that these children tended to have poorer housing, lower family income, and that their fathers were more likely to have had (at the time of the child's birth) semi- and unskilled occupations – all factors that have been found to be associated with poorer school performance (Davie et al. 1972). Generally, the attainments of children living with widowed mothers were similar to those of children from intact families, but there were some indications of slightly adverse effects on the performance of boys. It seems likely then that the tensions and difficulties associated with divorce are responsible for most of the association between father absence and lower attainments but that lack of interaction with the father may also play some part, at least for boys (see (c) and (f)i, ii, and iii, below).

c) In intact families, the reading and mathematics attainments of both sexes are favourably influenced when the father takes a 'big or equal with mother' part in the child's management. Findings come from the National Child Development Study (Lambert and Hart, 1976). Other studies have also found that children whose fathers are highly available have better academic achievements than children with less available fathers (Blanchard and Biller, 1971; Douglas et al. 1968; Landy et al. 1969). These findings suggest that the adverse effects of prolonged father absence may, sometimes at least, be partly attributable to the decreased or total lack of interaction with the father.

d) Among children from extremely disadvantaged groups, there are many factors which have a deleterious effect on the child's cognitive abilities and so father absence makes little or no impact (Crellin et al., 1971). Findings are conflicting on whether low-income, black children in the United States are (Deutsch and Brown, 1964, Sciara and Jantz, 1974) or are not (Solomon et al., 1972; Wasserman, 1972) affected by father absence. Research which makes adequate allowance for any greater

203

economic disadvantage in the father-absent families is necessary to resolve the problem.

e) The family situation of father–absent children does not affect all intellectual abilities evenly, but has the greatest adverse effect on quantitative abilities, particularly for middle-class children (Altus, 1958; Carlsmith, 1964; Gregory, 1965b; Landy *et al.*, 1969; Nelsen and Maccoby, 1966; Sutton-Smith *et al.*, 1968). Recent findings from the National Children's Bureau's study of one parent families (Ferri, 1976) appear to confirm this, living in a fatherless home being found to affect arithmetic rather than reading performance, especially in the case of middle-class children whose parents were divorced or separated. There are also indications that some groups of children whose fathers are absent from home, particularly those from the middle-classes, have slightly higher verbal abilities than children with fathers at home (Lessing *et al.*, 1970; Sutton-Smith *et al.*, 1968). The National Children's Bureau study findings again appear to be in line with the evidence from earlier studies.

f) A number of factors modify the influence of father absence on the child's intellectual abilities:
i) Age of child at onset of father absence. The most deleterious effects of father absence occur in the first five years of life (Blanchard and Biller, 1971) or even the first two (Santrock, 1972) at least when the cause of absence is divorce, separation or desertion. There is also some evidence that decreased interaction with the father in the intact family is deleterious early (before the child is 9 years old) rather than later (Landy *et al.*, 1969). Perhaps the mother is less able to compensate for the father's absence in the child's early years, when the reason is divorce or separation rather than death. When father absence is due to death, the boy may be more severely affected if the onset of father absence is later, when he is more aware of what has happened, rather than earlier (Santrock, 1972) (see also iii, below).

ii) Sex of child. Prolonged father absence appears to have adverse effects on boys rather than girls (Lessing *et al.*, 1970; Santrock, 1972). Boys, but not girls, from broken families were found to decline significantly more in intelligence test scores between the ages of six and twelve than children in intact families of similar socio–economic status in a longitudinal study (Rees and Palmer, 1970). In the National Children's Bureau study of one-parent families (Ferri, 1976) boys living with widowed mothers had lower arithmetic scores than girls, thus reversing the usual pattern for the sexes; boys (but not girls) whose fathers had died also made less progress in arithmetic between the ages of seven and eleven than their counterparts in two-parent families. Possibly these findings do indicate that the father's absence *per se,* and not just the stress associated with it, affects boys at least.

iii) Reason for father absence. Absence from home of the father because of divorce or separation is generally found to have some adverse effects on educational attainments (Ferri, 1976; Santrock, 1972) while the father's death may have little or no deleterious effects after allowance is made for material disadvantages (Douglas *et al.,* 1968; Santrock, 1972). These findings could be interpreted to mean that it is family tensions and insecurity (Douglas *et al.,* 1968) or the mother's negative attitude to males (Santrock, 1972) rather than a lack of interaction with the father himself that influences the child's cognitive abilities adversely. Nevertheless, the differential effect of father absence on boys and girls (see ii and iv) does suggest that the mother and other persons may not entirely be able to compensate for the lack of interaction with the father.

iv) Presence of a step-father. Findings are somewhat conflicting. There is some evidence that a step-father's presence raises the scores of previously father-absent children (Lessing *et al.,* 1970), although the effect seems to occur for boys rather than girls (Santrock, 1972). Findings from the National Survey of Health and Development (Douglas, cited by Murchison, 1974), in contrast, suggest that the presence of a step-father has deleterious effects, particularly where the father has died, but include no separate analyses by sex. There has been no attempt to study the effect of other adult male relatives who may act as father substitutes. Nor has the effect of the amount and quality of contact with the absent father himself been explored.

v) Social class. The father's absence probably does affect middle- and working-class children differently (Ferri, 1976; Lessing *et al.,* 1970) but the differential class effects need systematic exploration.

vi) Sibling composition. This may influence the impact of father absence on the child's cognitive abilities (Sutton-Smith *et al.,* 1968) but it has been little investigated so far.

vii) The mother's behaviour and attitudes. There is some evidence that the husbandless mother has higher educational aspirations for the child, is more involved in school affairs, and exerts more pressure on the child to achieve than the married mother of similar income level, except when there are severe limitations on time or income (Kriesberg, 1967 and 1970). Divorced or separated mothers from a middle-class background (rated on husband's occupation at the time of the child's birth), though, appear to have less contact with schools than middle-class mothers from intact homes (Ferri, 1976), possibly because they are more conscious of their anomalous position, or because, in some cases, they are having to cope with considerable deterioration in material circumstances.

g) The effect of the family situation on the intellectual attainments of some groups of father-absent children may be obscured in large-scale surveys (Coleman, 1966; Wilson, 1967) which group all father-absent children together, regardless of modifying factors. Additionally, the father-present group was confounded in these studies by including in it children with step-fathers (Herzog and Sudia, 1973). A re-analysis of the Coleman data, grouping children with step-fathers separately from those living with their natural fathers (Tabler *et al.*, cited by Herzog and Sudia, 1973) found that children from father-absent homes did have lower scores than those from father-present homes, but that the differences were very slight when compared with race differences.

2. The father's influence in the intact family

a) There is some evidence that father-child interactions may affect the child's intellectual functioning from a very early age, by fifteen months (Wachs *et al.*, 1971) or even the end of the first year (Spelke *et al.*, 1973).

b) Father-child interactions influence the intellectual development of children of both sexes, but the impact of the father's behaviour at various stages in the child's development may not be the same for the two sexes.
i) Boys. Father nurturance (Honzik, 1967; N. Radin, 1972a and 1973) and lack of restrictiveness are related to intelligence test scores in boys six years of age or younger. Boys' intellectual achievements in the pre-adolescent years, both verbal (Bing, 1963; Honzik, 1967) and analytical (Corah, 1965; Dyk and Witkin, 1965; Goldstein and Peck, 1973) are possibly influenced more by the early mother-child than the father-child relationship. The degree to which the mother allows the child autonomy appears to play an important part in the development of analytical abilities in the boy, but the father's support of the mother in child-rearing apparently encourages this type of maternal behaviour (Dyk and Witkin, 1965), while his behaviour may also have a more direct influence (Corah, 1965). There is some evidence that verbal abilities are fostered in the pre-adolescent boy when the father as well as the mother interacts a great deal with the son, while over involvement with the parents may depress number ability (Walberg and Majoribanks, 1973).
ii) Girls. There is some evidence of the father's influence on the girl's intellectual attainments, both verbal (Bing, 1963; Honzik, 1967) and analytical (Corah, 1965) from as early as the third year of life (Reppucci, 1971) and some indication that certain aspects of his behaviour may have more effect on the girl than the boy. Achievement motivation in primary school age girls has been found to be more closely related to high involvement with the father (who shows both positive, warm and critical, rejecting behaviour) than the mother, while in boys it appears to

be more often related to high involvement with the mother (Crandall, 1972).

Evidence of the father's role in the child's cognitive development has often emerged from studies primarily focussing on the mother's influence (e.g. Bing, 1963; Dyk and Witkin, 1965; Goldstein and Peck, 1973). Further direct study of the father's influence is needed to clarify which aspects of the father's behaviour affect the child's intellectual development and the exact stage in the child's life at which they exert their influence.

c) By the time the child reaches pre-adolescence too much parental intrusiveness may be detrimental for achievement and achievement motivation (Busse, 1969; Crandall et al., 1964; Solomon et al., 1971). Findings suggest that children of this age need both parental interest in and encouragement of their achievements (Douglas et al., 1968; Hermans et al., 1972; Rosen and D'Andrade, 1959) and freedom to work in their own way and make their own decisions (Busse, 1969, Crandall et al., 1964; Hermans et al., 1972; Rosen and D'Andrade, 1959; Solomon et al., 1971). Somewhat dissimilar behaviour from the parents may be advantageous for the development of high-achievement motivation (Rosen and D'Andrade, 1959; Solomon et al., 1971), the father's role often being to ensure that the child has sufficient autonomy. The exact combination of interest and non-interference that is optimal for the child's intellectual development may well differ for the sexes and between social classes and ethnic groups (Solomon et al., 1971; Stein and Bailey, 1973).

C. Sex-role development – Summary of findings

1.The effects of father absence

a) Father-absent boys tend to be less masculine than father-present boys in sex-role orientation (underlying feelings of masculinity or femininity) but little different in the more overt aspects of sex-role, sex-role preference and sex-role adoption.

i) Sex-role orientation (underlying perception, not necessarily conscious of male or femaleness of self, measured by various projective tests – Biller, 1970 and 1971; Biller and Borstelmann, 1967; Lynn, 1969). Father-absent boys are found to be less masculine in sex-role orientation than father-present boys of similar age and social class (Barclay and Cusumano, 1967; Biller, 1968a and 1969a; Burns, 1972; Burton, 1972; Nash, 1965; Santrock, 1970). Exceptions are two studies using figure drawings as the projective measure (Donini, 1967; Lawton and Sechrest,

1962) but in the former the father-absent boys were more variable in sex-identification than the father-present boys.

ii) Sex-role preference (desire to adhere to cultural sex-standards, measured by self-rating scales of interests and attitudes – Biller, 1970 and 1971; Biller and Borstelmann, 1967; Lynn, 1969). Few differences have been found between father-absent and father-present boys in sex-role preferences (Altus, 1958; Barclay and Cusumano, 1967; Biller, 1968b and 1969a; Dean, 1971; Greenstein, 1966; Miller, 1961; Wohlford *et al.*, 1971).

iii) Sex-role adoption (masculinity or femininity of an individual's behaviour, as viewed by others, measured by observer's ratings of overt behaviour – Biller, 1970 and 1971; Biller and Borstelmann, 1967; Lynn, 1969). On the whole, there are also few differences between father-present and father-absent boys in sex-role adoption (Biller, 1968a, 1968b, 1969a; Keller and Murray, 1973; Wohlford *et al.*, 1971), although much appears to depend here on the age of the child at the onset of father absence (Hetherington, 1966; McCord *et al.*, 1962) (see (c) i, below).

b) The slight differences found between the sex-role preferences of young father-present and father-absent boys (Biller, 1968b and 1969a; Santrock, 1970) tend to disappear by adolescence (Barclay and Cusumano, 1967; Dean, 1971; Greenstein, 1966; Miller, 1961), at least in lower-class subjects (Altus, 1958). Differences in sex-role orientation probably remain in adolescence (Barclay and Cusumano, 1967; Donini, 1967), although further investigation is needed here. There is no evidence available about the sex-role adoption of father-absent boys in later adolescence.

c) A number of factors modify the influence of the father's absence on the boy's sex- role development:
i) Age of boy at onset of father absence. Early father absence (before the child is 5 or 6 years old) has a greater effect on the boy's masculinity than later absence (Biller and Bahm, 1971; Hetherington, 1966). Late father absence (after the child is 6 years old) tends to be associated with high aggressiveness in both sex-role orientation (Santrock and Wohlford, 1970) and sex-role adoption (Hetherington, 1966; McCord *et al.*, 1962). An unexplored possibility deserving further investigation is that late father absence leads to higher aggressiveness only in white boys (the tables in one study – Hetherington, 1966 – suggests that only the white and not the black late father-absent subjects were more aggressive than the father-present boys), perhaps because so many other factors in the family and social situation of black boys in the United States (where the studies were carried out) may give rise to aggression.
ii) Reason for absence. This has been little investigated but there is

some evidence that father absence due to divorce, separation or desertion is more likely to produce exaggerated aggressiveness or sex-role deviancy (Santrock and Wohlford, 1970; Schoolman, 1969) than father absence due to death. Perhaps this is because the mother is more likely to be rejecting or 'deviant' when the family is broken by divorce, rather than by death (see v, below). Where the father has died and the mother is also rejecting or 'deviant', the child is particularly likely to display a combination of feminine and aggressive behaviour (McCord *et al.* 1962).

iii) Presence of step-father (Nash, 1965; Santrock, 1970) and older brothers (Santrock, 1970; Wohlford *et al.*, 1971) is related to greater masculinity in young father-absent boys.

iv) Social class. Father absence appears to have a greater effect on middle- than on working-class boys (Altus, 1958), but further research is necessary to establish or disprove this.

v) The mother's attitudes and behaviour. The mother's encouragement of masculinity has some effect on sex-role preference and sex-role adoption (Biller, 1969a), but not on sex-role orientation (Biller, 1969a), at least while the boy is young. Maternal rejection, 'deviancy', or personality difficulties may be related to sex-role conflict in the boy, regardless of the child's age at the onset of father absence (McCord *et al.*, 1962; Schoolman, 1969)

vi) Intelligence. Differences in sex-role development of father-absent and father-present boys may be partly due to differences in intelligence between the groups (Kohlberg, 1967; Santrock and Wohlford, 1970), but even when the groups are matched for intelligence some differences remain (Biller, 1969a; Biller and Bahm, 1971; Burns, 1972).

d) Father absence has little effect on the sex-role development of girls (Burton, 1972; Hetherington, 1972; Santrock, 1970).

2. The father's influence in the intact family

a) The father's overall importance in the family (as measured by the boy's perception of father power in decision-making, competence, nurturance and limit-setting) is strongly related to masculinity of all three aspects of sex-role in the young boy (Biller, 1968b and 1969b). The aspects of the father's influence that have the strongest relationship to sex-role are perceived paternal decision-making and competence (Biller, 1968b and 1969b). Paternal dominance over the mother in decision making (as observed in an experimental situation) is also related to sex-role (Biller, 1968b, 1969b; Hetherington, 1965), but not as strongly as perceived father-dominance (Biller, 1969b), possibly because the latter is the better measure of the father's actual influence in the family. Father nurturance, both as perceived by the boy and the mother (Biller, 1968b and 1969b;

209

Mussen and Distler, 1959; Mussen and Rutherford, 1963) and influence in limit- setting, as perceived by the boy (Biller, 1968b and 1969b) and the mother (Mussen and Distler, 1960) are related to high masculinity of sex-role orientation but are not separately related to high masculinity in the other aspects of sex-role (Biller, 1968b and 1969b). Possibly there is a curvilinear relationship between father nurturance and sex-role adoption, affection from the father being related to moderate rather than extremely high or low overt masculinity, at least by the time the boy reaches pre- adolescence (Bronson, 1959). The majority of these studies have assessed the father's role in the family by comparing his influence in various aspects of family functioning to that of the mother. Findings from the studies which assess the father's behaviour separately from that of the mother (Bronson, 1959; Mussen and Distler, 1960) suggest that it is the father's interaction with the child, rather than his influence over the mother in a particular area, at least as far as father nurturance is concerned, that affects the child's sex-role development.

b) Sex-role orientation is the aspect of sex-role development most affected by family functioning (Biller, 1969b, 1971). This is consistent with the studies of father absence which find sex-role orientation to be more affected than other aspects.

c) Masculinity of the father's interests (Biller, 1971; Mussen and Rutherford, 1963) or encouragement of masculine activities by either parent (Biller, 1968b; Mussen and Rutherford, 1963) has little effect on the sex-role orientation of boys.

d) For girls, the father's influence in family affairs has less effect on sex-role development than it has with boys (Biller, 1971; Hetherington, 1965), but the encouragement of participation in sex-typed activities has a stronger influence on sex-role than it has with boys (Biller, 1971; Mussen and Rutherford, 1963).

e) Sex-role development and adjustment. The evidence indicates that it is sex-role orientation (underlying feelings of masculinity or femininity) that is mainly affected by the father's behaviour in the family, or father absence, as far as the boy is concerned, while sex-role behaviour in the girl is little affected by the father's behaviour. Some doubt arises about the validity of findings that father-absent boys (or those whose fathers are little involved in family functioning) are less masculine in sex-role orientation than father-present boys (or those whose fathers are considerably involved in family functioning), as measurement is made on projective tests which require interpretation from an investigator whose judgements may be biased by pre-conceptions (Herzog and Sudia, 1971 and 1973). Evidence against this view is the consistency with which independent researchers, using different tests, have found differences between the father-present and father-absent boys, and the fact that the tests meaningfully differentiate sub-categories of father-absent boys, e.g. early and late father-absent boys (see p. 208). Presuming then that there is a real difference between the father-absent and father-present boys, how far is masculinity, particularly masculinity of sex-role orientation, related to good adjustment? There are a number of studies which show that masculinity of various aspects of sex-role behaviour is related to good personal and social adjustment in pre-school (Flammer, 1971; Inselberg and Burke, 1973; Vroegh et al., 1967), pre-adolescent boys (Biller and Barry, 1971; Connell and Johnson, 1970; Gray, 1957; Sears, 1970), although some findings are equivocal (Webb, 1963). There is also some evidence, though it is tentative, which indicates that it is underlying masculinity rather than masculinity of overt behaviour which is related to good adjustment in boys (Flammer, 1971; Inselberg and Burke, 1973), and that underlying masculinity need only be moderate rather than high for good adjustment (Inselberg and Burke, 1973). In adult life it is very doubtful, though, whether behaviour in accordance with the stereotype of masculinity can be considered desirable (Herzog and Sudia, 1971 and 1973), and there is evidence that boys with rigidly masculine overt behaviour have, in fact, poorer emotional and social adjustment as adults than boys with less masculine overt behaviour (Mussen, 1961 and 1962). However, the boys who were highly masculine in sex-role preferences in this study differed little from the boys with more feminine sex-role preferences in their masculinity of sex-role orientation, and there were indications of considerable discrepancy between the underlying and overt aspects of sex-role behaviour in some of the overtly masculine boys. A possible interpretation then is that it may have been an underlying insecurity of masculinity in these boys which hampered their achievement of flexibility of behaviour and good adjustment in adult life. This possibility deserves further exploration. Evidence is far too sketchy, though, for any definitive conclusions to be reached on whether low masculinity as measured by projective tests is associated with adjustment difficulties in adult life.

D. Emotional and social adjustment – Summary of findings

1. The effects of father absence

a) On the whole the father's absence from home appears to have little effect on the children's emotional and social adjustment (apart from the immediate impact) but the child living in a fatherless home may be somewhat more likely to experience difficulties in social relationships.

i) The social adjustment (rated by teachers) of a nationally representative sample of eleven-year-olds living with their mothers alone differed little from that of children living in two-parent families after allowance had been made for disadvantaging background factors such as lower social class, poorer housing, lower income (Ferri, 1976). Nor were the two groups distinguished in most aspects of behaviour at home (rated by mothers), though in a few areas divorced or separated mothers reported their children, especially girls, to be having greater difficulties. There was some evidence that these mothers were worried about the situation and its effects on the child and the differences may have reflected their anxieties rather than indicating that the family situation was having adverse effects on the children.

ii) Father absence does not appear to be related to behaviour problems in adolescents (Burchinal. 1964). Symptoms of anxiety appear to be no more frequent in early adolescent working-class father-absent boys than in those from intact families, except where the mother is rejecting or 'deviant' (McCord *et al.*, 1962). Findings of greater anxiety in five-year-old father-absent children than in father-present children (Koch 1961) may be related to the high incidence of covert maternal rejection apparently found in this small sample (twenty-two children and their mothers).

iii) There is possibly some relationship between father absence and bed-wetting (Douglas, 1970). No separate social class analyses were made, though, in Douglas' study, and no account was taken of the deterioration of living standards in the father-absent families, which may also bear some relationship to bed-wetting. Children living in fatherless homes in the National Children's Bureau study of one-parent families (Ferri, 1976) also showed a slightly higher level of bed-wetting than those in two-parent families, but the father's absence appeared to be associated with persistence of the condition rather than giving rise to it.

iv) Father absence generally has little effect on the child's self-concept (Kelly, 1970; Thomes, 1968). A greater frequency of low self-esteem was found among father-absent adolescents in one study (Rosenberg, 1965) only when the mother had been very young at the time of family breakdown (suggesting that financial hardship may have been the crucial factor here), or, in the case of divorce, where there was strong religious opposition to this (suggesting that social stigma may have been the cause).

v) Father absence may be associated with difficulties in peer group relationships in pre-adolescent (Hetherington, 1966) and adolescent boys (Miller, 1961; Mitchell and Wilson, 1967). Father-absent adolescent girls appear to be insecure in their relationships with the opposite sex (Hetherington, 1972; Nelsen and Vangen, 1971). Father-absent adolescents have also been found to be striving for, rather than satisfying, their need for attention from the opposite sex (Bartlett and Horrocks, 1958).

b) Delinquency. There is only a slight or no over-representation of father absence among delinquent boys, at least among those from the working class (Herzog and Sudia, 1971 and 1973; West and Farrington, 1973). Fallacious conclusions about delinquents have often been reached by generalising from studies of institutionalised delinquents as West (1969) has pointed out. Considerably higher rates of broken families are found among institutionalised delinquents than amongst the controls (e.g. Jonsson, 1967) precisely because delinquents are selected for institutionalisation partly on the basis of their home circumstances. Studies using as their samples unselected groups of normal children (Douglas *et al.*, 1966; Gibson, 1969; Gregory, 1965a; West and Farrington, 1973) have also found that children from broken families are more likely than those from intact families to become delinquent but the difference is only significantly greater when family break-up is due to divorce or separation rather than death — and the relationship appears to be partly at least due to low income rather than the family situation (Chilton and Markle, 1972; West and Farrington, 1973), within the working class. There is some evidence of a stronger association between delinquency and broken homes among the middle rather than the working class (Douglas, 1970). There are no available findings to indicate how far this is attributable to the change in economic circumstances occuring at the break-up of the middle-class family or to the greater impact of the family situation in the middle class.

c) A number of factors modify the effects of father absence on the child's emotional and social adjustment:
i) Age of child at the onset of father absence. This has been little investigated in relation to the child's emotional and social adjustment. If there is any association between father absence and delinquency, it appears to be with late rather than early father absence (Anderson, 1968; McCord *et al.*, 1962).
ii) Sex of child. The same sex parent tends to have the greatest impact on certain aspects of the child's emotional and social adjustment — peer group relations (Hoffman, 1961), leadership qualities (Bronfenbrenner, 1961) and possibly psychiatric disorder (Rutter, 1966) and delinquency (Gregory, 1965a).
iii) Reason for father absence. The stronger relationship between delinquency and father absence due to divorce or separation rather than father absence due to death appears to be partly at least accounted for by the greater economic disadvantage of the former situation. Tension and

discord in the family before its break-up (Rutter, 1971) and greater difficulty for the mother in maintaining a harmonious family atmosphere after divorce may also be partly responsible for the relationship. Some studies of adolescents (Kopf, 1970; Nye, 1957) have found no relationship between the child's emotional and social adjustment and the reason for father absence. There seems to be a possibility that divorce and separation have a greater effect on middle-class children (see v, below).

iv) Presence of a step-father. There is some evidence that the presence of a step-father has an adverse effect on self-esteem (Rosenberg, 1965), enuresis (Douglas, 1970) and delinquency (Glueck and Glueck, 1962; McCord et al., 1962). However other studies have found that a step-father makes little or no difference to the child's emotional and social adjustment (Nye, 1957; Perry and Pfuhl, 1963, Wilson et al., 1975). Further investigation is needed. The child's age at his mother's remarriage, the quality of the mother-child relationship, and her attitude to the step-father are all likely to affect the relationship established with the step-father and its influence on the child (Biller, 1974).

v) Social class. The father's absence, especially where it is due to divorce or separation, may have a greater influence on middle- than working-class children. In the National Children's Bureau study of one-parent families, children from non-manual homes living with divorced or separated mothers had poorer social adjustment than other fatherless groups (Ferri, 1976). This is possibly due to the greater adverse change in material circumstances experienced by some non-manual families as the result of divorce, or it may be due to the greater consciousness of their anomalous position felt by the middle-class mother and her children. Douglas' findings on delinquency are in the same direction (see (b) above).

vi) The mother's behaviour and attitudes. These are of crucial importance for the child's emotional and social adjustment in the father-absent family (Kopf, 1970; McCord et al., 1962; Pedersen, 1966). In the intact family, the father can shield the child from the impact of an emotionally disturbed (Pedersen, 1966), rejecting or 'deviant' (McCord et al., 1962) or over-protective mother but in the father-absent family the child feels the full impact of her influence. The mother's adjustment to the situation after the father leaves also affects the child (Kopf, 1970) but this has hardly been explored.

2. The father's influence in the intact family

a) Father affection is the most important parental influence on a boy's peer group relationships (Hoffman, 1961; Leiderman, 1959) and leadership qualities (Bronfenbrenner, 1961). Father nurturance (as perceived by the child) is related to good self-concept in both adolescent boys (Reuter and Biller, 1973) and girls (Fish and Biller, 1973). Warmth from either parent, though, appears to be related to good self-concept in pre-adolescents of either sex (Sears, 1970). These findings are in line with those from studies of father absence – father absence is more likely to affect adversely a boy's peer group relationship than his self-concept, as warmth from the mother is sufficient for a child to achieve a good self-concept.

b) The father's participation in management of the children was found to be related to good social adjustment at school in the follow-up at eleven of the National Child Development Study sample (Lambert and Hart, 1976). Other studies have found that positive involvement of the father with the child, when combined with nurturance, is related to good peer adjustment (Hoffman, 1961), self-concept (Coopersmith, 1967) and personality adjustment (Reuter and Biller, 1973) in boys. However, it appears that the father needs to be both relatively available and relatively nurturant for good adjustment, the mere presence of the father at home, or a nurturant but seldom-at-home father being insufficient (Reuter and Biller, 1973). Evidence is conflicting on whether father dominance over the mother in family functioning is (Hoffman, 1961) or is not (Sears, 1970) related to good adjustment in boys. Some reconciliation of these findings is possibly provided by another study (Klein et al., 1973) in which behaviour problems were fewer in boys where the father was dominant but the mother passive than when the opposite pattern prevailed, but were still fewer when both the mother and the father were dominant in behaviour. Further research is necessary (see also (f) below).

c) In girls, at least those from professional middle-class families, excessive affection from the father may have a debilitating affect on leadership qualities (Bronfenbrenner, 1961) and independence (Baumrind and Black, 1967). A moderate level of affection is probably most conducive to the development of these qualities, but further investigation with subjects from a wider social-class range is needed.

d) Unsatisfactory parental behaviour appears to be related to delinquency in boys even after family income has been taken into account (West and Farrington, 1973). The behaviour of both parents is important but it is unclear from present research whether one parent has more influence than the other (Andry, 1960, 1971; Glueck and Glueck, 1962; West and Farrington, 1973). Inadequate affection from the father is associated with delinquency in boys (Andry, 1960, 1971; Bandura and Walters, 1959; Glueck and Glueck, 1962; Hetherington, et al., 1971; West and Farrington, 1973). Over-strict (Bandura and Walters, 1959; Glueck and

Glueck, 1968; Hetherington, *et al.*, 1971; West and Farrington, 1973), inconsistent (Andry, 1960, 1971; Glueck and Glueck, 1968; West and Farrington, 1973) and emotionally harsh (West and Farrington, 1973) discipline from the father also appear to be associated with delinquency in boys. Fathers who never take part in leisure activities with their sons also appear to be more likely to have delinquent boys than those who do take part with them (West and Farrington, 1973). There is also a strong association between serious parental conflict and delinquency (Rutter, 1971; West and Farrington, 1973).

e) The mental health and child-rearing attitudes of the father, as well as the mother, are related to emotional adjustment in the child. For younger children the mother may have the greater influence. In one study (Wolff and Acton, 1968) psychiatric disorders were found to be more common amongst mothers but not fathers of primary-school-age Edinburgh children (average age − eight) referred to a hospital psychiatric department, though a higher proportion of fathers as well as mothers did have sociopathic disorders. In another study, ten-year-olds with psychiatric disorders (on teacher or parental ratings) from two different areas, the Isle of Wight and an inner London Borough, were more likely than randomly chosen controls from the same areas to have parents with neurotic disorders (though the difference was significant only for mothers), and fathers who had committed 'offences' (Rutter *et al.*, 1975) Other studies have found that psychiatric illness (Rutter, 1966), personality adjustment (Anderson, 1969) and child-rearing attitudes of the father (Peterson *et al.*, 1959) are more strongly related than those of the mother to emotional problems in boys. Further studies are needed of children of different ages, which make separate analyses for the sexes, and which examine associations with different types of child psychiatric disorder.

f) Several family interaction studies (using observational techniques while the family members are engaged on an experimental task) suggest that a coalition between the parents, in which one takes the leadership and is supported by the other, and agreed channels of communication, rather than a contest for power among all family members, including the children, is generally related to good adjustment in the pre-adolescent child (Murrell and Stachowiak, 1967; Odom *et al.*, 1971; Schuham, 1970). A review of twenty-seven studies comparing interaction in families with a disturbed (non-schizophrenic) and a non-disturbed child (Jacob, 1975) suggests that fathers are more influential in normal families, particularly in relation to the child. Over-domination in fathers, though, may also lead to disturbance in sons (Alkire, 1969; Biller, 1974; Hetherington *et al.*, 1971). In normal families the child appears to gain influence as he reaches adolescence (Jacob, 1974). Clarification is needed of patterns of family relationships conducive to good adjustment in children of different ages. Future studies should make separate analyses for the sexes and differentiate the disturbed families into homogeneous sub-groups (Jacob, 1975).

E. Conclusions and implications

The father's influence in the intact family

Overall, research findings using different approaches are consistent enough to justify the conclusion that the father has a direct influence – in addition to his indirect influence, as the mother's economic and emotional support – on the child's development, probably from the earliest years.

The statement that 'at the very minimum "fathering" is relevant to the child's cognitive functioning' (Radin, 1972a) is most probably over-cautious. Generally, it appears that high verbal achievement is fostered by a close interaction with, and verbal stimulation from, an adult in the early years. Although it is probably the mother who is the main influence here, particularly for boys, there are indications that the father's influence is by no means negligible. Numerical and analytical abilities, in contrast to verbal abilities, appear to be fostered primarily by lack of restrictiveness, by giving the child the freedom to explore the environment on his own. Here, too, there is evidence of the father's influence, both direct and also indirect, his support of the mother in child-rearing probably giving her the self-confidence to allow more autonomy in the child. In fact, fathers have been found to allow more autonomy in pre-school children of both sexes than mothers (Rothbart and Maccoby, 1966) so their influence may be of particular importance here. In the later primary-school years it is well-established that interest and encouragement from both mother and father are associated with good school achievement, but there are indications that pressurising the child into intellectual activities and over-intrusiveness, at least by both parents, are counter-productive. Further clarification of the effect of the combined behaviour of the parents is necessary but, for boys at least, it is over-intrusiveness by the father that appears to be detrimental for both achievement and achievement motivation, while encouragement of independence and autonomy in decision-making may be beneficial.

While findings by no means incontrovertibly show that the father's behaviour is antecedent to the child's behaviour rather than merely a reaction to it, there is evidence against the latter interpretation. Findings from longitudinal studies (e.g. Honzik, 1967; Radin, 1973) indicate that father behaviour in the early years does affect later intellectual

217

functioning (although the father's influence is not, of course, necessarily operative at the time it is actually measured), and there is some internal evidence that the father's behaviour is not simply a response to the child's intellectual functioning (e.g. in the Solomon *et al.* study, 1971, parents who thought their children to be of low ability did not participate with them significantly more, and parental intrusiveness cannot be regarded as a reaction to low achievement). Insufficient longitudinal data and a number of studies with subjects of one sex only leave much in doubt, though, about the timing of the influences exerted by the father's behaviour and the apparently differential effect on the sexes.

Again it can be said, at a minimum, that fathering is relevant to the child's, particularly the boy's, sex-role development, and emotional and social adjustment. There is evidence that the father's child-rearing practices and mental health (unlikely to be a mere response to the child's behaviour) are almost, if not as important as the mother's in relation to emotional problems and delinquency, especially for boys. The warmth of the father-child relationship (measured in at least two studies, Sears, 1970, and West and Farrington, 1973, before the child behaviour under investigation) appears to have an important influence on the child's adjustment. Affection from the father has been found to be associated with good peer adjustment, leadership qualities, personal adjustment and masculine sex-role orientation in boys, while inadequate affection is associated with delinquent behaviour. There are also indications, which would have important implications if confirmed, that warmth from the father is insufficient for good adjustment unless he can also spend a certain minimum level of time with the boy. The girl too seems to be affected by the warmth of the father-child relationship but here there appears to be some danger that over-affection, at least in the middle-classes, will have a depressing effect on the child's independence and leadership qualities.

The effects of father absence

On the whole the studies of father absence suggest that lack of the father-child relationship has relatively little effect on the child's cognitive, emotional and social development, when the material deprivations of father absence have been taken into account. Where adverse effects do appear to be the result of the family situation rather than of economic circumstances, these are usually, although not always, found to be greater when father absence is due to divorce, separation or desertion than when it is due to death. This suggests that the adverse effects are connected with the circumstances associated with the family disruption – including possibly the tension and conflict prior to the family breakdown, the greater difficulty afterwards in maintaining a harmonious family atmosphere, the more negative attitudes of the mother, and feelings of 'differentness' in the children, especially where community disapproval is strong – rather than the absence (or reduction) of the father-child relationship. However, there remain some adverse effects of father absence for which the most plausible explanation does appear to be the lack of father-child relationship itself. The greater effect of father absence on the educational attainment of boys than of girls, and the difficulties experienced in opposite sex relationships by girls whose fathers have died, as well as those whose fathers have left the family, are examples.

Nevertheless, taken overall, the adverse effects of father absence are slighter than might be expected if the father is an important influence on the child's development in the intact family. Does this mean then that the apparently considerable influence of the father is, after all, an artifact of faulty research design? In fact, it is an over-simplication to expect the father's influence in the intact family to be measured by differences between father-present and father-absent children in attainment or adjustment, although many investigators have adopted this view. The father's absence cannot be conceptualised as an unfilled gap in family relationships but means, actually, that there is a complex change in relationships. This involves the mother herself, and others, including, relatives, neighbours and friends, and even the children themselves, taking over some aspects of the father's role (Kriesberg, 1970). However, findings from one study (Goldstein and Peck, 1973) illustrate that the father's absence involves more complicated changes than this. Boys' analytical ability scores have been found in several studies to correlate significantly with those of their mother's, but Goldstein and Peck found that there was such an association only when the father was present in the family, while in father-absent families, in which the mother's influence would be expected to be stronger, no correlations were found between the children's and the mother's scores.

Fortunately, the change in relationships that occurs when the father is absent appears to result quite often in the creation of a family situation which is relatively satisfactory for the child. Findings suggest that the mother's attitudes and her ability to cope with the situation are crucial factors in how far the loss is made up. The somewhat scattered indications of slightly adverse effects, not apparently explicable by material adversity or the stresses of family disruption, on various aspects of development, do show, though, that it is not always possible to make up entirely for the loss of the father-child relationship.

Policy implications

This review has attempted to isolate the effects of father absence *per se* on the development of children from those due to lower income, poorer housing conditions, and other material adversities that are undoubtedly the outcome of father absence in a high proportion of families (Department of Health and Social Security, Finer Report, 1974). It is not possible from the research reviewed here to make any estimate of the extent to which these material disadvantages affect the cognitive, emotional and social development of father-absent children. However, there are many indications that, where these material disadvantages are not adequately taken into account in the research design the father-absent children compare less favourably with the father-present children (Ferri, 1976). There is also ample evidence from other research that adverse environmental circumstances are associated with lower educational attainments, poorer social adjustment and delinquency (Douglas, 1964; Douglas et al., 1968; Davie et al., 1972; West and Farrington, 1973). Any attempt to offset the deleterious effects on a child of living in a father-absent family must include effective measures to relieve material hardship, as the Finer report recognised.

The findings of this review highlight the importance of the mother in the father-absent family as a determinant of the child's attainment and adjustment. Measures which relieve the physical and emotional strain on mothers and give them the opportunity to reconstitute their lives are likely also to be of immeasurable value to the children. Employment may be beneficial to the husbandless mother because it is likely to increase her self-esteem and widen her circle of social contacts, and there is, in fact, some evidence that it also improves the family relationships and attainments of the child (see review on Shared Care, Part II). To enable a higher proportion of husbandless mothers to work without increasing the physical strain on them, and without jeopardising the care of the children, a number of measures are needed – removal of financial deterrents, increase in part-time work opportunities, greater flexibility of working hours, day-care facilities for part of as well as the full working day, provision of play centres for school-age children after school and in the holidays, and home help. Of course, some husbandless mothers, particularly those with children under school age, may prefer not to work, and it is essential that they should be enabled to stay at home without financial strain. They too will need relief on occasion from the care of the children and the confines of the home and many of the measures suggested for employed mothers are also applicable to those who remain at home. It is more doubtful if direct help to father-absent children would be beneficial for there are indications from the research that anything which adds to the feelings of 'differentness' of these children should be avoided.

The importance of the father's influence in the intact family suggests that there should be more concerted attempts at preparation for parenthood among boys. However, most essential is the acknowledgement that the father needs opportunities to develop a continuing and sympathetic relationship with the child. The evidence from research gives some indication that an affectionate but hardly-ever-at-home father is insufficient for the development of good adjustment, particularly for boys. This means that fathers must be able to earn a reasonable living for their families without excessive over-time in the evenings or at weekends. Fathers, as well as mothers, should also have the right to some time off work to visit the school, or a clinic. There can be little doubt that a relationship with two concerned adults who have somewhat differing experiences, is of benefit to the child.

Annotations

(Only the one study that is exceptionally sound methodologically has been annotated in this section.)

FERRI, E. 1976. *Growing up in a One-Parent Family*, NFER Pub. Co. Slough. 196 pp; Humanities Press, Atlantic Highlands, NJ.

An investigation of the prevalence of one-parent family situations at the age of eleven among children from the National Child Development Study (consisting of all babies born during the week of 3–9 March 1958 in England, Wales and Scotland), of the social environment of these children and of the effect of the family situation on their development. At this age, 5.4 per cent of the children in the sample were being cared for by one parent alone, without the support of a parent substitute of the opposite sex living in the same household (the definition of one-parent families adopted in the study), 4.7 per cent of the total sample being cared for by the mother alone. Among fatherless families (to whom attention is confined in the remainder of this summary) just over half were due to marital breakdown, 35 per cent to death of the father and 9 per cent were illegitimate.

Comparisons were made on the background and development of the fatherless children with children in the sample who were being cared for by both their 'natural' parents. More children living with divorced and separated mothers had fathers with semi- and unskilled jobs than those in two-parent families. Widows tended to be older, and divorced and separated mothers younger, than mothers in intact families. A much higher proportion of fatherless children (47 per cent) than of children from complete families (6 per cent), had been dependent on Supplementary Benefits at some time during the previous year, the loss of the father enormously increasing the risk of becoming dependent on state support for both manual and non-manual families (rated on father's occupation at the time of the child's birth). The proportion of families dependent on Supplementary Benefits was especially high in manual working-class families where the mother was divorced or separated. Both widows and divorced and separated mothers from a non-manual background had a higher employment rate than mothers from two-parent families but among mothers from manual homes only widows had a higher rate of employment. Divorced or separated mothers dependent on Supplementary Benefit suffered a reduction in income if they earned more than a certain amount (£2 at the time of the investigation) but this did not apply to mothers receiving the Widowed Mother's Allowance. Children fatherless due to marital breakdown or illegitimacy, but not those whose fathers had died, were worse off in every aspect of housing – including type and tenure of accommodation, availability of basic amenities and necessity of bed-sharing – whether they were from a non-manual or manual background. There was evidence that divorce or separation carried the risk of loss of house ownership, and of deterioration in amenities available (losses occurred to about 25 per cent of children becoming fatherless between seven and eleven, compared with only 4–5 per cent of children whose families remained intact). Lone mothers visited the school as often (with the exception of divorced and separated mothers from a non-manual background) as mothers from intact families and differed little in aspirations for further education and training, though a lower proportion of divorced and separated mothers wanted their daughters to stay on at school beyond fifteen or have further education.

These findings indicate that fatherless children tend to be disadvantaged in such factors as social class, income and housing and, to some extent, parental aspirations, compared with children in two-parent families. Previous research has found that these factors are associated with educational attainments and social adjustment. To assess the effects of family situation *per se* on development then allowance has to be made for these factors. Fatherless children were found to have lower educational attainments (National Foundation for Educational Research, reading and arithmetic tests) and social adjustment (Bristol Social Adjustment Guides) than children in two-parent families in the present study. When allowance was made for background factors, though, the differences between the various family groups in reading attainment and social adjustment were no longer statistically significant. Low income appeared to be a particularly important factor in accounting for the poorer performance of fatherless children, this being the only single factor whose omission from the analyses resulted in the relationship between family situation and reading attainment or family situation and social adjustment again becoming significant. However, there was some evidence that the family situation itself, particularly the stresses and tensions associated with marital breakdown, did have some effect on the children's development, though its influence was relatively small compared with such factors as social class or family size. The differences between the arithmetic scores of children in the various family situations was reduced but remained statistically significant when all the other factors had been taken into account, children fatherless as a result of marital breakdown having lower scores than those of children in two-parent families. (There was also a tendency in the same direction for reading scores though it was not significant.) There was also some evidence that the father's absence *per se* may have some adverse effects, at least on the arithmetic attainments of boys. Children whose fathers had died were generally similar in educational performance to children in intact families, but boys' arithmetic scores tended to be lower than those of girls, thus reversing the usual relationship with sex. Boys living with widowed mothers also tended to make less progress in arithmetic between the age of seven and eleven than boys in complete families, though the two groups of girls made similar progress. Children of both sexes who were fatherless because of divorce or separation made poorer progress than their counterparts in two-parent families, the disadvantageous circumstances surrounding marital breakdown probably outweighing any differential effect of the father's absence on the sexes. Full-time maternal employment was associated with better academic performance for children of widows and children who were illegitimate, and with better adjustment as well for the latter group. Maternal employment did not appear to affect the attainments or adjustment of children living with divorced or separated mothers. It appears that the material benefits to the family and psychological benefits to the mother of full-time employment are again outweighed by the stresses surrounding marital breakdown for the children in this group.

References

(When a title is annotated, this is indicated at the end of the entry by the relevant page number printed in bold type.)

ALKIRE, A. A. 1969. 'Social power and communication within families of disturbed and nondisturbed preadolescents', *Journal of Personality and Social Psychology* 13, 4, 335–49.

ALTUS, W. D. 1958. 'The broken home and factors of adjustment', *Psychological Reports* 4, 477.

ANDERSON, L. M. 1969. 'Personality characteristics of parents of neurotic, aggressive, and normal preadolescent boys', *Journal of Consulting and Clinical Psychology*, 33, 5, 575–81.

ANDERSON, R. E. 1968. 'Where's Dad? Paternal deprivation and delinquency', *Archives of General Psychiatry* 18, 641–9.

ANDRY, R. G. 1960, 1971. *Delinquency and parental pathology. A study in forensic and clinical psychology*, Staples Press, London; Crane Russak & Co., New York. 189 pp.

BANDURA, A. and WALTERS, R. H. 1959. *Adolescent aggression*, Ronald Press Company, New York. 475 pp.

BARCLAY, A. and CUSUMANO, D. R. 1967. 'Father absence, cross-sex identity and field-dependent behavior in male adolescents', *Child Development* 38, 1, 243–50.

BARTLETT, C. J. and HORROCKS, J. E. 1958. 'A study of the needs status of adolescents from broken homes', *Journal of Genetic Psychology* 93, 153–9.

BAUMRIND, D. and BLACK, A. E. 1967. 'Socialization practices associated with dimensions of competence in preschool boys and girls', *Child Development* 38, 2, 291–327.

BILLER, H. B. 1968a. 'A note on father absence and masculine development in lower-class Negro and white boys', *Child Development* 39, 3, 1003–6.

BILLER, H. B. 1968b. 'A multiaspect investigation of masculine development in kindergarten age boys', *Genetic Psychology Monographs* 78, 89–138.

BILLER, H. B. 1969a. 'Father absence, maternal encouragement, and sex-role development in kindergarten age boys', *Child Development* 40, 539–46.

BILLER, H. B. 1969b. 'Father dominance and sex-role development in kindergarten age boys', *Developmental Psychology* 1, 2, 87–94.

BILLER, H. B. 1970. 'Father absence and the personality development of the male child', *Developmental Psychology* 2, 181–201.

BILLER, H. B. 1971. *Father, Child and Sex-Role*, Heath-Lexington Books, Lexington, Mass. 193 pp.

BILLER, H. B. 1974. *Paternal Deprivation: Family, School, Sexuality and Society*, D. C. Heath, London. 226 pp.

BILLER, H. B. and BAHM, R. H. 1971. 'Father absence, perceived maternal behavior, and masculinity of self-concept among junior high school boys', *Developmental Psychology* 4, 2, 178–81.

BILLER, H. B. and BARRY, W. 1971. 'Sex-role patterns, paternal similarity and personality adjustment in college males', *Developmental Psychology* 4, 1, 107.

BILLER, H. B. and BORSTELMANN, L. J. 1967. 'Masculine development: an integrative review', *Merrill-Palmer Quarterly* 13, 4, 253–94.

BING, E. 1963. 'Effect of childrearing practices on development of differential cognitive abilities', *Child Development* 34, 631–48.

BLANCHARD, R. W. and BILLER, H. B. 1971. 'Father availability and academic performance among third-grade boys', *Developmental Psychology* 4, 3, 301–5.

BRONFENBRENNER, U. 1961. 'Some familial antecedents of responsibility and leadership in adolescents', in L. Petrullo and B. M. Bass (eds) *Leadership and Interpersonal Behavior*, Holt, Rinehart, New York. 239–71.

BRONSON, W. C. 1959. 'Dimensions of ego and infantile identification', *Journal of Personality* 27, 532–45.

BURCHINAL, L. G. 1964. 'Characteristics of adolescents from unbroken, broken and reconstituted families', *Journal of Marriage and Family Living* 26, 1, 44–51.

BURNS, R. 1972. 'The effect of father's absence on the development of the masculine identification of boys in residential treatment', *Dissertation Abstracts International* 32, 7–B, 4179–80.

BURTON, R. V. 1972. 'Cross-sex identity in Barbados', *Developmental Psychology* 6, 3, 365–74.

BUSSE, T. V. 1969. 'Child-rearing antecedents of flexible thinking', *Developmental Psychology* 1, 5, 585–91.

CARLSMITH, L. 1964. 'Effect of early father absence on scholastic aptitude', *Harvard Educational Review* 34, 1–21.

CHILTON, R. J. and MARKLE, G. E. 1972. 'Family disruption, delinquent conduct and the effect of subclassification', *American Sociological Review* 37, 93–9.

COLEMAN, J. S. 1966. *Equality of Educational Opportunity*, US Government Printing Office, Washington, DC. (especially pp. 293–302)

CONNELL, D. M. and JOHNSON, J. E. 1970. 'Relationship between sex-role identification and self-esteem in early adolescents', *Developmental Psychology* 3, 2, 268.

COOPERSMITH, S. 1967. *The Antecedents of Self-Esteem*, W. H. Freeman, London. 283 pp.

CORAH, N. 1965. 'Differentiation in children and parents', *Journal of Personality* 33, 2, 300–8.

CRANDALL, V. C. 1972. 'The Fels study: some contributions to personality development and achievement in childhood and adulthood', *Seminars in Psychiatry*, 4, 4, 383–97.

CRANDALL, V., DEWEY, R., KATKOVSKY, W. and PRESTON, A. 1964. 'Parents' attitudes and behaviors and grade-school children's academic achievements', *Journal of Genetic Psychology* 104, 1, 53–66.

CRELLIN, E., PRINGLE, M. L. K. and WEST, P. 1971. *Born Illegitimate: Social and Educational Implications*, NFER Pub. Co., Slough; Humanities Press, Atlantic Highlands, NJ. 173 pp.

225

DAVIE, R., BUTLER, N. and GOLDSTEIN, H. 1972. *From Birth to Seven*, Longman in association with National Children's Bureau, London; Humanities Press, Atlantic Highlands, NJ. 586 pp. **p. 312**

DEAN, K. 1971. 'Father absence, feminine identification and assertive-aggressiveness: a test of compulsive masculinity among institutionalized Negro juvenile delinquents', *Dissertation Abstracts International* 31, 9–A, 4912–3.

DEPARTMENT OF HEALTH AND SOCIAL SECURITY. 1974. *Report of the Committee on One Parent Families* (Chairman, M. Finer) (Cmnd 5629–I) HMSO, London, Vols I and II.

DEUTSCH, M. and BROWN, B. 1964. 'Social influences in Negro-White intelligence differences', *Journal of Social Issues* 20, 2, 24–35.

DONINI, G. P. 1967. 'An evaluation of sex-role identification among father-absent and father-present boys', *Psychology* 4, 13–16.

DOUGLAS, J. W. B. 1964. *The Home and the School*, MacGibbon and Kee, London. 224 pp.

DOUGLAS, J. W. B. 1970. 'Broken families and child behaviour', *Journal of the Royal College of Physicians* 4, 3, 203–10.

DOUGLAS, J. W. B., ROSS, J. M., HAMMOND, W. A. and MULLIGAN, D. G. 1966. 'Delinquency and social class', *British Journal of Criminology* 6, 294–302.

DOUGLAS, J. W. B., ROSS, J. M. and SIMPSON, H. R. 1968. *All Our Future*, Peter Davies, London. 252 pp.

DYK, R. B. and WITKIN, H. A. 1965. 'Family experiences related to the development of differentiation in children', *Child Development* 36, 1, 21–55.

FERRI. E. 1976. *Growing up in a One Parent Family*, NFER Pub. Co., Slough; Humanities Press, Atlantic Highlands, NJ. 196 pp. **p. 221**

FISH, K. D. and BILLER, H. B. 1973. 'Perceived childhood paternal relationships and college females' personal adjustment', *Adolescence* 8, 31, 415–20.

FLAMMER, D. P. 1971. 'Self-esteem, parent identification and sex role development in preschool age boys and girls', *Child Study Journal* 2, 1, 39–45.

GIBSON, H. B. 1969. 'Early delinquency in relation to broken homes', *Journal of Child Psychology and Psychiatry* 10, 3, 195–204.

GLUECK, S. and GLUECK, E. 1962. *Family Environment and Delinquency*, Routledge and Kegan Paul, London. 328 pp.

GLUECK, S. and GLUECK, E. T. 1968. *Delinquents and Nondelinquents in Perspective*, Oxford University Press, London. 268 pp.

GOLDSTEIN, H. S. and PECK, R. 1973. 'Maternal differentiation, father absence and cognitive differentiation in children', *Archives of General Psychiatry* 29, 370–3.

GRAY, S. W. 1957. 'Masculinity-feminity in relation to anxiety and social acceptance', *Child Development* 28, 2, 203–14.

GREENSTEIN, J. M. 1966. 'Father characteristics and sex typing', *Journal of Personality and Social Psychology* 3, 3, 271–7.

GREGORY, I. 1965a. 'Anterospective data following childhood loss of a parent. I. Delinquency and high school dropout', *Archives of General Psychiatry* 13, 99–109.

GREGORY, I. 1965b. 'Anterospective data following childhood loss of a parent. II. Pathology, performance and potential among college students, *Archives of General Psychiatry* 13, 110–9.

HALEY, J. 1972. 'Critical overview of present status of family interaction', in J. L. Framo, *Family Interaction*, Springer, New York. 13–49.

HERMANS, H. J. M., TERAAK, J. J. F. and MAES, P. C. J. M. 1972. 'Achievement motivation and fear of failure in family and school', *Developmental Psychology* 6, 3, 520–8.

HERZOG, E. and SUDIA, C. E. 1971. *Boys in Fatherless Families*, US Department of Health, Education and Welfare, Office of Child Development, DHEW Publications No. (OCD) 72–33. Children's Bureau, Washington, DC. 120 pp.

HERZOG, E. and SUIDA, C. E. 1973. 'Children in fatherless families', in B. M. Caldwell and H. N. Ricciuti (eds) *Review of Child Developmental Research, III*, University of Chicago, Chicago. 141–232.

HETHERINGTON, E. M. 1965. 'A developmental study of the effects of sex of the dominant parent on sex-role preference, identification and imitation in children', *Journal of Personality and Social Psychology* 2, 2, 188–94.

HETHERINGTON, E. M. 1966. 'Effects of paternal absence on sex-typed behaviors in Negro and white preadolescent males', *Journal of Personality and Social Psychology* 4, 1, 87–91.

HETHERINGTON, E. M. 1972. 'Effects of father absence on personality development in adolescent daughters', *Developmental Psychology* 7, 3, 313–26.

HETHERINGTON, E. M., STOUWIE, R. J., and RIDBERG, E. H. 1971. 'Patterns of family interaction and child-rearing attitudes related to three dimensions of juvenile delinquency', *Journal of Abnormal Psychology* 78, 2, 160–76.

HOFFMAN, L. W. 1961. 'The father's role in the family and the child's peer-group adjustment', *Merrill-Palmer Quarterly* 7, 97–105.

HOLLINGSHEAD, A. B. and REDLICH, F. C. 1958. *Social class and mental illness: a community study*, Wiley, New York. 442 pp.

HONZIK, M. P. 1967. 'Environmental correlates of mental growth: prediction from the family setting at 21 months', *Child Development* 38, 2, 337–64.

INSELBERG, R. M. and BURKE, L. 1973. 'Social and psychological correlates of masculinity in young boys', *Merrill-Palmer Quarterly* 19, 1, 41–7.

JACOB, T. 1974. 'Patterns of family conflict and dominance as a function of child age and social class', *Developmental Psychology* 10, 1, 1–12.

JACOB, T. 1975. 'Family interaction in disturbed and normal families: a methodological and substantive review', *Psychological Bulletin* 82, 1, 33–65.

JONSSON, G. 1967. 'Delinquent boys, their parents and grandparents', *Acta Psychiatrica Scandinavica* 43, 195, 264 pp.

KELLER, P. A. and MURRAY, E. J. 1973. 'Imitative aggression with adult male and female models in father absent and father present Negro boys', *Journal of Genetic Psychology* 122, 217–21.

KELLY, J. M. 1970. 'Self-concept development in parent deprived children: a comparative study', *Graduate Research in Education and Related Disciplines* 6, 1, 30–48.

KLEIN, M. M., PLUTCHICK, R. and CONTE, H. R. 1973. 'Parental dominance – passivity and behavior problems of children', *Journal of Consulting and Clinical Psychology* 40, 3, 416–19.

KOCH, M. B. 1961. 'Anxiety in pre-school children from broken homes', *Merrill-Palmer Quarterly* 7, 4, 225–31.

KOHLBERG, L. 1967. 'A cognitive-developmental analysis of children's sex-role concepts and attitudes', in E. E. Maccoby (ed) *The Development of Sex Differences*, Tavistock Publications, London; Stanford University Press, Stanford, Calif. 82–173.

KOPF, K. E. 1970. 'Family variables and school adjustment of eighth grade father-absent boys', *Family Coordinator* 2, 145–50.

KRIESBERG, L. 1967. 'Rearing children for educational achievement in fatherless families', *Journal of Marriage and the Family* 29, 288–301.

KRIESBERG, L. 1970. *Mothers in Poverty*, Aldine, Chicago. 356 pp.

LAMBERT, L. and HART, S. 1976. 'Who needs a father?' *New Society* 37, 718, 80.

LANDY, F., ROSENBERG, B. G. and SUTTON-SMITH, B. 1969. 'The effect of limited father absence on cognitive development', *Child Development* 40, 941–4.

LAWTON, M. J. and SECHREST, L. 1962. 'Figure drawings by young boys from father-present and father-absent homes', *Journal of Clinical Psychology* 18, 304–5.

LEIDERMAN, G. 1959. 'Effect of parental relationships and child-training practices on boys' interactions with peers', *Acta Psychologica* 15, 469–70.

LESSING, E. E., ZAGORIN, S. W. and NELSON, D. 1970. 'WISC subtest and IQ score correlates of father absence' *Journal of Genetic Psychology* 117, 181–95.

LYNN, D. B. 1969. *Parental and Sex Role Identification: a Theoretical Formulation*, McCutchan, Berkeley, California.

MCCORD, J., MCCORD, W. and THURBER, E. 1962. 'Some effects of

228

paternal absence on male children', *Journal of Abnormal and Social Psychology* 64, 5, 361–9.

MILLER, B. A. B. 1961. 'Effects of father absence and mother's evaluation of father on the socialization of adolescent boys', *Dissertation Abstracts* 22, 1257–8.

MITCHELL, D. and WILSON, W. 1967. 'Relationship of father absence to masculinity and popularity of delinquent boys', *Psychological Reports* 20, 1173–4.

MURCHISON, N. 1974. 'Illustrations of the difficulties of some children in one-parent families', in Department of Health and Social Security, *Report of the Committee on One-Parent Families*, HMSO, London, Vol II. 363–91.

MURRELL, S. A. and STACHOWIAK, J. G. 1967. 'Consistency, rigidity and power in the interaction patterns of clinic and nonclinic families', *Journal of Abnormal Psychology* 72, 3, 265–72.

MUSSEN, P. 1961. 'Some antecedents and consequents of masculine sex-typing in adolescent boys', *Psychological Monographs*, Whole no. 506.

MUSSEN, P. 1962. 'Long-term consequents of masculinity of interests in adolescence', *Journal of Consulting Psychology* 26, 5, 435–40.

MUSSEN, P. and DISTLER, L. 1959. 'Masculinity, identification and father-son relationships', *Journal of Abnormal and Social Psychology* 59, 350–6.

MUSSEN, P. and DISTLER, L. 1960. 'Child-rearing antecedents of masculine identification in kindergarten boys', *Child Development* 31, 89–100.

MUSSEN, P. and RUTHERFORD, E. 1963. 'Parent-child relations and parental personality in relation to young children's sex-role preferences', *Child Development* 34, 589–607.

NASH, J. 1965. 'The father in contemporary culture and current psychological literature', *Child Development* 36, 1, 261–97.

NELSEN, E. A. and MACCOBY, E. E. 1966. 'The relationship between social development and differential abilities on the scholastic aptitude test', *Merrill-Palmer Quarterly* 12, 4, 269–84.

NELSEN, E. A. and VANGEN, P. M. 1971. 'Impact of father absence on heterosexual behaviors and social development of preadolescent girls in a ghetto environment', *Proceedings, 79th Annual Convention of the American Psychological Association* 6, 1, 165–6.

NYE, F. I. 1957. 'Child adjustment in broken or unhappy unbroken homes', *Marriage and Family Living* 19, 356–61.

ODOM, L., SEEMAN, J. and NEWBROUGH, J. R. 1971. 'A study of family communication patterns and personality integration in children', *Child Psychiatry and Human Development* 1, 4, 275–85.

OSOFSKY, J. D. 1972. 'Relationships between fathers' reported and observed behaviors with daughters', *Proceedings, 80th Annual Convention of the American Psychological Association* 1, 133–4.

PEDERSEN, F. A. 1966. 'Relationships between father-absence and emotional disturbance in male military dependents', *Merrill-Palmer Quarterly* 12, 4, 321–31.

PERRY, J. B. and PFUHL, E. H. 1963. 'Adjustment of children in "solo" and "remarriage" homes', *Marriage and Family Living* 25, 221–3.

PETERSON, D. R., BECKER, W. C., HELLMER, L. A., SHOEMAKER, D. J. and QUAY, H. C. 1959. 'Parental attitudes and child adjustment', *Child Development* 30, 119–30.

RADIN, N. 1972a. 'Father-child interaction and the intellectual functioning of four year old boys', *Developmental Psychology* 6, 2, 353–61.

RADIN, N. 1973. 'Observed paternal behaviors as antecedents of intellectual functioning in young boys', *Developmental Psychology* 8, 3, 369–76.

REES, A. H. and PALMER, F. H. 1970. 'Factors related to change in mental test performance', *Developmental Psychology Monographs* 3, 2, pt 2, 57 pp.

REPPUCCI, N. D. 1971. 'Parental education, sex differences, and performance on cognitive tasks among two year old children', *Developmental Psychology* 4, 2, 248–53, **p. 120**

REUTER, M. W. and BILLER, H. B. 1973. 'Perceived paternal nurturance-availability and personality adjustment among college males', *Journal of Consulting and Clinical Psychology* 40, 3, 339–42.

ROSEN, B. C. and D'ANDRADE, R. 1959. 'The psychosocial origins of achievement motivation', *Sociometry* 22, 185–218.

ROSENBERG, M. 1965. *Society and the Adolescent Self-Image*, Princeton, New Jersey, 326 pp.

ROTHBART, M. K. and MACCOBY, E. E. 1966. 'Parents' differential reactions to sons and daughters', *Journal of Personality and Social Psychology* 4, 3, 237–43.

RUTTER, M. 1966. *Children of Sick Parents: An Environmental and Psychiatric Study*, Oxford University Press, London. 146 pp.

RUTTER, M. 1971. 'Parent-child separation: Psychological effects on the children', *Journal of Child Psychology and Psychiatry* 12, 233–60.

RUTTER, M., YULE, B., QUINTON, D., ROWLANDS, O., YULE, W. and BERGER, M. 1975. 'Attainment and adjustment in two geographical areas: III. Some factors accounting for area differences', *British Journal of Psychiatry* 125, 520–33.

SANTROCK, J. W. 1970. 'Paternal absence, sex typing and identification', *Developmental Psychology* 2, 2, 264–72.

SANTROCK, J. W. 1972. 'Relation of type and onset of father absence to cognitive development', *Child Development* 43, 455–69.

SANTROCK, J. W. and WOHLFORD, P. 1970. 'Effects of father absence:

influence of the reason for and the onset of the absence', *Proceedings of the 78th Annual Convention of the American Psychological Association* 5, 1, 265–6.

SCHOOLMAN, J. L. 1969. 'The relationship of the development of masculinity to father absence in preadolescent boys', *Dissertation Abstracts International* 30, 6–B, 2917.

SCHUMAN, A. I. 1970. 'Power relations in emotionally disturbed and normal family triads', *Journal of Abnormal Psychology* 75, 1, 30–7.

SCIARA, F. J. and JANTZ, R. K. 1974. 'Father absence and its apparent effect on the reading achievement of black children from low income families', *Journal of Negro Education* 43, 2, 221–7.

SEARS, R. R. 1970. 'Relation of early socialization experiences to self-concepts and gender role in middle childhood', *Child Development* 41, 2, 267–89.

SOLOMON, D., HIRSCH, J. G., SCHEINFELD, R. and JACKSON, J. C. 1972. 'Family characteristics and elementary school achievement in an urban ghetto', *Journal of Consulting and Clinical Psychology* 39, 3, 462–6.

SOLOMON, D., HOULIHAN, K. A., BUSSE, T. V. and PARELIUS, R. J. 1971. 'Parent behavior and child academic achievement, achievement striving and related personality characteristics', *Genetic Psychology Monographs* 83, 2, 173–273.

SPELKE, E., ZELAZO, P., KAGAN, J. and KOTELCHUK, M. 1973. 'Father interaction and separation protest', *Developmental Psychology* 9, 1, 83–90. **p. 98**

SPREY, J. 1970. 'The study of single parenthood: some methodological considerations', in B. Schlesinger, *The One Parent Family. Perspectives and Annotated Bibliography*, University of Toronto Press. 13–25.

STEIN, A. H. and BAILEY, M. M. 1973. 'The socialization of achievement orientation in females', *Psychological Bulletin* 80, 5, 345–66.

SUTTON-SMITH, B., ROSENBERG, B. G. and LANDY, F. 1968. 'Father-absence effects in families of different sibling compositions', *Child Development* 39, 4, 1213–21.

THOMES, M. M. 1968. 'Children with absent fathers', *Journal of Marriage and the Family* 30, 1, 89–96.

VROEGH, K., JENKIN, N., BLACK, M. and HANDRICH, M. 1967. 'Discriminant analyses of preschool masculinity and femininity', *Multivariate Behavioral Research* 2, 3, 299–313.

WACHS, T. D., UZGIRIS, I. C. and HUNT, J. McV. 1971. 'Cognitive development in infants of different age levels and from different environmental backgrounds: an explanatory investigation', *Merrill-Palmer Quarterly* 17, 4, 283–317. **p. 122**

WALBERG, H. J. and MARJORIBANKS, K. 1973. 'Differential mental abilities and home environment: a canonical analysis', *Developmental Psychology* 9, 3, 363–8.

WARNER, W. L., MEEKER, M. and EELS, K. 1949. *Social class in America*, Chicago, Science Research Associates.

WASSERMAN, H. L. 1972. 'A comparative study of school performance among boys from broken and intact black families', *Journal of Negro Education* 41, 2, 137–41.

WEBB, A. P. 1963. 'Sex-role preferences and adjustment in early adolescents' *Child Development* 34, 3, 609–18.

WEST, D. J. 1969. *Present Conduct and Future Delinquency*, Heinemann, London; International Universities Press, New York. 207 pp.

WEST, D. J. and FARRINGTON, D. P. 1973. *Who Becomes Delinquent?* Heinemann, London; Crane, Russak & Co. 265 pp.

WILSON, A. B. 1967. 'Educational consequences of segregation in a California community', in US Commission on Civil Rights, *Racial Isolation in Public Schools*, Appendices, Vol 2, US Government Printing Office, Washington, DC. 165–206.

WILSON, K. L., ZURCHER, L. A., McADAMS, D. C. and CURTIS, R. L. 1975. 'Stepfathers and stepchildren: an exploratory analysis from two national surveys', *Journal of Marriage and the Family* 37, 3, 526–36.

WOHLFORD, P., SANTROCK, J. W., BERGER, S. E. and LIBERMAN, D. 1971. 'Older brothers' influence on sex-typed, aggressive and dependent behavior in father-absent children', *Developmental Psychology* 4, 2, 124–34.

WOLFF, S. and ACTON, W. P. 1968. 'Characteristics of parents of disturbed children', *British Journal of Psychiatry* 114, 593–601.

YARROW, M. R. 1963. 'Problems of methods in parent-child research', *Child Development* 34, 1, 215–26.

Part IV
Teachers' expectations and pupil performance

A. Introduction

The idea that teachers' attitudes and beliefs about the level of their pupils' ability will affect the pupils' actual attainments is by no means new (Pidgeon, 1970). The first claim to provide experimental evidence of this, though, was made by Rosenthal and Jacobson (1968). In essence, these researchers predicted to teachers at the beginning of the school year that certain of their pupils, actually randomly selected, would make unusual intellectual gains within the coming year, and these predictions were fulfilled. The effect of the study was immediate and dramatic. It received considerable publicity in the American popular press and inspired a whole body of research on teachers' expectations. The study itself was also severely criticised, mainly on the grounds of its technical deficiencies (Thorndike, 1968, 1969; Claiborn, 1969; Jensen, 1969; Snow, 1969; Elashoff and Snow, 1971). The vehemence of the attack, however justified the particular criticisms, suggests that the basic idea of the study caused much hostility.

The Rosenthal and Jacobson study was far more than an ingenious experiment but was one with important educational implications. In their book, the authors suggested that the generally poor school performance of disadvantaged children might be due not only to their social background, to cultural and linguistic impoverishment, and lack of motivation to do well at school. Teachers' attitudes and behaviour might also be a contributing factor towards the children's lack of success in school. Simply changing the teachers' expectations, without doing anything else for the disadvantaged child, could lead to an improvement in intellectual performance. It is this idea that teachers might be to blame to some extent, however unconsciously, for the low success of the disadvantaged child, rather than this arising from the limitations of the child himself that appears to arouse such passionate feelings.

It is unfortunate that the methodological criticisms of a study with such important practical implications appear to be justified. The basic weakness lies in the difficulty in attempting to alter teachers' expectations for the children in their classes. Evidence from the study suggests that the teachers took little notice of the predictions presented to them (Nuermberger, 1969; Snow, 1969) and it is doubtful whether the teachers' expectations were actually modified to any great extent.

233

Re-analyses of the study data, using a number of slightly different statistical approaches (Elashoff and Snow, 1971) do provide some evidence that the favourable-expectancy children in the first and second grades at least may have obtained a slight benefit from the experimental manipulation. However, according to Elashoff and Snow, even these analyses are of uncertain validity owing to the inadequacy of the original study design. It remains unclear whether teachers' expectations were actually altered at all in the Rosenthal and Jacobson study, and whether pupils did benefit from any modifications that did occur. The study did not show, as claimed, that it is possible to modify teachers' expectations with dramatic effects on the pupils, but rather that altering teachers' expectations is no easy task. The merit of the study is that it gave a tremendous impetus to research on the possible effects of teachers' expectations. Although in some cases the researchers' main aim appears to have been the refutation of the Rosenthal and Jacobson findings, others have attempted to design studies which enable the effects of teachers' expectations to be investigated more effectively.

In several of the replication studies the attempt to modify the teachers' expectations was even weaker than in the original study, the predictions being presented to the teachers at the end of the school year when the teachers' own expectations of the children were too well-established to be experimentally changed (Claiborn, 1969; Fielder et al., 1971). The authors of another replication study (José and Cody, 1971) demonstrate that the expectations of the majority of teachers had not been changed and correctly conclude that generalisations cannot be made about the effect of experimentally induced expectations unless it is ensured that the expectations have been effectively established. Nevertheless, the authors of the two studies mentioned above conclude from very weak attempts at altering teachers' expectations that 'the expectancy effect is not as pervasive as suggested in Rosenthal and Jacobson's original study' (Fielder et al., 1971) or, more sweepingly that the results 'do not support, nor suggest that there is, an expectancy effect' (Claiborn, 1969). In fact, these replication studies provide no evidence on whether teachers' expectations do affect pupil performance. Rather, the main point they prove is that teachers' expectations are not completely malleable, capable of immediate modification at the experimenter's whim.

In contrast to these findings there is evidence that when it is possible to establish experimental expectations, the effect on both teaching behaviour and pupil attainment is dramatic (Beez, 1970). This study, though, took place in an experimental situation, the teachers having no prior knowledge of the pupils. In the classroom situation, however, the experimental prediction is just one influence on the teacher which has to compete with her own expectations for the children as well as the children's behaviour. There is just one study (Meichenbaum et al., 1969), carried out in the rather special circumstances of a training school for adolescent girl delinquents which does appear to have succeeded in altering teachers' expectations in a classroom situation by taking great care in the way in which the favourable expectations were introduced to the teachers. Here, too, an immediate effect on both teaching behaviour and pupil attainment and behaviour was found. Unfortunately, the experimental period in this study was extremely brief, and it does not show whether the experimental expectancies can remain effective for more than a week or two.

As there is considerable difficulty in modifying teachers' expectations of children in the classroom, a more hopeful approach would appear to be an attempt to determine the effect of the teachers' own expectations on their pupils. This approach is increasingly being adopted by researchers. Some recent studies have investigated the relationship between teachers' expectations of future academic performance and the child's attainments and found a close association between them (Dusek and O'Connell, 1973; Willis, 1973), teachers' expectations being better predictors of academic achievement than IQ scores (Krupczak, 1973). The association between teachers' expectations and pupil performance does not necessarily mean, of course, that the teachers' expectations were influencing the pupils' attainments. The teachers may simply have been making accurate estimates of the children's academic abilities. There are, though, a few studies which do actually show that teachers' expectations can affect pupils' attainments. In one study, not in fact specifically concerned with the Rosenthal and Jacobson controversy (Burstall, 1968) it was found that children's attainments can be affected by the beliefs of teachers about the academic consequences of certain characteristics of the children, in this case teachers' beliefs about the success of low-ability children in learning French. Similarly, Palardy (1969) found that boys' reading achievements were influenced by their teachers' beliefs about boys' ability to learn to read as successfully as girls. A more recent study (Sutherland and Goldschmid, 1974) has found that expectations of teachers which are discrepant from ability, as measured by intelligence tests, can affect intellectual growth. Interestingly, it was negative discrepant teacher expectations which could not, of course, ethically be introduced in studies attempting experimental manipulations of teachers' expectations, rather than positive expectations that made a significant difference to intellectual development. It has also been found (Seaver, 1973) that children's school achievements may be influenced by teachers' knowledge of their older brothers and sisters, and the expectations derived from this knowledge.

Evidence that teachers do not base their estimations of children's ability entirely on intellectual factors comes from Barker Lunn's (1970) study of streaming in British primary schools. Although teachers

235

were found in the main to be accurate in their estimates of children's ability in relation to performance on an English test, where they were inaccurate, the tendency was to under-estimate working-class children and over-estimate middle-class children. These negative discrepant expectations for the working-class children may well have contributed to the decline in the reading performance of the working-class children relative to that of the middle-class children between the ages of 7 and 10. Findings from a number of studies in which teachers have been asked to make judgements about the future progress of hypothetical children from school records, test scores or answers to questions also show on the whole that teachers' estimations are influenced by non-ability factors.

Observational studies of classrooms (Rist, 1970; Nash, 1973) have found that teachers' expectations, partially based on non-intellective factors, may affect groupings of children and teacher behaviour towards them. A number of studies which have attempted to measure teacher behaviour either in the ordinary classroom situation (Brophy and Good, 1970; Willis, 1970) or in experimental teaching situations (Rothbart *et al.*, 1971; Rubovits and Maehr, 1971 and 1973; Chaikin *et al.*, 1974) have findings which suggest they behave differentially to those for whom they have high and low expectations, although the exact ways in which teacher behaviour is affected require clarification. It seems likely that the impact of teacher behaviour on the child has to be understood in the context of his general experiences in the classroom (Weinstein, 1976).

Taken as a whole, a considerable amount of evidence that teachers' expectations do influence their behaviour and pupils' actual achievements is accumulating. Obviously, in the actual school situation, the process is very complicated. Not all teachers will have the same beliefs about the academic consequences of certain attributes of the children. Nor will the same expectations necessarily influence the behaviour of all teachers in the same way (Meichenbaum *et al.*, 1969). Factors which may influence the teacher's judgement do not have the same strength of effect. There is evidence, for example, that reporting a child's IQ score by itself has little effect but that combined with a prediction it is much more powerful in shaping teachers' expectations (Beggs, 1972). Teachers' observations of children for whom they have no prior knowledge appear to be only selectively influenced by information given (Salvia, 1973), but expectations are influenced more than observations (Mason, 1973). The extent to which teachers' expectations will affect pupil performance in the classroom is as yet unclear, but there is little doubt that they do have an influence.

Studies on teachers' classroom behaviour appear to be a particularly fruitful line of research. They suggest that even if teachers' initial estimates of children's ability are not biased by non-intellectual attributes of the children, teachers may still be inadvertently widening the gap between children. Nash (1973) indicates how the teacher may create quite different school environments for the children she views favourably and those she views unfavourably. To give one example, unfavourably-perceived children who created a disturbance in the classroom were reproved by name, while the same behaviour from a favourably-perceived child merely brought an anonymous reproval to the class as a whole, a difference in treatment that could have a considerable effect on a child's self-perception.

The implications of this research for educational policy cannot be doubted. Teachers must be made aware of the non-intellectual factors which may bias their judgements of a child; of possible differences in their behaviour to those for whom they have different expectations; and of their power to influence children's attainments. The individual teacher, though, is under the constraints of the educational system. The competitiveness of the system in this country, the emphasis in grouping by ability even in unstreamed classes must encourage teachers to expect differences between children and to widen rather than close gaps.

Expectations about achievement in the educational system possibly have more substantial effects than their influence on individual teachers. Expectations of low achievement by non-grammar-school pupils may have been a factor in their being allocated fewer resources than grammar-school pupils in some local authorities (Byrne, 1974). These policies inevitably resulted in lower achievements than could be accounted for by ability. How far such inequalities, based on expectations about achievement, are being overcome in the British comprehensive school system, where this has been fully introduced, is an important area for future research.

In the following review, the material is grouped into six sections:
i) the controversy around the Rosenthal and Jacobson study;
ii) replications of the Rosenthal and Jacobson study;
iii) other attempts to alter experimentally teachers' expectations;
iv) the effects of teachers' own expectations;
v) the communication of the teachers' expectations to the children;
vi) factors determining teachers' expectations.

In each section, brief comments on the material included are followed by annotations, presented, in this part of the review, in chronological order. Studies which do not fit neatly into a single category are placed in the section which is in accordance with the main interest of the researcher. At the end of Part IV all references are, as usual, listed in alphabetical order.

B. Controversy around the Rosenthal and Jacobson study

Essentially, the Rosenthal and Jacobson study claimed to show that

237

children reported to class teachers as having unusual potential for intellectual growth (supposedly on the basis of a test designed to predict academic spurting) did make greater gains in intellectual growth than controls over the school year, even though they were actually chosen at random and differed from the controls only in that the prophecy was made for them.

Unfortunately, the whole foundation of the study is somewhat shaky, for it is doubtful whether the experimenters' prognosis for the pupils had much effect at all on the expectations of most of the teachers. This point has been made by two critics of the study (Nuermberger, 1969; Snow, 1969) who have drawn attention to the report, near the end of the book, which describes the teachers' reactions to the lists of the 'potential bloomers'. Not only could the sixteen teachers recall no more than eighteen of the original seventy-two names two years after the beginning of the experiment but some, overburdened with memos, had merely glanced at the lists and thrown them away. Rosenthal and Jacobson's only comment is: 'had we known how casually our lists of names would be treated, we might have thought twice about the likelihood of obtaining any IQ gains as a function of teachers' expectations'. They do not express any more serious doubts and do not even entertain the possibility that the basis of the study may have been undermined by the failure to modify teachers' expectations to any great extent.

It may have been, of course, that the lists did have some immediate impact at least on a number of the teachers despite their having little memory of them later on. For there is some evidence that favourable teachers' expectations did bring an advantage to the youngest children (the first and second grades) even from the re-analyses of the data made by critics of the statistical analyses of the original study (Elashoff and Snow, 1971). A significant but slight expectancy advantage still held after procedures were adopted which minimised the effect of the many extreme pre- and post-test IQ scores found for the younger children, due to the inadequate norming at this age level of the intelligence measure used (Flanagan's Tests of General Ability) – one of the major sources of criticism of the study (Thorndike, 1968; 1969; Snow, 1969; Elashoff and Snow, 1971). Nevertheless, uncertainty remains about the validity of these re-analyses, due to the weaknesses of the original study design (Elashoff and Snow, 1971).

Whether the weak experimental intervention carried out by Rosenthal and Jacobson did influence first and second-grade teachers to the extent that the favourable-expectancy pupils in their classes benefitted slightly must, then, remain uncertain. The only definite conclusion to be drawn from the study is that the effect of teachers' expectations on pupil performance is an issue meriting further research.

Annotations

ROSENTHAL, R. and JACOBSON, L. 1968. *Pygmalion in the Classroom. Teacher Expectation and Pupils' Intellectual Development*, Holt, Rinehart and Winston, New York. 240pp.

Each class teacher in a primary (public elementary) school in a predominantly lower-class area was presented at the beginning of the school year with a list of names of a number of pupils in the class, supposedly children predicted by a previously administered test (purportedly the 'Harvard Test of Inflected Acquisition', but actually an intelligence test – Flanagan's Tests of General Ability (TOGA)) to be those likely to show 'academic blooming' in the near future, but, in fact, 20 per cent of the class chosen at random.

Eight months after this list was presented to teachers, the favourable-expectancy children were found to have made significantly greater gains in intellectual growth than the controls (re-testing on the TOGA being administered one year after the original testing). The favourable-expectancy children gained significantly more than the controls in total IQ in eleven out of the seventeen classes tested; in verbal IQ in twelve out of eighteen classes; and in reasoning IQ in fifteen out of seventeen classes. The benefit of the favourable expectancy was greatest, though for the six- to eight-year-old (first and second grade) children. The benefits of the favourable expectancy also varied with other attributes of the children. Girls tended to show greater expectancy advantage in reasoning IQ and boys in verbal IQ, the areas in which they were already strongest. There was a tendency for the Mexican children to have greater expectancy advantage than the non-Mexican children, and boys who looked more 'Mexican' benefitted more than those who looked less Mexican. There was also some tendency for middle-track (ability group) children, particularly girls, to have greater expectancy advantage than children in high or low tracks.

The effects of the favourable expectancy were already beginning to appear four months after the presentation of the lists to the teachers, re-testing on the TOGA showing that the 'special' children made greater gains than the controls in total and reasoning IQ, though the difference was small and non-significant. A final re-testing on the TOGA two years after the initial pre-testing and twenty months after the teachers were presented with the names of the 'potential bloomers' showed that only the original eleven to twelve-year-old (fifth-grade) children continued to benefit from the favourable expectancy. The tendency for the middle-track children to benefit was stronger than at the end of the first year, and the favourable-expectancy, high-track boys actually showed an expectancy disadvantage. Where comparison was possible, the advantage of the favourable expectancy children was found to be greater on objective measures of achievement (Iowa Tests of Basic Skills) than on teachers' assessments of academic achievement. This suggests that the effect of favourable teachers' expectation on pupil performance cannot be accounted for by biased teacher assessment. The teachers did administer the IQ tests to the children themselves but they were scored by independent research assistants. Re-testing of three classes by an independent examiner also produced very similar results to those obtained by the teachers' own testing. Nor can the expectancy effect be attributed to teachers' devoting more of their time to experimental than control children, at least from the teachers' estimates of how they allocated their time. In fact, from teachers' recollections two years after the experiment began, teachers appear to have paid very little attention to the names presented to them. It is suggested that the teacher may communicate expectancy in a subtle and complex manner to the child and that further investigation of possible mechanisms is necessary.

GUMPERT, P. and GUMPERT, C. September 1968. 'The teacher as Pygmalion: comments on the psychology of expectation', *Urban Review* 3, 21–25.

Argument that the proper unit of analysis of the Rosenthal and Jacobson study should have been the classroom average and not the score of the individual child, as all children in a class are affected by the teachers' and other children's behaviour. When the data were re-analysed, using the classroom average as the unit of analysis, many of the statistically significant results no longer held, but the main effects were still statistically significant. It is concluded that the study satisfactorily shows that the teacher expectancy effect does take place.

THORNDIKE, R. L. November, 1968. 'Review of Rosenthal, R. and Jacobson, L., Pygmalion in the classroom', *American Educational Research Journal* 5, 4, 708–11.

Criticism of the Rosenthal and Jacobson study on the grounds that the main effects of the favourable expectancy appear only for the youngest children (grades one and two), while Flanagan's Tests of General Ability, the intelligence test used, appear not to function at this level, extrapolation down from the published norms giving, for example, some excessively low pre-test reasoning IQ scores.

NUERMBERGER, R. M. February 1969, 'Review of Pygmalion in the classroom', *Personnel and Guidance Journal* 47, 575–8.

Argues that the Rosenthal and Jacobson research is based on a faulty premise. The authors assumed that once the teachers knew which children were about to make an 'academic spurt' they would subtly influence the children's behaviour – but, at the experiment's end, it was found that the teachers, over-burdened with memos, had merely glanced at the lists and thrown them away.

SNOW, R. E. April 1969. 'Unfinished Pygmalion. Review of R. Rosenthal and L. Jacobson, Pygmalion in the classroom: teacher expectation and pupils' intellectual development', *Contemporary Psychology* 14, 4, 197–9.

Main points of criticism of the Rosenthal and Jacobson study are: i) inadequacy of the norms of Flanagan's Tests of Ability for the younger children; ii) the statistical analysis itself; iii) presentation of material – findings reported in the text cannot be verified from the data given. It is also noted that Rosenthal and Jacobson fail to face the full implications of their findings that teachers could not recall, and hardly glanced at, the lists of 'potential bloomers'.

ROSENTHAL, R. November, 1969. 'Empirical vs decreed validation of clocks and tests', *American Educational Research Journal* 6, 4, 689–92.

Main points of this reply to Thorndike (1968, above) are:-
i) the evidence for the expectancy advantage was found on the much criticised reasoning IQ not just in the first and second grades, which are said to be least well-measured, but in fifteen of the seventeen classes tested – or, leaving aside the first two grades, for ten of the eleven classes; ii) the 'worthless' pre-test IQs for the first-grade children were able to predict at a considerably better than chance level the track to which the children were later assigned by teachers (who did not know the test results).

THORNDIKE, R. L. November, 1969. 'But you have to know how to tell the time', *American Educational Research Journal* 6, 4, 692.

Reply to Rosenthal (1969, above), mainly concerned with adequacy of norms published in Flanagan's Tests of General Ability at the younger age levels.

JENSEN, A. Winter, 1969. 'How much can we boost IQ and scholastic achievement?', *Harvard Educational Review* 39, 1 ('Expectancy gain', 107–8).

Questions a number of aspects of the Rosenthal and Jacobson study, including the statistical techniques, use of the same form of group administered IQ test for each testing, and teacher-administration of tests.

GEPHART, W. May 1970. 'Will the real Pygmalion please stand up', *American Educational Research Journal* 7, 3, 473–5.

. Accusation that Rosenthal (1969) in reply to Thorndike claims that expectancy advantage was found in reasoning IQ in fifteen of seventeen classes but that tables in the book (pp 75 and 77) show that only the favourable-expectancy children in grades one and two benefitted. It is concluded that the expectancy effect is the investigator's misinterpretation of what data are because of some established expectation, not some mystical change in the behaviour of subjects.

ROSENTHAL, R. August, 1970. 'Another view of Pygmalion', *Contemporary Psychology* 15, 8, 524.

Reply to Snow (1969, see above) making similar points as in reply to Thorndike (Rosenthal, 1969) and also disputing Snow's criticisms of some of the statistical analyses in the book.

ELASHOFF, J. D. and SNOW, R. E. (1971) *Pygmalion Reconsidered.* Charles A. Jones, Ohio (chapters I-V, pp. 1–47 and Appendix A pp. 86–124).

A methodological criticism of *Pygmalion in the Classroom* is presented in the first five chapters, while an Appendix reports a re-analysis of the raw data, supplied to the present authors by Rosenthal and Jacobson. The main criticisms concern:
i) Reporting of the research. The study was reported in a misleading manner – conclusions are over-stated and do not agree from place to place. Insufficient data is given to the reader from which to determine the validity of the statistical procedures. There is a misuse of the p-value – it is implied that the observed difference is the true difference, while the p-value only gives the likelihood of a larger difference being found if there is actually no difference between the means of two samples.
ii) Design and sampling problems. It is not clear how the children were assigned to the experimental group – the experimental children were supposed to be a 20 per cent random sample, but the number was varied for each classroom to make the lists of 'potential bloomers' more plausible to the teachers, and it is uncertain how this was carried out. Imbalance in design – the original inequalities and sampling loss during the experimental period mean that the experimental and control groups were not comparable on a number of factors, of which the most important is probably ability track. In view of the uncertain sampling plan, lack of balance and possibility of non-random subject losses, the consistently higher pre-test scores of the experimental subjects present serious difficulties which attempts at statistical correction may not erase.
iii) Measurement problems. The group intelligence test used, Flanagan's

Test of General Abilities (TOGA), has not been fully normed for the youngest children. Some of the pre-test IQs obtained for the first-grade children were extraordinarily low and could have been obtained by guessing. The IQ scores were unstable over time in many instances. Other mental ability information which was easily obtainable was not used to examine the validity of the TOGA scores and of how valid changes of TOGA scores were as measures of intellectual growth, e.g. the experimental group did not show a significantly greater proportion of upward changes in ability track than did the control group, and so track changes do not support the contention that the experimental children benefitted from the favourable expectancy. The validity of the experiment in general is doubtful – the teachers felt that they had paid little or no attention to the lists of 'potential bloomers'.

Overall, the problems of unbalanced sampling design, 20 per cent subject loss, many extreme scores, and low reliability mean that it is not clear that any analysis or significance test on these data can be accepted as wholly valid. From the re-analyses carried out, using a number of slightly different statistical approaches, there was no evidence of an expectancy effect for grades three to six, but some indication of an expectancy effect for grades one and two did emerge. While it cannot be concluded that the analysis has demonstrated an expectancy effect, sufficient evidence has been provided to justify further research.

ROSENTHAL, R. and RUBIN, D. B. 1971. 'Pygmalion reaffirmed', in J. D. Elashoff and R. E. Snow, *Pygmalion Reconsidered*, Charles A. Jones, Ohio. (Appendix C pp. 139–55).

The various statistical procedures used by Elashoff and Snow strongly support the hypothesis of positive effects for favourable teacher expectancies, but these authors repeatedly instruct their readers not to believe the results of their own analysis because of 'doubtful randomisation' and 'imbalance' in experimental conditions in Rosenthal and Jacobson's original study. The children were assigned to the experimental conditions by tables of random numbers and dozens of tests of the distribution of the pre-test scores gave no indication of failure of randomisation. In the one replication study mentioned by Elashoff and Snow, two of the six teachers involved were aware of the purpose of the research, as the author explains in his doctrinal thesis, but fails to mention in his later published report (Claiborn, 1969). The weight of replication evidence from studies both in everyday and laboratory situations is, in fact, very heavy – over a third of the studies reached or exceeded $p < .05$ in the predicted direction, a result that would be virtually unobtainable if there were no effects from experimental expectancies.

243

C. Replications of the Rosenthal and Jacobson study

There are six published studies using a design similar to the Rosenthal and Jacobson research. The experimental children, actually selected at random, were presented to teachers as those who were likely, from the findings of a test designed to predict unusual intellectual growth (actually an intelligence test), to make an academic spurt in the near future, and their gains on IQ and other attainment measures were compared with those of the controls over the experimental period. Two of the studies (Claiborn, 1969; Mendels and Flanders, 1973), particularly the latter, tried to overcome some of the difficulties for statistical analysis presented by the Rosenthal and Jacobson design. In the Mendels and Flanders study, the favourable expectancy and control groups were equivalent both in number of children and pre-test IQ scores, and an intelligence test was used (Cognitive Abilities Test) which had more adequate norms for the younger children than the test used (Flanagan's Tests of General Ability) in the original study.

Only in two of the replication studies (Conn et al., 1968; Mendels and Flanders, 1973), the former having Rosenthal himself as a member of the research team, were any tendencies found for the experimental children to make greater intellectual gains than the controls and these were very slight, failing to reach statistical significance. It is of interest, though, that these slight trends were found in the Mendels and Flanders study, the most carefully carried out of any of the replication studies. Not only were attempts made at overcoming the design and measurement weaknesses of the original study, but an effort was made to ensure that the teachers took some notice of the experimental expectancies – they were asked to send a postcard back to the experimenters with the names of the 'potential spurters' listed.

Nevertheless, even in the Mendels and Flanders study, only a weak attempt was made to establish artificially the favourable expectations, as the authors acknowledged. The investigators in another of the replication studies (José and Cody, 1971) at least tried to find out whether the favourable experimental expectations had been established by administering a questionnaire to the teachers after the experimental period. This showed there had been a failure to establish the favourable expectancy for the majority of teachers and José and Cody correctly pointed out that it is necessary to ensure that teacher expectancies have actually been modified before drawing any conclusions about their effects. Rosenthal (Evans and Rosenthal, 1969) once again, though, appeared to be happily unconcerned that most of the teachers in his study failed to recollect the names of the 'potential bloomers'. In the remaining replication studies (Conn et al., 1968; Claiborn, 1969, Fielder et al., 1971) the attempt at establishing the favourable expectations was even more feeble. The favourable predictions were presented to the teachers a considerable time after the beginning of the school year, when teachers must have already had their own well-established expectations for the children.

An additional weakness in most of the replication studies is the very short experimental period, only two months in one study (Claiborn, 1969) and four months in two others (Fielder *et al.*, 1971; José and Cody, 1971) between the presentation of the names to the teachers and the re-testing of IQ.

Some of the researchers (Claiborn, 1969; Fielder *et al.*, 1971) do appear to be aware of the limitations on their studies imposed by the introduction of the expectancy late in the school year and the short experimental period. What is puzzling is why they chose these conditions for their research if they seriously hoped to find out whether teachers' expectations do affect pupil performance.

In the study most widely cited as refuting the Rosenthal and Jacobson findings (Claiborn, 1969) two out of six of the teachers were at least partially aware of the true purpose of the experiment, as the author admits in his doctoral thesis but not in his much more widely known journal article (Rosenthal and Rubin, 1971). It is difficult not to conclude that he was more concerned with disproving the Rosenthal and Jacobson findings than in investigating any possible effects of teachers' expectations.

Although the replication studies have largely negative findings, they in no way show that strongly held expectations of teachers do not influence pupil performance.

Annotations

CONN, L. K., EDWARDS, C. N., ROSENTHAL, R. and CROWNE, D. 1968. 'Perception of emotion and response to teachers' expectancy by elementary school children', *Psychological Reports* 22, 27–34.

In this study, six- to thirteen-year-old children attending a school in an upper middle-class area were administered an IQ test (Flanagan's Tests of General Ability) four months before the end of the school year and were re-tested both at the end of the same and the following school years. The children randomly assigned to the favourable-expectancy group tended to gain more in IQ than the control children after four months but less on the second re-testing, similarly to the high ability group of the Rosenthal and Jacobson study. Findings of the study also suggest that ability to perceive and interpret non-verbal communication of emotion may be a factor in the process by which teachers' expectations influence their pupils' attainments.

CLAIBORN, W. L. 1969. 'Expectancy effects in the classroom: a failure to replicate', *Journal of Educational Psychology* 60, 5, 377–83.

In this study, IQ changes (Flanagan's Tests of General Ability) over the experimental period of two months were not significantly greater for the randomly selected favourable-expectancy group than for the controls. Observation of teacher-pupil interactions showed no greater change for the experimental than for the control group after the introduction of the expectancy. Subjects were six- to seven-year-old (first grade) pupils from three schools in middle-class areas. The author points out that the IQ tests used, statements about the 'potential bloomers', and percentage designated as potential bloomers were the same as in the Rosenthal and Jacobson study. Major differences were, though, that the favourable expectancy was introduced in the second semester of the school year, well after the teachers would have formed their impression of the children; re-testing of IQ took place after only two months; pre-test IQ was substantially higher. It is concluded that the study findings are equivocal.

EVANS, J. T. and ROSENTHAL, R. 1969. 'Interpersonal self-fulfilling prophecies: further extrapolation from the laboratory to the classroom', *Proceedings, 77th Annual Convention of the American Psychological Association.* 371–2.

Subjects in this study were 477 children (from kindergarten age to about eleven years) attending two schools in a middle-class area of a Mid-western city. After one year, boys in the favourable-expectancy group were found to have made significantly greater gains in reasoning IQ (Flanagan's Tests of General Ability) than controls, but favourable-expectancy girls gained less than controls. Findings were similar in the two schools.

BAKER, J. P. and CRIST, J. L. 1971. 'Teacher expectancies: a review of the literature', in J. D. Elashoff and R. E. Snow, *Pygmalion Reconsidered*, Charles A. Jones, Ohio (chapter VI, pp. 48–64).

Summaries and criticisms of studies relevant to the hypothesis that teachers' expectations affect pupils' behaviour and progress are presented under the following headings:
1) replications of the Rosenthal and Jacobson research (nine studies); 2) studies of the effect of expectancy on teachers' perceptions of their pupils (seven); 3) studies of the effect of teachers' expectancies on various measures of pupil behaviour and achievement (six); 4) studies of the influence of expectancies on teachers' treatment of their pupils. It is concluded that teachers' expectancies probably do not affect their pupils' IQ scores – but that only weak to moderate expectations were induced in

the replication studies, and it has not yet been tested whether strongly occurring natural expectancies can influence intellectual growth. Observed teacher and pupil behaviour, and pupil achievements, particularly on teacher-controlled measures, are likely to be affected by naturally occurring teachers' expectations, or strong experimentally induced expectations. It is recommended that the Rosenthal and Jacobson's paradigm be abandoned; instead there should be research into the effects of naturally occurring expectancies on the teacher-pupil interaction process and on teacher-controlled achievement measures. The question for future research is not whether there are expectancy effects but how these operate in the school situation. With further understanding, school administrative arrangements and teacher training programmes could be devised which would avert the effects of negative teacher expectations.

FIELDER, W. R., COHEN, R. D. and FEENEY, S. 1971. 'An attempt to replicate the teacher expectancy effect', *Psychological Reports* 29, 1223–8.

19 per cent of 796 pupils from thirty-six classes of three schools, randomly selected, were presented to teachers at the beginning of the school term as showing exceptional potential for intellectual growth. Pre-testing of IQ (Flanagan's Tests of General Ability), by the investigators, took place two weeks before the beginning of the spring term and re-testing four months later. Gains in total IQ, reasoning IQ and verbal IQ showed no expectancy advantage for the experimental children as a whole, nor for those in grades one and two considered separately. Nor did the experimental children from either the school in the middle-class area or from two schools in deprived areas with substantial Mexican-American populations benefit from the favourable expectancy. The authors note that their study took place in the spring term, by which time it may have been more difficult to implant the expectancy advantage. They also point out that one term may be too short a period for the expectancy advantage to appear.

JOSE, J. and CODY, J. J. 1971. 'Teacher-pupil interaction as it relates to attempted changes in teacher expectancy of academic ability and achievement', *American Educational Research Journal* 8, 1, 39–49.

One hundred and forty-four six to eight-year-old (first and second grade) pupils from eighteen classes were randomly selected as subjects, four pupils from each class being assigned at random to the favourable-expectancy group and four to the control group. Four months after the favourable expectancy was presented to teachers no significant differences were found between the score gains of the experimental and

247

control groups in either intelligence (Flanagan's Tests of General Ability) or achievement (reading and arithmetic sub-tests of Metropolitan Achievement Tests).

Observation of teacher-pupil interactions during the experimental period showed few differences in the teachers' behaviour to the control and experimental groups. A questionnaire administered to teachers after the end of the experiment showed that only seven of the eighteen teachers had expected the experimental children to 'bloom' academically. It is concluded that generalisations cannot be made about the effects of teachers' expectancies until research is conducted which effectively modifies teachers' expectancies.

MENDELS, G. E. and FLANDERS, J. P. 1973. 'Teachers' expectations and pupil performance', *American Educational Research Journal* 10, 3, 203–12.

In this replication study, the favourable-expectancy children tended to make slightly greater gains in IQ (Cognitive Abilities Test) than the control children over the experimental period of six months. There were no statistically significant differences between the two groups in teachers' grades or reading level at the end of the experimental period, but the direction of mean differences favoured the experimental group. In four classes, teachers reported that the favourable-expectancy children made greater gains than the other children. Subjects were 108 six-to seven-year-old (first grade) children attending classes for the educationally deprived in ten different schools. There were no significant differences in the pre-test IQ between the experimental and control groups, and both contained the same number of children.

D. Other experimental attempts to alter teachers' expectations

The studies presented in this section are heterogeneous in design, though they have in common the experimental modification of teachers' expectations. A number are quite similar to the Rosenthal and Jacobson research, but differ sufficiently in one or more ways to preclude their being categorised as replication studies (Anderson and Rosenthal, 1968; Meichenbaum *et al.*, 1969; Fine, 1972; Kester and Letchworth, 1972; Pellegrini and Hicks, 1972; Dusek and O'Connell, 1973; Rosenthal *et al.*, 1974). Main points of difference included: attainment rather than intelligence tests being used to measure the effect of the favourable expectancy (Kester and Letchworth, 1972; Meichenbaum *et al.*, 1969; Dusek and O'Connell, 1973); a slightly different presentation of the favourable expectancy, subjects being reported to teachers as 'bright'

(Kester and Letchworth, 1972) or as those who would make progress in reading (Fine, 1972); the study taking place not in a normal school situation but in a day camp for retarded boys (Anderson and Rosenthal, 1968) a training school for adolescent delinquent girls (Meichenbaum *et al.*, 1969) or an experimental enrichment programme for disadvantaged children (Pellegrini and Hicks, 1972). All but one of these studies (Meichenbaum et al., 1969) had largely negative findings.

The crucial difference between the study by Meichenbaum *et al.*, and the others appears to lie in the effective establishment of the experimental expectations. This was successfully achieved in the Meichenbaum *et al.*, study by presenting the favourable expectancy to the teachers at a group meeting during which teachers were encouraged to express their reactions to the girls named. After some initial surprise at the inclusion of some girls for whom they had previously had low expectations the teachers managed to find evidence from the girls' past behaviour of their potential for blooming. This procedure appeared to overcome the disadvantage of carrying out the experiment at the end of the school year, when teachers' own expectancies were already well-established, and appeared to be sufficient to enable the favourable expectancy girls to show greater gain than the controls in an objectively marked examination in as short a period as two weeks.

In two other studies (Pitt, 1956; Fleming and Anttonen, 1971a,b,c) the former being a forerunner to the Rosenthal and Jacobson study, the technique of reporting inflated IQs for the experimental children to the teacher was used. Here, too, findings were negative. Again, there is some doubt as to whether the experimental expectancies were effectively established. The experimental children were not new to the school in either study, and the knowledge that teachers already had of their abilities may have been too well-established to be affected by the mere reporting of inflated IQs. There is some evidence from another study (Beggs *et al.*, 1972) that awareness of IQ in itself has little influence on teachers' expectations of pupil achievement.

In the two remaining studies (Beez, 1970; Schrank, 1970) the expectancies seem to have been effectively established, and both produce evidence that the favourable expectancies benefitted pupil performance. Schrank's study used a rather different design from those discussed so far. Instruction groups of Air Force cadets were given ability labels, in accordance with the usual practice, but the students were, in fact, randomly assigned to groups. It was found that only when the instructors as well as the students believed in the ability labels did the higher-ability labelled groups perform better academically than the lower-ability labelled groups.

Beez's (1970) study is perhaps the most dramatic demonstration that experimentally induced expectations can affect teaching behaviour and pupil attainment, but it is also farthest from the ordinary classroom situation. The tutors in this study had no prior knowledge of the children with whom they worked on a number of experimental tasks, and in these circumstances they appear to have been considerably influenced by the fake psychological evaluations provided for each child. Of course, this does not mean that teachers' own expectations necessarily have a similarly dramatic effect in the classroom for they are subject to continual modification by better knowledge of the child.

It is interesting that some of the studies in this section which failed to show that experimental expectations influenced the pupils' performance did find some indication that the teachers' own expectations were influencing the pupils' attainments (Fleming and Anttonen, 1971a; Dusek and O'Connell, 1973). In the first-mentioned study it was found that teachers' opinions of intelligence tests influenced their pupils' attainments on intelligence and academic achievement tests. In the latter study, an attempt was made to determine the teachers' own expectations of their pupils. These expectations were found to correlate significantly with the pupils' actual academic achievements. There was some evidence that these expectations were determined by the children's ability, rather than by non-ability factors (Dusek and O'Connell, 1973; O'Connell et al., 1974). Subjects were, though, children with at least a full year's school experience, by which time the effect of teachers' expectations for the children may have become incorporated into their school records.

Annotations

PITT, C. C. V. 1956. 'An experimental study of the effects of teachers' knowledge or incorrect knowledge of pupil IQs on teachers' attitudes and practices and pupils' attitudes and achievements', *Dissertation Abstracts* 16, 2387–8.

Carried out some time prior to the Rosenthal and Jacobson research, this study found no effects on the achievement scores or teachers' marks of eleven- to thirteen-year-old (fifth and sixth grade) boys which could be attributed to teachers' knowing or not knowing the boys' IQs or to the reporting of inflated or deflated (by 10 points) IQs to teachers. The study was carried out over a period of six months with 320 boys from an elementary school system in a suburban area of Toronto, Ontario, as subjects.

ANDERSON, D. F. and ROSENTHAL, R. 1968. 'Some effects of interpersonal expectancy and social interaction on institutionalized retarded children', *Proceedings of the 76th Annual Convention of the American Psychological Association* 3, 479–80.

Institutionalised retarded boys who were both assigned to the favourable-expectancy group and who experienced an enriched social environment decreased in reasoning IQ (Flanagan's Tests of General Ability) over the eight weeks of the experimental period compared with boys who were in the favourable-expectancy or enriched-environment groups only, or controls who received no special treatment. The subjects were twenty-eight retarded boys, aged nine to sixteen years, attending a summer camp. Boys in the favourable-expectancy group increased in social competence (Cain Levine scale) compared with the controls, and received less attention from day-camp counsellors. It is concluded that manipulation of expectations can produce a dramatic effect in a relatively short time but that the nature of the effect depends on the particular situation.

MEICHENBAUM, D. H., BOWERS, K. S. and ROSS, R. R. 1969. 'A behavioral analysis of teacher expectancy effect', *Journal of Personality and Social Psychology* 13, 4, 306–16.

Subjects in this study were fourteen adolescent institutionalised delinquent girls, all taught by four teachers. The study was conducted at the end of the school year when teachers had formed their own assessments of the girls' intellectual potential. Instead of randomly selecting the experimental group, teachers' assessments of the girls' potential were determined, and three girls identified by teachers as having high potential and three girls identified by teachers as having low potential were selected as the favourable-expectancy students. Teachers' expectations were effectively modified. The names of the 'potential bloomers' were presented to teachers at a group meeting by their chief psychologist, the teachers being given the chance to discuss their reactions. Girls in the experimental group improved significantly more than those in the control group over the two-week period following the presentation of expectancies on objectively scored tests of academic performance, though not on subjectively scored tests, and in the frequency of appropriate classroom behaviour. Teachers did not increase in the amount of attention they gave to the favourable-expectancy group, but the quality of the interactions changed, though the nature of the change varied for the individual teachers.

SCHRANK, W. R. 1970. 'A further study of the labeling effect of ability grouping', *Journal of Educational Research* 63, 8, 358–60.

A report of two experiments conducted at the US Air Force Academy. In the first experiment students from high-ability-labelled groups performed significantly better academically (teachers' grades and examination grades) than students from low-ability-labelled groups although students were actually randomly assigned to the groups regardless of ability. In the second experiment few differences were found between the academic performances of students in the higher- and lower-ability-labelled groups. The major difference between the experiments was that instructors were informed in the second, but not in the first, experiment of the random nature of the groups. The teachers' expectations of pupil performance and consequent teaching methods and standards of grading appear to be the crucial factor in producing differences in academic performance between the groups.

BEEZ, W. V. 1970. 'Influence of biased psychological reports on teacher behavior and pupil performance', in M. B. Miles and W. W. Charters, Jr. comps, *Learning in social settings*, Allyn and Bacon, Boston. 328–34. Also summary in *Proceedings of the 76th Annual Convention of the American Psychological Association* 1968, 605–6.

An experimental study inspired by the Rosenthal and Jacobson research, but with an entirely different design. Sixty teachers attending graduate summer classes were randomly assigned as individual tutors to Head Start children. Half of the children, randomly selected, were presented to the teachers as being of 'high ability' and half of 'low ability'. Each was given a folder containing a faked psychological evaluation of the child – all were described as average in IQ but for the 'low-ability' group the debilitative effects of cultural deprivation and poor school prognosis were emphasised, while positive aspects of the child's behaviour and a good school prognosis were given for the 'high-ability' group. Teachers were asked to work individually with the children on two experimental tasks. Significantly higher scores were obtained on the symbol-learning task by the 'high-ability' group (5.9) than by the 'low-ability' group (3.1). Teachers of the two groups differed dramatically in teaching behaviour, those with the favourable-expectancy group attempting to teach 10.43 words and those with low expectancy group only 5.66. Teachers rated the favourable-expectancy children significantly higher than the low-expectancy children on achievement, social competence and intelligence. They retained these evaluations even though all children completed the second, puzzle, task successfully. It is concluded that the experiment shows the drastic effects that may arise from 'labelling' children, though in a normal school situation these may be somewhat modified by teachers' better knowledge of the child.

FLEMING, E. S. and ANTTONEN, R. G. 1971a. 'Teacher expectancy or my fair lady', *American Educational Research Journal* 8, 2, 241–52.

Part of a larger study (see below) attempting to investigate the teacher expectancy effect in a classroom situation, but using a different design from the Rosenthal and Jacobson study. 1087 seven to eight-year-old (second grade) children from Cleveland public schools in low and middle socio-economic status areas were randomly assigned to one of four groups: i) Kuhlmann-Anderson Intelligence Test scores reported back to teachers; ii) IQ test scores inflated by 16 points reported back to teachers; iii) Primary Mental Abilities percentiles reported to teachers; iv) no test information reported to teachers. All testing took place at the beginning of the school year, and re-testing was administered eight months later. The different treatments had no significant effect on IQ. Children whose teachers had a high opinion of IQ tests (modified Goslin Teacher Opinion Scale), though, had higher final IQ scores than children whose teachers had a low opinion of IQ tests. Teachers reported the inflated IQs to be less accurate than the other types of information given.

FLEMING, E. S. and ANTTONEN, R. G. 1971b. 'Teacher-expectancy effect examined at different ability levels', *Journal of Special Education* 5, 2, 127–31.

Further findings from the study summarised above. Subjects were divided into high- (IQ 110 +), middle- (IQ 90–109) and low- (IQ below 90) ability groups. The inflated IQ group did not gain significantly more in IQ than the other three groups at any of the ability levels. Thus there is no support for Rosenthal and Jacobson's finding that middle-ability children gain most from favourable teacher expectancy.

FLEMING, E. S. and ANTTONEN, R. G. 1971c. 'Teacher expectancy as related to the academic and personal growth of primary age children', *Monographs of the Society for Research in Child Development* 36, 5, (serial no. 145), 31 pp.

Another part of the study described above is reported here. The inflated IQ group did not significantly exceed the other three groups in achievement (sub-tests of the Stanford Achievement Test) or teacher grades or self-concept. Tests were administered in October, February and May, and teachers' grades were obtained for February and June. Children whose teachers valued IQ tests highly, though, tended to have higher achievement scores than children whose teachers had a low opinion of IQ tests. While external manipulation of teachers' expectancies, then, appears to have no effect on pupil performance, the teachers' attitudes to IQ does have an effect. Further exploration is needed of the process by which these attitudes of teachers affect their pupils' achievements.

FINE, L. 1972. 'The effects of positive teacher expectancy on the reading achievement and IQ gains of pupils in grade two', *Dissertation Abstracts International* 33, 4-A, 1510–11.

Seven- to eight-year-old children presented to teachers as those who would make significant progress in reading during the school year failed to make greater gains on reading ability than the control children over an experimental period of five months. The experimental children whose names were remembered by teachers did not make greater gains than those whose names were not remembered. Children about whom the prediction was believed, though, made greater gains on reading comprehension and teachers' perceptions of reading ability than those for whom the prediction was not believed. Subjects were 180 children from five urban schools, randomly assigned to the experimental and control groups.

KESTER, S. W. and LETCHWORTH, G. A. 1972. 'Communication of teacher expectations and their effects on achievement and attitudes of secondary school students', *Journal of Educational Research* 66, 2, 51–5.

In the first week of the school year, all selected classes of thirteen- to fourteen-year-old (seventh grade) pupils were administered a number of tests including the Otis-Lennon Mental Abilities Test and the Stanford Achievement Test and these tests were re-administered to study subjects nine weeks later. Half of the pupils found to be of average ability were randomly assigned to the experimental group and half to the control group. Names of the experimental subjects were presented to English and mathematics teachers as those of 'bright' students whose classroom behaviour was to be observed in a study in the following weeks. At the end of the experimental period, no significant differences were found between the performances of the two groups on tests of language and mathematics. Nor did the experimental students show more favourable attitude changes (measured on semantic differential scales) to these subjects. Teachers, though, did spend more time communicating with the experimental students than the controls, and more time communicating in a positive, accepting, supportive manner (non-verbal as well as verbal communication was included in the analysis).

PELLEGRINI, R. J. and HICKS, R. A. 1972. 'Prophecy effects and tutorial instruction for the disadvantaged child', *American Educational Research Journal* 9, 3, 413–9.

A study which suggests that an important element in the teacher-expectancy effect may be selective coaching by teachers of the favourable-expectancy children for the IQ re-testing. In the present research children in the favourable-expectancy group only made greater gains than the controls over the experimental period when the tutors were also familiarised with items from the IQ tests used. Significantly greater gains were made in only one of the two tests used, the Peabody

Picture Vocabulary Test, the picture identification necessary for this being a more teachable skill than the reasoning needed for the other test, the Wechsler Intelligence Scale for Children similarities sub-test. The subjects, forty-four disadvantaged nine-year-old children taking part in an experimental enrichment programme were randomly assigned to one of the four groups. IQ testing was carried out by independent examiners before the beginning of the programme and after an experimental period of seventeen weeks during which the children received at least two hours individual tutoring per week.

DUSEK, J. B. and O'CONNELL, E. J. 1973. 'Teacher expectancy effects on the achievement test performance of elementary school children', *Journal of Educational Psychology* 65, 3, 371–7.

This study of the teacher-expectancy effect suggests that manipulation of teachers' expectations does not influence pupils' academic performance but teachers' own expectations may influence pupils' subsequent performance. The Stanford Achievement Test (SAT) was administered to seven- to eight-year-old second grade) and ten- to eleven-year-old (fourth grade) children two weeks after the beginning of the school year, disguised to teachers as a test to measure potential gains in language and arithmetic scores during the school year. During the testing period, each teacher was asked to rank her pupils according to her expectations for their academic achievements at the end of the school year. Within each class, half of the children ranked 1–16 by the teacher were randomly assigned to the favourable-expectancy group and half to the control group. When re-tested on the SAT four and eight months later, there were no significant differences in score gains between the experimental and control children. Children ranked higher by teachers, though, had higher scores on each administration of the SAT. Teachers reported that they based their expectations on the child's previous performance and his work at the beginning of the school year. Teachers' rankings were significantly correlated with scores on the first SAT testing suggesting that they were, at least partly, determined by the level of academic ability shown by the child.

O'CONNELL, E. J., DUSEK, J. B. and WHEELER, R. J. 1974. 'A follow-up study of teacher expectancy effects', *Journal of Educational Psychology* 66, 3, 325–8.

A follow-up of the Dusek and O'Connell (1973) experiment (see above). In the previous study second and fourth grade pupils presented to teachers near the beginning of the school year as having a favourable expectancy did not make greater gains during the school year on standardised tests (Stanford Achievement Test) than the controls. On the other hand, the teachers' own rankings of pupils according to their expectations of the pupils doing well academically during the school year were closely related to actual achievements. In the present study scores on the SAT in the following school year (during the third and fifth grades) were significantly related to the teacher rankings of the previous year. Scores of the children presented to teachers in the previous year as having a favourable expectancy again did not differ from those of the control children. Findings of the two experiments indicate that simply telling teachers that pupils will perform well does not alter actual pupil performance. Teachers' own rankings of pupils are, though, strongly related to later academic achievement, even when the pupils are no longer under the tutelage of the teachers who made the original rankings. It is concluded that teachers make accurate predictions of pupils' academic potential, and that they are not biased in their expectations by non-relevant factors such as social class.

ROSENTHAL, R., BARATZ, S. S. and HALL, C. M. 1974. 'Teacher behavior, teacher expectations, and gains in pupils' rated creativity', *Journal of Genetic Psychology* 124, 115–21.

A study similar in design to the original Rosenthal and Jacobson research, but teachers were told that a randomly selected 20 per cent of the pupils in each class were likely to make unusual gains in creativity in the near future. The study took place in an inner city school in which all the teachers and nearly all the pupils were black. After eight months only 'potential bloomers' in the fifth grade made greater gains in creativity than the control children (creativity was judged by professional creative artists from children's drawings made at the beginning and end of the school year). The fifth grade 'potential bloomers' were also the only experimental group to make greater gains than controls in IQ (Flanagan Tests of General Ability), suggesting that their increase in creativity was not merely a fluke. Observations of classroom behaviour showed that teachers treated the children who were expected to make unusual gains in creativity slightly more negatively than the control children. This supports the findings of Rubovits and Maehr (1973) that white children for whom there is a favourable expectancy are treated more positively by teachers but black children for whom there is a favourable expectancy are treated more negatively. Teachers tended, though, in the present study to be more active towards the 'potentially creative' children.

E. The effects of teachers' own expectations

It has been seen in the previous sections that the fundamental weakness in the Rosenthal and Jacobson paradigm is the difficulty in attempting to alter teachers' expectations in a classroom situation. In all but one of the subsequent studies of similar design, the weak manipulation of teachers' expectancies failed in the main to have any influence on pupil performance. Some evidence did emerge from the studies already reviewed that teachers' own expectations are quite closely related to pupil attainments, but it was unclear if this was due to the influence of the expectations or if it merely showed that teachers' expectations are generally based on an accurate prediction of ability. In this section, a number of studies are presented which have found evidence that naturally occurring expectations of teachers which are based partially at least on factors other than ability can affect pupil performance.

In the study closest in design to the Rosenthal and Jacobson research (Sutherland and Goldschmid, 1974) it was found that children for whom teachers had negative discrepant expectations (i.e. teachers' ratings of ability were below those obtained on intelligence tests) decreased in IQ over a five-month period compared with children of similar ability level (as measured by the intelligence tests) for whom teachers' ratings and IQ scores were in concordance. Another study (Seaver, 1973) utilised a naturally occurring source of possible discrepancy between a child's ability and teachers' expectations – the teachers' knowledge of the child's older siblings – to investigate the effect of teachers' own expectations. Findings showed that pupils taught by the same teachers as their older siblings had higher academic achievements than pupils taught by different teachers if their older siblings had been bright and lower achievements if their siblings had been dull.

Two studies (Burstall, 1968; Palardy, 1969) have found evidence that different teacher beliefs about pupil performance can affect that performance. In the latter study, which was directly inspired by the Rosenthal and Jacobson research, boys' success in learning to read was found to be influenced by whether or not the teacher believed that boys learn to read as successfully as girls. Similarly, in a study not primarily concerned with the effects of teachers' expectations, Burstall found that an important factor in the attainments of low-ability children in French was the head-teacher's belief in the ability of these children successfully to learn French.

Several other studies provide indirect evidence of the possible influence of teachers' expectations, derived partially at least from non-ability factors, on pupil performance. In the major British study of streaming in the primary school (Barker Lunn, 1970) it was found that whether they were in streamed or unstreamed schools the reading performance of working-class children tended to fall off in relation to that of middle-class children between the ages of seven and ten years. It was also found that although teachers' ratings of children's ability were accurate in the majority of cases when compared with performance on an English test, where discrepancies did occur, teachers were more likely to underestimate ability in working-class children and overestimate ability in middle-class children. Barker Lunn interprets these findings as indicating that the relative decline in the reading performance of the working-class children can be attributed in part to the negative discrepant expectations of the teachers.

In an American study (Rist, 1970) in which a class of black ghetto children was observed over a two-and-a-half-year period, it was found that the kindergarten teacher grouped the children permanently at three separate tables according to her expectations of their 'success' after only 8 days at school. Her expectations appeared to be based on social factors, such as dress, ease of interaction with the teacher, frequency of speech in Standard American English and the family's socio-economic status, rather than on actual ability (the three groups did not differ significantly in intelligence test scores even by the end of the kindergarten year). These groupings, made so early in the child's school career, remained more or less unchanged throughout the next two school years. They came to be justified, though, not in terms of teachers' expectations, but of apparently 'objective' records of previous school work including, by the beginning of the second grade, reading test performance.

Pidgeon's work (1970) is important because it suggests that not only may teachers' expectations for individual children in their classes influence pupil performance but that the attainments of a class as a whole may be influenced by teacher expectations. In one of his investigations it was found that where class grouping in the primary school within year groups is by age, the older children tend, by the end of the junior school years, to be advanced in relation to the reading scores expected for their age while the younger children tend to perform below the level calculated for their age. A possible explanation is that the teachers expected and obtained a higher performance from the older children.

It is noteworthy that in only one of the studies in this section were teachers' own expectations found to be unrelated to pupil attainments (Schwarz and Cook, 1972), and as the pupils were educationally retarded, expectations were probably too low to make any effect likely.

Annotations

BURSTALL, C. 1968 *French from Eight. A National Experiment.* Occasional Publications Series No. 18, NFER Pub. Co., Slough.

In this evaluation of French teaching in primary schools, an important factor in the success of 'low-ability' children (those with scores lower than one standard deviation below the mean on three or more of five general ability tests) was found to be the attitude of the head-teacher. Where the head-teacher had low expectations for the level of attainment of low-ability children in French, a higher proportion of these children was found in the 'low-scoring' group (test scores lower than one standard deviation below the mean) and a lower proportion in the 'high-scoring' group (test scores higher than one standard deviation above the mean) than in schools where the head had high expectations for low ability children. The forty-two schools whose heads had negative attitudes contained 50.25 per cent of the low-scoring group and only 21.7 per cent of the high-scoring group. The eighty schools whose heads had positive attitudes contained 49.75 per cent of the low-ability children in the low-scoring group and 78.30 per cent of the high-scoring, low-ability children.

PALARDY, J. M. 1969. 'What teachers believe – what children achieve', *Elementary School Journal*, 69, 370–4.

The reading achievements of six- to seven-year-old boys taught by teachers who believed that boys are less successful in learning to read than girls, were found to be significantly lower than those of girls in the same classes. The reading achievements of these boys were also lower than those of boys taught by teachers who believed that boys are as successful in learning to read as girls. The four groups of children, fifty-three boys and fifty-one girls, taught by teachers who believed boys to be as successful as girls, and fifty-eight boys and fifty-one girls taught by teachers who believed boys to be less successful than girls, were similar in age, socio-economic background, and reading readiness at the beginning of the school year. They were also equated statistically for IQ before the comparisons on reading achievement were made. The teachers, all women with similar qualifications, were using the same reading scheme.

BARKER LUNN, J. C. 1970. *Streaming in the Primary School*, NFER Pub. Co., Slough; Humanities Press, Atlantic Highlands, NJ. 508 pp.

This report of a longitudinal study comparing the intellectual, personal and social progress of children in thirty-six non-streamed primary schools with that of children in thirty-six streamed, but otherwise similar, primary schools throughout their junior school careers, contains some indirect evidence of the possible influence of teacher expectations on pupil performance. It was found that the reading performance of middle-class children (social classes I, II and III) showed a relative improvement between the ages of seven and ten years, while that of working-class children (social classes IV and V) showed a relative deterioration. This may have been partly attributable to the lower expectations that teachers held for some working-class children. A comparison of teachers' ratings of children's ability with their actual performance on the English test, carried out at the end of the third year, showed that teachers rated the majority of children accurately. Where teachers' ratings were discrepant, though, they were more likely to underestimate working-class children and to overestimate middle-class children. This underestimation of working-class children probably contributed to the tendency for children from social classes IV and V to be placed disproportionately frequently in bottom classes in schools which practised streaming. Findings of the study also showed that children allowed to remain in a stream although 'wrongly allocated' (as measured by their performance on the English or arithmetic tests) tended eventually to conform to the standards of the stream. On the other hand, children promoted to a higher stream tended to make very good progress, and those demoted to a lower stream tended to deteriorate whether or not the transfer was justified by the children's test performance prior to the move.

PIDGEON, D. A. 1970. *Expectation and Pupil Performance*, NFER Pub. Co., Slough; Humanities Press, Atlantic Highlands, NJ (especially chapters 1, 6, 8 and 9).

The author argues that there is a basic difficulty in attempting to show, as Rosenthal and Jacobson have done, that the teacher expectancy effect operates with individual children – if comparisons are made within classrooms, the number of experimental subjects must be very small and it is difficult to set up a viable experimental design. Additionally, teachers must be given false information about individual children and, if this is to be believable, it is unlikely to produce statistically significant results. It is suggested that evidence may best be obtained from the study of an existing situation which possesses the required conditions, although this is likely to be rarely found. Alternatively, possible consequences of teachers' expectations influencing pupils' achievements under certain conditions may be deduced and an examination made of whether these consequences in fact occur. Chapter 6 presents evidence that in later years in the primary school, when children within a year group are grouped by age, those in the 'oldest' class exceed the achievement scores calculated for their age, but those in the 'youngest' class perform below the level calculated for their age. In schools adopting random or ability grouping, however, effects of length of schooling disappear when age is taken into account. It is suggested that the explanation may lie in the expectations of teachers, who see the older children as being able to work at a higher level than the younger children. Chapter 8 presents evidence that dispersion of scores is greater in streamed than in unstreamed schools in England. The dispersion is also greater in England, where streaming is widely practised, than in other Western countries that employ a grade promotion system. It is argued that the difference stems from the attitudes of the teachers. In the grade system, the teachers' objective is to ensure that all children complete the grade successfully; in the streamed system, teachers expect those in the high streams to have high attainments and those in low streams to have low attainments.

RIST, R. C. 1970. 'Student social class and teacher expectations: the self-fulfilling prophecy in ghetto education', *Harvard Educational Review* 40, 411–51.

Observational study over a period of two-and-a-half years of a group of black children attending a ghetto school. The author contends that the kindergarten teacher labelled the children as 'fast-learners' or 'slow-learners' after only a few days in the class, not on any criteria of academic potential, but on expectations of school achievements based on social criteria, and that these expectations became self-fulfilling prophecies. The teacher's expectations were derived from social criteria known before the children entered the school – whether the family was receiving welfare assistance, whether they had a telephone, medical care of the child, size of family and whether intact – and on early impressions of the child's appearance and behaviour in the classroom – dress, manners, ease of interaction with adults, ability in verbal communication. The groups formed in this way were not only physically separated from each other by being placed at separate tables but were also treated differently by the teacher, the 'fast-learning' group receiving most of her attention. IQ testing at the end of the kindergarten years showed that there was no significant difference between the 'fast-learning' and the 'slow-learning' groups, although the scores were skewed slightly higher in the 'fast-learning' group. In the first and second grades, the children almost invariably remained in the same ability groupings, although the judgements of teachers were now based on the children's past academic performance.

BEGGS, D. L., MAYER, G. R. and LEWIS, E. L. 1972. 'The effect of various techniques of interpreting test results on teacher perception and pupil achievement', *Measurement and Evaluation in Guidance* 5, 1, 290–7.

In this study, it was found that teachers' knowledge of pupils' IQ scores influenced their subsequent estimates of pupils' IQ but had less effect on their estimates of pupil achievements. Presenting the teachers solely with alphabetical lists of their pupils and predictions (based on actual IQ scores though these were not given to teachers) of their future work had little effect on the teachers' estimates of IQ or achievements. Presentation of both IQ scores and predictions, however, had a considerable effect. Subjects were 990 seven- to eight-year-old children (second grade) in thirty-three classes. Results of IQ testing on Flanagan's Tests of General Ability administered early in the school year were reported to teachers by school counsellors in one of five different ways, while no test results were reported for a sixth group. No differences were found among the six groups in gains on achievement tests (Metropolitan Achievement Tests) administered at the time of the IQ testing and again four months later.

SCHWARZ, R. H. and COOK, J. J. 1972. 'Teacher expectancy as it relates to the academic achievement of EMR students', *Journal of Educational Research* 65, 9, 393–6.

In this study, teachers' expectations for the academic progress of their pupils were not significantly correlated with the pupils' actual achievement gains (Wide Range Achievement Test) over the school year. Rosenthal's hypothesis that teachers' expectations affect the pupils' performance is not borne out by this study. Subjects were 136 six- to eight-year-old, educable, mentally-retarded (IQ 48–82) children and their teachers.

KRUPCZAK, W. P. 1973. 'Relationships among student self-concept of academic ability, teacher perception of student academic ability and student achievement', *Dissertation Abstracts International* 33, 7–A, 3389.

In this study, teacher perception of student academic ability (modified Brookover self-concept-of-ability scale) was found to be a better predictor of student achievement (reading and arithmetic sub-tests of Stanford Achievement Test) and grade point average than IQ scores, thus supporting Rosenthal's hypothesis that teachers' expectations can affect pupils' achievements. Subjects were 520 twelve- to thirteen-year-old (sixth grade) black, white and Spanish pupils from a public school system in Florida.

NASH, R. 1973. *Classrooms Observed. The Teacher's Perception and the Pupil's Performance*, Routledge and Kegan Paul, London. 138 pp.

An observational study of children and their teachers in primary schools and the first year of comprehensive school. Generally, it was found that a child's self-image was closely related to the teacher's perception of him. Teachers' perceptions of a child (measured by Kelly's repetory grid technique, which uses the teacher's own constructs for rating children) were found to be related to aspects of the child's personality more than to aspects of his ability. A relationship was found between the teacher's perception of the child and the child's attainment (Schonell Reading Test and the teacher's ranking of class position). While no relationship was found between a child's actual social class and his attainment, a significant relationship did exist between the teacher's perception of the child's social class and his attainment. In the comprehensive school, teachers appeared to be selecting children they viewed unfavourably for the remedial class. The remedial-class children were perceived much more unfavourably than children of similar IQ and primary-school class position who remained in the ordinary classes. It is concluded that teachers should be made more aware of their power to shape a child's school career.

SEAVER, W. B. 1973. 'Effects of naturally induced teacher expectancies', *Journal of Personality and Social Psychology* 28, 3, 333–42.

This study attempted to determine the effects of naturally occurring teachers' expectancies on the pupils' academic progress, rather than to experimentally manipulate teachers' expectations as in most previous research. It was found, as hypothesised, that achievements (Stanford Achievement Test and teachers' grades) of six- to seven-year-old (first grade) children whose older siblings had been taught by the same teachers were significantly affected by teacher expectations arising from prior experience with the older siblings. Controls were younger siblings whose older siblings had been taught by different teachers. The sample consisted of seventy-nine pairs of siblings from two schools in a high socio-economic status area.

WILLIS, S. L. 1973. 'Formation of teachers' expectations of students' academic performance', *Dissertation Abstracts International* 33, 9–A, 4960.

Teachers' rankings of six- to seven-year-old (first grade) pupils' academic achievement made in the first two weeks of the school year, correlated significantly with the pupils' scores on the Metropolitan Readiness Test. Rankings were highly stable over time, though modified somewhat by knowledge of test scores. Initial rankings were made with little information about the children's academic ability as there was no public kindergarten system in the area. Subjects were seventy-four women teachers from elementary schools in middle-class communities.

WILLIAMS, T. 1976. 'Teacher prophecies and the inheritance of inequality', *Sociology of Education* 49, 3, 223–36.

Using data from 10,500 Toronto high-school students, it was found that teacher cognitive expectations (pupil's chance of completing the university entrance year at school) and normative expectations (of pupil's adherence to norms of classroom behaviour) added nothing to the explanation of student achievement test scores beyond that due to students' ascribed (father's occupation, parents' education) and achievement (academic aptitude, stream (track), educational and occupational aspiration, past school performance) characteristics. In contrast, teachers' expectations of conformity to classroom norms, as well as their expectations of students' academic performance, had an important effect on the grades assigned to students by the teachers, exceeded for males only by the effect of the student's past performance. It could be argued that the effects of teacher expectations do not represent self-fulfilling prophecies but are reflections of better teacher knowledge of students – but if this is the case, they should logically add to the explanation of student achievement test scores as well. It could also be argued that teacher expectations do not affect achievement scores in high school because teacher expectations in the early years at school have already had their effect on achievement and contributed to students' achievement characteristics – but if this is so why do they continue to affect teacher evaluations? While teacher expectations both of student performance and behaviour appear to influence their evaluation of students these expectations themselves were not based on the social background characteristics of the students (though parental income was not taken into account in the analysis) but on their achievements in school.

F. How do teachers communicate their expectations to the pupils?

Studies in the previous section suggest that teachers' own expectations do affect the attainments of their pupils. This raises the question of the mechanism through which teachers' expectations influence pupils' academic performance. Studies presented in this section, as well as a number reviewed earlier (Conn et al., 1968; Claiborn, 1969; Meichenbaum et al., 1969; Rist, 1970; José and Cody, 1971; Kester and Letchworth, 1972; Nash, 1973) are concerned with whether and how teachers' behaviour is affected by expectations for their pupils.

Several studies (Rothbart et al., 1971; Rubovits and Maehr, 1971 and 1973; Chaikin et al., 1974) have investigated teacher-pupil interactions in especially designed experimental teaching situations. The evidence is consistent in showing that higher-ability-labelled students are treated more favourably than lower-ability-labelled students, at least when they are white. Rothbart et al., though, found that teachers spent more time talking to and looking at students for whom they had high expectations while Rubovits and Maehr found that the high-expectancy students were requested to respond more often and were given more praise. Findings of the Chaikin *et al*. study suggest that one of the means through which teachers communicate their approval of the high-expectancy students may be by non-verbal behaviour, such as leaning towards these students, looking and smiling at them more.

Findings from these artificial teaching situations, in which teacher-student contact is of short duration, cannot be taken as necessarily valid in the ordinary classroom, especially as the teachers in the studies were relatively inexperienced (Dusek, 1975). There is some evidence, though, that the behaviour of more experienced teachers can be influenced, at least in the short-term, in the same manner. In a study of similar design (Medinnus and Unruh, 1971, cited by Brophy and Good, 1974b) the subjects were 20 Head Start teachers and the pupils two boys from each of their classes, one designated to the teacher as a high-ability and the other as a low-ability child, although both actually had average intelligence test scores. The teachers gave more praise and less criticism to the boys they believed to be of high ability while working with them individually on a block-sorting task.

In four of the studies which attempted to manipulate teachers' expectations (Claiborn, 1969; Meichenbaum *et al*., 1969; José and Cody, 1971; Kester and Letchworth, 1972) observations were also carried out on teacher-pupil interactions. In two of these (Meichenbaum *et al*., 1969, and Kester and Letchworth, 1972) teachers altered in their behaviour to pupils with favourable expectancies. Kester and Letchworth found that teachers behaved in a more positive-accepting manner to the allegedly 'bright' pupils than the controls, even though this did not result in higher academic gains, at least during the nine weeks of the study period. Meichenbaum *et al*.'s findings are of particular interest because they show that each of the four teachers teaching the same group of girls responded differently to the favourable-expectancy information; two increasing in positive interactions with the 'late bloomers', one decreasing in negative interactions and one actually decreasing in positive interactions. The other two studies (Claiborn, 1969; José and Cody, 1971) produced largely negative findings, the teachers' interactions with the favourable-expectancy children not changing more than those with the controls. These, as discussed earlier, were studies in which the favourable experimental expectations failed to become established for most of the teachers.

A number of studies have attempted to investigate in measurable terms whether teachers' own expectations affect their behaviour in the classroom (Brophy and Good, 1970, 1974a; Willis, 1970; Alpert, 1974; Weinstein, 1976). Findings of the first detailed study carried out (Brophy and Good, 1970) suggest that teachers do give preferential treatment to those for whom they have high expectations but that, for this age group (six- to seven-year-olds) at least, the difference in teacher behaviour is not so much in the number of contacts with teachers but in how the teachers interacted with them. Children for whom the teachers held higher expectations received more praise for answering correctly, less criticism for wrong answers, and more opportunity to make a second response when incorrect or unable to reply to a first question. They received no feedback to an answer much less frequently than the low-expectancy children. Findings from Willis' study, from the brief report available, appear to be in broad agreement, as do those from several unpublished studies by independent researchers cited by Brophy and Good (1974a).

Later work, though, including a number of studies by Brophy and Good and their colleagues, has shown that these particular differences in behaviour to high- and low-expectation pupils are by no means universally found among teachers, although a minority do appear to show this pattern of differences. Alpert (1974) categorised, defined and scored teacher behaviour differently from Brophy and Good (1970) but it is nevertheless clear that her findings are contradictory to theirs. The bottom reading group received at least as much 'good' teaching as the top group, including praise, support and encouragement. Similarly, in a recent study Weinstein (1976), using the Brophy and Good measures of teacher-child interaction, found that teachers gave the bottom-reading group members more praise for correct answers and less often left them without any feedback than children in other groups.

Weinstein's work suggests that, despite the similarity between the groups in a number of the teacher-child interactions measured, teachers did differ in the types of contact they had with pupils in the different groups, and that these differences would indicate to pupils the types of expectations held for them. Her work indicates that the experiences of pupils in different ability groups has to be looked at much more closely before the impact on the pupils of different kinds of teacher behaviour can be judged. For example, praise for bottom-reading group members is not necessarily supportive and encouraging but may convey low expectations, especially where it is given for less than correct answers. Delay in providing feedback to top-reading group members may convey high expectations and allow the pupil to make a successful response. Teachers' expectations for the different groups in the class may be conveyed to pupils by their general behaviour and statements to the whole class, thus making clear to pupils their place in the hierarchy.

Two studies, one American (Rist, 1970) and one British (Nash, 1973), which have observed classroom behaviour without attempting to measure specific aspects of teacher-pupil interaction, show how teachers may create quite different school environments for children who are favoured and for those who are not favoured. Nash's findings suggest that teachers sometimes treat the same behaviour from different children differently, according to their perceptions of the children. Brophy and Good (1974a) also give evidence from one of their studies showing that pupils for whom teachers have low expectations are more often criticised when they misbehave than are middle-expectation children who misbehave in the classroom.

Beez's (1970) study also suggests one way in which teachers' expectations may affect pupils' academic performance. He found that teachers in an experimental situation actually attempted to, and succeeded in, teaching a larger amount of material to the supposedly 'high-ability' students than to those believed to be of low ability. These findings need validation in an ordinary classroom.

Most of the studies so far discussed have assumed that differing teacher behaviour will affect pupils' attainments, but have not actually investigated the link. Two recent studies (Alpert, 1975; Firestone and Brody, 1975) were specifically concerned with the influence of teacher-pupil interaction on attainment, with contrasting results. In the latter study negative interactions with the teacher in kindergarten were related to poorer achievement scores in the first year at primary school even after IQ had been controlled. In the former study, teachers were encouraged to increase their use of 'good' teacher behaviour to bottom-reading group pupils over a period of ten weeks, but this failed to influence the pupils' reading attainment. It is doubtful if these findings provide evidence against teacher-pupil interactions influencing pupil performance, though, for it is by no means certain that the behaviour of the teachers changed to any great extent. Teachers were only observed briefly, on two occasions, during the intervention period. Weinstein's research also suggests that even if changes did occur in some kinds of teacher behaviour this would not necessarily affect the children's performance unless teachers' attitudes to the group also altered.

Overall, findings suggest that teachers' expectations often do affect their teaching behaviour. The exact ways in which teacher behaviour is affected, though, needs further investigation in studies in actual classroom situations. The extent to which teachers' behaviour is differentiated may well be affected by the social-class composition of the school population, by school organisation and by the philosophy and attitudes of both the school and the individual teacher. This too requires investigation.

Annotations

BROPHY, J. E. and GOOD, T. L. 1970. 'Teachers' communication of differential expectations for children's classroom performance: some behavioral data', *Journal of Educational Psychology* 61, 5, 365–74.

Observations of teacher-pupil interactions were carried out in four classes of six- to seven-year-olds (first grade) on three boys and three girls rated high in achievement and on three boys and three girls rated low in achievement. Children rated high created more response opportunities for themselves, especially work-centred interactions with teachers. Teachers tended to initiate more contacts with the lows than the highs, but the only significant difference between the groups was that the lows received more criticisms of their behaviour. The main difference in teacher-initiated interactions with the two groups was in quality rather than quantity. The highs were more frequently praised when correct and less frequently criticised when incorrect or unable to respond. Teachers were also more persistent in eliciting responses from highs than lows. The highs did better than the lows on objective measures of achievement (correct answers, Stanford Achievement Test). It is concluded that teachers do communicate differential performance expectations for different children through their classroom behaviour.

GOOD, T. L. and BROPHY, J. E. 1971. 'Questioned equality for grade one boys and girls', *Reading Teacher* 25, 3, 247–52.

This study failed to confirm the suggestion of some researchers that the superior performance of girls compared to boys in the early stages of reading is due to teachers' discrimination against boys. Observations of teacher-pupil interaction in four classes of six- to seven-year-olds showed that teachers did not differ in their treatment of boys and girls or high and low achievers during reading instruction. Teachers did criticise boys more in other classroom activities even though the boys gave more correct answers but this was due to the more disruptive behaviour of the boys rather than to teacher bias against them.

ROTHBART, M., DALFEN, S. and BARRETT, R. 1971. 'Effects of teacher's expectancy on student-teacher interaction', *Journal of Educational Psychology* 62, 1, 49–54.

In this study, thirteen student teachers each supervised a discussion with four adolescent students, two arbitrarily designated as 'lacking in intellectual potential'. Observation and analysis of teacher-pupil interactions showed that the teachers tended to spend more time talking to the high- than to the low-expectation students, and that high-expectation students tended to talk more. Teachers did not differ, though, in the amount of encouragement given to students in the two groups.

RUBOVITS, P. C. and MAEHR, M. L. 1971. 'Pygmalion analyzed:

toward an explanation of the Rosenthal-Jacobson findings', *Journal of Personality and Social Psychology* 19, 2, 197–203.

A study which suggests that teachers' expectations do affect teacher behaviour in some ways. Undergraduate students, acting as teachers in an experimental teaching situation, were found to request significantly more statements from and praise significantly more often, pupils labelled as gifted than pupils labelled nongifted, though the labels were applied at random without regard to actual abilities. The total attention given to the two groups did not differ significantly, indicating that quality rather than amount of interaction is the crucial difference in behaviour. The authors point out that a replication study is necessary to determine whether these findings also apply to experienced teachers.

WILLIS, B. J. 1970. 'The influence of teacher expectation on teachers' classroom interaction with selected children', *Dissertation Abstracts* 30, 5072A.

In this observational study of classroom interaction, it was found that teachers gave more favourable treatment to the children in their classes whom they considered to be the most efficient learners than to those they considered to be the least efficient learners. Teachers ignored the behaviour of the 'least-efficient' children more often and made more frequent verbal responses to the behaviour of the 'most-efficient' children.

ROSENTHAL, R. 1973. 'The Pygmalion effect lives', *Psychology Today* 7, 4, 56–63.

Eighty-four studies, out of 242 carried out, have found that teacher or experimenter expectations made a significant difference to the subjects' performance. This is a level seven times greater than chance and indicates, argues the author, that the Pygmalion effect does exist in certain circumstances. Evidence from current research suggests that four factors produce the Pygmalion effect (at least five studies provide findings supporting each of these factors and no more than 20 per cent of relevant studies provide contradictory findings). Teachers favour students for whom they have high expectations by:
i) the provision of a warmer emotional climate for them; ii) provision of more feedback, especially praise, about student performance; iii) teaching a greater amount of and more complex material; iv) encouraging greater responsiveness from these students.

RUBOVITS, P. C. and MAEHR, M. L. 1973. 'Pygmalion black and white', *Journal of Personality and Social Psychology* 25, 2, 210–18.

A replication and extension of an earlier study by the same authors (see above). In the present study, two of the pupils in the experimental teaching situation were black and two white, one black and white pupil being labelled 'gifted' without regard to actual ability. The undergraduate students who were acting as teachers were found to give less attention to, ignore more, praise less, and criticise more, black than white pupils. It was the black pupils labelled 'gifted' who received least attention and praise and most criticism. It is noted, though, that this pattern was not displayed by all the teachers. The undergraduates, acting as teachers, also had little experience of teaching or of blacks, and the findings may be unique to them.

ALPERT, J. L. 1974. 'Teacher behavior across ability groups: a consideration of the mediation of Pygmalion effects', *Journal of Educational Psychology* 66, 3, 348–53.

Teachers were found in this study to treat their top- and bottom-reading groups similarly. They spent similar amounts of time with the two groups, used a similar amount of instructional materials and gave similar amounts of praise, encouragement, support and other kinds of verbal behaviour likely to promote reading performance to them. As there were fewer pupils in the bottom (average 8.87) than in the top (average 13.87) groups, the pupils in the bottom group actually received preferential treatment. The results contradict findings of previous studies (Brophy and Good, 1970; Rist, 1970) that high-ability pupils receive preferential treatment from teachers.

BROPHY, J. E. and Good, T. L. 1974a. 'Naturalistic studies of teacher expectation effects', Chapter 4 in *Teacher-Student Relationships: Causes and Consequences*, Holt, Rinehart and Winston, New York. 78–128.

This chapter includes an account of follow-up studies carried out by the authors and their colleagues to the initial Brophy and Good (1970) research (see above), which suggested that teachers treat pupils for whom they have high expectations more favourably than those for whom they have low expectations. Findings of the first replication study conducted in nine first-year classes in three primary schools suggest that the tendency to favour pupils for whom they have high expectations is not universal among teachers, though it is found in some teachers. Generally, in this study, the teachers tried to compensate for the tendency of high-expectation pupils to demand their attention by seeking out those for whom they had low expectations. Unlike the findings of the original study there was no tendency for low-expectation pupils to receive less praise following correct answers, and they tended to receive more, rather than less, teacher feedback. Three teachers did tend to favour the high-expectation students, showing behaviour similar to that found in teachers in the initial study. Two further studies, with second and fifth year students, confirmed that the pattern of favouring pupils for whom they have high expectations and inappropriately teaching low expectation pupils is confined to a few teachers. Studies with older pupils suggested that differences in teacher behaviour to high- and low-expectation pupils are more likely to be found in quantitative than in qualitative measures at this stage. In a study of seventh-year pupils, the high-expectation group dominated the teachers attention, and though they compensated to some extent, this was not sufficient to correct the balance.

CHAIKIN, A. L., SIGLER, E. and DERLEGA, V. J. 1974. 'Nonverbal mediators of teacher expectancy effects', *Journal of Personality and Social Psychology* 30, 1, 144–9.

The subjects – forty-two undergraduates – were asked to give individual tutoring for a five minute period to a ten-year-old student who was described as being either bright or dull or about whom they were given no expectations. Subjects expecting their pupils to be bright leaned forward more, looked their pupils more in the eye, nodded their heads more and smiled more, during the tutoring session than subjects expecting their pupils to be dull, or having no expectations of them. The kinds of behaviour shown more frequently to the bright pupils have been found in previous research to indicate approval and liking. Although their non-verbal behaviour showed greater liking of the students they expected to be bright, the subjects may not have been aware of their feelings – verbal ratings of liking did not distinguish between the supposedly bright and dull pupils.

ALPERT, J. L. 1975. 'Teacher behavior and pupil performance: reconsideration of the mediation of Pygmalion effects', *Journal of Educational Research* 69, 2, 53–7.

A number of researchers have found a relationship between teacher expectations and teacher behaviour, and have suggested that teacher behaviour affects pupil performance, but the latter relationship has rarely been investigated. The aim of the present study was to determine whether an increase in certain kinds of teacher behaviour, judged by experts as likely to increase pupils' reading performance, would actually affect the achievements of low-ability pupils. The 'good' teacher behaviour consisted of: more reading group time; more 'best' reading group time (at times when teacher felt most motivated to teach); more instructional materials in the reading group; fewer pupils in the reading group; more 'good' verbal behaviours. Eight second-grade teachers in New York Catholic schools serving a middle-class area were asked to increase their 'good' teaching behaviour to their bottom-reading group pupils, while nine teachers and their bottom-reading group pupils were used as controls. After a period of ten weeks no effects of the intervention were found on the reading group performance of the experimental children. The question arises as to whether the experimental teachers actually changed their behaviour, for daily observations were not carried out during the intervention period (they were actually only visited twice and telephoned twice). The daily logs kept by the teachers do suggest, though, that they increased the amount of 'good' teaching behaviour (although there was no change in the number of pupils in the reading groups), and these logs appear to be reliable, the teachers recording deviations from the suggested changes in teacher behaviour.

FIRESTONE, G. and BRODY, N. 1975. 'Longitudinal investigation of teacher-student interactions and their relationship to academic performance', *Journal of Educational Psychology* 67, 4, 544–50.

Seventy-nine five- to six-year-old children, mainly black, were observed in their classrooms over a period of a year (for two-hour sessions every three weeks), in the second half of the kindergarten year and the first half of the first grade. An intelligence test (Lorge Thorndike) was administered to the children at the beginning of the observation period and an achievement test (Metropolitan Achievement Test (MAT)) three months after the end of this period. Children who experienced the most negative interactions with teachers during the second half of kindergarten were those who did most poorly on the achievement test (MAT) in the first grade. When IQ was controlled, knowledge of the percentage of negative interactions contributed from 3.6 per cent to 7.0 per cent of the variance of the scores on the MAT subtests. With the influence of IQ controlled the number of times the child was chosen to demonstrate something in class in the kindergarten period was positively and significantly related to MAT subtest scores on word knowledge and total reading. Also the number of interactions of all types that the child experienced during this period was related to scores on the maths subtest of the MAT. As IQ was controlled the teacher-pupil interactions cannot be solely reflections of ability. It is possible that teacher behaviour towards the child is influenced by teacher expectations for him, and that the way a child is treated by the teacher affects his confidence and interest, and through this his achievement. However, it is also possible that the behaviour of the teacher to the child is a result of some characteristic in the child, independent of IQ but related to achievement (e.g. over-aggression) and that it is this characteristic, and not the interaction with the teacher, that affects achievement.

WEINSTEIN, R. S. 1976. 'Reading group membership in first grade:

teacher behaviors and pupil experience over time', *Journal of Educational Psychology* 68, 1, 103–16.

Observations were made of teacher behaviour (interactions with individual pupils, using the Brophy and Good (1970) system) in three first-year classrooms in a primary school situated in a predominantly working-class area of Connecticut. The observations were made for a five-months period (on twelve occasions for the entire morning and early afternoon), from the beginning of the school year. A relatively fixed reading group membership did not emerge until the end of the first month and changes continued during the next four months (affecting 35.8 per cent of the pupils), but re-assignment of middle-group children occurred much more frequently than re-assignment of high- or low-group children, and none of the low-group members reached the high group in this period. Reading group membership contributed a statistically significant 25 per cent to the prediction of pupil reading performance (measured at mid year) over and above the initial differences in reading readiness among the pupils. The gap between the performance of the groups widened during the period of the study. Low-group members tended to be favoured by the teachers, being given more response opportunities, more instruction time and also (unlike the Brophy and Good findings) more praise for correct answers and at the end of a reading turn despite poor performance, and being left less frequently without feedback. Nevertheless it is suggested that the teachers conveyed their lower expectations to these children in various ways. High rates of praise for less than perfect answers may, for example, be perceived by pupils as conveying low expectations. Teachers' statements to the whole class about the reading groups may also indicate to the pupils their different expectations for the groups.

G. What determines teachers' expectations?

It has already been suggested (see Section E) that teachers may base their evaluations of children's future achievements, at least to some extent, on their beliefs about the relationship between certain non-ability factors and academic achievement. There is evidence that teachers' judgements of the ability of children in their classes are influenced by sex (Palardy, 1969), social class (Goodacre, 1968; Barker Lunn, 1970, Rist, 1970) and the child's adaptation to new situations (Gordon and Thomas, 1967).

Findings from an observational study of a British primary school (Murphy, 1974) that teachers do not consciously evaluate children's ability in terms of their social-class background and that they are capable of differentiating their judgements of children's ability from those of behaviour are hardly convincing evidence that teachers' expectations are entirely unbiased. It has not been suggested that teachers deliberately rank children's ability in accordance with their social class but that indications of social class are among the characteristics of a child which sometimes subtly influence the teacher's estimation.

A number of studies in which subjects are asked to evaluate the future attainments of a hypothetical child from such evidence as school reports, test scores or answers to school questions have also found that non-ability factors such as socio-economic status (McLaughlin *et al.* 1970; Harvey and Slatin, 1975), speech characteristics (Crowl and MacGinitie, 1974), colour (Henderson and Long, 1973), and physical attractiveness (Clifford and Walster, 1973) may influence the judgements even of experienced teachers, though some studies have failed to find such a bias (Dietz and Purkey, 1969; Heintz, 1974).

One study (Mason, 1973) has shown that warnings to teachers about the effects of teacher bias may not result in teachers being any less influenced in their expectations for a child by a faked psychological report. While these findings do not necessarily apply in the ordinary classroom situation, where teachers have the opportunity to gain better knowledge of their pupils, they do suggest that some teacher biases may be difficult to change. A later study (Mason *et al.* 1976) found that more experienced teachers (more than three years' teaching) were less influenced in their expectations for children by a fictitious psychological report than were less experienced teachers. However, the authors suggest that this does not necessarily mean that more experienced teachers are less biased, for it may have been their other biases which prevented the faked psychological report from making much impact. In another study (Harvey and Slatin, 1975) it was the less-experienced teachers in lower-class schools who were more reluctant to make judgements about children on the basis of social class. Further studies of how teachers make evaluations of children in actual classrooms are needed.

Annotations

BERGAN, J. R. and SMITH, J. O. 1966. 'Effects of socio-economic status and sex on prospective teachers' judgements', *Mental Retardation* 4, 1, 13–15.

Seventy-two prospective teachers rated a hypothetical seven-year-old educable mentally retarded child (IQ between 65 and 75) as more intellectually competent and socially acceptable when the child was described as coming from a high socio-economic status background than when described as having low socio-economic status. Sex of the hypothetical child did not affect teacher ratings.

GORDON, E. M. and THOMAS, A. 1967. 'Children's behavioral style and the teacher's appraisal of their intelligence', *Journal of School Psychology* 5, 4, 292–300.

In this study it was found that teachers' estimates of children's intelligence were influenced by non-intellective behavioural characteristics of the children. Children who adapt quickly to new situations tended to be overestimated in intelligence and those who only gradually become involved in a new activity to be under-estimated. Subjects were ninety-three kindergarten children and their two experienced teachers.

DIETZ, S. M. and PURKEY, W. W. 1969. 'Teacher expectation of performance based on race of the student', *Psychological Reports* 24, 694.

Teachers' expectations for the future academic performance of pupils were found to be uninfluenced by race in this study. The subjects, 147 white graduate students with teaching experience, were asked to rate the scholastic performance of a hypothetical adolescent boy from a written description of his background and characteristics, the word 'Negro' being inserted in the description of the boy presented to half of the subjects.

McLAUGHLIN, J. A., MILLER, C. K. and CHANSKY, N. M. 1970. 'Prognoses made by special educators', *Mental Retardation* 8, 5, 20–4.

Eighty-seven postgraduate students taking a course in special education were presented with two matched pairs (two male and two female) of case histories, similar in age (about eight years old) and IQ (70–80 range), but with one member of each pair having a lower-class background and the other a middle-class background. Generally, the middle-class boy was seen most favourably, followed by the middle-class girl, and the lower-class girl, with the lower-class boy being seen least favourably.

CLIFFORD, M. M. and WALSTER, E. 1973. 'The effect of physical attractiveness on teacher expectations', *Sociology of Education* 46, 248–58.

This study suggests that teachers' expectations for a child may be influenced by the child's physical attractiveness. The subjects – 404 teachers – were presented with the school record and photograph of an eleven- to twelve-year-old (fifth grade) child. Teachers had more favourable expectations about the IQ, length of schooling, interest of parents and popularity of physically attractive rather than of physically unattractive children.

275

MASON, E. J. 1973. 'Teachers' observations and expectations of boys and girls as influenced by biased psychological reports and knowledge of the effects of bias', *Journal of Educational Psychology* 65, 2, 238–43.

A study which found that teachers' observations of children taking a test were little influenced by biased psychological reports of the children, but their expectations for the children were influenced by these reports. Subjects who were lectured on the effects of bias in the classroom tended to rate the child's test performance more independently of the psychological report than those not lectured about the effect of bias, but the lecture had no effect on the teachers' expectations for the child. The subjects – seventy-nine teachers and student teachers – were shown a videotape of a kindergarten-age child taking a test and were asked to evaluate the child's performance and give their expectations for the child's academic achievement at the end of the school year.

SALVIA, J., CLARK, G. M. and YSSELDYKE, J. E. 1973. 'Teacher retention of stereotypes of exceptionality', *Exceptional Children* 39, 8, 651–2.

Subjects, 165 special and general education students, were shown a videotape and asked to rate the performance of three children each seen taking three tests. One group of subjects was told that the children were 'gifted', one group that they were 'normal', and a third group that they were 'mentally retarded', although all children were actually normal six- to ten-year-olds. The effects of the labels differed for the individual children. They produced no difference in the ratings for one child. The other two children were rated more favourably when labelled 'gifted' and less favourably when labelled 'retarded' on some aspects of their performance, although these were not the same for the two children. It is concluded that the effects of labelling are selective rather than pervasive.

HENDERSON, E. H. and LONG, B. H. 1973. 'Academic expectancies of black and white teachers for black and white first graders', *Proceedings of the 81st Annual Convention of the American Psychological Association* 8, 685–6.

Forty-eight female teachers, one half black, from the Southern states of the United States were asked to predict the probability that children would learn to read in the first grade from their readiness test scores and ratings of classroom behaviour. Both black and white teachers had lower expectancies for low-scoring black children than for low-scoring white children; also both groups of teachers had lower expectancies for low-scoring, lower-class black children than for white children with similar characteristics.

JACOBS, F. J. and DEGRAAF, C. A. 1973. 'Expectancy and race: their influences on intelligence test scores', *Exceptional Children* 40, 2, 108–9.

Thirty-two qualified school psychologists (sixteen black, sixteen white) watched two videotapes, one of a white ten-year-old boy and the other of a black ten-year-old boy, taking the Wechsler Intelligence Scale for Children (WISC). Psychologists told that a child had a history of doing well at school scored the child higher on the WISC, particularly on the verbal scale, than those told a child performed poorly at school. The expectancy effect was greater when the psychologists were scoring children of the same ethnic group as themselves.

CROWL, T. K. and MACGINITIE, W. H. 1974. 'The influence of students' speech characteristics on teachers' evaluations of oral answers', *Journal of Educational Psychology* 66, 3, 304–8.

Tape-recorded answers to typical school questions were judged by experienced teachers as being of significantly higher quality when spoken by upper-middle class white students than when spoken by lower socio-economic status black students.

HEINTZ, P. 1974. 'Teacher expectancy for academic achievement of mentally retarded pupils', *Mental Retardation* 12, 3, 24–7.

Seventy-two experienced, special-class teachers completed a questionnaire designed to measure their expectations of the ultimate reading achievement of a hypothetical educable mentally-retarded child (IQ between 65 and 75). Unlike the prospective teachers of an earlier study (Bergan and Smith, 1966) these experienced teachers were not influenced in their judgements by the socio-economic status of the hypothetical pupil. Teachers differed considerably, though, in their expectations of reading achievement for the hypothetical pupil. Over half of the teachers thought that the retarded pupil would not be able to achieve the reading level expected on the basis of mental age. It is suggested that teachers' expectations of ultimate reading achievement for educable mentally retarded pupils may well influence the complexity of learning experiences they provide for their pupils.

MURPHY, J. 1974. 'Teacher expectations and working-class under-achievement', *British Journal of Sociology* 25, 3, 326–44.

Observations of and informal interview with teachers in a British primary school indicated that teachers do not think in terms of social class when assessing their pupils' academic performance and social conduct. Nor does the teacher's appraisal of a child's behaviour influence her judgement of that child's academic ability. Additionally, teachers' preferences for their pupils were found to correlate only weakly with class positions while objectively assessed IQ scores correlated highly with class positions. It is concluded that, in this primary school at least, working-class under-achievement cannot be attributed to negative teacher expectations.

HARVEY, D. G. and SLATIN, G. T. 1975. 'The relationship between child's SES and teacher expectations: a test of the middle-class bias hypothesis', *Social Forces* 54, 1, 140–59.

Ninety-six teachers were shown photographs of eighteen children, half black and half white. Teachers' expectations of the children's academic performance and social adjustment were related to their perceptions of the children's social class. Teachers in lower-class schools, especially less-experienced teachers, were more reluctant to make judgements about children than teachers in middle-class schools.

MASON, E. J., LARIMORE, D. L. and KIFER, E. 1976. 'Teaching experience and teachers' expectations for grades in academic subject areas', *Contemporary Educational Psychology* 1, 369–75.

Seventy-nine subjects, taking introductory courses in educational psychology, were presented with a fictitious psychological report of a child before watching a videotape of the child being tested on the Boehm Test of Basic Concepts. Subjects given an unfavourable psychological report to read had lower expectations for the child's grades at the end of the first school year than subjects given favourable or neutral reports. Subjects with more experience of teaching (more than three years) were less influenced by the psychological reports than those with less experience.

References

(When a title is annotated, this is indicated at the end of the entry by the relevant page number in bold type.)

ALPERT, J. L. 1974. 'Teacher behavior across ability groups: a consideration of the mediation of Pygmalion effects', *Journal of Educational Psychology* 66, 3, 348–53. **p. 270**

ALPERT, J. L. 1975. 'Teacher behavior and pupil performance: reconsideration of the mediation of Pygmalion effects', *Journal of Educational Research* 69, 2, 53–7. **p. 271**

ANDERSON, D. F. and ROSENTHAL, R. 1968. 'Some effects of interpersonal expectancy and social interaction on institutionalised retarded children', *Proceedings of the 76th Annual Convention of the American Psychological Association* 3, 479–80. **p. 250**

BAKER, J. P. and CRIST, J. L. 1971. 'Teacher expectancies: a review of the literature', in J. D. Elashoff and R. E. Snow, *Pygmalion Reconsidered*, Charles A. Jones, Ohio (chapter VI, 48–64). **p. 246**

BARKER LUNN, J. C. 1970. *Streaming in the Primary School*, NFER, Slough. 508 pp; Humanities Press, Atlantic Highlands, NJ. **p. 259**

BEEZ, W. V. 1970. 'Influence of biased psychological reports on teacher behavior and pupil performance', in M. B. Miles and W. W. Charters, Jr. (comps) *Learning in Social Settings*, Allyn and Bacon, Boston, 328–34. Also, a summary in *Proceedings of the 76th Convention of the American Psychological Association*, 1968, 605–6. **p. 252**

BEGGS, D. L., MAYER, G. R., and LEWIS, E. L. 1972. 'The effects of various techniques of interpreting test results on teacher perception and pupil achievement', *Measurement and Evaluation in Guidance* 5, 1, 290–7. **p. 261**

BERGAN, J. R. and SMITH, J. O. 1966. 'Effects of socio-economic status and sex on prospective teachers' judgements', *Mental Retardation* 4, 1, 13–15. **p. 274**

BROPHY, J. E. and GOOD, T. L. 1970. 'Teachers' communication of differential expectations for children's classroom performance: some behavioral data', *Journal of Educational Psychology* 61, 5, 365–74. **p. 267**

BROPHY, J. E. and GOOD, T. L. 1974a. 'Naturalistic studies of teacher expectation effects', Chapter 4 in *Teacher Student Relationships: Causes and Consequences*, Holt, Rinehart and Winston, New York. 78–128. **p. 270**

BROPHY, J. E. and GOOD. T. L. 1974b. *Teacher Student Relationships: Causes and Consequences*, Holt, Rinehart and Winston, New York. 400 pp.

BURSTALL, C. 1968. *French from Eight: A National Experiment.* Occasional Publication Series no. 18, NFER Pub. Co., Slough. **p. 258**

BYRNE, E. M. 1974. *Planning and Educational Inequality: A Study of the Rationale of Resource Allocation*, NFER Pub. Co., Slough; Humanities Press, Atlantic Highlands, NJ. 386 pp.

CHAIKIN, A. L., SIGLER, E. and DERLEGA, V. J. 1974. 'Nonverbal mediators of teacher expectancy effects', *Journal of Personality and Social Psychology* 30, 1, 144–9. **p. 271**

CLAIBORN, W. L. 1969. 'Expectancy effects in the classroom: a failure to replicate', *Journal of Educational Psychology* 60, 5, 377–83. **p. 246**

CLIFFORD, M. M. and WALSTER, E. 1973. 'The effect of physical attractiveness on teacher expectations', *Sociology of Education* 46, 248–58. **p. 275**

CONN, L. K., EDWARDS, C. N., ROSENTHAL, R. and CROWNE, D. 1968. 'Perception of emotion and response to teachers' expectancy by elementary school children', *Psychological Reports* 22, 27–34. **p. 245**

CROWL, T. K. and MACGINITIE, W. H. 1974. 'The influence of students' speech characteristics on teachers' evaluations of oral answers', *Journal of Educational Psychology* 66, 3, 304–8. **p. 277**

DIETZ, S. M. and PURKEY, W. W. 1969. 'Teacher expectation of performance based on race of student'. *Psychological Reports* 24, 694. **p. 275**

DUSEK, J. B. 1975. 'Do teachers bias children's learning?' *Review of Educational Research* 45, 4, 661–84.

DUSEK, J. B. and O'CONNELL, E. J. 1973. 'Teacher expectancy effects on the achievement test performance of elementary school children', *Journal of Educational Psychology* 65, 3, 371–7. **p. 255**

ELASHOFF, J. D. and SNOW, R. E. 1971. *Pygmalion Reconsidered*. Charles A. Jones, Ohio (chapters I–V, pp. 1–47, and Appendix A, pp. 86–124). **p. 242**

EVANS, J. T. and ROSENTHAL, R. 1969. 'Interpersonal self-fulfilling prophecies: further extrapolation from the laboratory to the classroom', *Proceedings of the 77th Annual Convention of the American Psychological Association*, 371–2. **p. 246**

FIELDER, W. R., COHEN, R. D. and Feeney, S. 1971. 'An attempt to replicate the teacher expectancy effect', *Psychological Reports* 29, 1223–8. **p. 247**

FINE, L. 1972. 'The effects of positive teacher expectancy on the reading achievement and IQ gains of pupils in grade two', *Dissertation Abstracts International* 33, 4–A, 1510–11. **p. 253**

FIRESTONE, G. and BRODY, N. 1975. 'Longitudinal investigation of teacher-student interactions and their relationship to academic performance', *Journal of Educational Psychology* 67, 4, 544–50. **p. 272**

FLEMING, E. S. and ANTTONEN, R. G. 1971a. 'Teacher expectancy or my fair lady', *American Educational Research Journal* 8, 2, 241–52. **p. 252**

FLEMING, E. S. and ANTTONEN, R. G. 1971b. 'Teacher-expectancy effect examined at different ability levels', *Journal of Special Education* 5, 2, 127–31. **p. 253**

FLEMING, E. S. and ANTTONEN, R. G. 1971c. 'Teacher expectancy as related to the academic and personal growth of primary-age children', *Monographs of the Society for Research in Child Development* 36, 5 (serial no. 145). 31 pp. **p. 253**

GEPHART, W. 1970. 'Will the real Pygmalion please stand up', *American Educational Research Journal* 7, 3, 473–5. **p. 242**

GOOD, T. L. and BROPHY, J. E. 1971. 'Questioned equality for grade one boys and girls', *Reading Teacher* 25, 3, 247–52. **p. 268**

GOODACRE, E. J. 1968. *Teachers and Their Pupils' Home Background.* NFER Pub. Co., Slough. 170 pp.

GORDON, E. M. and THOMAS, A. 1967. 'Children's behavioral style and the teacher's appraisal of their intelligence', *Journal of School Psychology* 5, 4, 292–300. **p. 275**

GUMPERT, P. and GUMPERT, C. 1968. 'The teacher as Pygmalion: comments on the psychology of expectation', *Urban Review* 3, 21–5. **p. 240**

HARVEY, D. G. and SLATIN, G. T. 1975. 'The relationship between child's SES and teacher expectations: a test of the middle-class bias hypothesis', *Social Forces* 54, 1, 140–59. **p. 278**

HEINTZ, P. 1974. 'Teacher expectancy for academic achievement of mentally retarded pupils', *Mental Retardation* 12, 3, 24–7. **p. 277**

HENDERSON, E. H. and LONG, B. H. 1973. 'Academic expectancies of black and white teachers for black and white first graders', *Proceedings of the 81st Annual Convention of the American Psychological Association* 8, 685–6. **p. 276**

JACOBS, F. J. and DE GRAAF, C. A. 1973. 'Expectancy and race: their influence on intelligence test scores', *Exceptional Children* 40, 2, 108–9. **p. 277**

JENSEN, A. 1969. 'How much can we boost IQ and scholastic achievement?', *Harvard Educational Review* 39, 1 ('Expectancy gain', pp. 107–8). **p. 241**

JOSE, J. and CODY, J. J. 1971. 'Teacher-pupil interaction as it relates to attempted changes in teacher expectancy of academic ability', *American Educational Research Journal* 8, 1, 39–49. **p. 247**

KESTER, S. W. and LETCHWORTH, G. A. 1972. 'Communication of

teacher expectations and their effects on achievement and attitudes of secondary school students', *Journal of Educational Research* 66, 2, 51–5. **p. 254**

KRUPCZAK, W. P. 1973. 'Relationships among student self-concept of academic ability, teacher perception of student academic ability, and student achievement', *Dissertation Abstracts International* 33, 7–A, 3388–9. **p. 262**

McLAUGHLIN, J. A., MILLER, C. K. and CHANSKY, N. M. 1970. 'Prognoses made by special educators', *Mental Retardation* 8, 5, 20–4. **p. 275**

MASON, E. J. 1973. 'Teachers' observations and expectations of boys and girls as influenced by biased psychological reports and knowledge of the effects of bias', *Journal of Educational Psychology* 65, 2, 238–43. **p. 276**

MASON, E. J., LARIMORE, D. L. and KIFER, E. 1976. 'Teaching experience and teachers' expectations for grades in academic subject areas', *Contemporary Educational Psychology* 1, 369–75. **p. 278**

MEICHENBAUM, D. H., BOWERS, K. S. and ROSS, R. R. 1969. 'A behavioral analysis of teacher expectancy effect', *Journal of Personality and Social Psychology* 13, 4, 306–16. **p. 251**

MENDELS, G. E. and FLANDERS, J. P. 1973. 'Teachers' expectations and pupil performance', *American Educational Research Journal* 10, 3, 203–12. **p. 248**

MURPHY, J. 1974. 'Teacher expectations and working-class under-achievement', *British Journal of Sociology* 25, 3, 326–44. **p. 277**

NASH, R. 1973. *Classrooms Observed. The Teacher's Perception and the Pupil's Performance*, Routledge and Kegan Paul, London. 138 pp. **p. 262**

NUERMBERGER, R. M. 1969. 'Review of Pygmalion in the classroom', *Personnel and Guidance Journal* 47, 575–8. **p. 240**

O'CONNELL, E. J., DUSEK, J. B. and WHEELER, R. J. 1974. 'A follow-up study of teacher expectancy effects', *Journal of Educational Psychology* 66, 3, 352–8. **p. 255**

PALARDY, J. M. 1969. 'What teachers believe – what children achieve', *Elementary School Journal* 69, 370–4. **p. 259**

PELLEGRINI, R. J. and HICKS, R. A. 1972. 'Prophecy effects and tutorial instruction for the disadvantaged child', *American Educational Research Journal* 9, 3, 413–9. **p. 254**

PIDGEON, D. A. 1970. *Expectation and Pupil Performance*, NFER Pub.

Co., Slough; Humanities Press, Atlantic Highlands, NJ (especially chapters, 1, 6, 8 and 9). **p. 260**

PITT, C. C. V. 1956. 'An experimental study of the effects of teachers' knowledge or incorrect knowledge of pupil IQs on teachers' attitudes and practices and pupils' attitudes and achievements', *Dissertation Abstracts* 16, 2387–8. **p. 250**

RIST, R. C. 1970. 'Student social class and teacher expectations: the self-fulfilling prophecy in ghetto education', *Harvard Educational Review* 40, 411–51. **p. 261**

ROSENTHAL, R. 1969. 'Empirical vs decreed validation of clocks and tests', *American Educational Research Journal* 6, 4, 689–92. **p. 241**

ROSENTHAL, R. 1970. 'Another view of Pygmalion', *Contemporary Psychology* 15, 8, 524. **p. 242**

ROSENTHAL, R. 1973. 'The Pygmalion effect lives', *Psychology Today* 7, 4, 56–63. **p. 269**

ROSENTHAL, R. and JACOBSON, L. 1968. *Pygmalion in the Classroom. Teacher Expectation and Pupils' Intellectual Development*, Holt, Rinehart and Winston, New York. 240 pp. **p. 239**

ROSENTHAL, R. and RUBIN, D. B. 1971. 'Pygmalion reaffirmed', in J. D. Elashoff and R. E. Snow, *Pygmalion Reconsidered*, Charles A. Jones, Ohio (Appendix C, 139–55). **p. 243**

ROSENTHAL, R., BARATZ, S. S. and HALL, C. M. 1974. 'Teacher behavior, teacher expectations and gains in pupils' rated creativity', *Journal of Genetic Psychology* 124, 115–21. **p. 256**

ROTHBART, M., DALFEN, S. and BARRETT, R. 1971. 'Effects of teacher's expectancy on student-teacher interaction', *Journal of Educational Psychology* 62, 1, 49–54. **p. 268**

RUBOVITS, P. C. and MAEHR, M. L. 1971. 'Pygmalion analyzed: toward an explanation of the Rosenthal-Jacobson findings', *Journal of Personality and Social Psychology* 19, 2, 197–203. **p. 268**

RUBOVITS, P. C. and MAEHR, M. L. 1973. 'Pygmalion black and white', *Journal of Personality and Social Psychology* 25, 2, 210–18. **p. 269**

SALVIA, J., CLARK, G. M. and YSSELDYKE, J. E. 1973. 'Teacher retention of stereotypes of exceptionality', *Exceptional Children* 39, 8, 651–2. **p. 276**

SCHRANK, W. R. 1970. 'A further study of the labeling effect of ability grouping', *Journal of Educational Resarch* 63, 8, 358–60. **p. 251**

SCHWARZ, R. H. and COOK, J. J. 1972. 'Teacher expectancy as it relates to the academic achievement of EMR students', *Journal of Educational Research* 65, 9, 393–6. **p. 262**

SEAVER, W. B. 1973. 'Effects of naturally induced teacher expectancies', *Journal of Personality and Social Psychology* 28, 3, 333–42. **p. 263**

SNOW, R. E. 1969. 'Unfinished Pygmalion. Review of R. Rosenthal and L. Jacobson, Pygmalion in the classroom: Teacher expectation and pupils' intellectual development', *Contemporary Psychology* 14, 4, 197–9. **p. 241**

SUTHERLAND, A. and GOLDSCHMID, M. L. 1974. 'Negative teacher expectation and IQ change in children with superior intellectual potential', *Child Development* 45, 3, 852–6.

THORNDIKE, R. L. 1968. 'Review of Rosenthal, R. and Jacobson, L. Pygmalion in the classroom', *American Educational Research Journal* 5, 4, 708–11. **p. 240**

THORNDIKE, R. L. 1969. 'But you have to know how to tell the time', *American Educational Research Journal* 6, 4, 692. **p. 241**

WEINSTEIN, R. S. 1976. 'Reading group membership in first grade: teacher behaviors and pupil experience over time', *Journal of Educational Psychology* 68, 1, 103–16. **p. 273**

WILLIAMS, T. 1976. 'Teacher prophecies and the inheritance of inequality', *Sociology of Education* 49, 3, 223–36. **p. 263**

WILLIS, B. J. 1970. 'The influence of teacher expectation on teachers' classroom interaction with selected children', *Dissertation Abstracts* 30, 5072A. **p. 269**

WILLIS, S. L. 1973. 'Formation of teachers' expectations of students' academic performance'. *Dissertation Abstracts International* 33, 9–A, 4960. **p. 263**.

Part V
Disadvantage and intervention

A. Intellectual disadvantage

1. Introduction
Educational attainments and social class

It is undisputed that working-class children, particularly those from the unskilled working class or belonging to a minority ethnic group, tend to have much lower school achievements than middle-class children. Recent evidence shows that social-class differences in attainments are already occurring at the infant school stage. The chances of a seven-year-old being a poor reader were found to be six times as great if he came from an unskilled working-class background rather than a middle-class professional background in the National Child Development Study of a nationally representative sample of children in England, Scotland and Wales (Davie *et al.*, 1972).

An Inner London Education Authority survey (1972) of children just entering secondary schools found that boys from a manual, working-class background had an average reading age about ten months behind that of boys from a non-manual background while the manual working-class girls were about twelve months behind the non-manual girls (on the Neale Analysis of Reading Ability). Immigrant children from a manual background were even further behind, their reading age being approximately a year lower than that of manual, working-class, non-immigrant children.

A somewhat earlier British study also using a nationally representative sample found considerable differences in school achievements between children from non-manual and working-class backgrounds (Douglas, 1964; Douglas *et al.*, 1968). Differences were present at the age of eight and were maintained or even increased up to the age of fifteen (findings disputed by Horobin *et al.*, 1967; but recently confirmed by Fogelman and Goldstein, 1976).

Studies carried out in the United States have very similar findings.

Explanations of educational disadvantage

While there is no dispute that children from unskilled working-class backgrounds, particularly from minority ethnic groups, tend to have relatively poor school achievements the explanation for these findings is a subject of intense disagreement. Very broadly, the types of explanation offered can be placed in three categories.

The first type of explanation was the dominant viewpoint of the 1960s and the theory on which most programmes of compensatory education in the United States was based. Exponents of this position (e.g. Bloom *et al.*, 1965; Hess *et al.*, 1968a; Kirk and Hunt, 1975) hold that the low school achievements of poor children can be attributed to deficits in their cognitive, linguistic and motivational skills and that these are determined in the main by the children's early environmental experiences. These experiences, which tend to be associated with poverty in our society, are given the overall label of 'cultural deprivation'. They include a lack in the number and variety of objects and places with which the infant comes into contact, and, most importantly, in the amount and quality of verbal interaction with adults.

Interest in the second type of explanation was intensified partly at least from disappointment with the results of the compensatory education programme. Genetic, not environmental, factors it was argued (Jensen, 1969; Eysenck, 1971) were the main cause of the cognitive deficits of the unskilled, working-class or black child. It was conceded, though, that school achievements are affected by non-cognitive factors, such as motivation and values, as well as intelligence, and that these are largely determined by environmental influences.

The third type of explanation, like the first, attributes the low educational attainments of poor children to environmental causes. According to this viewpoint, though, unskilled, working-class and ethnic minority-group children do not suffer from any cognitive or linguistic deficits (Baratz, 1969 and 1970; Ginsburg, 1972; Labov, 1970). Any human society provides experiences sufficient for normal cognitive and linguistic development. The essence of this view is that lower working-class and ethnic-minority children come from backgrounds that are 'culturally different' but that their culture is not 'deficient' compared to middle-class culture. Apparent differences on IQ and other standardised tests arise primarily because the lower-class and minority-group child is not motivated towards test taking. Difficulties in reading may be accentuated by linguistic differences between non-standard dialects and standard English (Labov, 1969 and 1970; Stewart, 1969; Baratz, 1969 and 1970). It is admitted, though, at least by Ginsburg, that the lower-class environment may be deficient in one aspect, the parents providing fewer reading experiences for the child prior to school entry. However, it is not 'compensatory education' that is needed but a change in the school environment, so that it is adapted to the ways of thinking, language and needs of poor children.

These are very different diagnoses then of what constitutes disadvantage, having very different policy implications. In Part V, evidence on the cognitive and linguistic abilities of disadvantaged children will be reviewed and an attempt made to see how far these three theories can be substantiated or disproved.

2. Do low intelligence test scores 'explain' low educational attainments?

Intelligence test performance, social class and ethnic group.

Many studies have shown that scores on intelligence tests or other standardised measures of mental performance tend to decrease with social class. Confirmation of this is found in several fairly recent British studies. Social-class differences on tests of ability were found both at secondary- (Douglas *et al.*, 1968) and primary-school level (Douglas, 1964) in the study using a nationally representative sample. An average difference of about 14 IQ points was found between social class I and II children and those from social classes IV and V in a study of children attending local education authority primary schools in Aberdeen (Horobin *et al.*, 1967). Differences, in fact, appear to be already present in three-year-olds, though not earlier (Hindley, 1965). Studies from the United States show that minority, particularly black, children have lower intelligence test scores than white children of similar socio-economic status (Deutsch and Brown, 1964; Dreger and Miller, 1960, 1968).

According to the 'genetic' theorists (i.e. Jensen and his associates, not all geneticists) intelligence tests are measuring innate ability, and the poor school achievements of unskilled working-class and black children can be explained by their below average ability. This argument, put forward in Jensen's 1969 article, ran counter to the prevailing view. Most psychologists in the 1960s accepted that there is no sharp distinction between ability and achievement. Unlike attainment tests, intelligence tests are not direct measures of what the child has learned in school but they do measure what the child has learned from his general experiences.

Tests were originally designed to provide a standardised measure by which to determine whether a child could profit from normal school education. They are still generally validated against measures of scholastic achievement either directly or through validation against other established tests. The tendency towards relatively poor performance on intelligence tests by lower-working-class and minority-group children could arise then because their environment has failed to provide opportunities for the development of certain cognitive skills and mental strategies required in school work to the same extent as a middle-class environment. It could also arise, though, because these children are less familiar with certain types of problem, or with the kinds of objects and words used in tests. Working-class children could also be less at ease in the test situation and less motivated to do well. A number of studies have explored these possibilities.

Contents of tests, and motivation in test taking as causes of social class differences

When subjects were given the opportunity to become familiar with the test contents, differences between upper and lower-class kindergarten children were in fact almost eliminated on a perceptual-discrimination task using as its material stylised and highly abstract drawings of everyday objects (Primary Mental Ability) (Covington, 1967). However, familiarisation with the language and materials used in an individually administered intelligence test (Wechsler Preschool and Primary Scale of Intelligence) benefitted middle-class, pre-school children as much as those from the working class in another study (Kinnie and Sternlof, 1971). Revision of the content of standard intelligence test items to reduce their 'middle-class' bias and make them more meaningful to children from all social classes only differentially improved the performance of lower-class eleven-year-olds when they were also allowed practice and were motivated to do well on the test by being promised a reward if they did their best (Haggard, 1954). Studies which have allowed practice on tests to children from non-Western cultures have produced similar findings. Gains are found due to practice and coaching but they are generally little different in size from those made by British children in similar experiments. Motivation, combined with practice, though, appears to have had some success in differentially raising the scores of non-Western children (Vernon, 1969).

Motivation to perform well, without the provision of practice or revision of test content was found, in fact, differentially to benefit the lower social-status children in Haggard's study. A procedure for administering the Stanford Binet Intelligence test which was intended to improve the child's motivation by giving him a feeling of success was actually found to increase the scores of disadvantaged pre-school children as much as did nursery-school experiences over a seven months period (Zigler and Butterfield, 1968).

The findings of another study (Hertzig et al., 1968) not only emphasise the importance of motivational factors in test-taking but show that the mere establishment of rapport with the examiner does not in itself overcome differences in response to intelligence testing. Three to four year old Puerto Rican children from unskilled and semi-skilled working-class families and middle-class white American children of similar age were administered the Stanford Binet Intelligence test. Although the Puerto Rican children were tested by a Puerto Rican examiner with whom they were already well acquainted in the language with which they were most familiar (English or Spanish) they attempted to do what was asked of them significantly less often than the middle-class children, particularly when a verbal response was required. Of course, these findings cannot necessarily be generalised to lower-class children in general.

Role of experimenter and intelligence test performance

Lower-class black children may not only be less motivated to do well in a test situation than middle-class children but they may suffer an additional disadvantage when the experimenter is white. The performance of black American, lower-class, pre-school children (Moore and Retish, 1974) and of West Indian school children in Britain (Watson, 1972) has been found to improve when the examiner is black. The effect was greatest for the older West Indian children (fourteen to fifteen year olds) when the situation was more stressful, i.e. when the children were told that they were taking an IQ test rather than doing a research exercise. In an American study (Solkoff, 1972) both black and white eight to eleven-year-olds had better scores (on the Wechsler Intelligence Scale for Children) when the examiner was black. In this case, though, the situation was non-stressful, the children being told that they were to 'play some games' rather than being given a test. In another study (Caldwell and Knight, 1970) it made no difference to the performance of eleven-year-old black American children whether the examiner was black or white, but the findings were confounded by the two examiners being of opposite sex. Overall, the evidence suggests that a black examiner may differentially benefit black children in formal testing situations.

Are there social class differences in intellectual competence?

Three studies which have examined social class differences in the intellectual functioning of young children, taking exceptional care to ensure as far as possible that all subjects were at ease and responding in the testing situation, should give some indication of whether there are social class differences in those cognitive skills required for performance on IQ tests. Nevertheless, it is doubtful if motivational and attitudinal social class differences, built up through the child's life experiences, can be entirely overcome by efforts to achieve rapport in the testing situation, and this needs to be borne in mind when interpreting the findings.

At first, these three studies appear to have contradictory findings. A large IQ difference (Stanford Binet) between the highest and lowest-social-status groups was found for black three-year-olds in the study carried out by Golden, Birns and their colleagues (1971). Also, Jewish,

Puerto Rican, Chinese and black high social-status six to seven year olds performed better than low-social-status children of the same ethnic group on tests of verbal, reasoning, number and spatial ability in the study conducted by Lesser and his associates (1965). In contrast, Palmer (1970) found a significant difference only in language facility (as measured by the Peabody Picture Vocabulary Scale) and not on the Stanford Binet Intelligence test or other measures of cognitive ability between the high and low-status, black, pre-school subjects.

The apparent discrepancy is probably due to the marked difference in the composition of the lower social status groups in the three studies. In Palmer's study, all working-class children are included in the lower social-status category (Hollingshead Index of Social Status, Classes IV and V), while Golden, Birns and their colleagues have three lower social-status groups – working-class (Hollingshead, Class IV), lower-class, non-welfare (Hollingshead, Class V) and lower-class welfare (also Hollingshead, Class V). The gap of 23 IQ points found in the Golden et al. study is between the middle-class and the lowest social status group, consisting entirely of families living on welfare. The IQ gap between the middle-class and the stable working-class group is only 9 points. Thus these studies re-affirm that it is the poorest children who are most likely to be at disadvantage on certain intellectual tasks.

Is the intellectual disadvantage of the lower-working-class children almost entirely in verbal ability, as Palmer suggests? Lesser and his colleagues found that the lower-class children in each ethnic group (who were virtually all entirely from the lowest socio-economic level on the Hollingshead Index, except for the Jewish group) were somewhat less competent than the middle-class children not only in vocabulary but in other skills. However, although the contents of tests were designed in this study so that it would be familiar to children from all social classes and ethnic groups, the tests were quite heavily dependent on verbal instructions (Sitkei and Meyers, 1969) and in some cases on verbal labelling. It is difficult to be certain how far the social class differences found here are due to differences in verbal ability and how far there are actual differences in other areas.

How important are social class differences in linguistic skills?

It seems clear that the main social class difference between children aged up to six or seven years is in performance on tests of language ability. There appears to be a difference in vocabulary, as the work of Lesser et al. (1965) showed. A more recent series of experiments by Kirk, Hunt and their associates (Hunt et al. 1975a, 1975b; Kirk et al., 1975a, 1975b; Kirk and Hunt, 1975) found that four-year-old Head Start children (whose parents were mainly unskilled or unemployed) were much poorer at naming colours, positions, shapes and numbers than middle-class children. This does not necessarily mean that socially disadvantaged children differ from middle-class children in the extent of their vocabulary, for they may possibly know as many words, though some are those of their own 'culture'. There does not appear to be any definite evidence here. In any case, as Kirk and Hunt suggest, not knowing some of the words that are used in school in the early years may cause confusions, which could lead to cognitive disadvantages. The main social class difference in language which emerges from the literature, though, is in the purpose for which language is used, in the extent to which it is used for problem solving and the manipulation of ideas, at least those of the kind that occur in the school situation (see Section B, on Language Disadvantage, for an extensive discussion of this). A recent study (Golden *et al.*, 1974) even found a social-class difference at the age of two in the ability to use specific labels to help in the perceptual discrimination of unfamiliar objects.

Environmental or genetic factors as a cause of differences in intelligence test scores?

Presuming then that some children from unskilled, working-class families do tend to be less advanced in certain of the cognitive skills required by IQ tests compared with middle-class children, can this be attributed to their environmental circumstances? Jensen (1969) has contended that genetic factors are four times as important as environmental factors in accounting for differences in intelligence test scores between individuals in a population and from this concludes that differences between social classes and ethnic groups are also largely due to genetic factors. This is an erroneous line of reasoning as many critics have pointed out (Furby, 1973; Layzer, 1972; Lewontin, 1970; Scarr-Salapatek, 1975; Barbara Tizard, 1973). Nevertheless as Jensen relies so heavily on evidence bearing on the question of the relative contribution of heredity and environment to variations in IQ between individuals within a population this cannot be ignored. A detailed discussion of the research, though, much of which was conducted in the 1920s and 1930s, is outside the scope of this review.

Barbara Tizard (1973) has argued that the four main lines of evidence put forward by Jensen to support his position that genetic factors are of overwhelming importance in determining IQ can equally support an environmental explanation. This evidence consists of:
(a) Kinship correlation tables which show that correlations between the IQs of individuals depend on the closeness of family relationship;
(b) 'Regression to the mean', the tendency for children to have IQs nearer to the population mean than those of their parents;

291

DISADVANTAGE AND INTERVENTION

(c) Findings that the IQs of adopted children and their natural parents are more highly correlated than the IQs of these children and their adoptive parents;

(d) Findings that the IQs of monozygotic (identical) twins brought up separately since infancy are highly correlated, the correlations being considerably higher than those between siblings brought up in the same family.

Scrutiny of this evidence by a number of critics has shown, at a minimum, that the findings are by no means as unequivocally in favour of genetic factors being of predominant importance as Jensen suggests. Jensen took his evidence of correlations between the IQs of individuals differing in the degree of relatedness mainly from Erlenmeyer-Kimling and Jarvik's (1963) review of 52 independent studies. The median correlation between unrelated persons reared apart is 0.01, between unrelated individuals reared together 0.24, between foster parents and children 0.20, between child and parent 0.50 and between monozygotic twins brought up together 0.87. It has been pointed out, though, (Layzer, 1972) that these are 'median' correlations, and that the 'actual' correlation is not necessarily close to the median though it is likely to lie within a range of values comparable to the range spanned by the actual measurements. The ranges around the median values are, in fact, very considerable. For example, the correlations reported for parent and child in twelve studies range from 0.22 to 0.8 (Clarke and Clarke, 1974). Layzer also questions whether it is meaningful to combine correlations when they are derived, as Erlenmeyer-Kimling and Jarvik indicate, from diverse, though largely white North American and European, populations and from studies using different measures of IQ. In any case (Barbara Tizard, 1973) the pattern of correlations could be explained in terms of greater similarities in the environments of closer relatives.

In the case of 'regression to the mean' few studies provide sufficient data (IQs of both parents and all their children) to determine whether this actually occurs. Barbara Tizard also points out that the explanation for regression to the mean, that it is unlikely that factors which are responsible for unusually high or unusually low IQs will work in the same direction for the children, is compatible with a high environmental contribution to IQ variance.

It is possible that the relatively high correlation between the IQs of adopted children and their natural parents is due to selective placement, the philosophy of adoptive societies having been to place children in homes similar in social background to that of the child's natural parents. Kamin (1974) has argued that the correlations of IQ between adoptive children and their adoptive parents are inevitably low because adoptive parents represent a relatively narrow range of environmental influence. He also shows that the correlations between the IQs of adoptive parents and their own children are low. However, this argument has been disputed by Fulker (1975) who says that the more usual comparison is with the correlations of IQs between control children and their true parents, and that these are substantially higher.

One of the main problems in studies of separated identical twins is that the environments in which the children are reared are usually rather similar, the twins often being brought up by people who are related to each other. Unfortunately, as several researchers have shown (e.g. Clarke and Clarke, 1974; Kamin, 1974), the one study which is often quoted as having largely avoided this problem (Burt, 1966) is open to criticism on other grounds. In particular, IQs were obtained not simply from standardised tests but were submitted to an assessment procedure which slightly raised the correlation between the separated twins (Clarke and Clarke, 1974; Layzer, 1972). Additionally, it is doubtful if the environments in which the separated twins were brought up were as dissimilar as has sometimes been supposed. Although there was no significant correlation between the social class ratings of the environments of the separated twins, there is no evidence that the adoption agencies were not carrying out their usual policy of trying to match the child's background and adoptive home, and the environments may well have been similar in characteristics which are likely to affect cognitive development such as child rearing practices and values (Bronfenbrenner, 1975; Layzer, 1972). Similar treatment, due to their similarity in physical appearance and other characteristics, may also be a factor increasing the correlation between the IQs of identical twins, whether they are separated (but in rather similar environments) (Layzer, 1972) or living in the same family (Schwartz and Schwartz, 1974). Here again then environmental influences probably account to a large extent for the high correlations found in IQs.

It is clear that the difficulty of disentangling genetic and environmental factors will present a major obstacle to the quantitative estimation of the heritability of IQ. Conventional heritability analysis, in fact, assumes that there is a random allocation of genetic endowments to environments (Anderson, 1974; Bronfenbrenner, 1975; Layzer, 1972; Barbara Tizard, 1973). Random allocation of children to environments, as discussed above, occurs in none of the studies – including those of identical twins reared apart and unrelated adopted children brought up together – on which Jensen bases his estimates of the heritability of IQ (Barbara Tizard, 1973). Jencks (1973), on the other hand, after attempting to make an allowance for selective placement, estimated the heritability of IQ to be 0.45, considerably lower than the Jensen estimate. However, even this will be an inflated estimate of heritability because the child's individual characteristics (determined partly, at least, by his genetic endowment) will influence his 'micro-environment' (Bronfenbrenner, 1975; Layzer,

1972, 1974), making the environments of separated twins more alike and those of unrelated children brought up together more dissimilar. To the extent that children self-select aspects of their environment in accordance with their genetic make-ups, it is perhaps not illegitimate to classify such influences as genetically caused. This is to over-simplify, though, for environments differ in the extent to which they permit the child to choose such environmental opportunities for himself. Additionally, the child's own characteristics will influence how he is treated by others, but it is not only that a genetic predisposition towards some skill may cause others to encourage its development, for characteristics of the child totally unrelated to that skill may affect the opportunities others provide for its development. It appears that in the present state of knowledge, genetic and environmental influences are inextricably linked.

Even if it were possible to separate genetic from environmental influences heritability estimates derived from sample populations can only be generalised to the population at large if the samples are representative (Bronfenbrenner, 1975; Layzer, 1972). In twin studies, which have most commonly been used to estimate heritability, generalisation to the population as a whole is only valid if the environmental differences that occur between twins are as great as those that occur for unrelated children of the same sex and age. In none of the studies of identical twins brought up apart, on which estimates have been based, has this condition been fulfilled. As already discussed, separated identical twins are usually placed in somewhat similar environments and the possible contribution of environmental differences in the population to variability among individuals is under-estimated. Where the estimate of the heritability of IQ is based on a comparison of non-separated monozygotic (identical) and dyzygotic (fraternal) correlations the environmental differences between the twins are only those that exist within a family and the contribution of environmental differences to individual variability in the general population is again under-estimated (Bronfenbrenner, 1975).

It is of interest that a very recent study (Adams et al., 1976) using this method of comparing the correlations of identical and fraternal twins arrived at a very much lower estimation of heritability for performance on general mental ability tests (devised by the National Foundation for Educational Research, with items very like those in standardised IQ tests) than Jensen's value of 0.80 for IQ. The twins were a nationally representative sample of eleven-year-olds, obtained from the National Child Development Study sample. Using Jensen's own method of estimation a heritability of 0.373 was obtained for non-verbal ability. On the verbal test the difference between the correlations of the identical and fraternal twins was non-significant. Had the fact that identical twins are usually given greater similarity of treatment been taken into account, the estimate would have been even lower. This is a further reason for over-estimation of heritability in studies based on identical versus fraternal twin comparisons. It is assumed that the greater similarity of identical twins is due solely to their greater genetic similarity, the likelihood that the environments of the identical twins will be more alike than those of the fraternal twins being ignored. Weaknesses of this particular twin study lie in its use of groups tests, meaning that verbal items rely on reading ability, which is generally estimated as having a lower heritability than IQ, and determination of zygosity of the twins by impressionistic methods (although misclassification appears to be uncommon). Its strengths lie in the nationally representative sample, and the uniformity in age of the subjects, thus avoiding the problems found in testing a wide range of subjects in other twin studies.

There can be little doubt that Jensen has considerably underrated the methodological problems in making a quantitative estimate of the heritability of IQ within a population. However, even if estimates of a high contribution of genetic factors to scores on intelligence tests could be accepted this says nothing about the effect of major differences or changes in environmental circumstances on IQ (Hunt, 1975; Layzer, 1972). A number of studies show how the level of cognitive development differs in individuals coming from the same population but having been brought up under very different environmental circumstances (Hunt, 1975). In one study, three samples of Greek children, largely from working-class families, were found to achieve the concept of object permanence at different ages according to the type of upbringing they had had (Paraskevopoulous and Hunt, 1971). Infants assigned on a chance basis a few days after birth to two institutions differed in the average age at which they reached this level of cognitive development in accordance with the amount of individual attention they received. Those in an orphanage with a child/care-taker ratio of 10:1 arrived at this stage forty-one weeks later than those in an orphanage with a ratio of 3:1. Home-reared children were twenty-five weeks further ahead. American lower-class children attending an educationally oriented day-care centre attained this level two years earlier than the Greek children in the unstimulating orphanage (Hunt, 1975). Although it cannot be said that these children came from a single population there is no reason to believe that Greek and American children differ in genetic endowment.

A recent study by Tizard and Rees (1974) also provides strong evidence of the influence of environmental factors on IQ. Three groups of children, all of whom had been placed in residential care before the age of four months, were compared in IQ (Wechsler) when they were four-and-a-half years old. Those who had been adopted into white middle-class families just after they were three years old had an average IQ of 115, those who had been restored to their working-class mothers, many of whom were single parents living on social security, had an average IQ of 100, while thcse who remained in residential care had an average IQ of 105. As mentioned earlier, a difficulty in using most studies of adopted children for the assessment of environmental effects is that it has been the policy to seek adoptive homes which are similar in socio-economic level to those of the children's natural parents. This means that effects which appear attributable to the 'superior' adoptive environment could actually be due to the children's 'superior' genetic endowment. In the Tizard and Rees study, though, the natural fathers of the adopted children appeared to be, if anything, somewhat lower in socio-economic status than those in the other groups. Also, when the IQs of some of the children had been assessed at the age of two, while they were still in residential care, no differences were found between those who were later to be adopted and the others. It is difficult to see how the IQ differences between the groups can be other than effects of the environment.

Environmental or genetic factors as a cause of black/white IQ differences

It has already been much emphasised that whatever the genetic contribution to IQ variance within a population group such as a 'race', no inference can be drawn about the cause of differences between groups (Layzer, 1972; Tizard, 1973; Scarr-Salapatek, 1975). One way of looking at the contribution of genetic and environmental factors to differences in average intelligence between groups is to compare the IQs of children of one ethnic group, adopted by the parents of the other ethnic group, with those of their adoptive and natural parents (Loehlin *et al.*, 1975). When a recent study was carried out on these lines (Scarr-Salapatek and Weinberg, 1975) it was found that black children adopted by white families had an average IQ of 106, compared with an expected 90 (calculated from educational and occupational level of parents) if they had stayed with their own families. This then is evidence in favour of at least part of the black/white difference being due to environmental factors.

In another study (Willerman *et al.*, 1974) the IQs of 129 children from black/white matings were tested at the age of four. Children whose mothers were white and fathers black had significantly higher IQ (by 9 points) than children of the opposite combination of parents. This suggests that maternal child-rearing practices may contribute to the differences in IQ found between black and white children, though the possibility cannot be ruled out that the white mother/black father combination of parents was better endowed intellectually.

A study of institutionalised children appears to indicate quite clearly, though, that the black/white differences in IQ usually found for young children originate from differences in their environmental experiences. It was found (B. Tizard, 1974) that when reared in the same environmental conditions, a relatively high-quality residential nursery, white and black two to five-year-old children are very similar on measures of language (Reynell) and non-verbal intelligence (Minnesota). Only on the non-verbal measure was there a significant difference between the groups and this was in favour of the black children. Similarly, in the study of four-and-a-half year olds who had been in residential care from the early months of life, no black/white IQ differences were found in any of the three groups: those who were adopted, those who were restored to their own mothers and those who remained in residential care (Tizard and Rees, 1974).

It is rare, of course, to find black and white children who have experienced similar environmental conditions. There are a number of studies, though, which indicate that the more similar the environmental circumstances of the ethnic groups, the less is the difference between the average IQs of the groups. Simply equating blacks and whites on socio-economic level is insufficient to eliminate environmental differences between the groups.

Black children in the United States tend to come from crowded homes, from broken homes, from larger families and to have working mothers more often than white children of a similar socio-economic level as Tulkin (1968) has shown. In his study, differences in intelligence (Lorge-Thorndike) and achievement were no longer statistically significant between eleven and twelve-year-old black and white children in the middle-class group when these environmental variables were held constant. Significant differences remained, though, between the black and white children in the lower social-class groups. Tulkin points out that black lower-class families generally have lower incomes than similar white families and that there is a higher incidence of prematurity among black babies, both variables not taken into account in the study but which could affect the intelligence test and achievement scores. Added to this is the whole history of oppression and being discriminated against that places blacks in the United States in a different position from other groups, even other minority groups (Rex, 1972).

Several recent studies of immigrant children in Britain have shown that differences found on intelligence tests between recent immigrants and British children in the same socio-economic level are eliminated (in the case of Asian children) or attenuated (in the case of West Indian children) when the immigrant children have lived in the U.K. for a number of years (Ashby et al., 1970; McFie and Thompson, 1970; Sharma, 1971, cited by Ghuman, 1975).

In the Ashby et al. study Indian children who had been in England for three years or less were significantly poorer than Scottish children, matched for age and social class, on all the measures used (Glasgow verbal reasoning, Moray House, Raven's matrices, Goodenough Draw-a-man). Indian children who had been in England for nine years or more, though, did not differ significantly on the tests from the Scottish children. McFie and Thompson found that West Indian children attending a child guidance clinic had considerably lower scores than English children of similar age on a number of sub-tests, both performance and verbal, of the Wechsler Intelligence Scale for Children. Immigrant children who had received all their schooling in the U.K., however, had significantly better scores than those who had started their education in the West Indies.

In a recent study (Ghuman, 1975) nine and eleven-year-old Punjabi Sikh boys living in Birmingham were found not to differ significantly on tests of mental ability using non-verbal materials (Raven's matrices, Block design sub-test of the Wechsler) from English boys coming from a similar socio-economic level, the unskilled and semi-skilled working-classes. The performance of boys of similar ages living in two villages in the Punjab and coming from farming families (as did the immigrant Punjabis originally) was significantly poorer on both these tests than that of the Punjabi boys in Birmingham.

Are there differences in patterns of ability between ethnic groups?

There is some evidence that ethnic groups may differ in patterns of ability. Lesser *et al.* (1965), in their carefully carried out investigation, found significant differences among Jewish, Chinese, Puerto Rican and black six- to seven-year-old children in their patterns of scores on tests of verbal, reasoning, number and spatial abilities. These differences held within both the middle- and lower-class groups although middle-class children from different ethnic groups were more alike in their scores than were lower-class children from different ethnic groups. Similarly, Marjoribanks (1972a), studying eleven-year-old Canadian boys from five ethnic groups (Canadian Indian, French Canadian, Jews, southern Italians, white Protestants with a British background) found differences between the groups in the patterns of scores on tests of verbal, reasoning, number and spatial abilities. On the other hand, no ethnic-related differences in patterns of ability were found among black and white four-year-olds studied by Sitkei and Meyers (1969). The difference in findings may be due to the differences in the tests used, suggesting that ethnic-related differences are probably confined to a few areas of cognition (Ginsburg, 1972). Also, the subjects were younger in this study and any distinctive features of the learning environments associated with particular ethnic groups will have had less time to influence them.

Marjoribanks, in his study, identified environmental characteristics of the home likely to be related to learning and found both that the ethnic groups differed in their profiles of these characteristics and that these characteristics were actually related to the mental ability scores. The distinctive learning environment that tended to be associated with an ethnic group was found to account in large part, though not entirely, for the differences in the patterns of mental ability scores. It is unlikely that all environmental factors which affect mental ability scores were included in the analysis and there appears to be no necessity to attribute the remaining differences between the groups to genetic influences.

To sum up on differences in mental ability scores: there appears to be a social class difference in some aspects of cognitive, particularly language, performance, even after motivational and situational factors which adversely affect the performance of the lower social class children have been taken into account as far as is possible and the middle-class bias in test content has been reduced. These differences appear to be attributable to environmental rather than genetic factors. Whether they mean that unskilled working-class and black children actually do tend to be less competent in some intellectual skills than middle-class children is a matter of some dispute. At any rate, cognitive skills are not used to the same extent by the disadvantaged child as by the middle-class child in the testing situation. The test scores of black children tend to be lower than those of white children because they generally suffer from environmental adversity to a greater extent and additionally because testing by a white examiner is more stressful for them. IQ tests are good predictors of school success not because they assess 'pure' cognitive ability but precisely because they are influenced by the same motivational, attitudinal and social factors that affect learning at school.

3. Level I (associative) and Level II (conceptual) abilities

Jensen's theory

Jensen (1969) has suggested that there is a fundamental psychological distinction between two kinds of learning ability, associative and conceptual. Associative, or Level I learning, involves rote memory tasks which require little if any transformation of the material by the learner. Examples of such tasks are digit-span memory, serial rote learning, free recall of uncategorised visually or verbally presented materials and paired associate learning. Conceptual, or Level II abilities, in contrast, require the learner to transform the material before making a response. Intelligence tests with a low cultural loading, such as Raven's Progressive matrices measure this kind of ability.

According to Jensen's (1969) first version of the theory the genetic factors underlying Level I ability are distributed roughly equally in all the social classes but, because of their importance in scholastic achievement under traditional methods of teaching, Level II abilities have become disproportionately frequent in the higher social classes. Jensen suggests that the failure of many working-class children at school is due to the over-emphasis on conceptual rather than associative learning. He advocates different kinds of teaching for children with different abilities. Where children possess Level II abilities these should be fully encouraged. For the rest, educational methods should be devised which capitalise on the children's associative abilities.

Jensen's argument is based on the evidence from research that lower-class children perform as well as middle-class children on tests that are supposed to measure associative ability but there are marked social class differences on tests measuring cognitive and conceptual abilities (Jensen and Frederiksen, 1973; Jensen, 1974; Nazzaro and Nazzaro, 1972; Rohwer et al., 1971). In a number of these studies, though, social class and ethnic group were confounded (e.g. Rohwer et al., 1971; Jensen and Frederiksen, 1973), the higher socio-economic level children being white and the lower socio-economic level children being black. Several researchers have found that Jensen's model does not hold within the black population. The lower social-class group has been found to perform more poorly on Level I tasks such as digit-span, the difference between the classes being as large on this measure as on Level II ability (Green and Rohwer, 1971). An absence of social class differences has been found on tasks supposed to measure Level II abilities, such as free recall of a categorised list (Mensing and Traxler, 1973).

Also, the correlation between performance on tasks of associative and conceptual ability has not, as would be predicted by Jensen's theory, been found to be higher among white higher socio-economic level children than among black lower socio-economic level children (Rohwer et al., 1971; Stevenson et al., 1971).

Findings such as these have led Jensen to modify his theory. He now states (Jensen, 1973, 1974) that the essential of the theory is the independence of Level I and Level II abilities. Level II abilities have some degree, though it is only slight, of dependency on Level I but Level I does not depend on Level II. Populations that have developed under different selective pressures for different abilities and are relatively separate from each other may be expected to differ in Level I and Level II abilities and in the degree of correlation between Level I and Level II. However, in industrial societies, social mobility is more dependent on Level II ability than on Level I and it can be expected that the higher socio-economic groups will differ from the lower more in Level II than in Level I abilities.

Jensen's recent studies (1973, 1974) have been empirical tests of these hypotheses. As predicted, white children have been found to differ from black children more in Level II than in Level I ability, and the correlation between Level I and Level II abilities is higher in the white population than the black. The finding that the Mexican population, which Jensen sees as being socio-economically (though this is not true culturally) further from the white population than is the black population, is nevertheless nearer to the white population in Level II ability appears to have caused a further shift in the theory. Differences between blacks and whites are now stated to be ethnic group rather than socio-economic differences. Within the white population, differences between the socio-economic groups are greater for Level II than for Level I ability, as predicted. In the black population, though, this relationship is not consistently found.

Is the Level I/Level II dichotomy justified?

It is doubtful if Jensen's classification into two types of abilities can be accepted. Two studies, using middle-class white and lower-class, mainly black, samples (Friedrichs et al., 1971; Stevenson et al., 1971) have shown that correlations among different learning tasks are low, indicating that there is a high degree of differentiation of abilities in children. There was, in line with Jensen's findings, a significant correlation between an associative learning task (paired associates) and a conceptual task (category sorting) in the middle-class white group – but there was also a correlation of remarkably similar magnitude in the lower-class population. These studies offer no support for a difference in learning processes in black and white children. They do give some indication, though, of ways in which the two groups differ. The disadvantaged children needed more instructions before they understood what to do, they found some of the tasks much more boring and they had to be taught the names of the objects used in some tasks before these could be administered.

It has also been pointed out (Rohwer, 1971) that Jensen's categorisation of particular tasks as involving only rote memory or conceptual ability is by no means unchallengeable. The Peabody Picture Vocabulary Test, which consistently produces black/white and social class differences does not appear to require a highly conceptual process – the subject has to select out of four pictures the one which best illustrates the meaning of a word. On the other hand, it can be queried whether paired associate learning, the task which most regularly fails to produce black/white and social class differences, really requires no transformation of material for successful response. In this task the subject is presented with a pair of pictures and then is tested by being shown one member and being asked to name the other. There is ample research evidence showing that people who perform well on this task construct images or form sentences involving the members of the pair, an activity that certainly appears to be conceptual in character.

Social class differences in 'use' of conceptual ability

According to Rohwer all tasks require conceptual activity for proficient performance. Lower-class and ethnic-minority children often differ from middle-class children not in that they do not possess conceptual skills but in that they spontaneously supply conceptual activity to a task less readily. The differences between the children is particularly large in tasks which require the application of a previously learned formal set of rules, as in problems of logic, Raven's matrices and categorised lists in free-recall tasks. The differences are less in tasks such as paired associate learning or the free recall of uncategorised lists, which require imaginative conceptual activity.

Evidence that lower-class black children do not spontaneously supply additional conceptual activity is provided in a study by Rohwer and Ammon (1971). A paired associate task was presented in five different ways, in four of which the child had to supply some kind of conceptual activity, without being instructed to do so, for successful performance. He had, for example, to supply the images of the objects when he only heard their names, or the names when he only saw the pictures. The performance of the middle-class children was slightly but significantly better on this kind of task. However, when the child both saw the pictures and heard the names he did not have to supply anything more and performance of the two social class groups did not differ. Similarly, in another study (Nazzaro and Nazzaro, 1972) middle-class children were found to be more successful on a paired associate task when members of the stimulus pair were related by the experimenter only in a phrase mediated by a conjunction and thus requiring further elaboration into a meaningful sentence for successful learning. When the elaboration was supplied by the experimenter, the members of the pair being related in a phrase mediated by a preposition, the two groups did not differ. These findings might perhaps be taken to support Jensen's view that the lower-class children are capable only of associative learning. However, Rohwer and Ammon (1971) found that instruction in elaborative activities for twenty minutes a day over only a five-day period was sufficient to bring the performance of the lower-social-class black children up to that of middle-class white children before training.

Rather similarly, in a task involving free recall of categorised lists (Moely *et al.*, 1969) it was found that children up to the age of ten or so, unlike eleven- to twelve-year-olds, did not spontaneously group into categories objects they would later be asked to recall. When they were explicitly told to group the objects in the study period, though, recall improved significantly, suggesting that the younger child possessed conceptual skills but did not use them in the task until instructed to do so. Whether a capacity that is possessed is actually used probably depends on the 'degree' of possession as well as the way the task is presented and the situation.

Just as instruction enabled the younger children in the Moely *et al.* study to make use of conceptual ability they possessed but did not spontaneously utilise, prior training enabled some lower-social-class children to equal the performance of similarly trained middle-class children on a task involving the free recall of categorised lists in another study (Scrofani *et al.*, 1973). During the two thirty-minute training sessions the children were required to sort pictures into conceptual categories and to suggest a conceptual category to which a picture displayed by the experimenter might belong. For this training to benefit performance on a free-recall task meant that the children had to transfer their conceptual sorting skill to a new type of problem, which appears to be the essence of Level II ability.

This type of training was only found to be effective, though, for about half of the lower social-class children: those who gave evidence of their conceptual ability in their performance on Piagetian multiple classification and multiple seriation matrices but who nevertheless without training were considerably inferior to the middle-class children in performance on the free-recall task. Findings again suggest that some lower-class children possess conceptual skills but do not use them to the same extent as middle-class children in some kinds of tasks.

About half the lower social-class children in the Scrofani *et al.*, study, though, gained little benefit from prior training on conceptual sorting. These were children who could not successfully complete the Piagetian tasks. It appears that the development of conceptual skills is somewhat delayed in these children. There appears to be absolutely no basis, though, for rushing to the conclusion that because these abilities are delayed the children are inherently incapable of them and should only be taught through associative learning.

The effects of Jensen's policy would be to retard even further the development of conceptual skills in some lower-class children. Findings of a recent study (Nelson and Klausmeier, 1974) illustrate the point. Lower social-class children used more immature bases (immediate perceptions rather than specific attributes or nominal categories) for classification of geometrical figures than middle-class children of similar age but their responses became more mature between the ages of eleven to fourteen, provided they received school instruction in geometry. Seventeen-year-old lower social-class students who had not received instruction in geometry did not progress beyond classifying at the perceptual level. The problem for researchers is to devise teaching methods which will help to develop the cognitive skills of disadvantaged children.

4. Piagetian studies

The cultural-difference theorists deny that there is any tendency for unskilled working-class or minority-group children to be less competent in certain intellectual abilities than middle-class children. Ginsburg (1972) argues that IQ and other standardised tests of mental ability over-emphasise differences between children. Differences found between children on IQ tests which cannot be attributed to motivational and situational factors measure only particular skills, mainly verbal ones, which may be rather superificial. Items in these tests are deliberately chosen to differentiate between children rather than to show the common mental skills possessed by almost all children at a particular developmental stage. Also IQ and other similar tests show only the product of mental operations and give no indication of the mental processes by which the child arrives at a solution of the problems.

Ginsburg (1972) suggests that Piaget's work, in contrast, focuses on the concepts that are basic in a particular area, rather than on superficial aspects. Piaget's main interest is not so much in whether the child is successful or not on the tests he devised as in the patterns of reasoning used to arrive at a particular response.

Piaget's theory

According to Piaget's theory children in the pre-operational stage of thought are qualitatively different in their thought processes from adults. Children below the age of six or seven fail to realise that quantity is invariant even though the shape or appearance of a substance changes. For example, if the child is presented with two identical beakers filled with the same amount of water the child after the age of three to four almost always realises that they are equally full. If the contents of one beaker is poured, say, into a taller thinner beaker, resulting in a higher water level, the child at this stage of development thinks that there is more water in the differently shaped beaker. Similarly, if one of two identical balls of plasticine is rolled into a sausage-shape the child thinks they no longer contain the same amounts of plasticine.

At about the age of seven or eight there is a major change in the child's thought processes and he realises that whatever shape container the water is poured into the amount remains the same. The child has now achieved the concrete operational stage of thought. He realises that the initial equivalence of the water is conserved despite the transformation in appearance.

The pre-operational child's thought is characterised by centration, he tends to focus on only one dimension of the situation, such as the height of the water. When he reaches the concrete operational stage the child's thought becomes de-centred. He is able to attend to several dimensions of the situation and to realise that a change in one dimension is compensated by a reverse change in another dimension. The pre-operational child also concentrates on the static aspects of the situation and ignores the dynamic, looking at the heights of the liquid and not at the pouring. His thought lacks reversibility, the knowledge that pouring the water back into the original beaker would restore the original equivalence, proving that it could not have been destroyed. The child at the concrete operational stage, in contrast, is reversible in his thought. In Piaget's view, attainment of concrete operational thought processes is necessary for all rational activity.

Social class differences in performance on Piagetian tasks

Studies comparing social class performance on Piagetian conservation or other tasks designed to probe the child's underlying thought processes should show whether there are social class differences in basic abilities. Ginsburg reviews a few studies concerned with social class differences in the attainment of the concrete operational stage on various Piagetian tasks. Two of the studies carried out in the United States (Beilin *et al.*, 1966; Rothenberg and Courtney, 1969) found poorer performance by children from the lower social class, but a third (Beilin, 1964) did not. In another study (Mermelstein and Shulman, 1967) black lower-class nine-year-old children who had received regular schooling were similar in performance on conservation tasks to black children from another region who had received only a few months schooling, due to closure of the public schools, both groups being much superior to six-year-olds from the same two regions. Findings from these studies are interpreted by Ginsburg as showing that any social class differences are minor ones and that all children, however deprived, eventually achieve the concrete operational stage.

The body of research on social class differences in Piagetian tasks has grown substantially in the last few years. The evidence only partially supports Ginsburg's conclusions. While all children do appear to go through the same course of development in their mental processes the findings consistently indicate that lower social-class children lag in performance compared with middle-class children.

In one study (Gaudia, 1972) six- to ten-year-old children from the lowest social class were found to be more than a year behind the norming group for the test used (Goldschmid and Bentler Conservation Concept Diagnostic Kit), and as this group is composed of children from all social strata it is likely that the gap between the lower-class and middle-class children would be even greater. Studies using classification tasks (Overton *et al.*, 1971; Raven, 1967, Wei *et al.*, 1971) conservation tasks (Almy *et al.*, 1966; Brace and Nelson, 1965; Pace, 1973; Rothenberg, 1969a) and tasks concerned with the understanding of distance and movement (Rothenberg, 1969b) have found social class differences without exception. Differences are found very early, lower-class children already showing up to a year's deficit in the growth of skills necessary for conservation, such as ability to reproduce a row and in the understanding of the linguistic concepts 'same' and 'more' during the two-and-a-quarter to four year period (Rothenberg and Courtney, 1969).

In fact there is some evidence for social class differentiation during the sensori-motor stage, Wachs and his colleagues (1971) finding differences in means-ends behaviour in infants from seven months onwards. However, neither these authors nor Golden and Birns (1968) found any difference between the classes in the attainment of the concept of object permanence.

Role of language in Piagetian tasks

The evidence of social class differences on Piagetian tasks, at least from when the child is two-and-a-half years old or so, appears to be clear-cut. However, there is one complicating issue. In a study in which the higher and lower social-class children were matched for verbal ability no differences between the classes were found in performance on conservation and seriation tasks (Haney and Hooper, 1973). Verbal ability was related to conservation performance but its influence was small compared with age.

Do these findings mean that verbal ability facilitates the attainment of concrete operational thought, and that an important element in the poorer performance of Piagetian tasks of the lower social-class children is their lower verbal ability? Alternatively, it could be that language ability is merely a reflection of cognitive capabilities. A third possibility is that lower social-class children differ from higher social-class children mainly or partially in their ability to understand the language used in Piagetian tasks rather than in their attainment of cognitive structures. In the Mermelstein and Shulman study (1967) a higher proportion of the lower social-class black children succeeded on an entirely non-verbal conservation task than on the standard Piagetian verbal tasks.

There is clear evidence of social class differences in the understanding of words like 'same' or 'more' which are used in the Piagetian tasks (Rothenberg, 1969a; Rothenberg and Courtney, 1969). However, it seems unlikely that the social class differences can be attributed solely to communication differences. There appear to be no studies which have employed non-verbal techniques to make social class comparisons on the attainment of conservation. Fewer lower- than middle-class ten- to eleven-year-olds achieved maximum or near-maximum performance, though, on non-verbal multiple classification and multiple seriation tasks in one study (Scrofani et al., 1973). Social class differences were also found in two other studies of multiple classification which partially, at least, used non-verbal techniques to assess the children's level of development (Overton et al., 1971; Wei et al., 1971). Evidence from studies using predominantly non-verbal tasks indicative of whether the child has attained concrete operational thought – the ability to anticipate water level in jars tilted at angles (Beilin et al., 1966), and understanding of concepts of distance and movement (one of the tasks in Rothenberg, 1969b) suggests that there are social class differences in the rate of development.

There is also considerable evidence that the role of language ability in the performance of Piagetian tasks goes much beyond simply being able to understand and respond to the examiner's questions. Findings from a number of studies which have attempted to train non-conserving children to conserve also suggest that language ability facilitates the attainment of conservation, though improving the child's knowledge of comparative and dimensional terms does not by itself lead to conservation (Sigel et al., 1966; Sonstroem, 1966; Sinclair de Zwart, 1969).

Sinclair de Zwart interprets her findings as indicating, in accordance with Piaget's views on the role of language, that full understanding of comparative terms such as 'more', 'less', 'as much as' is only acquired when the child has reached the concrete operational level of thought rather than being a determinant of achievement of that level. Nevertheless her studies (with Inhelder) show, as she herself acknowledges, that training in the use of certain verbal terms may have the function of directing the child's attention to relevant aspects of the problem situation. Non-conserving children were taught expressions used by most conservers but few non-conservers: comparative terms (e.g. 'more than'), differentiated terms for different dimensions (e.g. 'little' and 'thin' rather than 'small' for both dimensions), and co-ordinated dimensions (e.g. 'this pencil is longer and thinner, the other is short and thick' rather than describing only one dimension or separate sentences describing first length and then thickness). Difficulty was experienced in teaching the children the comparative and co-ordinated structures. Only a few children learned to conserve. The children's answers showed, though, that they now noticed the co-varying dimensions, the liquid went up higher in the narrower glass, but this did not result in their arriving at a conserving judgement.

Sigel and his associates aimed in their study to teach the mental operations that are presumed to be the requisites of conservation. Four of five non-conservers were able to succeed on one or more conservation tasks administered two weeks after the training programme while none of the controls managed to conserve on any task. The authors conclude that the encouragement given to the children to label similarities and differences between objects played an important part in their realisation of the multiplicity of the attributes of objects and that changes in one attribute might be associated with changes in another.

Sonstroem's training experiment provides more direct evidence of the role of language in acquiring conservation. The study aimed to teach the child the mental operations of 'inversion' (reversibility) and 'compensation' (changes in one dimension must be compensated for by changes in another) that are considered essential for acquiring conservation. Materials used in both the conservation tests and training experience were two similar balls of clay, one being changed into a different shape and then converted into a ball again, the child being asked after each alteration which had more clay or whether they had the same amount. It was hypothesised that the child's physical performance of the appropriate mental operations would facilitate his acquisition of conservation. To act out 'inversion' only required the child to manipulate the clay himself but 'compensation' involved the experimenter providing verbal labels for the compensating attributes when the shape altered (e.g. when one ball was converted to a pencil this was labelled 'the longest ' and the other 'the fattest'). Almost 80 per cent of the children who were allowed to manipulate the clay themselves and who were also provided with verbal labels for the compensating attributes during training succeeded on the conservation post-test although they had failed on the pre-test (the difference between the tests was that the experimenter changed one of the balls into a 'hot dog' in pre-test and 'snake' or 'jump-rope' in the post-test). Manipulation alone and labelling alone, though, provided learning rates similar to those found in children neither allowed to manipulate the clay themselves nor provided with labels (25 per cent). Sonstroem suggests that providing the child with many different words forces him to think of the clay in many different ways and eventually to realise that it can have a multiplicity of shapes and still be the same clay. However, without the physical experience of reversibility verbal labelling had little success in helping the children to attain conservation.

Peisach's (1974) study of knowledge of dimensional terms in five- to eight-year-old children leads to similar conclusions. Language ability helps the child, particularly the younger child, to consider more than one dimension of an object at the same time but it is only one aspect of the development of conservation. Findings also appear consistent with studies of deaf children. Furth's work (1973) indicates that when special methods are adopted which enable them to understand the instructions in a task of conservation of the quantity of liquid deaf children are found to be one or two years behind hearing children. Furth's own view is that linguistic skills are not necessary for the attainment of concrete operational thought. However, manual communication may provide deaf children with a linguistic system (Dale, 1972) and it is doubtful if they can be characterised as being without linguistic skills as Furth does. Rather, their less developed linguistic system probably contributes to the relatively slight retardation found.

These findings suggest then that the lower verbal ability in lower social-class children may be one of the factors tending to cause slower cognitive development. Differences may have been exaggerated in some studies, though, difficulties in verbal communication being confused with failure of cognitive understanding.

Possession and 'use' of cognitive structures

There is at least a possibility that some lower-class children who perform poorly on the Piagetian tasks requiring concrete operational thought processes do so not because they have failed to develop the requisite cognitive structures at the same time as the middle-class children but because they do not always use the abilities they possess. It has been postulated (Overton et al., 1971) that these structures take time to become consolidated after they first emerge and that during this period a tendency to rely on perceptual features of the task – which is characteristic of the earlier pre-operational stage – remains. During the transition from pre-operational to concrete operational thought whether the child operates logically will be influenced by perceptual and other features of the task and situation. Once the cognitive structures have become consolidated task and situational factors play little part in determining whether they are used.

Some support for these hypotheses was obtained in a study conducted by one the authors (Overton). Reduction in perceptual features in a Piagetian multiple classification matrix task was found to improve the performance of six- to seven-year-old children, who would be expected to be in the transitional period. For younger children, who would still be at the pre-operational stage, and for older children, in whom the ability to operate in a logical manner should have become consolidated, performance was not affected by a reduction in perceptual features.

It may then be that the environment fails to provide some lower-class children in the transitional stage with techniques to orient them away from perceptual features to the extent that it does for the middle-class child.

Causes of social class and ethnic group differences

In most studies the ethnic groups of the social classes were unspecified although in some (Rothenberg, 1969a; Rothenberg and Courtney, 1969; Overton *et al.*, 1971) the higher social status groups were predominantly white and the lower status groups mainly black. In Gaudia's study black children from the lowest social class were behind both white and American Indian children of similar social class. A possible explanation, in line with the previous discussion, is the lower average verbal ability of the black children. Findings of one study (De Lemos, 1969) have been used to support the view (Eysenck, 1971) that mental differences between groups can be attributed to genetic factors. Part-blooded Aboriginal children (with the equivalent of one white great-grandparent) were found to perform significantly better on conservation tasks than full-blooded Aboriginal children living in apparently identical circumstances. However, these findings have not been replicated in other studies (Dasen, 1972; De Lacey, 1971).

In another study (Ghuman, 1975) Punjabi immigrant boys living in this country did not differ in a conservation of area task from English boys of similar socio-economic background but boys from the same ethnic groups as the immigrant children, still living in Punjabi villages, had a performance that was poorer than either of the groups in Britain.

None of these findings then appear to substantiate Eysenck's position that the differences between ethnic groups on conservation tasks are primarily due to genetic factors.

Attainment of the concrete operational thought-stage and school progress

How much does it matter if lower social-class children are somewhat slower in their attainment of concrete operational thought processes? While it seems very likely that the lower social status children do eventually catch up on these processes their slower development must surely be one of the factors hindering them in their school work at a particular point in time. It is doubtful if this can so easily be caught up. There is some direct evidence, in fact, that children who perform less well on conservation tasks when they are five-years-old are handicapped in both learning to read and arithmetic (Dimitrovksy and Almy, 1975a and 1975b). Conservation training which aims at teaching all the underlying pre-requisites was as successful with lower social-class as with middle-class five-year-olds in one study (Rothenberg and Orost, 1969). Work on these lines could be of great importance in intervention.

5. Conclusions

The performance on certain intellectual tasks of some, certainly not the majority, of children from an unskilled, working-class background does seem to be lower than that of middle-class children, even when efforts have been made to eliminate material unfamiliar to the child and put him at his ease. For some of these children, the problem appears to be that they do not use the abilities they possess. Whether this is because these abilities are held less 'securely' or it is due to unidentified motivational or other factors remains unclear. For other children it does appear that there is a slower development of cognitive abilities, although it seems very likely that some 'catching up' eventually occurs (Douglas *et al.*, 1968; Kagan and Klein, 1973). It is difficult to reach any definite conclusions because so few studies have had as their subjects those suffering from multiple social handicaps.

The available evidence suggests that both the 'cultural deficit' and 'cultural difference' theories have made valuable contributions to the understanding of educational disadvantage. For the majority of working-class children, any differences in intellectual performance from middle-class children that are found are probably due to motivational and 'know how' factors. Health disadvantages, and the lesser opportunities for interaction, particularly verbal interaction with adults, cannot, though, be ignored as having an effect on some children, particularly those with most social disadvantages. 'Cultural difference' theorists tend to forget that the 'way of life' of poor, unskilled working-class people is not simply a matter of different culture and traditions but is rather an adaptation to poverty. Environmental causes appear to more than account for the intellectual disadvantages that are found and leave little room for a 'genetic' interpretation.

Annotations

COLE, M., GAY, J., GLICK, J. A. and SHARP, D. W. 1971. *The Cultural Context of Learning and Thinking*, Basic Books, New York, 304 pp.

The authors' overall conclusion from this work is that different cultural groups differ not in the presence or absence of certain cognitive processes but in the circumstances in which particular processes are used. Intensive study was undertaken of the culture and language of the Kpelle tribe of the Republic of Liberia, and a large number of learning experiments were conducted with Kpelle subjects of different ages and with different lengths of, or no, attendance at Western-style schools. Experience of Western education was found to produce large differences in learning behaviour, although the amount of schooling that produced the differences varied with type of task. In discrimination learning tasks, children with moderate degrees of education used more generalised learning procedures while non-educated Kpelle children learned item by item. However, non-educated children did use a more generalised mode of learning in a few instances, so it cannot be concluded that they are incapable of such usage but only that they use general concept-based procedures less frequently. In studies of free recall, it was found that Kpelle high school students have learned to produce structures for themselves which they can use for the efficient storage and retrieval of information. The non-educated Kpelle have not learned spontaneously to produce such structures but they can use them when they are provided by the natural situation, as in story remembering. Other experiments suggest that non-educated Kpelle use 'situation-bound' rather than hypothetical thinking in certain naturally occurring situations.

Similarly, the authors suggest, the poor performance of minority groups in the United States is due to situation factors. However, it is not sufficient to demonstrate, as have some researchers, that children from these groups show learning skills in the street that they do not show in the classroom. It is necessary to use research methods similar to those in the present study to come to some understanding of the circumstances in which these skills are shown and to find ways of teaching the child to use these skills at school.

DAVIE, R., BUTLER, N. and GOLDSTEIN, H. 1972. *From Birth to Seven. The Second Report of the National Child Development Study (1958 cohort).* Longman in association with National Children's Bureau, London (from chapters 4, 5, 10 and 15); Humanities Press, Atlantic Highlands, N.J.

In this report of the development of children in the National Child Development Study (born in one week in March 1958) social class was found to have an important effect on school attainments at the age of seven. Children from Social Class V (unskilled manual) were found to be nearly seventeen months behind the children from Social Classes I and II (professional and technical) in reading ability (Southgate reading test). The chances of a child being a poor reader were six times as great if he came from Social Class V than if he came from Social Class I. Generally there was a sharp differentiation in attainments between children from the manual working-classes (Social Classes III (Manual), IV and V) and those from the non-manual classes (Social Classes III (Non-Manual), II and I), with children from Social Class V being at particular disadvantage. Children from Social Class V were very much more likely to live in overcrowded homes or those lacking sole use of basic amenities than those from Social Class I. These conditions had an effect of about nine months reading retardation independent of the influence of social class, sex, country (England, Scotland or Wales), type of accommodation and tenure, and, in the case of basic amenities, family size.

GAUDIA, G. 1972. 'Race, social class, and age of achievement of conservation on Piaget's tasks', *Developmental Psychology* 6, 1, 158–65.

126 six- to ten-year-old children from New York state, all members of the lowest social class (Warner scale), one third American Indian, one third black and the remainder white, were tested on the Conservation Concept Diagnostic Kit devised by Goldschmid and Bentler. Performance of the sample children was similar to that of the norming group, aged five-and-a-half to seven-and-a-half years, which represented all strata of society. This suggests that the lower-class children are slower in acquisition of conservation than more advantaged children. The black children were behind the other two groups in the attainment of conservation, and this difference increased with age. The black children were also lower in their verbal ability scores (Peabody Picture Vocabulary Test) than the other groups, and it is possible that a language-mediated variable is responsible for the retardation in their conservation performance. However, differences between the ethnic groups were not as large as those between the entire lower-class sample and the norming group.

GOLDEN, M., BIRNS, B., BRIDGER, W. and MOSS, A. 1971. 'Social class differentiation in cognitive development among black preschool children', *Child Development* 42, 1, 37–45.

In a previous study, three groups of black infants, one from families receiving welfare, one from lower educational-achievement families and one from higher educational-achievement families, were found not to differ significantly either on the Cattell Infant Intelligence scale or the Piaget Object scale at twelve, eighteen or twenty-four months. When 89 of the original 126 children were tested at approximately three years of age on the Stanford Binet Intelligence scale, highly significant differences were found between the socio-economic groups even though every effort was made to establish rapport with the children and elicit responses from them. Mean IQ scores (after re-classification on the Hollingshead Index of social status) were: middle-class 116, working-class 107, lower-class/non-welfare 100, lower-class/welfare 93. Social-class differentiation in intellectual ability appears to begin between the ages of eighteen and twenty-four months, the correlation between the mother's intelligence (Peabody Picture Vocabulary Test) and the child's intelligence (Cattell) increasing after eighteen months.

GREEN, R. B. and ROHWER, W. D. 1971. 'SES differences on learning and ability tests in black children', *American Educational Research Journal* 8, 4, 601–9.

A test of Jensen's hypothesis that Level I ability (associative ability–capacity for rote learning) is distributed equally in all socio-economic groups while Level II abilities (higher conceptual functioning) are not. Subjects were ten year old black children attending the same school, twenty belonging to the lowest socio-economic level, twenty to the lower-middle socio-economic level (Warner scale). Three tests were administered to each child, two requiring only Level I ability (paired-associate task; digit span task) and one requiring Level II abilities (Raven Coloured Progressive Matrices). As would be expected from Jensen's hypothesis, all three groups had similar scores on the paired-associate task but differences were found in performance on the Raven Matrices, the lowest socio-economic group having scores significantly lower than those of the other two groups. However, in contradiction to Jensen's hypothesis, the lowest socio-economic level also performed significantly below the lower-middle and middle-socio-economic level groups on the digit span task. The socio-economic groups differed more on this task than they did on the Level II task. Either Jensen's hypothesis is inadequate or it holds only in white and not in black populations.

HANEY, J. H. and HOOPER, F. H. 1973. 'A developmental comparison of social class and verbal ability influences on Piagetian tasks', *Journal of Genetic Psychology* 122, 235–45.

Both socio-economic level and verbal ability have been found to influence performance on Piagetian tasks of concrete operations. The present study was designed to assess the relative influence of these two variables. Eighty low socio-economic status subjects and eighty middle socio-economic status subjects, matched for verbal ability and grade level (kindergarten to fourth grade – five to ten years old) were individually administered seven Piagetian tasks (measures of seriation and conservation abilities). Middle and lower socio-economic status subjects did not differ significantly on performance on any of the tasks, but high verbal-ability subjects were superior to low-level verbal-ability subjects on all of the tasks. However, the impact of verbal ability was relatively minor compared with that of school grade. Previous research findings of significant influence of socio-economic status may have confounded socio-economic level with verbal ability. The question of whether it is language skills that lead to logical operations capabilities, or the converse, remains debatable.

HERTZIG, M. E., BIRCH, H. G., THOMAS, A. and MENDEZ, O. A. 1968. 'Class and ethnic differences in the responsiveness of preschool children to cognitive demands', *Monographs of the Society for Research in Child Development*, serial no: 117, 33, 1, 69 pp.

Behavioural style in response to cognitive demands (Stanford Binet intelligence test) was found to differ in two groups of three-year-old children, 116 from middle-class, mainly professional American families and 60 from working-class, mainly unskilled and semi-skilled, Puerto Rican families. The middle-class children made a higher proportion of work responses (attempts to do what was asked of them) to the cognitive demands than the Puerto Rican children. Overall, they made a greater number of verbally expressed responses, including more frequent spontaneous remarks about the task in hand. Verbal responses by the middle-class children when they failed to work were more often made in terms of lack of competence, while Puerto Rican more often made irrelevant remarks when they failed to work. Passive unresponsiveness was a more frequent response among the Puerto Rican than the middle-class children. The middle-class children made work responses equally often to verbal and non-verbal tasks while the Puerto Rican children made work responses more frequently to non-verbal tasks. The differences between the middle-class and the Puerto Rican children remained when IQ and ordinal position were controlled. The authors suggest that the Puerto Rican children possessed language but had difficulty in using it in response to demands for cognitive performance.

Differences between the middle-class and the Puerto Rican children could not be accounted for by differences in obstetrical histories, level of intelligence, ordinal position, adequacy of housing or family disruption. Nor could the differences have arisen from the test being conducted in an unfamiliar language to the Puerto Rican children for it was administered in the language in which each child was most competent (Spanish or English) by an examiner who was well-known to him. Possibly differences in child-rearing practices are responsible for the differences in behavioural style. The Puerto Rican mothers were much less task-oriented, less concerned with developing self-care skills in the children, less actively involved in their play, regarding it as a source of amusement rather than education. The Puerto Rican mother's language was social and affective rather than task directed.

Whatever its origins it is speculated that the behavioural style of the Puerto Rican children if maintained will be regarded as lack of motivation, surlines and silliness by teachers and is thus likely to lead to school failure. The solution, it is suggested, is not to try to alter the pattern of response of the Puerto Rican children but to find a method of instruction appropriate for them. Investigation is needed to find out whether the stylistic pattern observed in this study is characteristic of disadvantaged children in general or specific to Puerto Rican children.

JENSEN, A. R., 1974, 'Interaction of Level I and Level II abilities with race and socio-economic status', *Journal of Educational Psychology* 66, 1, 99–111.

Jensen has hypothesised the existence of two types of mental abilities. Level I ability is the capacity for rote learning and memorising – it involves no transformation of input. Level II abilities involve the mental manipulation of inputs, conceptualisation, reasoning and problem solving. Findings of previous research by the author and his associates have suggested that groups differing in socio-economic status differ less in Level I than in Level II abilities, and that there is a higher correlation between Level I and Level II abilities in middle- than in low socio-economic status groups.

The present study was designed to test Jensen's theory of mental abilities in a total school population. The subjects were 1,489 white, largely middle-class and upper-middle-class children and 1,123 black, predominantly lower-middle and lower-class children, virtually all the ten- to thirteen-year-olds attending the fourteen elementary schools in Berkeley, California. Subjects in each of the ethnic groups were divided into three socio-economic levels on the basis of parental occupations. Level I ability was measured by digit-span memory tests and Level II ability by the Lorge-Thorndike Intelligence Test. White/black differences were found to be highly significant on both Level I and Level II abilities but the difference in intelligence was more than twice that in memory. Within both the ethnic groups the higher/lower socio-economic level difference was twice as great for the intelligence as for the memory test. These findings are not in accordance with the original version of the theory (Jensen, 1969) which stated that higher and lower socio-economic groups differ in Level II but not in Level I ability. They do, though, conform to the essential of the theory that populations can differ in these two classes of mental abilities and that the direction of differences is such that higher and lower socio-economic groups will differ more in Level II than in Level I ability. As hypothesised there was a higher correlation between Level I and Level II ability (and regression of Level I upon Level II) in the white than in the black population. This was largely attributable to the difference between the entire white population and the lower socio-economic level black group. Within the black population there was a higher correlation between Level I and Level II abilities in the high- and middle-socio-economic groups than in the lower-socio-economic level group but no systematic differences were found within the white population. Although there was some evidence of functional dependence of non-verbal intelligence on memory the relationship did not appear to be very strong.

JENSEN, A. R. and FREDERIKSEN, J. 1973. 'Free recall of categorised and uncategorised lists: a test of the Jensen hypothesis', *Journal of Educational Psychology* 65, 3, 304–12.

In this study free recall of categorised and uncategorised lists was used to test Jensen's hypothesis that there are two fundamental types of mental abilities, Level I (rote learning and memory) and Level II (analysing, reasoning, abstraction and conceptual thinking). Previous research has suggested that low- and middle-class groups (and representative black and white groups) differ more in Level II than in Level I abilities. Also the correlation between Level I and Level II abilities is generally found to be higher in high-social-class groups than in low-social-class groups. Categorised lists are composed of items belonging to a small number of general categories, the items being presented sequentially in random order to the subject. Spontaneous provision by the subject of superordinate categories to facilitate recall gives clear evidence of conceptual or Level II ability. Uncategorised lists, on the other hand, are composed of items which bear little relationship to each other and cannot be grouped into obvious superordinate categories. Acquisition and recall, therefore, primarily involves Level I or rote learning ability.

Subjects of the present study were 120 eight- to nine-year-old (second grade) and ten- to eleven-year-old (fourth grade) children, half white and middle-class and half black and predominantly lower-middle or lower-class. As expected, performance of the black and white groups on the uncategorised list, the Level I task, did not differ significantly at either Grade 2 or Grade 4 levels. Performance of the two groups did not differ on the categorised list, the Level II task at Grade 2 but the middle-class, white children were significantly superior at Grade 4. At Grade 4 level also, the white, middle-class children showed significantly more clustering on recall of the categorised list than the black lower- and lower-middle-class children, showing that they made spontaneous clustering to facilitate recall to a greater extent. Categorised and uncategorised lists look much alike to the subjects, and the instructions given for both the tests were identical, so the performance difference on the Level II task at Grade 4 level cannot be attributed to the greater anxiety of the black lower class subjects or to their lack of test-taking motivation.

KIRK, G. E. and HUNT, J. McV. 1975. 'Social class and preschool language skill: i) Introduction', Kirk G. E., Hunt, J. McV, and Lieberman, C. 1975a. 'Social class and preschool language skill: ii) Semantic mastery of color information', Hunt, J. McV., Kirk, G. E. and Volkmar, F. 1975b. 'Social class and preschool language skill: iii) Semantic mastery of position information', *Genetic Psychology Monographs* 91, 2, 289–98, 299–316, 317–37.

A series of studies designed to test the validity of two explanations which have been put forward to explain why socially disadvantaged children do poorly at school in general. One suggests that the poor conditions in which they are reared leads to cognitive defects in early childhood. The other denies that these children are deficient in cognitive or language skills and proposes that school failure arises because disadvantaged children, especially black children, speak a nonstandard English dialect which makes learning to read in standard English difficult.

The second and third articles report research which investigated whether or not the semantic mastery of elementary abstractions, colour and position, were the same in four-year-old children with poor, uneducated parents as in children with middle-class, well-educated parents. Disadvantaged children were found not to differ from middle-class children in the perceptual identification of colour, but a markedly smaller percentage of the disadvantaged children showed an understanding of colour terms heard or were able to name correctly all the colours. White and black disadvantaged children did not differ in their semantic mastery of colour information. The disadvantaged children showed that they understood the examiners and their deficit in colour understanding cannot be attributed to failure to understand standard English. Findings on social class differences in semantic mastery of position information were very similar. It is concluded that children from socially disadvantaged backgrounds do have cognitive deficits and that their school difficulties cannot be attributed merely to dialect differences.

LESSER, G. S., FIFER, G. and CLARK, D. H. 1965. 'Mental abilities of children from different social class and cultural groups', *Monographs of the Society for Research in Child Development*, serial no: 102, 30, 4, 115 pp.

A study aimed to make a valid evaluation of the intellectual abilities of children from different cultural and social class backgrounds by devising tests free from cultural or class bias and creating optimal testing conditions. Eighty six- to seven-year-old New York children, from each of four ethnic groups, Chinese, Jewish, black and Puerto Rican, half from each group being middle-class and half lower-class (chosen so that there was maximum possible social class separation within each ethnic group) were tested on four aptitude scales: verbal, reasoning, number and space conceptualisation. The contents of the tests were selected so that they would be familiar to all the children. No reading or writing was required, instructions were kept simple and the test was administered in the language most familiar to the child. Ample practice was provided for each sub-test and examiners were instructed not to proceed with scored items unless the child was familiar with the material, understood the task and was willing to be tested.

Middle-class children were found to be superior to the lower-class children on all the scales and sub-tests. Ethnic group membership also influenced the level of each mental ability. In relation to the other groups, Jewish children were superior on verbal abilities, and Chinese children were superior on spatial abilities. The black children were average on verbal abilities, and, relative to the other groups, weaker on other abilities. Puerto Rican children were relatively weak on all abilities, particularly on verbal abilities. On each ability scale the scores of the middle-class children from the four ethnic groups were more alike than those of the lower-class children from the four groups. Patterns of mental ability differed for the four groups, but within each ethnic group the middle-class and the lower-class children showed the same patterns of ability.

MARJORIBANKS, K. 1972a. 'Ethnic and environment influences on mental abilities', *American Journal of Sociology* 78, 2, 323–37.

In this study ethnic groups – Canadian Indians, French Canadians, Jews, Southern Italians and white Anglo-Saxon Protestants – were found to differ both in their mental ability profiles and in levels of mental ability test scores (verbal, number, spatial and reasoning abilities as measured by SRA Primary Mental Abilities subtests). Ethnic groups also differed in their profiles of home environment characteristics. Home environment factors – encouragement of achievement, activeness, intellectuality and language usage – were found to account for a large percentage of the variance in verbal and number ability scores. When learning environment in the home was taken into account, ethnic group membership no longer made a contribution to the variance in spatial ability, and its influence on verbal, reasoning and number ability was much reduced. The environmental characteristics of the home contributed to the variance in mental abilities both 'independently' and through the association between environmental patterns and ethnicity. Subjects were 100 eleven-year-old boys from five ethnic groups, half of the subjects in each group coming from a middle-class and half from a working-class background.

MENSING, P. M. and TRAXLER, A. J. 1973. 'Social class differences in free recall of categorised and uncategorised lists in black children', *Journal of Educational Psychology* 65, 3, 378–82.

Jensen has hypothesised that Level I (rote-learning) ability is distributed similarly in all social classes but Level II (conceptual) abilities are distributed differently in middle- and lower-social-class groups. He has

319

shown in a recent study (Jensen and Frederiksen, 1973) that lower- and middle-class children perform similarly on a task requiring the free recall of uncategorised items (said to tap Level I ability) but differed significantly on a task requiring free recall of categorised items (said to tap Level II ability). In the present study, however, black lower- and middle-class children were found to differ neither in their ability to recall an uncategorised nor a categorised list. Social class differences were found, though, on two measures of intellectual ability, the Slosson Intelligence Test and Raven Coloured Progressive Matrices. Findings of the present study cast doubt on whether Jensen's model of the differential distribution of Level I and Level II abilities is adequate, at least for a black population. Subjects of the study, twenty lower-class and thirty middle-class black eleven to twelve year olds, were randomly assigned to one of the two free-recall tasks.

OVERTON, W. F., WAGNER, J. and DOLINSKY, H. 1971. 'Social class differences and task variables in the development of multiplicative classification', *Child Development* 42, 6, 1951–8.

White middle-class children performed significantly better than black lower-class children on Piagetian multiplicative classification tasks at the age level eight to nine, but not earlier at the four to five or six to seven age levels. Multiplicative classification is the ability simultaneously to classify an object into two or more categories, which according to Piaget, is attained when the child reaches the concrete operational level of thought generally in the sixth or seventh years of life. Prior to this the child is unable to co-ordinate simultaneously several stimulus categories and tends to rely on the perceptual features of a task. It is suggested that when these cognitive structures first emerge they are in the process of being consolidated and may not always be used in actual performance. The child has the ability to operate in a logical manner but whether he actually does so depends on the task and the situation. A previous experiment by one of the authors (Overton) provides some supporting evidence. Reduction of perceptual features in a task resulted in improved performance by middle-class children at the six to seven age level, when structures are likely to be emerging, but not at the four to five age level, when they are presumably not present or at the eight to nine level, when they have become consolidated.

Two possible explanations for the poorer performance of the lower-class children are suggested. Their environment may provide sufficient opportunities for the development of the necessary cognitive structures at the same age as in the middle-class children but may fail to provide techniques to orient the child away from perceptual features. Alternatively, environment may not provide the lower-class child with sufficient opportunities for development of these cognitive structures at the same age as in the middle-class child. A combination of both explanations is also a possibility. Subjects were ninety-six children, half at each age level being black, lower-class children from an inner city area in the United States and half middle-class, white children from a suburban area.

PALMER, F. H. 1970. 'Socioeconomic status and intellective performance among Negro preschool boys', *Developmental Psychology* 3, 1, 1–9.

No clear and consistent social class differences in intellectual abilities were found in black children tested up to the age of three years, eight months. A low but significant relationship was found, though, between social class and language facility as measured by the Peabody Picture Vocabulary Test. The stability of the lower-class families in the sample and the relatively small association found between occupation and education in this group are possible explanations for the absence of the social class differences in intelligence found at later ages. Also, the disadvantage suffered by lower-class children because of their greater difficulty in adapting to the test situation, compared with middle-class children, may have been overcome in the present study by the efforts made to ensure that each child was comfortable and responsive to testing.

SCROFANI, P. J., SUZIEDELIS, A. and SHORE, M. 1973. 'Conceptual ability in black and white children of different social classes: an experimental test of Jensen's hypothesis', *American Journal of Orthopsychiatry* 43, 4, 541–53.

A study designed to test Jensen's theory that differences in conceptual problem solving ability (Level II ability) found, in a number of studies, between higher- and lower socio-economic level groups are genetically based. Lower socio-economic level ten-year-olds who had high scores on Piagetian non-verbal tasks (multiple classification and multiple seriation) performed as well as middle-class children on a Level II task (free recall of categorised pictures) when both groups had received training in concept formation. Untrained lower-class children, even though they had high scores on the Piagetian tasks, did not perform as well as middle-class children on the Level II free-recall task. These lower-class children gained more from training than the middle-class children. Training consisted of thirty-minute sessions on the two days prior to administration of the free-recall task, in sorting picture cards into conceptual categories and suggesting conceptual categories to which cards displayed might belong. After the short training the lower-class subjects were able spontaneously to transfer the skill learned to a more complex task in which it was used in a new way. According to Jensen, this capacity to call upon relevant sub-abilities and previous learning when faced with a new problem is the essence of Level II ability. It therefore seems very unlikely that these lower-class children inherently differ in conceptual ability from the middle-class children. Possibly they have had less experience of the usefulness of conceptual analysis, or lack specific skills, such as verbal labelling that middle-class children possess.

These findings apply only, though, to the 48 per cent of the lower-class sample whose performance equalled that of the middle-class children on the Piagetian tasks. The 52 per cent who had lower scores on the Piagetian tasks benefited less from training than the middle-class children. However, recent research has shown that environmental factors affect the rate of development of the abilities measured by Piagetian tasks and there is no need to assume that the differences between the lower-class and middle-class children are genetic in origin.

Subjects of the study were 87 middle-class and 123 lower-class ten- to eleven-year-olds from six elementary schools in Maryland, from which three groups of 36 children each, middle socio-economic level, low socio-economic level, high Piagetian performance and low socio-economic level, low Piagetian performance, were selected for the training experiment. Black and white children of similar socio-economic level (each group contained roughly equal numbers) did not differ in Level II abilities.

TIZARD, B. and REES, J. 1974. 'A comparison of the effects of adoption, restoration to the natural mother, and continued institutionalisation on the cognitive development of four-year-old children', *Child Development* 45, 1, 92–9.

Sixty-five children who had been admitted to institutional care before they were four-and-a-half months old and remained there until they were at least two years of age were tested on the Wechsler Preschool Primary Scale of Intelligence when they were approximately four-and-a-half years old. The mean IQ score of children who had been adopted was significantly higher than that of children who were still in institutional care; the mean IQ score of children who had been restored to their natural mothers was lower than that of the institutional group, but not significantly so. There was no evidence that selective placement by IQ accounted for the higher scores of the adopted children. The natural fathers of these children were, if anything, of lower social class than the natural fathers of children in the other two groups; a higher proportion of them were known to have unskilled or semi-skilled occupations. Also, testing of intelligence (Cattell) at two years of age had revealed no differences between the mean scores of children who were subsequently to be adopted, restored to their natural mothers or remain in institutional care. The IQ scores did bear a relationship to the 'breadth of experience' of the children in the three groups. The adopted children had more treats and literary experiences than those in the other groups, while the restored children had fewer toys and books and were read to less often.

TULKIN, S. R. 1968. 'Race, class, family and school achievement', *Journal of Personality and Social Psychology* 9, 1, 31–7.

A number of studies have found significant differences between black and white children on tests of intelligence and school achievement even though attempts were made to control for social class and sex. Findings of the present study suggest that when the environmental backgrounds of ethnic groups are adequately equated, differences between blacks and whites disappear. Significant differences in intelligence test (Lorge-Thorndike) and achievement (Iowa Tests of Basic Skills) were found between blacks and whites within both the upper and lower socio-economic levels. When differences between the blacks and whites in crowdedness, broken homes and maternal employment were taken into account, ethnic groups differences in intelligence and achievement disappeared within the upper socio-economic level but not within the lower socio-economic level. A number of environmental factors are discussed which may account for the differences between lower-socio-economic level black and white children. Subjects were 389 eleven- and twelve-year-old children attending Maryland schools.

B. Language disadvantage

Are disadvantaged children verbally deficient?

The research reviewed so far suggests that language is a major contributor to the difference in intellectual performance between middle-class and unskilled, working-class children. Evidence from a considerable number of recent studies centrally concerned with the linguistic skills of middle- and working-class children appears to confirm social class differences in the mastery of language.

Several studies have used tests to determine the young (four- to five-year-old) child's knowledge of syntax (correct arrangement of words in sentences) and morphology (rules for noun and verb endings). Social class differences in understanding are not always found (Bruck and Tucker, 1974) and where they are found appear to be largely, if not entirely, due to dialect difficulties (Nurss and Day, 1971; Osser *et al.*,

323

1969). Differences possibly exist, though, in the ability of the child himself to produce correct grammatical constructions (Bruck and Tucker, 1974; Nurss and Day, 1971). There is some evidence that poor lower-class children are still behind middle-class children in their ability to make use of syntactic knowledge at the age of eight, though they do appear to be catching up (Frasure and Entwisle, 1973).

Already at three years old, middle-class children are beginning to show greater complexity in their spontaneous speech (more use of clauses, expansion of the noun phrase and verb complex) (Tough, 1970). Analyses of speech samples obtained from five-year-olds show similar social differences (Brandis and Henderson, 1970; Jones and MacMillan, 1973). It has already been seen from studies reviewed in the previous section that, compared with middle-class children, five-year-olds attending Head Start programmes (parents mainly unskilled or unemployed) have poorer knowledge of words used for elementary abstractions such as colour and position (Kirk et al., 1975a; Hunt et al., 1975b) and seven-year-old lower-class children of words representing items that would be familiar to all children living in an urban environment in the United States (Lesser et al., 1965).

Greater proficiency in using more complex sentence structures (e.g. greater use of subordinate clauses and ability to use more complex subordinations) and/or diversity in vocabulary have been found in several studies analysing the speech or written work of secondary school-age-children (Bernstein, 1962b; Lawton, 1968; Loban, 1966; Smedley, 1969; Williams and Naremore, 1969b).

Not all studies show social class differences. Studies which have analysed the written work of children at the beginning of secondary school stage have found no differences on measures of syntactic maturity (Richardson et al., 1976; Robinson, 1965) or in the number of different adjectives used (Thomaneck, 1972). Nevertheless, no studies show differences in favour of working-class children on measures of structural complexity or vocabulary diversity.

'Restricted' and 'elaborated' codes — Bernstein's theories

Do these differences mean that working-class children, particularly those at the bottom of the social scale, have linguistic deficiencies compared with middle-class children, or are the findings merely artifacts of the testing situation? The theoretical work of Basil Bernstein, and the empirical work inspired, both directly and indirectly by his theories, throw considerable light on this question.

Bernstein argues that different forms of social relation generate different speech systems or linguistic codes. Where there are strong communal ties, self-conscious shared identity, and common assumptions, the need to verbalise subjective intent and make it explicit is removed. The speaker selects from a narrow range of syntactic alternatives, and often from a less diversified vocabulary. The need to plan speech is reduced and utterances are fluent, though the meaning conveyed may be disjointed. The speaker emphasises shared meanings based on solidarity with the listener in the use of expressions such as 'you know', 'isn't it?'. The restricted code is used by everybody in some situations. The lower-working-class family in Western capitalist societies, whose only strength lies in social solidarity, and who is cut off from much of the cultural heritage of society, orients itself particularly towards the use of a restricted code.

An elaborated code arises when differences between individuals are emphasised. The speaker is forced to elaborate his meanings and to make them explicit and specific, as he cannot rely on the shared context to add information to what he actually says. He is forced to select among a wider range of syntactic alternatives and vocabulary to express his meaning. A greater amount of verbal planning is needed. The speaker expresses his individuality and separation from the listener by using the term 'I think'. A restricted code is readily learned informally but an elaborated code requires a much longer period of both informal and formal learning. Use of an elaborated code occurs mainly in the middle-classes and those layers of society that are moving towards a middle-class position.

Middle-class mothers, Bernstein suggests, tend to place greater emphasis on language use in the socialisation process. They make verbally explicit the relationship between the child's particular act and certain general rules and explain the reasons for, and consequences of, these rules. Not only is the child's understanding of and ability to use language promoted but he is made aware of general principles and causal relationships. When he enters school, he will be attuned both to the teacher's language and the material taught. Working-class mothers tend to place less emphasis on language in dealing with the child's act, and to leave the principles on which their own actions are based implicit. The child comes to understand and use a language in which meanings are bound to a particular situation. This will result in difficulties when he enters school.

Social class differences in explicitness of meaning

The essence of the difference between the elaborated and restricted codes is in the explicitness of meaning that is expressed in the speech. Further work suggests that this may indeed be the crucial distinction between the speech of middle-class and some lower social-class children (Bruner, 1971) even if Bernstein's theory of the generation of the differences cannot be fully accepted (see Section IV). An analysis by Hawkins (1969), a colleague of Bernstein's, was the first clearly to demonstrate the social class difference. He furthered the work of Henderson (Brandis and Henderson, 1970) which had already shown that middle-class five-year-olds used significantly more adjectives, different adjectives, nouns and different nouns than working-class children of similar verbal ability during certain speech tasks. Hawkins examined nominal group (the noun, pronoun, adjective group) usage and found that working-class children used not only more pronouns and fewer nouns and adjectives but also that they used more pronouns with referents outside the text. These pronouns, which are termed 'exophoric' need knowledge of the situation outside the speaker's words to be correctly understood (e.g. 'They've scored' is perfectly comprehensible when watching a football match but may leave the listener baffled in other circumstances). Use of 'anaphoric' pronouns, those which refer to something mentioned earlier by the speaker (e.g. 'The boy kicked the ball and it broke the window') differed little between the classes, showing that the more frequent use of pronouns by the working-class children was not due to greater conciseness. Middle-class children, it seems, specify more precisely the things to which they refer and their speech is understandable outside the context in which it occurs.

Use of nouns has another consequence. Very few modifications or qualifications are possible when pronouns are used. The noun, in contrast, opens up the opportunity for detailed attributes to be specified. Hawkins' findings showed that the middle-class children took up this opportunity for elaboration.

These social class differences in nominal group usage have been confirmed in several studies of young children, carried out by independent researchers both British (Tough, 1970) and American (Bruck and Tucker, 1974; Jones and MacMillan, 1973). Tough found that even in three-year-olds there was a social class difference in the proportion of speech which required the support of the concrete situation for effective communication. 34.5 per cent of the 'items represented' by the children from unskilled and semi-skilled working-class homes needed information outside the child's words to be understood but only 20.9 per cent of the speech of children from middle-class homes showed a similar information loss. The use of exophoric pronouns was significantly higher among the working-class than among the middle-class children. Again the differences could not be attributed to intelligence as the middle- and working-class children were of similar ability.

In an American study (Bruck and Tucker, 1974) five-year-old middle-class children showed greater clarity and explicitness than working-class children in a task in which they had to describe a series of abstract designs. The middle-class children elaborated the nominal group to a greater extent and used fewer ambiguous (exophoric or with ambiguous referents) pronouns.

This type of analysis has not been undertaken with older children although earlier studies of adolescents (Bernstein, 1962a; Lawton, 1968) had found greater use of adjectives and uncommon adjectives by the middle-class subjects and more frequent use of the pronouns 'you' and 'they' by the working-class subjects. A more recently published study (Cook Gumperz, 1973) looked for evidence of the elaborated and restricted codes in the mothers of five-year-old children, and found that, as with the young children, the working-class mothers had a higher proportion of exophoric pronouns in their speech.

Social class differences in purposes for which language is used

What significance do these speech differences have for the children's education? The answer is perhaps most clearly contained in Joan Tough's (1973) illuminating discussion of her research findings. She shows that all the Leeds children in her sample between the ages of three and five use language to comment on the experiences they are having, to direct their own and others' actions, to maintain their own interests, comfort and pleasure and to establish and maintain a working relationship with others. Some social class differences are found in the children's speech even when it is being used for these purposes. The middle-class children are more explicit and they elaborate more (they use more nouns and adjectives) even though this is not necessary for these uses. What is important, though, is that the middle-class children frequently use language for purposes which are rare in the working-class and which do demand explicitness and elaboration. They are able to move away from their present experience to something that is associated with it in some way. They can draw on past experience to extend the meaning of the present, they can develop a scene for play which is entirely in the imagination. They offer explanations and justifications. By the age of five, the advantaged child can set out a problem in his imagination, he can put forward alternative solutions and work out some of their possible consequences. Language not only enables him to express his thoughts to others but they are made explicit to himself and can be reflected on and changed. Similarly in an actual situation some middle-class children are able to pick out the relevant features, to synthesise them into possible meanings, to suggest alternative interpretations. Tough suggests that it is not that lower working-class children cannot elaborate the nominal group or make complex utterances but that they do not generally use language for purposes which require this. It is the purposes which are important, though, not the complexity of the language itself. The lower social-class child rarely uses language for these

327

purposes because language is much less the medium both of control and play in his home, compared with the middle-class child.

Other studies also give an indication of the different way in which middle- and working-class pre-school children use language. In an American study (Hertzig et al., 1968) not only did the middle-class children respond to the tasks on the Stanford Binet intelligence test by words rather than by actions or gestures more often than the lower-class Puerto Rican children (who were tested in the language most familiar to them) but they twice as often made spontaneous extensions to past experiences. Schachter et al., (1974) found that two- to five-year-old American middle-class children observed in pre-school classes differed from lower working-class children in their spontaneous speech to others mainly in that they significantly more often used explanations, justifications and rationalisations.

The greater ability of middle-class children to use language to analyse and synthesise is seen in several studies. In one (Krauss and Rotter, 1968) seven- and twelve-year-old middle-class children were found to be better at naming, and at identifying the designs from names given by the lower working-class children than were these children themselves.

Another experiment (Heider, 1971), analysing ten-year-olds' descriptions of these same abstract designs and also of faces, had similar findings. Middle-class descriptions of stimuli in this study tended to be better understood partly because a stimulus was described in two different ways in the majority (84 per cent) of cases. The middle-class children usually gave a metaphorical description of the stimulus as a whole (e.g. it looks like a house) and made physical descriptions of parts. Lower-class children mainly (79 per cent of responses) gave only inferential descriptions of the whole. Another experiment (Heider et al., 1968, cited by Cazden, 1972) showed that this was not because the lower-class children could not operate analytically, could not pick out the relevant features, but because they did not use the information they had unless given considerable prompting.

Children in Heider's (1971) experiment who gave a high percentage of part descriptive responses also tended to produce more elaborated noun phrases and more complex grammatical forms, even compared with other children in the same social class. It is interesting that (as Cazden, 1972, points out) one unexpected effect of a language intervention programme designed to elaborate and broaden language skills in five- to seven-year-old lower working-class children (Gahagan and Gahagan, 1970) was to produce precisely this kind of descriptive ability in some of the children. In a task describing stick figures they gave detailed, meticulous descriptions of the parts of the figure separately and of the relationship of parts to the body rather than describing the figure as a whole.

Are social class differences in language use products of the testing situation?

The studies reviewed suggest that middle-class children more often use language for problem solving, for the manipulation of ideas about things that are not present. But how far is the speech obtained in such studies representative of the way the children use speech in their everyday lives? Tough's data on three-year-olds was obtained from a session in which a set of play materials was provided and the child played together with a selected companion in the presence of the investigator. Recordings were also made of the speech of the children who attended nursery school (half the sample) during their normal activities and no child was included in the study unless his speech in the experimental session appeared to be a fair representation of his general language behaviour. Schachter *et al.*, (1974) recorded children's speech during their normal free play sessions in the pre-school centres. For these young children it would be hard to conclude that it was the circumstances of testing which were inhibiting certain uses of language in the less socially favoured.

This is far from denying, of course, that the situation in which it occurs has a most important influence on the speech produced, and that it may differentially affect children from different social backgrounds (Cazden, 1970, 1972). In an American study of five-year-old children (Jones and MacMillan, 1973) social class differences were greater on one measure of linguistic complexity (length of communication unit) in a more formal situation (the child was asked to tell the investigator all he could about three pictures) than in a more informal one (the adult was removed and the child asked by a classmate to tell all he could about three pictures). However, it was in the third situation, which appeared to be the most naturalistic, the child being asked to tell a friend about an experience he had enjoyed, with no adult present, that differences were greatest on the linguistic measures of complexity.

The lower social-class children were found to use relatively fewer nouns and more pronouns than in the other situations, and the differences from the middle-class children were greater in this aspect of speech as well. Thus although the topic demanded greater explicitness than the description of pictures it, in fact, received less from the lower social-class children. It would appear that the lower social-class children are less able to describe abstract events than the middle-class children. The social class difference found here cannot be attributed to the situation, which was relatively informal and had reduced differences on the picture description task. Also, though the topic may have been less interesting to the lower social-class than to the middle-class children the difference certainly seems unlikely to have been greater than in the picture description task.

These studies do suggest then, at least for young children, that there are social class differences in the ease with which language is used outside a concrete context. Is this also true for older children? Taken overall the evidence does point in this direction, but it is more difficult to be sure that differences are not solely due to the inhibiting effect of the testing or school situation on the working-class children or to their lesser degree of interest in the subject.

Lawton (1968) found social class differences in structural complexity and lexical diversity similar to Bernstein's (1962b) results, both in the speech produced by twelve- and fifteen-year-old London boys during a group discussion, and in their written work. Social class differences were greater on those subjects which could be written either abstractly or descriptively than on those in which only narrative/description was possible. Content analysis of the essays showed the writing of the middle-class boys at both age levels to be much more abstract and general, suggesting that when there is a choice the working-class boys move towards the more familiar description and structural simplicity.

Lawton's analysis of the boys' speech obtained in response to a sympathetic and encouraging interviewer is of particular interest. Parts of the interview required descriptive/narrative speech for a response while parts necessitated the use of abstract language if a response was to be made. Social class differences in speech obtained in the interview situation were in the same direction as those obtained in other parts of the study, but smaller. The differences were greater on the parts of the interview requiring abstract answers than on those needing descriptive answers. The most important finding, though, was that the working-class boys increased in structural complexity in the abstract parts of the interview. Content analysis, unlike that carried out on the written or discussion material, revealed little difference in the level of abstractness between the classes. The working-class boys may have had difficulty in using abstract language, for they often had to have several attempts before arriving at an appropriate answer. Nevertheless they did manage to use abstract language when there was little option and they were given encouragement to reply by the interviewer.

Some confirmation of Lawton's findings is found in other research. Social class differences, especially in vocabulary diversity, were found by Robinson (1965) in 'informal' letters written by twelve- to thirteen-year-old children to a friend, in which the subjects were left free to write as they chose. Differences were negligible, though, in a 'formal' letter in which the topic and manner of dealing with it were specified. Two American studies also show that the demands of the task can eliminate social class differences in language behaviour. Working-class children were found not to differ from middle-class subjects in the number of analytic responses given (Heider et al., 1968, cited by Cazden, 1972) or in the elaborative descriptions of television programmes (Williams and Naremore, 1969a), but they did require more prompting from the interviewer to reach the same level of performance.

Linguistic deficiencies or dialect differences?

It seems clear from the evidence that the main difficulty of lower working-class children does not lie in inadequate knowledge of syntax or even in inability to produce complex sentence structures. The important contribution of the American linguists (see Baratz, 1970; Labov, 1970) has been to show that linguistic deficiences of at least black lower-class children have been vastly over-exaggerated by writers such as Bereiter and Engelmann (1966). According to the linguists, failure of black, lower-class children to repeat sentences correctly in imitation tasks is due not to linguistic immaturity but to interference of the child's own dialect. This is a coherent linguistic system governed by rules similar to, but not identical with, those of Standard English. Research (Baratz, 1970; Labov, 1970) shows that there is a structure to the errors made when lower-class black children fail to imitate sentences correctly. The child is, in fact, indicating his understanding of the meaning of the sentence by 'translating' it into his own dialect. White middle-class children have been found to make similar 'translations', but into Standard English patterns, when asked to repeat non-Standard English sentences (Baratz, 1970). Studies with young children show that the difference in performance on imitation tasks between black lower-class and white middle-class children is markedly reduced when non-Standard English forms are accepted as correct (Nurss and Day, 1969; Osser et al., 1971). It is clear that if the child's dialect is not taken into account, his knowledge of syntax may be considerably under-estimated. This may well apply to many lower-class white children but little evidence is available so far.

Some studies have found that after entry to school, the black lower-class child's understanding of Standard English is as good as his understanding of black non-Standard English (Genshaft and Hirt, 1974; Weener, 1969). It has also been found to be as good as that of the white child of lower socio-economic status (Genshaft and Hirt, 1974) (who may himself, of course, suffer from dialect or other linguistic difficulties). These findings do not necessarily mean that dialect differences are without hampering effects. Understanding of single words or isolated sentences (with which these studies were concerned) cannot be taken as conclusive evidence that there are no difficulties in the comprehension of Standard English, as Edwards (1976) has pointed out. Much of the work of Labov has been concerned with showing how dialect differences may interfere with learning to read. This is likely, for example, where differences in pronunciation coincide with differences in grammatical form (Labov, 1969). Labov's work emphasises that if reading is to be taught effectively the teacher must have an understanding of the child's dialect. Otherwise she will be unable to determine whether deviations in reading are merely due to differences in pronunciation, which are unimportant, or to his failure to recognise grammatical signals. The situation may be similar for West Indian children in Britain (Edwards, 1976) though work on dialect differences has hardly begun in the UK.

Can it be concluded, then, as the American linguists claim, that the lower-class child's understanding of and ability to produce correct syntax is just as good as that of the middle-class child, difficulties only arising on occasion because of differences between the lower-class child's own dialect and Standard English? The evidence certainly suggests that most of the differences found in tests of understanding can be explained in this way. It is less certain that young, lower-class children, both black and white, do not have some difficulty in using their knowledge of syntax. Significant differences in ability to produce certain grammatical constructions remained between lower and middle-class pre-school children in the Nurss and Day (1971) study even after allowance had been made for the non-Standard dialect. Frasure and Entwisle (1973) also found that lower-class children, both black and white, were less able to put their knowledge of syntax into use than middle-class children up to the age of eight (though they were catching up), and that this could not be accounted for by dialect differences.

Language skills of the disadvantaged child

While it cannot be entirely ruled out that for young, lower-class children, at least, difficulties in using language for the manipulation of ideas are partly due to difficulties in producing complex syntactic structures, it is clear that this is not the main problem. There is considerable evidence that speech obtained during testing or in the classroom may considerably under-estimate the linguistic abilities of the lower-working-class child (Houston, 1970). Labov's (1970) dramatic example of how a monosyllabic eight-year-old black boy is transformed into an eager speaker when an interview is changed into an informal situation by the addition of crisps, a friend, taboo words and taboo topics is well-known. This phenomenon is not, of course, confined to black lower-class children in the United States. Joan Tough (1973) notes that at seven years of age the disadvantaged Leeds children used more complexity in their speech when they were on their own with a friend than in any other situation.

Sometimes, at least, complexity is used by the socially disadvantaged child for purposes very different from the problem-solving and exploring of abstract ideas that is necessary for school-work. For example, in black communities in the United States specialised forms of speech have developed amongst the youth who are organised into street gangs (Labov *et al.*, 1968, cited by Ginsburg, 1972). High value is placed on these verbal skills. One way in which this skill is exercised is in 'toasts', which are long epic poems, partly recited and partly invented. The emphasis is on the way something is said rather than on what is said. Intonation, pauses, facial expressions and gestures are an essential part of the performance.

Of course, this is not the only way in which disadvantaged children use complex speech in their own social environment. Labov (e.g. 1970) provides illustrations of the ability of black youth to produce complex arguments on abstract hypothetical questions. This is important but it does not answer the question of whether lower social-class children, black and white, use language to the same extent as middle-class children for abstract purposes, for the manipulation of ideas. The little evidence available suggests that there are social class differences in familiarity with these uses of language. The evidence on the different purposes for which young, middle- and lower working-class children use language, and on the preference of older working-class children for descriptive/narrative rather than abstract language do point in this direction. Without doubt, though, differences in actual performance between the social classes are often accentuated by the middle-class orientation of the schools and lack of interest in the subject matter used to lower working-class children. The research tentatively suggests some ways in which the school can help to develop the analysing and synthesising ideas of those lower-class-children who seem to have difficulties. The main problem, after all, is to enable the child to learn successfully at school. As Cole *et al.* (1971) put it 'the problem of transferring skills applied on the streets to the classroom is not solved by demonstrating the existence of the same skill on the streets. The child must be taught to apply these skills in the classroom'.

Annotations

BARATZ, J. C. 1970. 'Teaching reading in an urban Negro school system', in F. Williams (ed.) *Language and Poverty*, Markham, Chicago. 11–24.

The argument in this paper is that the failure in teaching the inner-city black child in the United States to read stems not from the intellectual deficit of the child but from inadequacies of the teaching methods. Negro non-Standard English spoken by the black child differs from Standard English spoken by the teacher in its sound system, grammar and

333

vocabulary. The differences arise not because the black child is deficient in language development but because Negro non-Standard English has different rules from Standard English.

Findings from an experiment in which nine- to ten- and eleven- to twelve-year-old children were asked to repeat as exactly as they could tape recorded sentences, half of which were in Standard English and half in Negro non-Standard English, indicated, as expected, that the white children were superior in repeating Standard English and the black non-Standard English. Error responses for both the black and white children were not random but followed a definite pattern. The experiment showed that all children 'translate' language that is outside their primary code and indicates that black children suffer from a difficulty in code switching not a language defect. When black children attempt to use Standard English, there is interference from their own dialect. It is suggested that the black child should be taught to read initially in his own dialect, and that a transition to reading in Standard English be made later.

BERNSTEIN, B. 1962a. 'Linguistic codes, hesitation phenomena and intelligence', *Language and Speech* 5, 31–46, (also reprinted in B. Bernstein 1971. *Class, Codes and Control*, Vol I, Routledge and Kegan Paul, London. 76–94; Schocken Books, New York).

An experiment designed to test the theory that there are social class differences in language use, the lower working-class being more or less confined to a restricted code while the middle-class use both a restricted and an elaborated code. Syntactic elements used by a speaker of a restricted code to express his meaning are relatively predictable, while in the case of an elaborated code the speaker chooses from a more extensive range of alternatives and the syntactic elements used are less predictable. A restricted code is generally used in a group whose members selfconsciously identify with each other, making it unnecessary to verbalise subjective intent to make it explicit. Verbal planning will be reduced and utterances fluent. Non-verbal expressions are important in indicating meaning. The content of the speech is likely to be descriptive and narrative rather than analytical and abstract. An elaborated code allows meaning to be expressed relatively explicitly according to the specific requirements of the listener. Greater verbal planning is required. The content may be, although it is not necessarily, abstract. The association between social class and code was investigated in this study using a technique originated by Goldman-Eisler, whose work suggested that summarising requires more time in pausing than description. Fluency and hesitation, therefore, differentiated levels of verbal planning.

Findings of the present study showed, as hypothesised, that lower working-class adolescent boys taking part in a group discussion spent less time pausing per word uttered and used a longer average phrase length than middle-class adolescent boys, particularly when groups were compared which were similar in both non-verbal (Raven's Progressive Matrices) and verbal (Mill Hill Vocabulary Scale) intelligence. Findings of this study confirm that middle-class and lower working-class groups differ in verbal planning and that the difference cannot be accounted for by intelligence. It seems that delay allows the middle-class greater lexicon and structural choice, and achievement of speech that is more appropriate to the particular occasion.

BERNSTEIN, B. 1962b. 'Social class, linguistic codes and grammatical elements', *Language and Speech* 5, 221–40, (also reprinted in B. Bernstein, *Class, Codes and Control*, Routledge and Kegan Paul, London, 1971. 95–117; Schocken Books, New York).

In a previous study, lower working-class and middle-class adolescent boys were found to differ in the use of hesitation during speech in a group discussion (see Bernstein, 1962a). The present study analysed the same speech samples for social class differences in lexical and grammatical usage. Middle-class subjects, in comparison with lower working-class subjects, were found to use more adjectives, more uncommon adjectives, more uncommon adverbs, more passive verbs, more complex verbal stems and more subordinate clauses. The middle-class subjects used a smaller proportion of personal pronouns and they more frequently selected 'I' from among the personal pronouns used. The lower working-class boys both more frequently selected 'you' and 'they' from among the personal pronouns used and used them more frequently than the middle-class boys. The working-class subjects used more terminal 'sympathetic circularity' sequences (e.g. 'you know', 'isn't it'), while middle-class subjects used 'I think' more often. Differences on most of the measures of grammatical and lexicon usage remained when two sub-groups, one from the working-class and the other from the middle-class sample, matched both on verbal and non-verbal intelligence, were compared. Very few differences were found, though, between the three sub-groups selected from the working-class sample (differing 20 points in non-verbal IQ) or between the two sub-groups selected from the middle-class sample (differing by 17 points in verbal IQ). Results of the study clearly indicate that class groups are differently oriented in their structural selection and lexicon choices, and that the difference in orientation is independent of intelligence.

BERNSTEIN, B. 1971. *Class, Codes and Control. Theoretical studies towards a Sociology of Language*, Routledge and Kegan Paul, London. 238 pp; Schocken Books, New York.

A collection of Basil Bernstein's papers, both theoretical and empirical, put together by the author to give a record of the development of his ideas on the relationship between language, social class and family structure.

BERNSTEIN, B. (ed.) 1973. *Class, Codes and Control. Vol 2. Applied studies towards a sociology of language*, Routledge and Kegan Paul, London. 377 pp; Schocken Books, New York.

A collection of papers by members of Basil Bernstein's research team, reporting the testing of particular aspects of his theoretical ideas by empirical work. Additionally, three theoretical papers are included.

BRANDIS, W. and HENDERSON, D. 1970. *Social Class, Language and Communication*. (chapter I 'Social class differences in form-class usage among five-year-old children' by D. Henderson; Chapter II 'Social class differences in form-class switching among five-year-old children' by D. Henderson; Chapter III 'Social class differences in communication and control', by B. Bernstein and W. Brandis), Routledge and Kegan Paul, London. 153 pp; Sage Publications Inc., Beverley Hills, Calif.

A report of the effects of social class, ability, sex of the child, and the mother's reported communication with her child on aspects of speech in the five-year-old child. The working-class sample was drawn from thirteen schools in a borough of East London and the middle-class sample from five schools in an outlying South East borough.

Analysis was made of the children's vocabulary (termed 'form-class') on three tasks each designed to elicit a different type of speech (narrative, descriptive and explanatory) (chapter I). Middle-class children, particularly those of high verbal ability (Crighton Vocabulary Scale) used more nouns, more different nouns, more different adjectives and more different verbs than working-class children. Within the 'nominal group' (nouns, adjectives and pronouns) the middle-class children were much more likely to use nouns and adjectives, thus both being more specific about whatever is being referred to, and more likely to assign attributes (e.g. working-class children are more likely to say 'they're eating' and middle-class children 'the people are having a nice meal'). The middle-class children's greater emphasis on development within the nominal group could increase their chances of producing a more developed and flexible clause structure later, with possible cognitive advantages. When only children whose mothers had high Communication Index scores (mothers who responded to the child's attempts to talk to them, and did not avoid difficult questions) were considered, social class differences diminished but differences within the 'nominal group' remained. Middle-class mothers with low Communication Index scores reduced the verbal elaboration of relationships in their children, particularly boys, and generally depressed the vocabulary of girls.

In the second part of the analysis (chapter II) it was found that more middle- than working-class children made a significant proportional change between tasks in the use of nouns, different nouns, verbs and different adverbs (termed 'form-class switching'). This suggests that the middle-class children may have been better able to express verbally their sensitivity to the different demands of the tasks.

The second part of the report (chapter III) is concerned with relationships between the mother's communication with and control of her child (as measured by mothers' responses to questionnaires given to them prior to the child's school entry) and a number of variables, including social class, ability of the child, the child's 'nominal group' usage and the mother's attitudes to education. Generally, working-class mothers were found to be more coercive with their children and to explain less to them. Ability of the child in the working class was found to be much more related to the mother's pattern of communication and control, her favourable educational orientation and developed nominal group usage in the child than ability in the middle class child. It appears that in the working class, the bright child is in a generally favourable position, but in the middle class all children, irrespective of ability are in a favourable position in regard to their future education, in relation to the working class. The mother's pattern of communication and control, though, was much more closely related to her educational orientation and developed nominal group usage in the child in the middle class than in the working class. These findings are interpreted as indicating that in the middle class the crucial person in determining how much stimulation and educational support the child receives is the mother. In the working class, one, though by no means the only, origin of relatively developed patterns of communication of the mother is the bright child, who acts as a stimulus to her.

BRUCK, M. and TUCKER, G. R. 1974. 'Social class differences in the acquisition of school language', *Merrill-Palmer Quarterly* 20, 205–20.

Forty kindergarten children (average age five years, five months), half from middle-class and half from working-class Canadian families, were administered, near the beginning of the school year and again near its end, a number of tests designed to measure children's understanding and usage of grammatical rules of English and ability to use language for effective communication. On the first testing, the middle-class children did significantly better than the working-class children in tests measuring their ability to produce correct grammatical constructions but did not differ from them in grammatical comprehension of classroom English. The two groups were similar in overall speech output, but the middle-class children used more nominal (noun, pronoun, adjective) groups, their speech was more elaborated and they used relatively fewer ambiguous pronouns (not referring to any previously used noun – exophoric pronouns – see Hawkins, 1973, or with an unclear noun referent). In describing unclear abstract designs the middle-class children gave more informative explanations but did not differ from the working-class children in the proportion of poor images given or ambiguous references made. Middle-class children included more relevant details in the story-telling than the working-class children but gave as many irrelevant details. In general the speech of the middle-class children was differentiated from that of the working-class children by greater explicitness. Over the school year, the children improved significantly on all tests of grammatical ability, the working-class children improving more rapidly than the middle-class on many of these tasks. There was improvement on some but not all of the tests of communication ability. This was due to an increase in relevant detail and explicitness rather than to a decrease in ambiguity and irrelevant detail. The lower-class children did not catch up to the same extent as on the tests of grammatical ability. It is suggested that all children, and especially those from the lower social classes, need help in schools on how to use speech more effectively for communication.

CAZDEN, C. B. 1970. 'The neglected situation in child language research and education', in F. Williams (ed) *Language and Poverty*, Markham, Chicago. 81–101.

It is argued that the school language problems of lower social-class children are not adequately explained by either the 'less language', 'cultural deprivation' or 'different language' theories. Studies have shown that social class differences in grammatical competence are not sufficient to explain school difficulties. It is true that many lower social-class children, especially black children, speak a dialect differing in some structural features from Standard English. However, both theories under-estimate the effects of the particular characteristics of the situation, as the child perceives it, on his speech. Studies suggest that the greater the personal involvement in a topic, the greater structural complexity in speech. Working-class children also produce greater elaboration and abstraction in their speech when the task is structured so that this is demanded of them. Characteristics of the listener also affect the complexity of the speech produced and there is tentative evidence that how conversation is initiated also has an effect. To design a language

ANGUAGE DISADVANTAGE

education programme it is necessary to decide in what situations and for what purposes children need to develop their communicative abilities.

DEWART, M. H. 1972. 'Social class and children's understanding of deep structure in sentences', *British Journal of Educational Psychology* 42, 2, 198–203.

This study suggests that working-class children may master the understanding of passive voice sentences, in which the grammatical subject and logical subject of the sentence are different, more slowly than middle-class children. Subjects were forty-four children of similar IQ, aged five-and-a-quarter to six-and-a-half years, half from a fee-paying preparatory of a grammar school and half from a primary school in a working-class area.

GAHAGAN, D. M. and GAHAGAN, G. A. 1970. *Talk Reform*, Routledge and Kegan Paul, London. 147 pp; Sage Publications, Inc., Beverley Hills, Calif.

Report of a language intervention programme based on the work of Basil Bernstein and designed to elaborate and broaden the spoken language of lower-working-class children handicapped educationally by their use of a restricted code. The programme was carried out for twenty minutes of the normal infant school day by the ordinary class teachers using only a limited amount of special materials. The sample consisted of 209 children in nine schools of an East London borough. Three schools formed the experimental group in which the three-year language programme was carried out. Three schools served as a 'pure' control group, only the testing necessary for evaluation of the programme being carried out in them. The remaining three schools formed a 'Hawthorne' control group, the teachers taking part in a special programme not connected with language training. This ensured that any differential gains made by the experimental children were not simply due to an increase in their teachers' motivation arising from their taking part in a research study. Activities devised for the language programme aimed to improve: i) the children's attention and auditory discrimination; ii) their ability to give verbal explanations and to express certain types of experiences such as emotions; iii) their vocabulary, sentence construction and understanding of logical operations.

Evaluation of the programme showed that the experimental children were superior to the 'Hawthorne' controls on a number of exploratory tests in which the children were obliged to use language and in which performance should be enhanced by superior linguistic skills. Specifically, they showed: higher-quality sentences linking pairs of items

339

and quicker learning in a paired associate task; better ability to discriminate verbally attributes of objects they could feel but not see; better performance on the more difficult problems in a verbal conceptual sorting task. Some tasks showed that children who had initially been lowest in language ability (English Picture Vocabulary Test) benefitted most from the language programme. At the end of the third year of the project, the incidence of low-scoring children on a standardised test of written language ability, the English Progress Test, was found to be lower in the experimental group than in either of the control groups, initial differences in language ability having been taken into account.

GENSHAFT, J. L. and HIRT, M. 1974. 'Language differences between black children and white children', *Developmental Psychology* 10, 3, 451-6.

In this experiment, black eleven- to twelve-year-old children in the United States did not differ from white children of similar age, non-verbal intelligence and socio-economic level, in ability to recall a fifteen-word list or to reproduce Standard English sentences containing the same words. Standard English words which would be familiar to speakers of non-Standard Negro English were selected for two tasks. White children were inferior to the black children in reproducing sentences in black dialect spoken by a black speaker. The study findings offer no support for the view that black children are deficient in language behaviour. They suggest, rather, that Negro non-Standard English is a different language from Standard English and that black children are bilingual.

HAWKINS, P. R. 1969. 'Social class, the nominal group and reference', *Language and Speech*, 12, 2, 125-35 (also reprinted in B. Bernstein (ed.) 1973. *Class, Codes and Control*, Vol 2, Routledge and Kegan Paul, London. 81-92; Schocken Books, New York).

Analysis of 'nominal group' (nouns, adjectives and pronouns) usage has shown that, independent of measured ability, there is a tendency for middle-class children to use the noun and its associated forms, while working-class children use the pronoun and forms associated with it (Brandis and Henderson, 1970, chapter I). Use of the noun is important because it allows much more elaboration (adjectives used as modifiers and qualifiers) than the pronoun. The present study extended the investigation of the nominal group by examining how and where the pronouns were being used. A pronoun, or other grammatical item such as 'this', 'that', can be used to refer backwards to something already mentioned (anaphoric reference, e.g. 'The boy kicked the ball and it broke the window'), forwards to something about to be mentioned (cataphoric reference), or outwards, to something not mentioned but in the environment of the speaker (exophoric reference, e.g. 'they've scored', when the speaker is standing on the edge of a football pitch). It was found that the working-class children were using more exophoric pronouns, which rely heavily for interpretation on the surrounding context, particularly in a task eliciting narrative speech (story telling from a set of pictures), but also in a descriptive task. Findings from the present study, which used a larger number of children from the same schools as in Henderson's study for the sample, also confirmed that middle-class children use significantly more nouns and words associated with nouns than working-class children, thus exploiting the possibilities of elaborating the nominal group more widely. It is concluded that these differences in speech of middle- and working-class children may well have important cognitive consequences.

HEIDER, E. R. 1971. 'Style and accuracy of verbal communication within and between social classes', *Journal of Personality and Social Psychology* 18, 1, 33–47.

A study designed to investigate whether middle-class speech is a better tool of communication than lower-class speech. Subjects were 143 ten-year-old children, approximately one-third from a professional background, and two-thirds lower-class children living in a government housing project (half black and half white). In the first experiment, subjects were asked to 'encode' novel abstract stimuli and faces, i.e. to describe one stimulus out of an array so that it would be recognised by a future listener. Middle-class children said more different things about the stimuli. Lower-class subjects gave mainly (over 70 per cent) whole/inferential responses (referring to whole and going beyond what was given to describe metaphorically). Middle-class children gave only about a quarter whole/inferential responses, over half of their responses being part/descriptive (referring to only part and describing physical properties of the stimulus). The majority of middle-class encodings were composed of both whole/inferential and part/descriptive units while only 21 per cent of lower-class encodings contained both kinds of units. Class differences in style occurred even when only the first units of the encodings were analysed, indicating that they were not simply due to differences in verbal fluency. Social class differences were not affected by the type of stimuli. Subjects who used a high percentage of part/descriptive units also tended to elaborate the noun phrase and to use 'complex' grammatical forms. In the second part of the experiment the same subjects were presented with one of six types of encodings, derived from the verbal descriptions given in the first part of the experiment, and asked which stimulus in an array was being described ('decoding'). Middle-class encodings were better identified than lower-class codings.

Also, middle-class subjects were better decoders than lower-class subjects, both of middle- and lower-class encodings. Sheer length of encodings did not affect communication accuracy but encoding units which contained both whole/inferential and part/descriptive styles were better understood. Middle-class part/descriptive encodings were particularly effective in communicating with other middle-class subjects. No encoding or decoding differences were found between the lower-class black and white children.

HOUSTON, S. H. 1970. 'A re-examination of some assumptions about the language of the disadvantaged child', *Child Development* 41, 947–63.

A re-examination of the assumptions and beliefs about language and communication of the disadvantaged child in the light of recent psycho- and socio-linguistic knowledge. It is argued that man has an innate biological capacity for linguistic acquisition, the operation of which is constant for all children. Language learning occurs merely by placing the child in the environment of the language and language deprivation does not exist. A number of standard comments on the language development of disadvantaged children are criticised by the author:
(1) The language of disadvantaged children is deficient – e.g. as shown by their unwillingness or inability to use language, short utterance length, and one word responses when they do. These comments are correct for the language used in the school, or in a testing situation, but not for the language the child uses naturally with his friends and family – where there are deviations from standard English they tend to be phonological rather than syntactic;
(2) The disadvantaged child does not use words properly – the actual difference is that the words are sometimes shaped differently;
(3) The language of the disadvantaged child does not provide him with an adequate basis for abstract thinking – based on a supposed lack of abstract terminology in his language. However, cognitive patterns cannot be extrapolated directly from linguistic patterns – if the language lacks a unitary term for a certain phenomenon it does not mean that the speakers are unaware of it or cannot deal with it. Innate ability to abstract, generalise and conceptualise is necessary to use language;
(4) Disadvantaged children tend to communicate non-verbally rather than verbally. There is no solid evidence here;
(5) The language of the disadvantaged child, as it represents his culture and environment, should be left alone. This is not correct because the child may lack some of the lexicon he needs to succeed in school or an occupation, and there may be social prejudice against the language he uses.

JONES, P. A. and McMILLAN, W. B. 1973. 'Speech characteristics as a function of social class and situational factors', *Child Development* 44, 1, 117–21.

It has been suggested (Labov, 1970) that the deficits found in the language of lower social-class children in a number of studies arise merely from the defensive attitudes these children adopt in a threatening test situation. To test this hypothesis, in the present study, speech samples of five-year-old children, sixteen from middle-class and eighteen from lower-class backgrounds, were obtained in situations differing from the highly structured to the naturalistic. Subjects were required to describe concrete stimuli (three coloured slides) to the interviewer in the first situation and to a friend in the second situation while in the third situation, they were asked to describe an abstract event (an enjoyable experience) to a friend. Results confirmed previous research findings (Bernstein, 1962b) that there are social-class differences in language usage, the speech of the lower-class children generally being less fluent and grammatically complex. Differences were sharpest in the third situation, in which an abstract event was described, the lower-class subjects producing significantly shorter communication units, making less use of subordination and using more pronouns, thus placing unrealistic reliance on the listener's awareness of the context. However, in contrast to Bernstein's (1962a) findings, it was the lower-class subjects who paused longer and more frequently. Possibly hesitation phenomena are indicators of emotional tensions and difficulties in expression rather than of verbal planning activity as Bernstein proposes.

LABOV, W. 1970. 'The logic of non-Standard English' in J. E. Alatis (ed) *Report of the 20th Annual Round Table Meeting on Linguistics and Language Studies*, Georgetown University Press, Washington. 1–39.

This paper argues against the view that the poor educational performance of black ghetto children is due to cultural deprivation, particularly 'verbal deprivation' arising from a lack of environmental stimulation in the early years. The author considers 'verbal deprivation' to be a dangerous myth which diverts attention from the real inadequacies of the educational system to the imaginary inadequacies of the child. The kind of monosyllabic verbal behaviour displayed by the lower-class child in an interview situation should not be taken as evidence of his verbal capacity but merely shows the child's ability to defend himself in a threatening situation. Evidence from recordings is provided showing radical changes in the speech of an eight-year-old ghetto boy in different situations: the monosyllabic speaker of the interview situation, even though the interviewer is a black adult known to the child, becomes a fluent English speaker when the situation is altered by the introduction of crisps, a friend and taboo words and topics.

It is conceded that ghetto children do have many verbal skills to learn if they are to succeed in school and that some of these − precision in spelling, practice in handling of abstract symbols, ability to state explicitly the meaning of words, and a richer vocabulary − are characteristics of middle-class speech. However, not all middle-class verbal style is useful for analysing and generalising, much being elaboration for its own sake. Analysis of the speech of a black ghetto adolescent and an upper-middle-class college-educated black shows that a complex argument can be presented clearly and effectively in non-Standard Negro English, while the modifications, qualifications and verbosity of middle-class Standard English may obscure meaning rather than making it explicit.

Differences between non-Standard Negro English and Standard English are not errors or the results of illogical behaviour but are due to some variations in the rules. Non-Standard English speakers fail to repeat sentences in Standard English 'correctly' precisely because they understand its meaning but then 'translate' into their own vernacular. Their dialect may utilise different devices to express meaning but the differences are in surface detail, not logic.

The 'verbal deprivation' theory is harmful because it justifies teachers' prejudice against the lower-class black children and their language and helps to turn teachers' expectations of low achievement into reality. Also, failure of compensatory education programmes based on the 'verbal deprivation' theory leads to the blame being put on the child and ultimately to theories of genetic inferiority of blacks. To teach black children successfully, a thorough knowledge of non-Standard Negro English as a coherent communicative system is necessary.

LAWTON, D. 1968. *Social Class, Language and Education* (especially chapter 6 'An experimental study of the speech and writing of some middle- and working-class boys'), Routledge and Kegan Paul, London. 181 pp.

In the first five chapters, the author reviews work on the relationship between language and social background, language and cognitive development, and critically examines Bernstein's work, both theoretical and empirical, on language and social class. Chapter VI reports the author's own research which was designed to provide evidence on Bernstein's theory of social class linguistic differences (see Bernstein, 1962b).

In accordance with Bernstein's thesis, this study provides clear evidence of differences in working- and middle-class usage of elaborated and restricted codes. The subjects were ten working-class, secondary-modern schoolboys (five aged twelve and five aged fifteen years) and ten middle-class boys at similar age levels, attending an independent fee-paying school, all four groups being matched for verbal (Mill Hill Vocabulary Scale) and non-verbal (Raven's Progressive Matrices) intelligence. In the first part of the study, working-class boys were found to write essays of shorter length. They selected words and structures from a narrower range of alternatives (less variety of adjectives and adverbs, more pronouns, less use of complex subordinate clauses and passive verbs). The content of their essays was less abstract. Similar social-class differences were found in the second part of the study when speech from group discussions was analysed. The differences were generally greater at the age of fifteen than at twelve but they were slightly less than in the study of written work. In the third part of the research, each boy was interviewed individually, some questions being designed to elicit descriptive and others abstract speech. Social class differences were in the same direction as in earlier parts of the study but smaller. As predicted, all subjects made linguistic adjustments to the different tasks but the middle-class children made greater adjustments, i.e. showed greater facility in code switching. Content analysis of answers showed that there were no differences in the kind or range of responses to the abstract questions but that the working-class boys appeared to have greater difficulty in answering, often making several attempts before achieving an appropriate response.

Findings of the study show the necessity to take context into account when analysing speech. It seems that when working-class boys are in an 'open' situation, they tend to use narrative/descriptive language but in a structured situation where they are forced to make an abstract response they are capable of doing so, although they may find it difficult. The study findings show that the potential attainments of working-class children may be much greater than their normal linguistic usage suggests.

NURSS, J. R. and DAY, D. E. 1971. 'Imitation, comprehension, and production of grammatical structures', *Journal of Verbal Learning and Verbal Behavior* 10, 68–74.

Four-year-old black and white lower-class children from a large Southern city in the United States were significantly inferior to a higher-status white group of children on measures of ability to imitate, comprehend and produce selected grammatical structures, when a standard American English scoring system was used. On a second scoring system, based on features of non-Standard lower-class dialects, lower-status white and black groups improved significantly on

345

production and the lower-status black group improved on imitation as well. However, scores of the high-status group on production ability were still considerably higher than those of the lower-status groups.

OSSER, H., WANG, M.D. and ZAID, F. 1969. 'The young child's ability to imitate and comprehend speech: a comparison of two subcultural groups', *Child Development* 40, 4, 1063–75.

White, middle-class children performed better than Negro, lower-class children on a task of imitation (even when allowances were made for non-Standard dialect) and a comprehension task.

ROBINSON, W. P. and CREED, C. D. 1968. 'Perceptual and verbal discriminations of "elaborated" and "restricted" code users', *Language and Speech*, 11, 3, 182–93. (also re-printed in B. Bernstein (ed) 1973. *Class, Codes and Control*, Vol 2, Routledge and Kegan Paul, London. 120–32; Schocken Books, New York).

Findings of this study suggest that the use of an elaborated code, whether due to an experimental language intervention programme or occurring naturally, is associated with better perceptual and verbal discrimination, even when IQ and social class are controlled. In the study task, each subject was presented with one member of a pair of pictures and then asked first to point to and afterwards to describe the differences between this picture and the other member of the pair. Subjects were six-year-old (second year) primary school children taking part in an experimental language intervention programme designed to encourage the use of an elaborated code. Each subject was matched with a control group child for intelligence (English Picture Vocabulary Test) and social class. In each group, four of the children were of high IQ and eight of low IQ, while four of the low IQ children were 'elaborated' and four 'restricted' code users. Separation into the two codes was made on the basis of grammatical analysis of language samples obtained on entry to infant school, the criteria being: number of subordinate clauses used; number of rank-shifted clauses; number of adverbial groups; number of verb tenses.

TOUGH, J. 1973. 'The language of young children, the implications for the education of the young disadvantaged child', in M. Chazan (ed) *Education in the Early Years*, Faculty of Education, University College of Swansea, 60–76.

It is suggested in this study that some children may be linguistically disadvantaged because of what they have learned to do with language rather than because of some deficiency in their knowledge of language.

Differences were already found at the age of three between children of professional parents and those whose parents came from the unskilled or semi-skilled working-classes in the way language was used in a semi-structured play situation. All the children used language to maintain their own interests, to establish and maintain a working relationship with the other children, to direct and accompany their play. Only the children from an advantaged background used language to justify their behaviour, to move away from the present situation to something that only had connections and associations with it, to create through their imagination a scene that could be shared with others. The last two usages demand that the child state his meaning clearly, and this explicitness becomes his normal mode of expression.

Differences between the groups can also be explained in terms of linguistic measures, such as mean length of utterances. However, although the disadvantaged children do not use complex structures to the extent that they make a high mean score there is evidence that this is not because they are unable to do so. It is rather that these children rarely meet uses which demand greater complexity. The home environments of the two groups provide quite different experiences that may be related to differences in values, and particularly to differences in 'control' strategies used by the mothers. Advantaged children are continually stimulated to use language to justify, explain, recall, compare, see alternative choices; in the disadvantaged home language is used to give instructions to the child, not to explore the meaning of a situation to him. Educational implications are that nursery-school teachers must set up an environment of interest to all the children and must then encourage every child to use language as a means of learning in the way that advantaged mothers do.

C. Health disadvantage

The part played by health factors in the child's intellectual and educational progress has been largely ignored in explanations of disadvantage. Attention has been drawn to this neglect in the writings of Birch and his associates (Birch, 1968; Birch and Gussow, 1970). A detailed examination of the research in this area is beyond the scope of the present review but to omit some mention of the greater health disadvantages of children from the lower social classes, and of their possible effect on intellectual development would result in a very one-sided review.

Low birth weight and prematurity

The disadvantage of low socio-economic-level children begins at birth

347

and perhaps long before this. Research in the UK has well established that prematurity and low birth weight (for pregnancy length) occur more frequently in the lower than the higher social classes (Davie *et al.*, 1972; Dinnage, 1970). Similarly, low birth weight is much more frequent among non-whites than among whites in the United States (Birch, 1968).

Sometimes a genetic abnormality, infection or other factor is responsible for both low birth weight or other perinatal complications and for a handicapping condition in the child. Low birth weight is in some cases, though, a causal factor in mental retardation (Dinnage, 1970); reduction in the incidence of mental handicap has been found when intra-uterine growth failure has been detected and birth induced (Rhodes, 1973). In a study of eight- to ten-year-old mentally subnormal children in Aberdeen (Birch *et al.*, 1970) it was concluded that one-eighth of the children had suffered neurological damage which could be attributed to the combined impact of several obstetric complications (assessed for each child by a physician, taking birth-weight into account). Ten of the eleven children whose subnormality appeared to be caused by obstetric problems came from the manual working classes. Half were severely subnormal (IQ below 50) and half mildly mentally handicapped (IQ 50–75).

The effects of low birth weight and obstetric complications are probably not confined to children who are obviously mentally handicapped. In the National Child Development Study (Davie *et al.*, 1972) low birth-weight was found to have a separate association with reading ability in seven year olds, after allowance was made for other influencing factors such as social class and birth order; for every one thousand grams (2.2. pounds) reduction in birth weight, reading ability was reduced by four months. Studies have shown that when children with obvious defects are excluded low birth weight children differ little from controls in general intellectual level, but there is some evidence of specific cognitive difficulties and emotional disturbance (Dinnage, 1970).

There is substantial evidence that low birth weight and other perinatal complications tend to have a more adverse effect on lower-social-class children than on those from a more privileged background (Davie *et al.*, 1972; Dinnage, 1970). The reasons for this need specification. Greater incidence of illnesses among lower-class children in the first few years, particularly in early infancy, and of hospital admissions (Douglas and Blomfield, 1958), lower utilisation of welfare clinics and other medical services except in acute illness (Davie *et al.*, 1972) and poorer nutrition may be among the relevant factors.

Disadvantage for the lower-social-class child begins before his own birth because low birth weight and the child's condition at birth are related to the reproductive efficiency of the mother. Shorter stature in the mother is related to an increase in prematurity, delivery complications

(Birch and Gussow, 1970), mild mental subnormality (IQ 60–75) and poor condition in the baby at birth (Birch *et al.*, 1970) even within the same social class. The mother's stature is, of course, affected by the adequacy of her nutrition during her childhood. The mother's age, her current state of health, her nutrition, and parity all influence the pregnancy and its outcome and all tend to be less favourable for children in the lowest social levels.

Nutrition and brain growth

Recent research (Dobbing and Sands, 1973) has shown that the baby's brain experiences its most rapid period of growth from midway through pregnancy until the child is well into his second year of life at least. Animal experiments have indicated that during this period of 'growth spurt' even comparatively mild under-nutrition may result in permanent intellectual and behavioural deficits (Birch and Gussow, 1970; Dobbing, 1971). This suggests that low-birth-weight babies who continue to be inadequately nourished in the first two or so years after birth may suffer from brain growth restriction which impairs later development (Dobbing, 1971). It cannot be ruled out that even in the UK some low-birth-weight babies are so affected, and the greater likelihood of poor nutrition could perhaps be one of the factors accounting for the more adverse outcome of this condition at the lower end of the social scale.

Direct evidence of long-term deficits in intellectual functioning resulting from malnutrition comes from the under-developed countries and mainly concerns children who have suffered episodes of severe under-nutrition in the early years. However, in most of these studies it is impossible to be sure whether the intellectual deficits found are attributable to nutritional rather than socio-cultural influences (Birch and Gussow, 1970; J. Tizard, 1974). A study carried out in Jamaica (Hertzig *et al.*, 1972) comes nearest to disentangling these factors. Primary-school boys who had been admitted to hospital in the first two years of life for clinical malnutrition, from homes that had good intellectual stimulation, had similar average intelligence scores to those of boys who had never suffered from malnutrition but came from intellectually impoverished homes. These boys who had recovered from malnutrition, though, had significantly poorer scores than those of control boys from intellectually stimulating homes but significantly better scores than those of previously malnourished boys from homes providing poor intellectual stimulation (Richardson, 1972, cited by J. Tizard, 1974).

Some evidence is also available that less severe malnutrition depresses intellectual functioning (Birch and Gussow, 1970; J. Tizard, 1974). The siblings of the boys who had suffered from malnutrition in the Jamaica study (Hertzig *et al.*, 1972) are likely to have suffered from

349

undernutrition. Their intelligence test scores were higher than those of their recovered siblings but lower than those of control boys who lived in the same neighbourhood. A study of Indonesian children (Liang *et al.*, 1967) found a relationship between the intelligence test scores of six- to twelve-year-old children and the adequacy of their nutrition both in the pre-school years and currently. Although the lower intellectual functioning of the less adequately nourished children is probably partly due to socio-cultural factors, it seems likely that nutrition plays a part.

Nutrition and health

Whether or not nutrition affects intellectual development through its direct effects on brain growth in the early years, it has an influence through its relationship to health. This does not only apply in the under-developed countries. While severe malnutrition is virtually unknown in the industrialised countries, there is evidence that mild forms of malnutrition do exist. A number of studies in the United States have shown dietary inadequacies among children from low-income families and a high prevalence of iron deficiency anaemia among lower-social-class infants (Birch and Gussow, 1970).

A recently published survey (Department of Health and Social Security, Committee on Medical Aspects of Food Policy, 1975) of a nationally representative sample of pre-school children in the UK found no evidence of under-nutrition among any social class, family size or income group. Although the intake of some nutrients was lower among children whose fathers (or mothers) earned less than £19 a week, nutrition was still generally above the Department of Health and Social Security recommended levels. Even in the lowest-income group, where the income of the head of the household was below £11 a week, the proportion of children with low nutrient intakes (defined as 80 per cent of average intake for each age group in the sample) was no greater than in the rest of the survey children.

Findings of this survey must, however, be viewed with some reservation. As the authors themselves point out, there was considerable erosion of the original sample which may have resulted in 'some bias in terms of the worst getting away'. Of the original sample of 2085, 147 could not be contacted. Information on the children's diets was obtained from only 63.4 per cent of the original sample which is hardly surprising when the work involved for the mother is considered. Not only had every single item of food prepared for the child to be weighed but so had all food left over, including the inedible such as apple cores. Findings showed that there was a bias in recording the diet in favour of the higher social classes and higher income groups. Height (which is recognised as an index of nutrition) did not show any consistent differences between those for whom a dietary record was and was not obtained. However, this absence of difference in height cannot be taken to mean that those with and without diet records were similar nutritionally. A far higher proportion of the latter group was not measured. Only five per cent of those for whom dietary records were obtained failed to be measured compared with 31 per cent of those for whom dietary records were not obtained.

It cannot be ruled out then that some disadvantaged children, even in the UK, have, in some aspects, too low a nutritional intake. Although the average intake of iron, unlike that of most nutrients, was found to be below the recommended level in the national survey, an earlier study of haemoglobin levels had revealed little or no evidence of anaemia in young children (Ministry of Health, 1968). A study of pre-school Glasgow children living in over-crowded slum homes (Arneil et al., 1965), in contrast, found a very high proportion (over 70 per cent) of anaemia among those aged one to two, although the incidence did show a marked decrease after the age of two-and-a-half. Further investigations of nutritional intake directly aimed at the most disadvantaged groups are necessary. Less adequate nutrition is known to be associated with bronchitis (Whitmore and Rutter, 1970) and may possibly be a contributor to the greater susceptibility to infections, particularly respiratory infections, found in the socially disadvantaged children in the National Child Development Study sample (Wedge and Prosser, 1973).

Health and cognitive development

Poor health, whatever its causes, cannot be ignored as a factor in the slower mental development of some socially disadvantaged children. In the early years the less healthy child may well be less able to develop a stimulating interaction with his care-taker, and be less active in exploring the physical environment (Birch, 1968; J. Tizard, 1974), both of which appear to be so important for the development of cognitive abilities (see Part I, The impact of very early life experiences on development). In the primary-school years, illness causes the most socially disadvantaged children, those from low income families, living in poor housing and coming from large or one-parent families, to be absent from school more than other children (Wedge and Prosser, 1973). This is likely further to depress the intellectual performance of these children as school absence among manual, working-class children is associated with lowered intelligence tests, and to a greater extent, school attainment scores (Douglas et al., 1968). The greater tendency for lower-class children to suffer from minor sensory defects, such as squint and speech difficulties

351

(Davie *et al.*, 1972) may also be a factor hindering their intellectual development.

The extent to which poorer health hampers the intellectual development of the most socially disadvantaged children within the normal intelligence range cannot be determined at present but it is unlikely that it has no effect. Consideration of the health disadvantages associated with poverty makes it improbable that the 'cultural difference' theorists' view that there is no tendency for children who are the most socially disadvantaged to be hindered in their intellectual development is correct. It also, though, reinforces the view that environmental deprivation is sufficient to explain any deficits found, making any resort to 'genetic' explanations superfluous.

D. Social and cultural disadvantage

1. Material disadvantage

There can be little doubt that it is the children at the bottom of the social scale who are the most disadvantaged educationally. In a nationally representative sample, seven-year-olds from Social Class V were found to be almost seventeen months behind children of the same age from Social Classes I and II in reading attainment (National Child Development Study – Davie *et al.*, 1972). Similarly, in a survey of children attending Inner London Education Authority primary schools (Barnes and Lucas, 1975) eight-year-olds from Social Class V had a reading score over eighteen points lower than that of children from Social Class I. Recently published findings from the National Child Development Study (Fogelman and Goldstein, 1976) indicate that the gap in reading attainment between children from Social Class V and those from a non-manual background has increased to three years by the time the children are eleven, thus confirming earlier evidence (Douglas, 1964) on a widening difference to this age.

The reasons for the association between social class and educational attainment are complex. Cultural and linguistic influences, whether these are seen as deficiencies or differences, are ascribed the chief responsibility by most writers in the field. It is important, though, that the material disadvantages faced by children from the lower social classes are not overlooked. Not only are many of the 'cultural traditions' of the socially disadvantaged likely to have their origin in poverty and its concomitants (Tulkin and Konner, 1973) but material circumstances may affect educational attainments through other channels, such as health (see previous section) or by producing emotional strains in .parents or children.

Several studies show that poor household amenities and overcrowded conditions are associated with both lower ability and attainment (Davie *et al.*, 1972; Douglas, 1964; Hess *et al.*, 1968a; Murray, 1974). Absence or shared use of basic amenities (hot water, bathroom, indoor toilet) was found to reduce reading performance of seven-year-olds by nine months in the National Child Development Study (Davie *et al.*, 1972). Overcrowding (more than 1.5 persons per room) had a similar effect. Adverse housing conditions, of course, may be associated with other adverse circumstances, material or cultural, and it could be these which are influencing educational attainment. In Douglas' earlier study using a nationally representative sample, the influence of poor housing (overcrowding and poor amenities) was separated from some of these other factors. Poor housing was found to affect adversely ability and attainment scores independently of family size, parental interest in the child's school work and the academic record of the school.

How then does poor housing affect ability and attainment? Poor housing may well be one of the reasons for the higher incidence of illness found amongst socially disadvantaged children (Wedge and Prosser, 1973). The stresses and strains produced by poor housing may affect both the parents and the children themselves. Overcrowding was associated with certain specific characteristics of maternal behaviour, such as authoritarian control techniques, and a feeling of 'powerlessness' in relation to school, which were associated with poorer cognitive development in four-year-old black children in an American study (Hess *et al.*, 1968a). Several studies have found that housing difficulties are associated with depression in mothers of young children (Richman, 1976). Both the ways in which their parents behave towards them and the environmental conditions themselves are likely to affect the children. Overcrowding was found to be related to aggression, lack of curiosity, impulsivity and extraversion in nine-year-old Scottish children in Educational Priority Area Schools, independently of family size, the kind of housing or neighbourhood quality, in one study (Murray, 1974). In Douglas' national survey, primary-school children with unsatisfactory housing conditions were thought by teachers to be lazy or poor workers and to lack concentration in school.

Home conditions may make it difficult or impossible to provide good facilities for homework. There is very little research evidence on the effects of this. In one study, though (Dale and Griffiths, 1965), almost half of the grammar school children who were demoted from a high to a low stream (and who were almost all from working-class families) had poor facilities for homework. A strong relationship was found in another study among secondary-school children from working-class homes between inadequate facilities for homework and apathy towards school work (Sumner and Warburton, 1972).

2. The cultural environment of the home

A number of British studies have found a strong relationship between the cultural environment of the home – the parents' interest in reading, their educational aspirations for the child, the amount of interaction with him – and ability and attainment at the primary school stage (Miller, 1971; Peaker, 1967; Wiseman, 1967). Findings from American studies are similar (e.g. Whiteman and Deutsch, 1968). Although achievement in the secondary school is closely related to that at primary school (Walberg and Marjoribanks, 1974), home environment during the secondary-school years continues to make a contribution to attainment (Ainsworth and Batten, 1974; Walberg and Marjoribanks, 1974).

It has also been found in these and other studies (e.g. Marjoribanks, 1972b) that ability scores and school attainment are more strongly related to the cultural environment than to socio-economic factors such as the father's occupation, parents' education, the material standards of the home. Home environment variables such as the parents' educational aspirations for the child (Barker Lunn, 1970; Douglas, 1964; Whiteman and Deutsch, 1968), time spent with the child in educational or cultural activities (Morton-Williams, 1967; Whiteman and Deutsch, 1968) and the level of literacy in the home (Morton-Williams, 1967) show a moderate relationship to socio-economic level. In Walberg and Marjoribanks' study (1974) family social status (father's occupation, education, family income) and the influence of family size explained statistically significant variance in the cultural environment of the home among a large sample of primary- and secondary-school children but left from 47 to 71 per cent of the variance in environment unexplained.

Where unskilled, working-class parents are able to achieve a high level of involvement with their children in intellectually stimulating activities (Whiteman and Deutsch, 1968) and an effective interest in their education (Douglas, 1964), the disadvantaging effects of low social class on ability and attainment are largely mitigated. Nevertheless, it is for the children from semi- and unskilled working-class families, whose parents themselves have had only elementary-school education, that overcrowding and poor housing conditions have the most effect on ability and attainment (Douglas, 1964). Limitations on time and energy in these circumstances are likely to make it very difficult for parents to engage in stimulating activities with their children however affectionate they are towards them.

It could be argued, of course, that the link between the cultural environment of the home and the child's ability and attainment is not a causal one. If intelligence is largely genetically determined then it is the more intelligent parents, those most likely to provide a culturally stimulating home environment, who will most probably have children with high ability, but the statistical association thus produced need have no causal connotations. Some evidence against this viewpoint has already been discussed in Section I of this review. In Ainsworth and Batten's (1974) study, it was also found that variables concerning parental ambition for the child's education, their interest and awareness in his school-work and the parents' and child's liking for reading were related to secondary-school attainment even when either the ability of the parents (parents' 11 + results) or the child (7 + intelligence) was held constant.

Of course, as Finlayson (1971) has pointed out it is wrong to treat parental aspirations and interest solely as causal influences, as has been assumed in much of the work that has been mentioned. The aspirations and interest shown could simply be reflections of how well the child is actually performing at school. In fact, the true position seems to be somewhere between the two, parental aspirations and interest both influencing and being influenced by the child's school achievements. In Ainsworth and Batten's study the magnitude of correlations between parental aspiration variables and secondary-school attainment was considerably reduced when the child's ability (at 7 +) was held constant but nevertheless, as already mentioned, remained statistically significant. Douglas (1964) found not only that parental interest was related to ability (in which the causal influence could be in either direction) but that children of similar ability level had a slight advantage in the 11 + examination if their parents were rated as being very interested (on teachers' judgements and visits to the school).

Barker Lunn's (1970) study showed that parental aspirations are affected by the evidence produced by the school of the child's achievements. Generally, streaming raised parental aspirations where the child's ability was high but depressed them where the child was below average. Social-class differences in aspirations were not just reflections, though, of the child's achievements. At each ability level higher-social-class parents were more likely to desire grammar-school places for their children, to want them to stay at school beyond the statutory leaving age and to hope for university or college places.

Although there undoubtedly are social class differences in aspirations for and interest in their children's education, it should be emphasised that it is only a minority of parents who are uninterested in their children's education. Only 15 per cent of seven-year-olds in the National Child Development Study had mothers who showed 'little or no interest' in their education and only 18 per cent wanted them to leave school as soon as possible (Davie et al., 1972). Amongst parents living in four educational Priority Areas less than a third wanted their children to leave school at the minimum age and only one to two-fifths of parents in each area did not think it important that the child should do well at school (Payne, 1974).

It is probably differences in parents' knowledge and ability to make their aspirations effective which is the crucial distinction. In an American survey (Coleman, 1966), it was found that black parents had greater interest in and aspirations for their child's education than white parents of similar socio-economic level but that parental interest had less effect on the achievement of black children than of white. Several British studies indicate that there are social class differences in parents' ability to translate their aspirations into practice. In one study, manual, especially unskilled, working-class parents living in Hartlepool, were found to know less about the workings of the educational system than middle-class parents (Pallister and Wilson, 1970). Middle-class parents are often able effectively to challenge decisions of teachers which they feel may adversely affect their children's career chances while working-class parents tend to leave this kind of decision to the school (Kelsall and Kelsall, 1971).

The experiences in Wakefield, a predominantly working-class town, in the first year of operation of a scheme in which parents were involved in the choice of the type of school the child should attend at 13 + , are also of interest (Whalley, 1970). After receiving information from the schools parents were asked to state (on the form provided) whether they wished their child to transfer to the senior high school, which offered a full range of courses, including GCE, or to remain at the local high school, which could only offer CSE courses. Surprisingly, the demand for places at the senior high school was only greater by thirty than the intake had been when it was a grammar school, even though places were available for twice this number. It was found that the vast majority of parents had accepted the advice of the high schools on whether to transfer their children, only six challenging the school's view that they should remain at the local high school.

In an American study (Jones, 1972) ten- to twelve-year-old boys with comparatively low verbal ability had mothers who were as knowledgeable about how they were getting on at school and had as frequent contacts with school staff as boys similar in non-verbal intelligence but comparatively high in verbal ability. But parents of the boys high in verbal ability provided greater opportunities for the development of language (encouragement of meal-time conversations, reading, provision of newspapers, use of library). This variable was identified as the best predictor of verbal ability, accounting for 51 per cent of the variance. Interested parents may be hampered in their attempts to help their children educationally by their own lack of knowledge or by material adversities. The most recent study by the Newsons (1977), published since this work was written, provides additional evidence on this – see Addendum, page 413.

3. Social class differences in the early environment

If there already tend to be differences in the intellectual performance of middle- and unskilled, working-class children at three to four years which cannot be accounted for by differences in familiarity with the material or ease in the test situation, then it seems likely that their origin lies in the experiences provided by the home environment. From recent evidence, there is little doubt that the level, variety, appropriateness and timing of stimulation provided for the child in the first two years affects the development of his cognitive processes and abilities in the early years of life and continues to have some influence into pre-adolescence at least. Generally, care-takers who provide this type of care are warm, loving and non-rejecting (see Part I – The impact of very early life experiences on development).

In the early months of life, the amount of touching, holding and other physical stimulation received by the child is related to his mental development at this age (Lewis and Goldberg, 1969; L. J. Yarrow, 1963). Evidence indicates that, if anything, lower-social-class infants are advantaged in the amount of physical stimulation provided by the mother in the first few months (Lewis and Wilson, 1972; Moss et al., 1969). Lewis and Wilson found an increase in maternal touching, holding, smiling and playing with decrease in social-class level in their study of three-months-old infants. Only in maternal vocalisations was there no social-class difference. Infants from the unskilled working class, in fact, tended to be somewhat superior in mental development (Bayley scale) to those from the upper middle class and were clearly so on a measure of attention. At ten months, no social class differences were found in the amount of time that mothers spent in close proximity to their infants or in the amount of physical contact (Tulkin and Kagan, 1972). Studies of infants from two weeks to three to four years old suggest that when children with similar parity are compared, there are no social-class differences in the extent of physical care-taking received by the child (Kilbride et al., 1971, cited by Streissguth and Bee, 1972; Tulkin and Kagan, 1972; Lawson and Ingleby, 1974).

A 'secure' attachment with his principal care-taker(s) appears to be the outcome of care-taking behaviour – sensitivity and appropriate responsiveness to the child's signals and provision of a high amount of social stimulation – which promotes cognitive development of the child in his first year and itself probably has a facilitating effect on this development. While there is no detailed study of whether there are social-class differences in the quality of the child's attachment to his mother (or main care-taker) there is no indication from available research that infants from a working-class background are any less attached to their mothers than middle-class infants (Messer and Lewis, 1972; Tulkin,

1973). The studies of early mother-infant interaction do not suggest that there are any social-class differences in maternal warmth, though this is not specifically measured. Middle-class and socially disadvantaged mothers have been found to differ little in their warmth to rather older (four to five years) children (Hess and Shipman, 1965; Kogan and Wimberger, 1969).

By the time the infant is ten months old there is evidence, though, that middle-class mothers do spend more time in interaction with their children, though not in physical interaction (Tulkin and Kagan, 1972). The main differences found were in the amount of maternal verbal interaction and in time spent 'entertaining' the infant, sometimes by means of a toy or object. These social-class differences could be of considerable importance for it appears to be verbal, not physical stimulation, that is the most important influence on mental development in the second year of life (Clarke-Stewart, 1973; Wachs *et al.*, 1971).

There is also evidence of the importance of the mother being involved in the child's play, for it is the stimulation with toys and objects that he receives from his mother rather than the number of these in the house that seems to be related to the complexity of the child's play (Clarke-Stewart, 1973). Findings by White and Watts (1973) that children who appear to be developing competently intellectually and socially spend more time with their mothers in 'intellectually stimulating' activities than infants developing less competently also support the view that the social-class differences found in maternal behaviour at this stage may be of importance (see also Part I, sections A and C).

Most of the work on social-class differences in early environmental experiences has dealt with somewhat older (four- to five-year-old) children. It has been inspired by Basil Bernstein's work (see section B) on differences in maternal communication styles and the extent to which they require the child to exercise, and thus develop, his cognitive abilities. In the well-known research by Hess, Shipman and their colleagues (Hess and Shipman, 1965; 1967; Hess *et al.*, 1968a) social-class differences were found in the use of control techniques. From an analysis of how mothers stated they would respond in various hypothetical situations, it was found that upper middle-class, black American mothers were much less likely to use imperative-normative control than lower-class, black mothers. These are commands for which no justification or explanation is given. This kind of control, it is suggested, simply requires the child to obey without having to undertake any complicated mental operations. Middle-class mothers were more likely than working-class mothers to use subjective-personal appeals. This kind of control takes into account the child's personal qualities, his feelings and reactions or the specific circumstances of the situation. The child is faced with the task of considering and weighing up alternative courses of action. The tendency to make greater use of imperative-normative control techniques was found to have a significant, though moderate, negative relationship to various measures of intellectual functioning in the child.

Similarly, in a more recent British study (Cook-Gumperz, 1973), middle-class mothers used, in their responses to hypothetical everyday problem situations, more personal control strategies, especially cognitively oriented strategies providing information for the child about the consequences of his act, while working-class mothers used more imperatives. Mothers from both social groups used the positional mode of control, in which rules are stated in terms of the general rather than particular attributes of child and case, but here too the middle-class tended verbally to elaborate the rule to a greater extent. Personal control strategies were found to be positively related to the child's verbal intelligence, particularly when an elaborated code was used.

These findings are based only on the mother's statement of how she would behave in a hypothetical situation and not on what she actually does. Hess and Shipman, however, also observed mothers interacting with their children in an actual, though experimental, situation, in which they were asked to teach their children three simple tasks, two involving sorting and one the copying of a geometric design. Social status differences were greatest (Hess et al., 1968a) in the extent to which the mother attempted to motivate the child by making the task appear enjoyable, by praising his successful efforts rather than criticising his failures and by the degree to which she gave specific instructions on what was involved in the task. Mothers who continually intruded in the task, telling the children to carry out certain physical operations, tended to be unsuccessful in teaching the task and to have children with low intellectual attainments. They were also more likely to come from the low social-status groups. A similar study (Bee et al., 1969) in which mothers were observed in teaching their children a house-building task has findings which appear, when taken overall, to corroborate these social-class differences.

Critics of this work (Ginsburg, 1972; Sroufe, 1970) point out that the teaching behaviour of mothers in these experimental situations is not necessarily representative of the mother's everyday behaviour. Ginsburg also emphasises that all of the mothers do teach their children the task to some extent and the social-class differences on a number of individual measures of teaching behaviour are not very great. Even where these are quite considerable, as in greater use of positive and less use of negative reinforcement by the middle-class mothers, they do not appear to be related to successful learning to any great extent. It is, however, probably not so much the differences in the individual aspects of teaching behaviour as the overall approach which is important. Hess and Shipman (1967) found in the copying task that a multiple correlation using three of

359

the teaching behaviours accounted for more of variance in performance scores than one using the intelligence scores of the mothers and children, and social class. Nevertheless, Ginsburg is correct to stress that there are similarities in the way all mothers teach and that all normal children do manage to learn a great deal.

To return to the first criticism: no doubt social-class differences are increased by the unfamiliarity of the university atmosphere to the lower-working-class mothers, especially in a test situation. Social-class differences in a free-play situation appear to be much smaller (Baldwin and Baldwin, 1973; Bee *et al.*, 1969) than those found when the mother is required to teach the child a particular task. Nevertheless, there is some evidence of social-class differences in maternal communication in everyday life. The Newsons' (1968) findings on child-rearing practices of mothers of four-year-old Nottingham children are based, it is true, on data obtained from interview with the mothers. Here, though, the emphasis is more on what actually has occurred between the mothers and their children rather than, as in the studies earlier discussed, what the mother says she would do in particular hypothetical situations. The findings do support the view that the middle-class mother places more emphasis on the use of reasoning in control, and also gives the child more opportunities for learning techniques of self-justification.

One study (Wooton, 1974) provides direct evidence of parental-child dialogue in everyday surroundings. By means of a radio microphone system recordings were made of all the speech taking place between four-year-old children and others in their own homes for a period up to four hours in a day on three separate occasions, no researcher being present. In line with other findings the middle-class parents in control situations showed a tendency to make more enquiries, especially about the child's feelings, to make fewer imperative and negative remarks and more strong suggestions which gave the child some discretion. Nevertheless, similarities between all parents in control techniques were much greater than social-class differences. By far the most frequent type of control statement made by parents from all social classes was the positive directive. Wooton's findings suggested that social-class differences outside the control context are probably more important than those within. Middle-class parents seized opportunities to extend the children's comments and questions to a considerably (and significantly) greater extent than the semi-skilled, working-class parents. One consequence of this, possibly having cognitive implications for the child, appeared to be that more of the middle-class children's questions arose out of parental comments, and questions which arose in this way tended to be more advanced than those originating independently of adult remarks. It is especially interesting that Wooton also found that only middle-class parents developed fantasy situations, making them occasions for demanding mental operations by the child. Joan Tough (1973) in her study of the use of language in young children found that middle-class children were much more able than those from a semi- or unskilled, working-class background to see problems in the imagination and work out their solution.

Wooton attributes the social-class differences to differences in views on the parental role. Historically, and in some cases at present, working-class parents have been forced to give priority to the physical needs of their children (Clarke-Stewart, 1973). Also, a number of studies have found that from the time when their children are very young middle-class parents are aware that their own activities have educational significance for the child, while working-class parents feel there is little they can do to modify the course of his development (Hubbard, cited by Tizard, 1975; Smith, 1975b; Tulkin and Kagan, 1972).

These studies suggest overall then that there are very considerable similarities in the early experiences of children from all social classes. However, differences in parental-child communication experiences may be sufficient to make middle-class children better prepared for the cognitive tasks of school than some children from a lower working-class background.

It is likely, though, that the contrasts in experience between the most socially disadvantaged children and those from more advantaged homes are greater than those seen in any of the studies reviewed here. Findings from the Hess and Shipman study suggest that maternal control techniques and teaching strategies tending to be associated with low cognitive performance in the child increase with decreasing social level. Even in this study, though, which did include a group of children from father-absent families living on public welfare, there is no indication that the most disadvantaged families were deliberately sought. Other studies have less disadvantaged working-class children as their subjects. The extent to which multiple social problems may affect early parental-child interactions has barely been explored as yet.

Annotations

AINSWORTH, M. E. and BATTEN, E. J. 1974. *The Effects of Environmental Factors on Secondary Educational Attainment in Manchester: a Plowden Follow-up*, Schools Council Research Studies, Macmillan, London. 212 pp.

Environmental influences on the secondary-school attainment of 1,544 children attending 53 schools were investigated, the subjects being those still available from the sample of 2,348 Manchester primary-school children studied on behalf of the Plowden Committee (Wiseman, 1967).

In the school-based analyses the main criteria of attainment were marks obtained in internal examinations in the first three years of secondary school, prior to the comprehensive reorganisation. A more intensive study of 143 individual pupils used a variety of criteria of attainment, including results of the external 16 + examinations.

Attainment was found to be overwhelmingly dependent on ability as measured by 11 + scores and so on the home and neighbourhood environmental factors which were found to be the major influence on ability in the earlier study. School environment was also crucially affected by the initial ability of the pupil intake, schools with higher ability pupils on entry not only having better qualified staff but also better physical provision and amenities. A disadvantageous early environment thus leads to a disadvantageous later school environment and secondary-school provisions compound rather than ameliorate disadvantage. School environment variables made very little contribution to attainment independent of their association with initial ability. However, in all types of school, irrespective of the initial ability of the pupils, better qualified teachers were associated with higher attainment.

The intensive study of individual pupils confirmed that many aspects of the home environment were related to attainment at all ages but showed that the effect of most of the variables derived from their association with the ability of the child at 7 + . Parental ambition, library membership, liking for reading, and, to a lesser extent, the child's own ambition, though, related to attainment independent of the child's ability (at 7 +) or parental ability (11 + selection). Ability, as measured by the child's 11 + results, was the most important influence on school-leaving age. However, a low level of parental ambition, literacy and material adequacy was associated with leaving at fifteen independent of initial ability. Entry to the sixth form was actually influenced as much by social class as by attainment.

BEE, H. L. *et al.* 1969. 'Social class differences in maternal teaching strategies and speech patterns', *Developmental Psychology* 1, 6, 726–34.

This study found social-class differences in maternal behaviour in both an unstructured (mother and child in a waiting room) and structured (problem-solving task in which mother was allowed to help child as much as she wished) situation, and in speech patterns. In the structured setting, the middle-class mothers adopted behaviour which encouraged the child to acquire strategies which could be adapted to other problem-solving situations. They allowed the child to take more time, offered suggestions that were less specific, and more often told their children what they were doing correctly, compared with the working-class mothers. In the unstructured situation, the middle-class mothers gave their children more attention. They were less controlling and disapproving. Speech patterns of the middle-class mothers were more complex (longer and more complex sentences, relatively more adjectives and fewer pronouns). It is suggested that the impoverished language environment and failure to encourage the learning of general techniques of problem-solving contribute towards lower cognitive functioning in the working-class children. Subjects were seventy-six working-class mothers (two-thirds black, and mainly eligible for Head-Start) and thirty-eight middle-class mothers (white, highly educated), and their children, aged four to five-and-a-half.

CHAZAN, M., LAING, A. and JACKSON, S. 1971. *Just Before School*, published for Schools Council by Basil Blackwell, London. 220 pp.

Four-year-old children, about to enter primary school in two to three months' time, living in four areas of Swansea designated 'deprived' by the local education authority, differed from children living in non-deprived areas (two middle-class and one 'settled working-class') in the extent to which the parents promoted interest in books and reading in the children. Significantly fewer of the children in the deprived than the non-deprived areas had attended nursery schools. The two groups of children did not differ, though, in play experiences, the use made of television and radio, contacts with other children or knowledge of the primary school prior to entry.

The findings show that disadvantaged children cannot be identified solely on the basis of living in areas designated 'deprived'. However, the differences that did emerge between the groups are of some importance. Also, the methodology of the study resulted in differences between the two groups being somewhat blurred. Children selected as subjects were in the main already registered at a primary school in the area several months before entry, thus probably excluding some of the most deprived. Inclusion of a fairly modern council estate in the 'deprived' areas and of a 'settled working-class' area in the control areas also attenuated differences between the groups in terms of social class, education of the parents and income. Comparison of the 'least-prepared' and 'best-prepared' children showed that rather more (though the difference was not statistically significant) of the former came from the deprived areas. Families of the 'least-prepared' were lower in social class, they had lower weekly incomes and their parents had attended school for a shorter period and had fewer qualifications. Children with 'most behaviour problems' had fathers with lower educational attainments, less financial security in the family and tended to be affected by a combination of problems to a greater extent than those with 'fewest behaviour problems'.

363

COOK-GUMPERZ, J. 1973. *Social Control and Socialization*, Routledge and Kegan Paul, London. 290 pp. (Foreword by Basil Bernstein, vii–x).

A study based on Bernstein's theory of social control and language use aimed at investigating social-class differences in mothers' control techniques and the cognitive consequences for the child of different techniques. Subjects were 236 mother-child pairs approximately half coming from a predominantly working-class and half from a middle-class London borough. Data on social control strategies were obtained through interview, the mothers being asked how they would react to the child in six hypothetical everyday problem situations; the children were asked, at the age of seven, how 'the mummy' would react in the same six situations.

Middle-class mothers (the social-class index rated on the occupation and education of both parents) used more personal control strategies (i.e. rules stated to fit the particular characteristics of the child and circumstances of the case), especially cognitively-oriented strategies providing information for the child about the consequences of his act. The working-class mothers used more imperative controls (i.e. the child is given no options and is controlled by superior force). Each social group predominantly used one mode of control but had a preferred strategy within other modes. Working-class mothers had preference for child-oriented affective appeals (i.e. evoking emotional response about the misdemeanour in the child) in the personal mode while middle-class mothers used command rather than physical or verbal punishment in the imperative mode. All social groups used the positional mode of control (i.e. rules stated in terms of general attributes of child and case) but in this mode, middle-class mothers tended to use more linguistically mediated controls. Social-class differences were few amongst the children but working-class children gave explanations markedly less often (Bernstein's Foreword).

Evidence was found that the mothers of the middle- and working-class children used two different speech codes, the middle-class using an elaborated code in which meanings are made explicit and the working-class a restricted code in which meanings are implicit. Indicators of the elaborated code were the higher degree of cohesiveness in the speech, allowing it to be understood apart from the context (greater use of anaphoric and cataphoric pronouns referring to items occurring earlier or later in the text), expressions of the speaker's individuality and separation from the listener (use of egocentric sequence 'I think') and attempts to qualify and develop meaning in the speech (use of conditional sequences, e.g. 'if', 'it depends', 'probably'). Indicators of restricted code were a lower degree of cohesiveness in the speech, making necessary sources of information outside the text and the expression of communal meaning based on solidarity between the speaker and the listener (use of socio-centric sequences such as 'you know', 'isn't it'). As expected, both personal and positional modes of control were associated with both language codes. The elaborated code, though, had a wider pattern of association with personal-control strategies, and those involving the most language mediation were associated with this code. The personal-control strategies associated with the restricted code were affective, relying on explanations of the emotion the child or other person would feel if the child persisted in his misdemeanour.

Personal-control strategies were found to be positively associated with the child's measured verbal intelligence, especially when mediated through an elaborated code.

DAS, J. P. 1973. 'Cultural deprivation and cognitive competence', in N. R. Ellis (ed) *International Review of Research in Mental Retardation, vol 6*, Academic Press, London. 1–53.

In the first part of this article, the author discusses what it is that constitutes cultural disadvantage. In the second part, a series of studies carried out by the author are reported, one aim of which was to clarify the role of economic prosperity, 'cultural' advantage, and non-intellective factors such as parental aspirations for and encouragement of the child's education on cognitive ability. Studies with rich high-caste, rich low-caste, poor high-caste and poor low-caste Hindu school-children as subjects indicated that economic prosperity and 'cultural' advantage both contributed independently to cognitive verbal ability but that economic prosperity was, on the whole, of greater advantage. Parental educational aspirations were not an important predictor of cognitive ability (Raven's Progressive Matrices) in the Hindu children. Parental educational expectations were, though, more closely related to educational achievements (California Achievement Test) than cognitive ability in white, lower-social-class Canadian children. As far as educational achievements were concerned, the low-social-class, white Canadian child benefitted more from high parental educational expectations than the high-social-class child.

HESS, R. D., SHIPMAN, V. C., BROPHY, J. E. and BEAR, R. M. 1968a. *The Cognitive Environments of Urban Preschool Children*, University of Chicago, 381 pp.

This study was designed to examine the processes through which socio-economic disadvantages affect the cognitive development of pre-school, black children in the United States. Subjects were 163 mothers and their four-year-old children coming from three different socio-economic levels: middle-class, settled, working-class and unskilled, working-class (sub-divided into father-present and father-absent groups). Within the working-class groups less crowded homes, fairly rich use of home resources in preparing the child for school and participation by the mother in community activities were related to a number of maternal characteristics which were found to be associated with better cognitive performance in the child.

The maternal characteristics favourable to the child's cognitive development included less frequent use of status-normative control strategies (norms and authority figures should be obeyed without question) and greater use of personal subjective strategies (calling attention to effects of the child's behaviour on himself and others) and feelings of personal effectiveness in dealing with the school. Middle-class mothers generally used types of control strategy and maternal teaching strategy which promoted cognitive development to a greater extent than those used by working-class mothers. Middle-class children differed significantly from children in each of the three working-class groups in IQ scores (Stanford Binet) but social-class differences in a cognitive task requiring verbal classification (Sigel) were greater than could be accounted for by the IQ differences.

Categorising ability in the child was positively related to the mother's use of abstract attitudes in a sorting task (Sigel). Maternal teaching behaviour, language style and attitudes to education were better predictors of the child's categorising ability than the mother's IQ or social class. Working-class mothers in comparison with middle-class mothers felt a lack of personal effectiveness in dealing with the school system, and this type of attitude was associated with compliance and uncertainty about his abilities in a test situation in the child.

HESS, R. D., SHIPMAN, V. C., BROPHY, J. E. and BEAR, R. M. 1968b. 'Mother's language and child's cognitive behavior', Chapter VII in R. D. Hess, V. C. Shipman, J. E. Brophy and R. M. Bear, *The Cognitive Environments of Urban Preschool Children*, University of Chicago. 147–70.

As part of a study designed to examine the processes by which social and economic disadvantage affect the child's early cognitive development, the relationship between maternal language style and the child's cognitive behaviour was investigated. Subjects were 163 mothers and their four-year-old children: 40 from the middle-class, 42 from the skilled, working-class, 40 from the semi- and unskilled, working-class, and 41 who were dependent on public assistance because of father absence. Three samples of the mother's speech were obtained: a description of a typical day in her life; her account of what was happening when shown a photograph of a mother and teacher in a classroom; her story to the child based on a picture depicting a lion and a mouse. Middle-class mothers scored consistently higher (with one exception) on all language measures, with the skilled, working-class mothers generally coming next.

The middle-class mothers spoke in longer sentences, used a wider range of adverbs, more different complex verb types and more complex syntatic structures. They also attended more to the stimuli in the test pictures, displayed more abstract concepts in their language usage and introduced more characters and objects not present in the lion-mouse picture, thus showing more imaginative thought elaboration. However, in the case of the mother-teacher photograph it was the working-class mothers who introduced more content, suggesting that if working-class subjects are interested enough, they are not necessarily stimulus-bound. The most striking relationship found was between the mother's language abstraction and the child's abstraction ability (as measured by ability to verbalise the sorting principle on a block sorting task and abstract categorising ability on Sigel Conceptual Sorting Task for Children). It was found that only the mother's language abstraction and not her abstracting ability (as measured by Similarities sub-test of Wechsler Adult Intelligence Scale), general verbal intelligence or the child's intelligence test score (Stanford Binet) was significantly related to the child's abstract categorising ability. It is suggested that there is an abstracting factor in the middle-class mother's language which is important in the development of abstraction behaviour of a high order in the child.

JONES, P. A. 1972. 'Home environment and the development of verbal ability', *Child Development* 43, 1081–6.

Mothers of ten- to twelve-year-old boys of high verbal ability had a higher interaction index (more disposed to encouraging the child to interact with his environment on a verbal-cognitive level) than mothers of boys with low verbal ability but equal intelligence. The main difference was that the mothers of the high-level boys viewed toys as serving a cognitive child-oriented function rather than an instrumental mother-oriented function. Mothers of high-verbal-level boys also had higher academic and career expectations and aspirations for their children and made more deliberate efforts for the use and development of language and vocabulary. The two groups of mothers did not differ in their knowledge of the child's school progress. Boys with lower verbal ability came from homes having a significantly lower occupational level. While mother's interest in their children did not differ between the two groups, they differed in the extent to which they provided opportunities for language development. This is probably related to the lower occupational status, and if they were given the money they would probably provide improved opportunities. 51 per cent of the variance in verbal ability scores was accounted for by the variable 'material and organisational opportunities for the use and development of language' while the addition of occupational status increased the percentage of variance accounted for to 59 per cent.

MARJORIBANKS, K. 1972b. 'Environment, social class and mental abilities', *Journal of Educational Psychology* 63, 103–9.

The learning environment of the home was found to account for 52 per cent of the variance in total intelligence test scores (SRA Primary Mental Abilities Test). However, environmental factors accounted for a large percentage of the variance in verbal and number ability test scores, but only a moderate percentage of variance in reasoning ability test scores and a low percentage in spatial ability test scores. Learning environment factors were more highly related to mental ability test scores than either social class or family structure (size of family, ordinal position in family, overcrowding) factors. Subjects were 185 eleven-year-old boys and their parents, 90 from a middle-class and 95 from a lower-social-class background.

WEDGE, P. and PROSSER, H. 1973. *Born to Fail?* Arrow Books in association with the National Children's Bureau, London. 64 pp.

Six per cent of eleven-year-old children in Britain were found to be socially disadvantaged in this study. Children in the National Child Development Study (all children born in the week 3–9 March 1958 in England, Scotland and Wales) who came from a one-parent or large family (five or more children) were badly housed (more than one-and-a-half persons per room or no exclusive use of hot water supply) and were in a low-income family (receiving free school meals or supplementary benefit) formed the socially disadvantaged group which was compared with the group of ordinary children (all non-disadvantaged children in the sample).

The disadvantaged children started their lives with a deficit having experienced unfavourable pregnancy and birth circumstances – young mothers, mothers who were heavy smokers, mothers with four or more previous pregnancies, less adequate antenatal care – to a greater extent than the ordinary children. At eleven, they lived in more cramped accommodation with fewer amenities, over half of the disadvantaged children having to share a bed compared with only one in eleven of the ordinary children.

Chronic ill-health and serious disability were four times as frequent among their fathers, one in ten of the fathers of disadvantaged children having been off work for a whole year compared with one in five hundred fathers of ordinary children. The disadvantaged children were shorter than the ordinary children, they were more likely to have suffered from a serious illness and to have a hearing or speech defect. One in twenty of disadvantaged children were said to be educationally subnormal compared with one in 150 of the ordinary group. Fewer of the disadvantaged children had any pre-school experience despite their greater need. Parents of disadvantaged children, especially fathers, were less likely to have visited the child's school and more wanted their child to leave as soon as possible, although five-sixths nevertheless wanted the child to stay on beyond the statutory leaving age. The disadvantaged children did less well in mathematics and reading tests, at the age of eleven on average being three-and-a-half years behind in reading. Nevertheless disadvantage and low attainment were not invariably associated, one in seven of the disadvantaged children doing better on reading tests than half the ordinary group, and some being at the highest level of attainment.

WOOTON, A. J. 1974. 'Talk in the homes of young children', *Sociology* 8, 2, 277–95.

Speech of working-class (semi-skilled) and middle-class (professional) parents and their four-year-old children was tape-recorded in their own homes using a radio microphone system (in the absence of a research worker). Middle-class children spoke more often to their parents in the home, particularly in play situations. Outside control situations, middle-class parents took more opportunities to extend dialogue themes. This led to middle-class children's 'why' questions being more dependent on previous non-interrogative remarks of their parents and more 'advanced' in content (as judged by two mothers of young children and two psychologists). Working-class children's 'why' questions tended to be more obvious or idiosyncratic because of their greater independence of information supplied by the parents.

Bernstein (1971) has argued that working-class parent-child relationships are more grounded in common assumptions and role expectations than is the case in the middle-class, making extended and individualised forms of speech less necessary. Evidence from the present study is contradictory, suggesting that it is the middle-class parent who more extensively transmits adult interpretations and meanings to the child. The working-class child's understanding of the world is less clearly articulated with parent's meanings. Social-class differences in parent-child relationships perhaps arise because middle-class parents see their role as educational while working-class parents assume that the child's natural talents will tend to emerge irrespective of the social environment.

E. Intervention

1. Introduction

American attempts to overcome the educational disadvantage of poor lower-class children by a programme of pre-school education are widely believed to have failed. This is based on a number of evaluations, particularly that carried out by the Westinghouse Learning Corporation (Horowitz and Paden, 1973) of the government-launched summer and full year Head-Start programmes. These have shown that by the third year at school (third grade) nine-to ten-year-olds who attended pre-school do not differ in their scores on various measures of intelligence from children who have not had the benefit of pre-school experience. The gains consistently shown after entry to the pre-school have more or less disappeared.

Yet it is also true that socially disadvantaged children invariably make significantly greater gains in intellectual performance during the first year of attendance at pre-school than children with similar characteristics who do not attend pre-school. These increased gains are probably partially at least due to greater ease with adults and greater motivation, as Zigler and Butterfield have suggested (1968) rather than being entirely attributable to cognitive development. However, even if the gains are due solely to motivational factors, they cannot be dismissed as worthless. They show that the initial score underestimated the child's ability. Additionally, the increased confidence and rapport with an adult is not something of importance only in a test. Research has shown (see Part IV 'Teacher expectations and pupil progress') that the relationship with the teacher may affect what is taught the child, how much he is encouraged and the self-image he has of his abilities.

Recent evidence from a number of experimentally designed pre-school programmes has, in fact, had some less depressing features (Ryan, 1974). While there are generally signs of a fade-out of differences between the pre-school and control groups by the third school year (grade) there is also some remaining advantage at this stage, particularly in academic achievement, which is surely the main point of the exercise. To hope for any more was unrealistic, as a number of researchers in the field have recently pointed out. As Gray (1974) puts it, An effective early intervention programme be it ever so good, cannot possibly be viewed as a form of inoculation whereby the child is immunised forever afterward to the effects of an inadequate home and a school inappropriate to his needs'. Learning in early childhood is important as a foundation on which later learning can occur but its existence cannot ensure that later learning will occur whatever the circumstances.

The most effective intervention study ever reported is Skeels's (1966) classic research. Children living in an unstimulating orphanage in the 1930s and functioning at the mentally retarded level were transferred to an environment that, unlikely though it may seem, was personally stimulating for them. They became 'house guests' in an institution for the mentally retarded, each child being individually placed in a ward with older girls and women. Each child received a great deal of attention, and most became attached to a particular adult. The children made large increases in intelligence test scores and eleven out of the thirteen were eventually adopted. Twenty years later, in the early 1960s, all were living normal adult lives. In contrast, controls who had remained in the orphanage which provided few opportunities for play or interaction with adults, were all of low socio-economic status or still institutionalised in adult life, only two out of the twelve ever having married.

The important point is that the successful outcome for the experimental group in the Skeels's study was not solely, or even mainly, due to the period (eighteen months on average) spent in the stimulating circumstances of being 'house guests'. The children continued to have an environment which encouraged cognitive development in their adoptive homes. Similarly, it was not just the early experience of the orphanage which depressed the intellectual performance of the control children but also their continuing lack of environmental stimulation throughout childhood either in the orphanage or as ordinary patients in an institution for the mentally retarded.

Similarly, it seems that the most successful intervention programmes are those which provide more than a year's pre-school provision. Sometimes this takes the form of an additional intervention beyond the age of five, sometimes of parental involvement in the programme, and quite often of both. Even so, the difficulties in family and social circumstances probably remain, as do inadequacies in the school after the programme ceases. Educational intervention in itself cannot solve society's problems. That it can make some improvements in the intellectual functioning of socially disadvantaged children, even if only for a relatively short time, does give some indication of their potential and of what is being wasted.

In the remainder of this review, a more detailed examination will be made of the intervention that has taken place in Britain. The American findings are too massive, and have in any case been too well reviewed already (see, for example, Bronfenbrenner, 1974) for them to be discussed in detail here. However, they often throw illumination on the British evidence and reference will be made to them where they do so.

2. Does nursery school attendance benefit disadvantaged children educationally?

Short-term benefits

Strangely enough, none of the recent pre-school studies in the UK have been designed to find out whether attendance is educationally more beneficial to the disadvantaged child than staying at home. The main studies, those carried out as part of the Educational Priority Area project, and the National Foundation for Educational Research study, did not include a control group of children remaining at home, or included one which appears to be a not-very-well matched afterthought (Halsey, 1972a; Smith, 1975a). What these studies did ask was which type of pre-school programme is most effective. Nevertheless it is the answer to the unasked question which comes most clearly from the findings.

The initial short-term benefit of attending nursery school, in line with the American experience, emerges from most of the studies. Gains in relation to national norms on standardised tests attributable to nursery school attendance, whether or not a special programme had been introduced, are found in several of the pre-school projects carried out in the Educational Priority Areas (areas of special need). The strongest evidence comes from the Dundee pre-school project (Harvey and Lee, 1974), all the nursery-school children making a gain of about ten points on a test claiming to measure general verbal ability (English Picture Vocabulary Test) and roughly similar improvements on other tests (sub-tests of the Wechsler Pre-school and Primary Scale of Intelligence). Starting from an average IQ of 95, below the national average, these disadvantaged children were entering infant school with an IQ of 105, above average. Considerably smaller (about four points on average) but consistent gains against national norms in verbal ability (EPVT) and also in language comprehension and expression (Reynell scales) were found in the London pre-school projects (Stevenson, 1975). The West Riding findings are rather less consistent but generally there was a move towards the age norms during the nursery school year (Smith, 1975a).

These findings suggest that the improvements in intellectual performance are due to nursery-school attendance but without control groups it is, of course, impossible to be sure. The national pre-school experiment (Halsey, 1972a) did include a small sample of children not attending playgroups or nursery schools but were located with some difficulty and appeared to have poorer home circumstances than those attending pre-school. Not too much weight can be given to the evidence that they declined over a nine months period on two tests (EPVT and Reynell comprehension) while remaining the same on a third (Reynell expressive language). Initital differences between the groups also cloud findings (of a small study carried out by two students from Leeds University Institute of Education) that children from the West Riding nursery school groups progressed over a four months period on the Stanford Binet Intelligence Test while children from a similar area not at pre-school remained at much the same level.

More convincing evidence is provided by virtually the only British study to investigate the short-term effects of nursery-school attendance as such (Cohen and Bagshaw, 1973). Children attending nursery school were found to have made greater gains than children of similar social class staying at home on a test of language and conceptualisation (Communication subscale of the Gunzburg Progress Assessment Chart).

In the Dundee pre-school project, it was found that longer exposure to nursery school resulted in greater improvements in scores. This suggests that a longer period of attendance benefits cognitive functioning, for longer attendance is hardly likely to cause greater test familiarity or make much difference to rapport with adults (Harvey and Lee, 1974).

Long-term benefits

Does nursery-school attendance have any longer-term educational benefits? An earlier study (Douglas and Ross, 1964) of children in a nationally representative sample, who had spent at least two hours a day in nursery schools or classes when they were four years old, found that at eight years old they had higher scores on tests of intelligence and attainment than children of similar social class without nursery experience. This advantage was lost by the time the children were eleven years old but as they tended to have poorer home circumstances than the children who had not attended nursery, the results suggest that pre-schooling was beneficial.

Findings from the West Riding pre-school projects (Smith, 1975a and d) are compatible with these. In fact, they contain some of the strongest evidence for the educational benefits of nursery-school attendance. In the year following the pre-school programme, when the nursery-school children entered the reception classes of the two Denaby infant schools, gains continued to be made, some of the groups reaching scores above the age norms both on the EPVT and Reynell Language Scales. This is not altogether out of line with the American research, for gains by pre-school as well as direct entry children are quite commonly found initially after entry to (primary) school (Bronfenbrenner, 1974). What is unusual, though, is that the gains of the Denaby children were often larger that those they had made during the pre-school year. The usual pattern of decline against test norms began after this. Nevertheless even at the end of the third year at school, scores of the children who had attended nursery school were still higher than those of children reaching this same

373

stage at the same schools in 1969, three years earlier, and who were mainly without nursery experience (scores obtained as part of EPA testing programme).

Although the differences between nursery attenders and non-attenders are likely to be 'washed out' in the next year or two (they disappeared in the pilot group – which experienced pre-school only for ten weeks in the summer – by the fourth year at infant school) they seem to have been maintained better in the West Riding project than in most of the American studies. The gain in the reception year is particularly encouraging.

To what can the better-than-usual West Riding results be attributed? The author (Smith, 1975a) rejects test familiarity as the explanation for the higher score of the nursery-school children, compared with other groups who had attended the same schools, at the end of the nursery year. Test familiarity did not prevent the later decline in scores. He suggests that an important reason may have been that almost all the children in the reception classes had attended one of the pre-school groups. This meant that teachers were able to progress more rapidly through the year's work. Also the nursery classes (except one) were situated in the same schools as the infant classes. The approach of the teachers in the nursery and reception classes was similar. Additionally, these were the first children to attend nursery classes at the schools, and they were the subject of a special educational programme, both of which may have made them of special interest to all the teachers in the schools.

In a later paper (Smith and James, 1975) it is pointed out that the extent to which gains in the pre-school are built upon depends on the characteristics of the particular primary school. This point deserves further elaboration. It can be seen from the descriptive account of the schools in the area given in the report of the West Riding EPA project, (Smith, 1975d) that the school which maintained gains better was one which enjoyed stable staffing and a good relationship with the community. The other primary school had experienced persistent staffing difficulties, and the teachers were new to the school at the beginning of the project period. The better quality of Denaby schools, compared with American schools, could be the partial explanation for the better than usual outcome in the project as a whole. There is one additional explanation, not mentioned by the author. All children of the right age in the catchment area of the two Denaby infant schools were included in the project, and the sample is likely to be higher in social class than those of the American studies. The American work shows that it is higher-rather than lower-working-class children who benefit most from pre-school education (Bronfenbrenner, 1974).

It is a pity that the West Riding study does not give any indication of the educational attainments of the children who had attended nursery school. The NFER project, the only other study to investigate the later effects of nursery schooling, did administer tests of reading and mathematics when the children were in their second year at infant school but detailed findings have not yet been published. It does appear, though, that nursery-school attendance, whether or not there was also a special programme, gave no advantage on these skills (Woodhead, 1976). Does this mean that the West Riding findings should be discounted? Not necessarily. The NFER pre-school children were scattered in twenty-one infant schools in Slough and many others outside. A considerable proportion of the children in the infant classes are likely to have been without any pre-school experience. Comments from the West Riding reception class teachers emphasise the importance of all children in the class having had this experience. Where this was so they felt that could accelerate the pace of work, but even a few children without pre-school experience prevented this.

Findings from the West Riding study suggest that pre-school nursery attendance lays the foundations on which academic skills can be based. Whether this is capitalised on will depend on later experiences. The special circumstances of the project enabled them to be built on here to a rather greater extent that is usual. Some of the more recent American studies suggest that with continuing intervention in the primary school, the academic achievements of disadvantaged children can be improved, at least for a time.

3. Effectiveness of different types of pre-school intervention

Structured versus traditional programmes

The main objective of the British research has been to evaluate the effectiveness of various special educational programmes in the pre-school. There is evidence from the American work that, in general, 'structured' pre-school programmes, those in which there are specific cognitive and/or linguistic goals, the children's activities being carefully planned and directed by the teacher, are more successful than 'traditional' nursery school programmes, with their emphasis on free-play and child-directed activities (Bronfenbrenner, 1974). 'Structured' programmes differ considerably among themselves, though, not only in specific goals but in the extent to which the teacher plans her own programme within the general guidelines and applies it to the needs of the particular children in her group, rather than having to adopt certain set procedures, and use specified materials and equipment (see Weikart, 1972). It should be emphasised that the British studies are not concerned with evaluating 'total' programmes covering all the daily activities of the child, but with special programmes introduced into, for the most

375

part, pre-existing nursery schools, classes or playgroups run on traditional lines, and taking up only a relatively small part of the nursery day.

The two major evaluation studies, the National Pre-school Experiment in the Educational Priority Areas (Halsey, 1972a) and the NFER study (cited by Tizard, 1975; Woodhead, 1976) both assessed the effectiveness of the Peabody Language Development Kit. This is an American programme, structured in the sense that it sets particular learning goals which are reached by a set sequence of lessons, each worked out in considerable detail. The teaching methods are not as formal, though, as in some of the American programmes with set lessons. The aims are the improvement of vocabulary and grammar, and of the ability to use language in various cognitive tasks. The equipment is provided with the kit and includes puppets, picture cards, posters, records of stories, songs and various noises. In both studies, some modification of the kit was made for use with English children, this being more extensive in the NFER study. Children were removed in smallish groups (twelve to fifteen in the EPA project) from normal nursery activities for the lessons, which lasted from fifteen to twenty minutes, and of which there were 180 in all. Thus the language programme was separate from the rest of the daily routine, though attempts were made to reinforce the skills taught in the remainder of the day in the NFER study, and to varying extents in the EPA groups.

Did the addition of this special programme improve the children's verbal ability to a greater extent than was achieved with the traditional nursery programme alone? In the short-term, there did appear to be some advantage. In the EPA study, the experimental groups almost all improved on tests of language ability (EPVT and Reynell scales) over the school year, while scores of the control groups without a special language programme were more variable. Additionally, each experimental group, with two exceptions, showed a greater improvement on these tests than its control, a group of similar type (nursery school, class or playgroup) but without a special programme. The failure of the differences to reach statistical significance is attributed by Halsey (1972a) to the small number of children in the groups resulting from the loss of subjects. The NFER study provides stronger evidence of the short-time success of the Peabody Kit, the experimental Slough nursery-school children making greater gains than their controls on the language measure used (the Illinois Test of Psycholinguistic Abilities).

An attempt was made in the National Pre-school Experiment to find out whether it was the content of the special programme itself or simply the novelty of the new experience and the increased opportunity for teacher-child conversations which accounted for the additional improvements in language ability. This was achieved by comparing the language attainments of children in the Birmingham Peabody groups with those of children in the same types of pre-school in the area who had experienced another carefully designed special programme. In this case, though, the objective of the programme was the teaching of number conservation rather than language skills. Generally, it was found that the Peabody groups progressed more than the number conservation groups on the language measures but the gap was much less marked than that between the Peabody groups and those without any special programme. This suggests that the gains attained with the Peabody are partly due to the content of the programme but that novelty, increased teacher-child interactions, and the familiarity a programme gives the child with a test-type situation, also play a part. For programmes necessitate co-operation with an adult in an individual or small group situation, concentration on a particular adult-chosen task and following of detailed instructions required in a test (Woodhead, 1976).

Evidence that children do appear to make the greatest gains on the skills the programme is designed to teach suggest that more has been acquired than better test-taking techniques (Woodhead, 1976). The Birmingham groups involved in the number conservation programme made considerably greater progress over the year on specially constructed number concept tests than the Peabody and control groups in the National Pre-school Experiment, who virtually did not change at all. Language programmes with rather different aims and approaches may also have different effects. In the West Riding EPA project (Smith, 1975a) comparison was made of the effects of the Peabody with another structured-language programme with a very different approach. The objectives were as clearly laid out as in the Peabody programme but emphasised the conceptual use of language rather than grammatical deficiencies. An individual tutoring method was used (adapted from that developed by Marian Blank–Blank and Solomon, 1968) allowing the material to be adapted to the child's level and the teacher to help him to bring him existing skills and knowledge to bear on a new problem. The main advantage of both the special language programme groups over the traditional nursery groups was on the Reynell Expressive Language scale, but the programme differentially affected the subscale scores. The Peabody group made the largest gains on the vocabulary section while the strength of the individual tutoring group lay in language complexity (likely to be encouraged by emphasis on language use) and descriptive content. Similarly, in an American study (Karnes, 1973) the magnitude of gains on subtests of the Illinois Test of Psycholinguistic Abilities made by children in two different structured programmes appeared to be related to the particular kinds of linguistic experience provided by these programmes.

'Structured' programmes or 'structure' for teachers?

Can it be concluded that the addition of an intensive teacher-directed programme with clearly defined cognitive or linguistic goals produces greater development for the child than the traditional nursery regime alone? The situation appears to be rather more complicated than this. In a number of instances, the more structured programme was no more effective than the traditional nursery. In one of the West Riding groups, the teacher thought the Peabody Kit an insult to the experienced teacher and used it in an offhand manner. The progress of this group was almost identical to that of the traditional nursery group. Programmed kits are not teacher-proof, as Weikart (1972) suggested they are. The Birmingham part-time nursery class control group actually showed greater improvement that the experimental part-time nursery class on two of the language measures. This case does not appear to be one of failure for the Peabody Kit but rather of success for a high-quality nursery which put particular emphasis on the development of language in the course of its ordinary activities.

Where teachers are committed to certain objectives and have sufficient skill perhaps special programmes are unnecessary? An American study (Weikart, 1972) compared the progress of disadvantaged children in two groups having structured programmes, but different approaches, and a third which had a traditional programme. The unusual feature was that in all three groups there were clearly defined weekly goals, teachers in each group planning on a daily basis the means of implementing the goals of their own programme. Over the first two years of the project all three groups made comparable, and very large, gains on several intelligence tests. However, in the third year, the children in the traditional group dropped behind those in the structured groups in intelligence test performance. During the second year, the teachers of the traditional group began to feel that there was less interest in their programme and their planning began to decline. Weikart concludes that the 'structure' of a programme is necessary for the teacher, not the child. A curriculum is necessary to help her in the translation of theoretical objectives into actual activities which will help the child to learn.

The experiences of the London EPA pre-school project (Stevenson, 1975) also suggest that a general objective, such as language development, and the intention to increase verbal interaction with the children is not sufficient. Apart from some additional gains in verbal comprehension (Reynell) the experimental children's progress on measures of language ability was no greater than those of children in the non-experimental nursery school classes. The programme did result in organisational changes in the classroom, in that the experimental teachers spent more time with the children, but this did not result in more one-to-one verbal interaction with them. It would seem that more definite cognitive and linguistic objectives and more detailed planning of how these can be brought about is necessary for the majority of teachers if children's language is to develop more than it does in the ordinary nursery.

Findings of a recent investigation of staff behaviour and linguistic development in nursery schools with different degrees of educational orientation (Tizard *et al.*, 1976) are in line with the above conclusion. Observation of staff behaviour showed that during their ordinary activities with the children, 'cognitive content' (time spent in helping the children to learn non-disciplinary behaviour) was greater in the most educationally oriented nursery schools than in the others. These educationally oriented nursery schools included a special language session daily, individually devised by the head, and aimed at developing such concepts as space, size, classification and number. Language scores of the working-class children in these centres (Reynell scales) were significantly higher that those of the working-class children attending the less educationally oriented centres; for middle-class children, attendance at the most educationally oriented centres made no significant difference. It is particularly important to note that none of the children tested had yet taken part in the special language programmes. It seems that the presence of the programme was able to influence the behaviour of the staff throughout their daily activities. This influence appeared to be of greater consequence for the working-class children. 'Cognitive' staff behaviour occurred less often in working-class nursery schools with no special programme than in similar middle-class schools. But there was more staff behaviour with a cognitive content in the working-class nursery schools which had a special programme than in middle-class schools without a programme.

These findings suggest that it is teacher behaviour rather than a detailed, intensive programme which promotes cognitive and linguistic development in disadvantaged children. However, more is necessary than a general orientation towards these objectives. The most skilful teachers may be able to work out their own activities but the less skilful or experienced need guidance on what the children should learn and on the activities likely to promote this end.

Long-term effects of special pre-school programmes

It has already been seen that the benefits of nursery school as such appeared to be retained in the first year of the infant schools in the West Riding, but not in Slough, and some explanations for the difference have been suggested. Children who had been in nursery groups with special educational programmes in the West Riding did not make greater gains than those from the ordinary nursery groups during the reception year, but they did appear to retain the gains previously made. In the next two years in the infant school, all the former nursery groups made a similar gradual decline in relation to the test norms (Smith and James, 1975).

The NFER study failed to find any advantage in academic attainments in the second year of infant school that could be attributed to the special programme. Children from the experimental groups performed no better on tests of reading and mathematics than children without any pre-school experience at all. Some of the American experimental research programmes have less depressing findings than these. Children who have been in structured pre-school programmes are found to have some advantage in academic attainments over children without any pre-school experience in the first school years, though this a generally diminishing from the second year (grade) (Gray and Klaus, 1970; Gray, 1974; Weikart et al., 1974). There is also some evidence of a significant advantage, continuing into the third year (grade) for those who have attended a pre-school with a structured programme compared with those who were at a pre-school with a traditional programme (Karnes, 1973; Karnes et al., 1974).

However, the American findings on the long-term effects of different kinds of pre-school programme re-affirm that it is over-simple to conclude that the most 'structured' are the most beneficial. They also show that programmes with the greatest immediate impact do not necessarily give the most advantage in the longer term.

In a recent comparative study, children in the two most highly structured programmes, the Bereiter-Engelmann (1966) and DAR (Gray and Klaus, 1970) made greater progress on numerical and linguistic skills in the pre-kindergarten years than children in the less structured Montessori or in the traditional nursery programmes, the Bereiter-Engelmann children also making most advance in intelligence test scores (Miller and Dyer, 1975). By the end of the second grade, though, the children from the Montessori programme had higher reading achievements than children in any other group, and they were also higher than the Bereiter-Engelmann children in intelligence test scores. The Montessori porgramme is less structured than the Bereiter-Engelmann or DAR programmes in that teachers do not maintain such rigid control over the actions of the children, children being allowed to choose their own activities and teaching being individualised. The materials are carefully prepared, though, so that children can learn certain specific concepts through their use.

Rather similarly, Karnes (1973) found in her comparative study that children in the two most highly structured programmes, one of which was a Bereiter-Engelmann programme while the other had been developed by Karnes, were superior to Montessori and traditional pre-school groups in intellectual functioning, language and school readiness skills at the end of the pre-kindergarten and kindergarten years. At the end of the first and second school years (grades) they were significantly superior to children from the traditional pre-school group (the Montessori follow-up could not be continued) in reading achievements. By the end of the third grade, though, the position had changed, intelligence test score differences between the groups having disappeared and only the children who had attended the Karnes pre-school group being significantly superior to the traditional pre-school children in reading achievement.

Karnes suggests that the greater emphasis on divergent responses and learning transfer in her programme may be responsible for its longer-term success. This is carefully sequenced towards particular objectives, the teacher having a high degree of control over the children's activities, but teaching takes place during the playing of various games rather than more formally. It is interesting that the Bereiter-Engelmann programme, in which there is intensive teaching to small groups of children, predominantly by means of verbal drills, was found to be associated with a decrease in inventiveness during the pre-school year in the Miller and Dyer (1975) study. This effect was still evident, though diminishing, at the end of the second year at school. The Montessori, which appeared to increase in academic benefit to the children, was associated with high scores in inventiveness both at the end of the pre-kindergarten and second school years. To evaluate the effectiveness of a pre-school programme, it may be necessary to look more widely beyond its immediate effects on IQ scores and academic type skills.

It should also be noted that one feature common to almost all the American programmes which have produced some benefits, is an emphasis on parental involvement, including in two of the projects (Gray, 1974; Weikart et al., 1974) home visits during the period of the pre-school intervention. Evidence from one study (Radin, 1972b) suggests that parental involvement in conjunction with a pre-school programme may not produce any immediate benefits but it may enhance the effects of subsequent schooling. The influence of parental involvement will be discussed in greater detail below.

4. Sustained intervention

Only the West Riding, of the British studies, has attempted to see if additional intervention in the primary school is more effective than pre-school intervention alone (Smith, 1975a and 1975c). Children in the reception class of one of the infant schools were matched in pairs on verbal ability (EPVT) and one member of each group was randomly allocated to the experimental group, which received short sessions of individual tutoring daily, while the other child was allocated to the controls. The experimental group again made larger gains, significantly so on the EPVT and Reynell comprehension scale. Again, too, these began to disappear, the groups having almost identical scores two years after the programme ended.

American studies have found that additional gains in intelligence test scores and larger gains in achievement are possible when intervention is extended into the first two years at school (Bissell, 1973; Bronfenbrenner 1974; Sprigle, 1974). Larger gains have been found in the kindergarten and first school year for children in Follow Through classes, the government-sponsored school intervention programme, than in children attending conventional classes. Children who had previously attended Head Start nurseries also made greater gains than those without Head Start experience.

The evaluations of the effects of the American Follow Through programmes that have been made so far (Bissell, 1973; Bronfenbrenner, 1974; Stallings, 1975) raise again the question of the most appropriate type of teaching methods for disadvantaged children. There seems little doubt that children in the kindergarten and primary school grades (five to nine year olds) make larger gains on tests of reading and mathematics achievement when they have been in more structured classrooms, in which there is more instruction, and more time devoted to the development of academic skills.

However, as Almy (1975) points out, caution is necessary before concluding that it is the more structured programme which best develops the academic skills of the disadvantaged child. The teaching programmes in such classes may be geared to the kinds of problem presented in the achievement tests. Children who have experienced a more flexible classroom which provides a wider variety of materials and activities and allows the child some choice may have strengths which are not reflected in scores on achievement tests in the early school years.

Indeed, the evidence shows that children in the more flexible Follow Through classes make greater gains on a test of non-verbal reasoning (Raven's Progressive Matrices) (Stallings, 1975). They also show more independence, co-operation and initiative in this type of classroom, although perhaps this is simply because they have more opportunities to do so (Resnick and Leinhardt, 1975). More flexible classrooms were also found to be associated, though, with fewer days' absence from school, an important indicator of attitudes to school. Other evaluations of Follow Through have also found more favourable changes in attitudes to school and learning among children who have been in less structured programmes (Bissel, 1973; Bronfenbrenner, 1974).

These findings again warn then against taking too hasty or narrow a view of the effectiveness of particular types of programmes. Perhaps a combination of clearly defined and detailed enough objectives together with a measure of freedom of activity for the child will provide the best long-term results. Much further experimentation and evaluation seems necessary here.

However, it appears unlikely that even an optimal educational intervention programme can, on its own, be sufficient for the most educationally disadvantaged children. In Herzog's (1974) intervention programme, two years of a traditional nursery pre-school was followed by three years with what appears to have been a structured but flexible programme. At the beginning of the fourth school year (grade) after one year in ordinary classes, only half of the lower-social-class children (those at the bottom of the social scale in terms of mother's education and over-crowding) had reached grade level (the level expected by teachers at this stage). It is hardly comforting, as Herzog and her colleagues point out, that an even greater proportion (two thirds) of control children, similar in social levels, were in this position.

In the study by Deutsch et al. (1974) the experimental children, who seem to have been particularly economically disadvantaged, were provided with a special curriculum tailored to fit individual needs from the pre-school years. Nevertheless, this did not enable them to do better academically than the original controls in the second year at school, while the intervention was still in progress. Intervention programmes make some difference to children with multiple social problems stacked against them, but, as Herzog and her colleagues say, without changes in social conditions outside school, it is hard to see that they can be maintained, except for a very few.

5. Parental involvement

Home-based intervention

Growing realisation that pre-school occupies only a very small proportion of the child's life, and that far too much had been expected from it, has led to an increasing emphasis on the parent's influence on the child's educational performance. If it is differences in the stimulation provided by the environment, particularly in the emphasis that is placed on verbal interaction with the child, which is responsible for the social-class differential in intelligence test performance already found in three-year-olds, then changes in parental behaviour could lead to longer-lasting effects in the child. Most of the experimental pre-school research carried out in the United States has incorporated an element of parental involvement in the design. Most held meetings to explain the purpose of the project, and tried to help parents to see the contribution they could make to the child's education. Some included home visits, either as a link between summer pre-school programmes (Gray and Klaus, 1970) or in addition to the pre-school (Weikart *et al.* 1974). In a few studies, though, home-based intervention has not been supplementary to the pre-school but the main approach.

It is clear that this strategy can produce large initial gains (Karnes *et al.*, 1970; Levenstein and Sunley, 1968; Levenstein, 1970). Are they better maintained, though, than the short-term gains made in the pre-school? There is no definitive answer available from research yet, but a detailed review by Bronfenbrenner (1974) brings out a number of important points. This type of intervention produces large gains in intelligence test scores when it occurs early, particularly when it begins before the child is three years old. It is also most effective, in terms of showing a smaller decrease when the intervention has ended, if the mother herself (or other caretaker), not a tutor, is the main agent of intervention. Working together on a common task, Bronfenbrenner suggests, strengthens the relationship between mother and infant, making each more responsive to the other. This means that the mother gears activities to the child's level and needs, and the child attends to what she is doing. Nevertheless, in the only study in which there are long-term findings (Levenstein, cited by Bronfenbrenner, 1974) no advantage was found from early home-based intervention in terms of academic achievement in the first school year, though intelligence test gains were maintained.

So far, only two British studies, one in Renfrewshire (Donachy, 1976) and the other carried out as part of the West Riding EPA project (Smith, 1975b) have evaluated parent intervention schemes. The approach adopted was rather different in the two studies. In the West Riding study, the children, who were eighteen months to two years old at the beginning, were visited in their homes over a period of almost a year. Usually, three kinds of games were brought on each visit, one to develop fine motor skills, one to test knowledge of colour, shape and size, and the third a book to assist in language, memory and perception. The mother was encouraged to work with the child as far as she was willing to do so. Where a toy or game had been particularly enjoyed, or where it needed further practice, it was left for use during the week.

In the Scottish study, mothers of three- and four-year-olds were asked to attend meetings at the child's future infant school with three of the infant teachers (or, in one group, with teachers at the nursery the child was attending) over a period of four months. The mothers selected a book to read at home with the child, and were given a programme dealing with vocabulary and simple concepts such as colour, size and space to be administered at home for thirty minutes each day.

In both the studies the experimental children gained significantly more than the controls in cognitive and linguistic skills (Merrill-Palmer, West Riding; Stanford Binet and Reynell Language scales, Renfrewshire). In the West Riding the intervention appeared to have had some effect on the mother-child relationship although not on the 'objective' environment (toys, books, organisation of the home). All mothers increased over the year the use of physical and verbal punishment, but this occurred to a lesser extent in the experimental mothers. Comments from parents showed that they now felt that they had a role to play in the child's education, a feeling that this and other studies (Hubbard, cited by Tizard, 1975) have found is often lacking in working-class parents.

There are no long-term follow-ups in British studies and no reason to think that this is the magic solution to the problems of educational disadvantage from the American experience. In any case, there appear to be considerable limitations to the use of home-based intervention as an alternative rather than as complementary to a pre-school programme. The West Riding children were predominantly from a skilled working-class background and although, in a sense, all working-class children are educationally disadvantaged, in that they tend to have somewhat poorer attainment and ability scores than middle-class children, this can be attributed to motivational and educational 'know-how' factors. It is the children at the bottom of the social scale who appear to be unable to use the abilities they possess in school, or who, in some cases, are perhaps somewhat slower than usual in the development of abilities (see section D) with whom the problem lies. It is precisely in the families of these children that there are difficulties in implementing a home-based intervention programme. Bronfenbrenner's review shows that where the mother is employed all the time, where she has poor home amenities or several young children to care for, she will not have the time or energy to go to a weekly meeting or even to attend to a home visitor. In such situations, practical help with social problems, and educationally oriented day care appear to be the predominant needs.

Parental involvement as a complement to pre-school education

This is not to say that every effort should not be made to involve the parents as far as possible in their children's education. Educationally oriented day care or nursery school may relieve the burden on some disadvantaged parents to the extent that they have more time for the child at home. For them, and for less disadvantaged parents, it may be possible to suggest some specific activities to be carried out at home. One American study found that home intervention carried on alongside pre-school education did not cause immediate gains in intelligence test scores to be greater but the parents did provide more educational materials at home and become less authoritarian (Radin, 1972b). In the subsequent year, children in the parent intervention group made greater gains than those with only pre-school experience.

385

In one of the West Riding pre-school studies (Smith, 1975e), parents were encouraged to take part in activities with groups of children, much time was spent by teachers in discussing the value of play activities and of how parents could help their children's language development, and teachers visited the homes regularly. The project was not planned to evaluate the effects of 'parental involvement' as such, but the high degree of parental interest could account for the large gains made by the 'control' group, especially in language comprehension, and for the fact that the 'experimental' group, similar in character except that it included 'individual tutoring' sessions, did little better. Not all parents can be involved to this extent but pre-school does provide innumerable opportunities for teachers to encourage parents to see the importance of their role. The essential is that teachers are aware of the need to do this.

Parental involvement in the primary school

The need for parental involvement does not stop, of course, once the child reaches the primary school stage. All the EPA projects made intensive efforts to get to know the parents of primary-school children and to explain to them what the schools were trying to achieve. The means included visits to the home by specially appointed home-school liaison teachers, publicity campaigns and attempts to bring parents into the schools. The London and Liverpool projects put most emphasis on getting parents to come to the school and from the reports (Halsey, 1972b; Midwinter, 1972) appear to have been reasonably successful. Response from parents to invitations to observe, and eventually participate in, classroom activities was enthusiastic in Liverpool, sometimes every child having a relative attend. Weekly evening meetings devoted to leisure activities attracted quite large numbers of parents and children in Deptford. Liverpool made a beginning with child-parent projects with local environment themes. No attempts were made to evaluate the effects of parental involvement on the children's attainments.

To see if bringing working-class parents into greater contact with the work of the school has favourable effects on children's academic achievements, there are two studies to turn to. The British research (Young and McGeeny, 1968) was a case study of one primary school in which four methods were used to bring about greater parental involvement: an open meeting for all parents early in the school year, private talks between parents and class teachers, meetings on teaching methods and home visits for some parents who had not taken the opportunities provided for coming to the school. While some improvements were made in relation to the age norms of standardised tests of intelligence and attainment which did not appear (by comparison with two other schools) to be entirely attributable to test familiarity, teacher enthusiasm rather than parental involvement cannot be ruled out as the cause. However, children whose parents had attended the meeting on reading methods did significantly better than those whose parents did not come. Interviews with some of these parents (and some who had attended meetings on arithmetic teaching) suggested that this was not only due to prior attitudes but that some changes had also been brought about. These often took the form of actively helping the child with his school work at home, but sometimes of putting less pressure on the child.

An American study (Smith, cited by Bronfenbrenner, 1974) in which socially disadvantaged parents were encouraged to support, but not actively teach, the child with his work, particularly reading, found significant gains in the reading achievement of seven- and eleven-year-olds, both in relation to norms and a control group.

The sparse evidence available does indicate that giving parents greater understanding of what the school is trying to do enhances the children's achievements. Attempts at parental involvement do carry a danger which these two studies appear to have avoided. While there is an enormous advantage in being able to discuss what he is doing with parents who have some understanding of the subject, and being able to turn to them when in difficulties, such parents may interfere too much with the child's work, not allow him to do anything on his own. This too may have detrimental effects on achievement and achievement motivation (Busse, 1969; Crandall, et al., 1964; Hermans et al., 1972; Solomon et al., 1971 – see Part III, The father's role). While the need for greater parental involvement is undoubtedly primary in the case of socially disadvantaged children, the child's need for autonomy must not be overlooked.

6. Postscript

How widespread is educational disadvantage?

It is clear from the work reviewed that there are some children who are severely handicapped educationally by a multiplication of social, cultural and health disadvantages, probably including an insufficiency of certain uses of language in the home, poor and overcrowded accommodation and an above average frequency of illness. However, it is a mistake to see educational disadvantage as being solely concentrated in an extreme group with an accumulation of problems. Not only do working-class children have parents who tend to know less about how to help them educationally, and who do not have the expectation of success of the middle-class but they, especially those from the unskilled, working-class, are much more likely to suffer from one or more of the material adversities associated with educational retardation.

Recent research has shown that the low average achievement scores of children from the semi- and unskilled, working classes, compared with those from the middle class are not solely due to a minority of children performing badly. When they were eleven years old, 52 per cent of the unskilled, working-class children in the National Child Development Study had low reading comprehension scores compared with 12 per cent of children from a professional or managerial background (Davie, 1973). West Riding second and third year juniors attending Educational Priority Area schools (in which a high proportion of children have one or more of the social characteristics associated with educational disadvantage) were, on average, almost six points behind juniors from the area attending non-EPA schools in English, even after the poorest readers (of which there were more in the EPA schools) had been excluded (Smith, 1975d).

This review has not been concerned with the many working-class children who do well at school in the early years. Twelve per cent of the eleven-year-olds from the unskilled working class, and 18 per cent from the semi-skilled, working-class, were found to have high reading comprehension scores in the National Child Development Study (Davie, 1973). The proportion of children in the middle score range was similar in all social classes. Of course, the lower working-class children who do well at school are more likely to be those who are relatively advantaged, both culturally and materially. Not all children do badly, though, even when their families suffer from severe material difficulties. In the study of socially disadvantaged children(living in one-parent or large families, with low income and poor housing) carried out by the National Children's Bureau (Wedge and Prosser, 1973) one in seven had better than average scores in reading, and the same was true in maths.

It should not be forgotten, though, that even working-class children who are doing well up to the end of the primary school years are very often prevented by social and material factors from making the best use of their abilities. Douglas' (Douglas *et al.*, 1968) national survey showed that even among children selected for grammar schools, the achievement scores of the manual working-class and middle-class children drew apart between the ages of eleven and fifteen. In the Robins' Report (Committee on Higher Education 1963), it was found that only 21 per cent of the semi- and unskilled working-class grammar school children graded in the top ability range at 11 + achieved two A levels, compared with 57 per cent of similar ability children from the professional and managerial classes. This was largely due to the much much higher proportion of lower manual working-class children leaving shcool before the age of eighteen, 77 per cent compared with 45 per cent of the upper middle-class children. Entering the sixth form has at least as much connection with social class as with school attainment (Ainsworth and Batten, 1974; Douglas *et al.*, 1968).

Can schools combat educational disadvantage?

To return to those working-class children who are the subject of this review, those who do badly at school, it is obviously completely unrealistic from the research reviewed to expect schools to overcome the effects of adverse material circumstances on their own. Do schools have any role to play, then? Several studies have found that the school environment makes very little difference to school achievement (Ainsworth and Batten, 1974; Barnes and Lucas, 1975; Coleman, 1966). However, these findings do not necessarily have to be interpreted to mean that schools are incapable of having any effect.

The primary school intervention research, particularly Stallings's (1975) recent study, suggests that classroom practices can have considerable effect on a child's educational attainments and attitudes. Stallings found that by the end of the third year at primary school (by the time the children were aged about ten) achievements in mathematics and reading, performance on a non-verbal reasoning test and school absence were at least as affected by classroom programmes as initial ability. At the secondary-school level, the Manchester study (Ainsworth and Batten, 1974) found that teacher qualifications had an increasing impact on attainment, particularly as the pupils' grew older, that was independent of 11 + ability. However, at least while a selective secondary school system was still in operation this study found that the lower the initial ability of the pupil intake, the worse the school environment in terms both of staff training and facilities.

It is unlikely that curriculum experimentation, better trained teachers and improved facilities throughout the educational system, from the pre-school to the secondary shool stage, would not improve the attainments of many socially disadvantaged children. Without an attack also on the social inequalities that give rise to disadvantages throughout the children's school careers, the effect on their lives, though, is likely, in most cases, to be limited.

Annotations

(Only British intervention studies have been annotated in this section)
COHEN, L. and BAGSHAW, D. 1973. 'A comparison of the achievements of nursery and non-nursery school children', *Durham Research Review* 6, 30, 735–42.

Twenty-eight three- to four-year-old children attending nursery school, some from relatively advantaged and others from relatively disadvantaged backgrounds, were matched with twenty-two non-nursery school children, similar in socio-economic background. At pre-testing, the two groups had similar scores on each section of the Gunzburg Progress Assessment Chart (PAC 1). On post-testing one year later, all the groups had made highly significant gains in their total scores on the PAC 1 but the gains of the experimental and control groups were similar. However, on the Communication sub-scale (concerned with language and conceptualisation) the gains of the experimental children were significantly larger than those of the controls. The gain of the middle-class experimental children was also significantly larger than that of the middle-class controls on this sub-scale but the difference between the two working-class groups was not significant although the trend was in a similar direction.

DONACHY, W. 1976. 'Parent participation in pre-school education', *British Journal of Educational Psychology* 46, 1, 31–9.

An investigation of the effects of a home-based intervention programme on three- and four-year-old children living in Renfrewshire. Mothers attended a weekly group meeting with some of the teachers at either the child's future infant school or his present nursery school. On each visit, mothers selected a book to be read at home with the child. They were also provided with a programme dealing with vocabulary, number, and relationships of time, space and size, to be administered at home for thirty minutes a day. Children taking part in the parent intervention programme made significant gains over a four months period in scores on the Stanford Binet Intelligence test and the Reynell Developmental Language Scales. Four-year-olds attending nursery school, but not receiving home-based intervention, made significant gains on the Stanford Binet but not on the Reynell Scales. Matched controls, living in a separate town, and receiving no form of pre-school intervention, failed to make gains on either measure. Similar gains were made by the middle-class (Social classes II and III) and working-class (Social classes IV and V) children taking part in the home intervention programme.

HALSEY, A. H. 1972a. 'The national pre-school experiment' in A. H. Halsey (ed) *Educational Priority, Vol. I: EPA Problems and Policies*, HMSO, London. 86–100.

The American programme, the Peabody Language Development Kit (PLDK) modified to some extent for use with British children, was introduced, for a one year experimental period, into seven nursery classes and playgroups in three of the areas – Birmingham, West Riding and Liverpool – in which the educational priority project was carried out. Evaluation was made by comparing the progress of the experimental children with that of children attending similar types of pre-school groups in which there was no special educational programme on two tests of language ability, the English Picture Vocabulary Test (EPVT) and the Reynell Developmental Language Scales (RDLS). Overall, the experimental and the control groups did not differ in the quality of equipment, environment, work or staff, but there was some tendency for the experimental children to come from a more favourable home background (fathers with rather higher occupational status, better housing, fewer from immigrant families).

Generally, the scores of the experimental groups improved on the tests over the year, while in some of the control groups scores rose and in others they fell. Generally, the scores of the PLDK groups improved more on the tests than did their controls (though only one difference was statistically significant due to the small number of children involved). However, the Birmingham part-time nursery control, which was of very high quality and which emphasised language development in its normal routine, improved slightly more than the PLDK group on the EPVT and the Expressive Language scale of the Reynell. This suggests that when there is already very good work in progress, the PLDK can add little.

Compared with three groups of similar type (a playgroup, a part-time nursery and a full-time nursery) in which a number concept programme has been introduced, the Birmingham PLDK groups made slightly greater improvement on the language tests, but the difference was smaller than that between the PLDK groups and the controls. This suggests that novelty and the increased teacher-child communication of the experimental programme account for part of the gains made by the PLDK groups but that the programme itself made an independent contribution.

Language development of seventeen Liverpool children not attending nursery school or playgroup deteriorated markedly over a nine-months period on the EPVT and the Verbal Comprehension scale of the Reynell. Too much emphasis should not be placed on this finding because these children appeared to come from a poorer social environment than those attending pre-school.

HARVEY, S. and LEE, T. R. 1974. 'An experimental study of educational compensation', in Morrison, C. M. (ed) *Educational Priority, Vol 5 : A Scottish Study*, HMSO, London. 124–68.

In the Dundee project, a pre-school programme for three- to five-year-old British children was specially developed. This consisted of a series of 'Themes', each concentrating on one particular aspect of the child's cognitive development. 'Themes' lasted about a week and each day the

391

theme was dealt with from one viewpoint in a 'playsem', an activity period lasting from twenty to eighty minutes.

In the original design, children from three nursery schools and a nursery class formed the experimental and proximal control groups. In each school, children were pre-tested and matched in pairs on date of entry to primary school, full- or part-time attendance at nursery school, sex and initial ability (on the English Picture Vocabulary Test). One child from each pair was randomly allocated to the experimental group and one to the control. A distal control group, which would be free from contamination by the programme, was formed by matching children from a nursery school, a nursery class and three playgroups on the same variables. Substantial loss of subjects during the experiment (about 200 out of over 500) meant that departures had to be made from the original matched-triple design, and alternative methods of analysis used.

Post-test scores (on entry to primary school or at the end of the project) showed differences in favour of the experimental group on five out of seven tests (EPVT, four non-verbal and one verbal sub-tests of the Wechsler Pre-school and Primary Scale of Intelligence, and the Wug Test, a test of English morphology), three comparisons with the distal control group reaching statistical significance. The experimental group also tended to make larger pre-test/post-test improvements although only one difference was statistically significant (with the distal control group on the Block Design of the W.PP.S.1). Comparison of progress made between the remaining matched pairs from the experimental and distal control groups showed slightly greater improvements in favour of the experimental children.

A notable finding was that all the nursery children improved about ten points on the EPVT, and a comparable amount on the other tests, bringing their scores from significantly below the national average to appreciably above. This improvement was greater for those who had entered at an early age or spent a longer period in the nursery school.

SMITH, G. 1975a. 'Pre-school: the main experiment' in G. Smith (ed) *Educational Priority, Vol 4: The West Riding Project*, HMSO, London. 97–120.

This research was designed to examine the effects of different forms of pre-school programme. Three types of programme were compared:
i) a 'traditional' nursery programme, ii) a nursery programme into which the Peabody Language Development Kit was inserted for fifteen to twenty minutes a day, iii) a nursery programme in which individual language tuition was provided for each child for fifteen to twenty minutes a day.

Both special programmes were concerned with language development, but the individual programme viewed language difficulties as primarily cognitive and motivational. Emphasis was placed on encouraging the child to generalise from what he already knew to new situations, and on developing appreciation of the functions that language can serve. The Peabody Kit, in contrast, places strong emphasis on 'drilling' children into 'correct' grammatical usage.

Pre-school provision was made for all the three- to four-year-olds in the catchment areas of two Denaby primary schools. In each school a traditional and a Peabody nursery class was set up. One of these classes ran in the mornings, the other in the afternoons, each having the same room and the same teaching staff. In one of the school areas only, a third nursery class, with the individual tutoring programme, was set up. This class was run on separate premises by the project team. Within each area, children were randomly allocated to the two or three groups.

In the area with the three nursery groups, all made similar small gains on the English Picture Vocabulary Test and larger ones on the Reynell Language Comprehension scale over the nursery year. On the Reynell Expressive Language Scale the two intervention groups made larger gains than the traditional nursery children, the Peabody group making the largest gain on the vocabulary section, and the individual group on language complexity. All the nursery groups moved nearer to the test 'norms' on the EPVT and the Renyell Comprehension, but the traditional group declined on the Reynell Expressive while the intervention groups gained. In the catchment area with only two nursery classes, there were no significant differences in gains on any test or sub-test between the intervention and traditional groups. Only on the Reynell Expressive Scale, in which the Peabody group remained at the same level while the traditional group fell back (but not significantly) is there any evidence of influence of the intervention programme. A possible explanation for the lack of effectiveness of the Peabody Kit here is the teacher's hostility to its use.

During the reception year in school, all groups continued to make gains, ending slightly above the age norms on most measures, the differences between the groups having disappeared. Compared with children at the same schools who had not attended nursery school, tested two years earlier as part of the EPA research, the nursery groups were well ahead at the end of the reception year. Their advantage remained, though it was declining, at the end of the third year in school.

SMITH, G. 1975b. 'Pre-school: the home visiting project' in G. Smith (ed) *Educational Priority, Vol 4: The West Riding Project*, HMSO, London. 135–66.

This project covered twenty children, aged between eighteen and twenty-seven months at its commencement, and living in the catchment area of a single school. A control group of children, living in a similar mining community some distance away, was formed, matched for age, sex and father's occupation.

The experimental children were visited every week for a period of one to two hours. Three different toys or games were presented each visit, one to develop fine motor skills, one to test knowledge of colour, shape and size and a book to encourage language, perception and memory. Toys and activities were presented one at a time, the child having to complete one activity before going on to the next. Suggestions were made to the child about how he might carry out an activity but he was encouraged to try out his own ideas. Mothers were asked to take part in the work and their interests and ideas were incorporated into the activities.

At the pre-testing, after the programme had begun at the beginning of 1971, the experimental and control groups had very similar scores on Merrill Palmer mental tests. Nine months later, on post-testing, the experimental group had made substantial gains and was about four months ahead of the control group in terms of mental age. A further home visiting programme was carried out after the post-testing until the autumn of 1972. At the second post-testing, after the completion of this programme and about fourteen months after the first post-test, both groups had substantially increased their scores but the experimental group was still about six standard points higher.

Few changes were found in the 'objective' home environment in either group over the first year of the project, although the experimental group was rated better on 'visual material in the home' at the post-test. In both groups, the mothers increased in use of verbal and physical punishment over the year but the trend was less pronounced in the experimental group.

SMITH, G. 1975c. 'Reception class: the individual language follow-up programme, 1970–1' in G. Smith (ed) *Educational Priority, Vol 4 : The West Riding Project*, HMSO, London (Section iii in Chapter 'Pre-school-primary school: further developments'). 175–83.

This project was set up to see whether gains made at pre-school could be maintained by continuing intervention into the school years. It was carried out in one of the Denaby schools that had taken part in the West Riding pre-school project (see Smith, 1975a). Children in the reception classes, almost all of whom had attended one of the pre-school groups, were paired on the basis of their score on the English Picture Vocabulary Test. One child from each pair was randomly allocated to the intervention group and one to the normal school programme, giving two groups both containing twenty children. The intervention consisted of individual language tutoring for ten to fifteen minutes a day. The individual group made larger gains on all three of the language scales used, the difference between the groups being statistically significant in the case of the EPVT and Reynell Comprehension Scale but not on the Reynell Expressive.

STEVENSON, J. 1975. 'The nursery school language work', in J. Barnes (ed) *Educational Priority, Vol 3: Curriculum Innovation in London's EPAs*, HMSO, London. 69–98.

An account of the London Pre-school Language Project, which aimed to accelerate language development, not by the introduction of a special programme, but by changing the verbal behaviour of teachers. The tacit assumption was that more frequent one-to-one conversation with the children would help their language development. Subjects were ten children from each of three classes in a Deptford nursery school, a further ten children from these classes being chosen to act as within-class controls. Ten children from each of the three other classes in the nursery school were chosen as controls. All children in the sample were randomly selected from those who were likely to remain at the nursery school throughout 1970–1. Children were similarly selected from the morning session of a playgroup in the area as experimental subjects and within-group controls, and from the afternoon session as controls. Children were pre-tested in September on the English Picture Vocabulary Scale (EPVT) and the Reynell Developmental Language Scales (RDLS) and post-tested in July 1971, or because the drop-out rate was so high, on leaving if this occurred in the second half of the spring term or later.

Generally, all the groups scored below the national average on the pre-tests and showed gains against the national norms on the post-tests, suggesting a beneficial effect for pre-school attendance. The experimental programme itself appeared to produce little additional beneficial effect, except perhaps on Verbal Comprehension (Reynell). Classroom observations during the spring term showed that the experimental teachers were available to the children more often than the control teachers. The experimental nursery assistants took over more administrative duties to release the teachers for interaction with the children. However, the experimental teachers were not involved in verbal one-to-one interactions more often than the control teachers. The experimental children were involved in verbal behaviour more than the control children, but they themselves initiated a smaller proportion of total interactions.

References

(When a title is annotated this is indicated at the end of an entry by the relevant page number printed in bold type.)

ADAMS, B., GHODSIAN, M. and RICHARDSON, K. 1976. 'Evidence for a low upper limit of heritability of mental test performance in a national sample of twins', *Nature* 263, 5575, 314–6.

AINSWORTH, M. E. and BATTEN, E. J. 1974. *The Effects of Environmental Factors on Secondary Educational Attainment in Manchester: A Plowden Follow-up*, Schools Council Research Studies, Macmillan, London. 212 pp. **p. 361**

ALMY, M. 1975. 'Commentary' in J. Stallings 'Implementation and child effects of teaching practices in follow through classrooms', *Monographs of the Society for Research in Child Development*, Serial no: 163, 40, 7–8, 120–3.

ALMY, M., CHITTENDEN, E. and MILLER, P. 1966. *Young Children's Thinking*, Teacher's College Press, New York. 153 pp.

ANDERSON, E. V. 1974. 'Genetics and intelligence' in J. Wortis (ed) *Mental Retardation and Developmental Disabilities. An Annual Review, VI*, Churchill Livingstone, Edinburgh/London. 20–43. Brunner/Mazel, New York, NY.

ARNEIL, G. C., McKILLIGAN, H. R. and LOBA, E. 1965. 'Malnutrition in Glasgow children', *Scottish Medical Journal* 10, 480–4.

ASHBY, B., MORRISON, A. and BUTCHER, H. J. 1970. 'The abilities and attainments of immigrant children', *Research in Education* 4, 73–80.

BALDWIN, A. L. and BALDWIN, C. P. 1973. 'The study of mother-child interaction', *American Scientist* 61, 6, 714–21.

BARATZ, J. C. 1969. 'A bi-dialectal task for determining language proficiency in economically disadvantaged Negro children', *Child Development* 40, 3, 889–901.

BARATZ, J. C. 1970. 'Teaching reading in an urban Negro school system' in F. Williams (ed) *Language and Poverty*, Markham, Chicago. 11–24. **p. 333**

BARKER LUNN, J. C. 1970. *Streaming in the Primary School*, NFER Pub. Co., Slough (chapter 12 'Attitudes of parents', 175–85). Humanities Press, Atlantic Highlands, NJ.

BARNES, J. H. and LUCAS, H. 1975. 'Positive discrimination in education: individuals, groups and institutions', in J. Barnes (ed) *Educational Priority, Vol. 3: Curriculum Innovation in London's EPAs*, HMSO, London. 237–87.

BEE, H. L. *et al.* 1969. 'Social class differences in maternal teaching strategies and speech patterns', *Developmental Psychology* 1, 6, 726–34. **p. 362**

BEILIN, H. 1964. 'Perceptual-cognitive conflict in the development of an invariant area concept', *Journal of Experimental Child Psychology* 1, 3, 208–26.

BEILIN, H., KAGAN, J. and RABINOWITZ, R. 1966. 'Effects of verbal and perceptual training on water level representation', *Child Development* 37, 2, 317–29.

BEREITER, C. and ENGELMANN, S. 1966. *Teaching Disadvantaged Children in Preschool*, Prentice-Hall, Englewood Cliffs, NJ. 312 pp.

BERNSTEIN, B. 1962a. 'Linguistic codes, hesitation phenomena and intelligence', *Language and Speech*, 5, 31–46 (Also re-printed in B. Bernstein, 1971, *Class Codes and Control, Vol 1*, Routledge and Kegan Paul, London. 76–94). Schocken Books, New York. **p. 334**

BERNSTEIN, B. 1962b. 'Social class, linguistic codes and grammatical elements', *Language and Speech* 5, 221–40 (also re-printed in B. Bernstein, 1971, *Class, Codes and Control, Vol 1*. Routledge and Kegan Paul, London. 95–117; Schocken Books, New York. **p. 335**

BERNSTEIN, B. 1971. *Class, Codes and Control. Theoretical Studies towards a Sociology of Language*, Routledge and Kegan Paul, London. 238 pp; Schocken Books, New York. **p. 335**

BERNSTEIN, B. 1973. *Class, Codes and Control, Vol 2. Applied Studies towards a Sociology of Language.* Routledge and Kegan Paul, London. 377 pp; Schocken Books, New York. **p. 336**

BIRCH, H. G. 1968. 'Health and the education of socially disadvantaged children', *Developmental Medicine and Child Psychology* 10, 5, 580–99.

BIRCH, H. and GUSSOW, J. D. 1970. *Disadvantaged Child: Health, Nutrition and School Failure*, Grune and Stratton, New York. 320 pp.

BIRCH, H. G., RICHARDSON, S. A., BAIRD, D., HOROBIN, G. and ILLSLEY, R. 1970. *Mental Subnormality in the Community. A Clinical and Epidemiologic Study*, Williams and Wilkins, Baltimore. 200 pp.

BISSELL, J. S. 1973. 'Planned variation in Head Start and Follow Through', in J. C. Stanley (ed) *Compensatory Education for Children Ages 2–10*, Johns Hopkins, Baltimore. 63–108.

BLANK, M. and SOLOMON, F. 1968. 'A tutorial language program to develop abstract thinking in socially disadvantaged pre-school children', *Child Development* 39, 2, 379–89.

BLOOM, B. S., DAVIS, A. and HESS, R. 1965. *Compensatory Education for Culture Deprivation*, Holt, Rinehart and Winston, New York. 179 pp.

BRACE, A. and NELSON, L. D. 1965. 'The preschool child's concept of number', *The Arithmetic Teacher* 12, 2, 126–33.

BRANDIS, W. and HENDERSON, D. 1970. *Social Class, Language and Communication* (chapter 1: 'Social class differences in form-class usage among five year old children' by D. Henderson; chapter 2: 'Social class differences in form-class switching among five year old children by D. Henderson; chapter 3: 'Social class differences in communication and control' by B. Bernstein and W. Brandis). Routledge and Kegan Paul, London. 153 pp; Sage Publications, Inc. Beverley Hills, Calif. **p. 336**

BRONFENBRENNER, U. 1974. *A Report on Longitudinal Evaluations of Preschool Programmes, Vol II. Is Early Intervention Effective?* DHEW Publication No. (OHD) 74–25, US Department of Health, Education and Welfare, Washington DC. 60 pp.

BRONFENBRENNER, U. 1975. 'Nature with nurture: a reinterpretation of the evidence', in A. Montagu (ed) *Race and IQ*. Oxford University Press, New York. 114–44.

BRUCK, M. and TUCKER, G. R. 1974. 'Social class differences in the acquisition of school language', *Merrill-Palmer Quarterly* 20, 205–20. **p. 337**

BRUNER, J. S. 1971. 'Poverty and childhood' in J. S. Bruner, *The Relevance of Education*, Allen and Unwin, London. 132–61; W. W. Norton & Co., New York.

BURT, C. 1966. 'The genetic determination of differences in intelligence: a study of monozygotic twins reared together and apart', *British Journal of Psychology* 57, 137–53.

CALDWELL, M. B. and KNIGHT, D. 1970. 'The effect of Negro and white examiners on Negro intelligence test performance', *Journal of Negro Education* 39, 21, 177–9.

CAZDEN, C. B. 1970. 'The neglected situation in child language research and education' in F. Williams (ed) *Language and Poverty*, Markham, Chicago. 81–101. **p. 338**

CAZDEN, C. B. 1972. *Child Language and Education*, Holt, Rinehart and Winston, New York. 314 pp.

CHAZAN, M., LAING, A. and JACKSON, S. 1971. *Just Before School*, Published for Schools Council by Basil Blackwell, Oxford. 220 pp. **p. 363**

CLARKE, A. M. and CLARKE, A. D. B. 1974. 'Genetic-environmental interactions in cognitive development' in A. M. and A. D. B. Clarke (eds) *Mental Deficiency, the Changing Outlook*, 3rd edn. Methuen, London. 164–205.

CLARKE-STEWART, K. A. 1973. 'Interactions between mothers and their young children: characteristics and consequences', *Monographs of the Society for Research in Child Development*, Serial no. 153, 38, 6–7. 109 pp. **p. 114**

COHEN, L. and BAGSHAW, D. 1973. 'A comparison of the achievements of nursery school and non-nursery school children', *Durham Research Review* 6, 30, 753–42. **p. 389**

COLE, M., GAY, J., GLICK, J. A. and SHARP, D. W. 1971. *The Cultural Context of Learning and Thinking*, Basic Books, New York. 304 pp. **p. 311**

COLEMAN, J. S. 1966. *Equality of Educational Opportunity*, US Department of Health, Education and Welfare, Washington DC. 737 pp.

COMMITTEE ON HIGHER EDUCATION, 1963. *Higher Education. Report ...* under the Chairmanship of Lord Robbins (Cmnd. 2154), HMSO, London. ('The so-called pool of ability' in Chapter 6; 'The future demand of higher education and the places needed to meet it', 49–54).

COOK-GUMPERZ, J. 1963. *Social Control and Socialisation*, Routledge and Kegan Paul, London. 290 pp. (Foreword by B. Bernstein, vii-x). **p. 364**

COVINGTON, M. V. 1967. 'Stimulus discrimination as a function of social class membership', *Child Development* 38, 2, 607–13.

DALE, P. S. 1972. *Language Development*, Dryden Press, London. (Especially chapter 8: 'The functions of language', 202–37.) 2nd edition 1976, Holt Rinehart & Winston, New York.

DALE, R. R. and GRIFFITH, S. 1965. *Down Stream*, Routledge and Kegan Paul, London. 97 pp.

DAS, J. P. 1973. 'Cultural deprivation and cognitive competence', in N. R. Ellis (ed) *International Review of Research in Mental Retardation, Vol 6*, Academic Press, London. 1–53. **p. 365**

DASEN, P. R. 1972. 'The development of conservation in aboriginal children: a replication study', *International Journal of Psychology* 7, 2, 75–85.

DAVIE, R. 1973. 'Eleven years of childhood', *Statistical News* 22, 14–18.

DAVIE, R., BUTLER, N. and GOLDSTEIN, H. 1972. *From Birth to Seven. The Second Report of the National Child Development Study (1958 cohort)* Longman in association with the National Children's Bureau, London (from chapters 4, 5, 10 and 15); Humanities Press, Atlantic Highlands, NJ. **p. 312**

DE LACEY, P. R. 1971. 'Verbal intelligence, operational thinking and environment in part-aboriginal children', *Australian Journal of Psychology* 23, 2, 145–9.

DE LEMOS, M. M. 1969. 'The development of conservation in aboriginal children', *International Journal of Psychology* 4, 4, 255–69.

DEPARTMENT OF HEALTH AND SOCIAL SECURITY, 1975. *A Nutrition Survey of Pre-school Children, 1967–8*. (A report by the Committee on Medical Aspects of Food Policy.) HMSO, London. 125 pp.

DEUTSCH, M. and BROWN, B. 1964. 'Social influences in Negro-white intelligence differences', *Journal of Social Issues* 20, 2, 24–35.

DEUTSCH, M., TALEPOROS, E. and VICTOR, J. 1974. 'A brief synopsis of an initial enrichment program in early childhood', in S. Ryan (ed) *A Report on Longitudinal Evaluations of Pre-school Programs. Vol 1. Longitudinal Evaluations*, DHEW Publication No. (OHD) 74–24, US Department of Health, Education and Welfare, Washington, DC. 49–60.

DEWART, M. H. 1972. 'Social class and children's understanding of deep structure in sentences', *British Journal of Educational Psychology* 42, 2, 198–203. **p. 339**

DIMITROVSKY, L. and ALMY, M. 1975a. 'Early conservation as a predictor of later reading', *Journal of Psychology* 90, 11–18.

399

DIMITROVSKY, L. and ALMY, M. 1975b. 'Early conservation as a predictor of arithmetic achievement', *Journal of Psychology* 91, 1st half, 65–70.

DINNAGE, R. 1970. *The Handicapped Child. Research Review, Vol 1*, Longman in association with National Bureau for Co-operation in Child Care (now National Children's Bureau), London. 414 pp.; Humanities Press, Atlantic Highlands, NJ.

DOBBING, J. 1971. 'Undernutrition and the developing brain', *British Nutrition Foundation Information Bulletin No 6*, 70–3.

DOBBING, J. and SANDS, J. 1973. 'Quantitative growth and the development of human brain', *Archives of Disease in Childhood* 48, 10, 757–67.

DONACHY, W. 1976. 'Parent participation in pre-school education', *British Journal of Educational Psychology* 46, 1, 31–9. **p. 390**

DOUGLAS, J. W. B. 1964. *The Home and the School*, MacGibbon and Kee, London. 224 pp.

DOUGLAS, J. W. B. and BLOMFIELD, J. M. 1958. *Children Under Five: The Results of a National Survey*, Allen and Unwin, London. 177 pp.

DOUGLAS, J. W. B. and ROSS, J. M. 1964. 'The later educational progress and emotional adjustment of children who went to nursery schools or classes', *Educational Research* 7, 1, 73–80.

DOUGLAS, J. W. B., ROSS, J. M. and SIMPSON, H. R. 1968. *All Our Future*, Peter Davies, London. 252 pp.

DREGER, R. M. and MILLER, K. S. 1960. 'Comparative psychological studies of Negroes and whites in the United States', *Psychological Bulletin* 47, 361–402.

DREGER, R. M. and MILLER, K. S. 1968. 'Comparative psychological studies of Negroes and whites in the United States: 1959–1965', *Psychological Bulletin Monograph Supplement* 70, 3, 2, 58 pp.

EDWARDS, V. K. 1976. 'Effects of dialect on the comprehension of West Indian children', *Educational Research* 18, 2, 83–95.

ERLENMEYER-KIMLING, L. and JARVIK, L. F. 1963. 'Genetics and intelligence', *Science* 142, 1477–9.

EYSENCK, H. J. 1971. *Race, Intelligence and Education*, Temple Smith, London. 160 pp.

FINLAYSON, D. 1971. 'Parental aspirations and the educational achievement of children', *Educational Research* 14, 1, 61–4.

FOGELMAN, K. R. and GOLDSTEIN, H. 1976. 'Social factors associated with changes in educational attainment between seven and eleven years of age', *Educational Studies* 2, 2, 95–109.

FRASURE, N. E. and ENTWISLE, D. R. 1973. 'Semantic and syntactic development in children', *Developmental Psychology* 9, 2, 236–45.

FRIEDRICHS, A. G. et al. 1971. 'Interrelations among learning and performance tasks at the preschool level', *Developmental Psychology* 4, 2, 164–72.

FULKER, D. W. 1975. 'The science and politics of IQ by Leon J. Kamin, New York: Halstead Press, 1974. pp. 183', *American Journal of Psychology* 88, 3, 505–37.

FURBY, L. 1973. 'Implications of within-group heritabilities for sources of between-group differences', *Developmental Psychology* 9, 1, 28–37.

FURTH, H. G. 1973. *Deafness and Learning*, Wadsworth, Belmont, Calif (chapter 6: 'Research in thinking processes', 52–71).

GAHAGAN, D. M. and GAHAGAN, G. A. 1970. *Talk Reform*, Routledge and Kegan Paul, London. 147 pp; Sage Publications Inc. Beverley Hills, Calif. **p. 339**

GAUDIA, G. 1972. 'Race, social class, and age of achievement of conservation on Piaget's tasks', *Developmental Psychology* 6, 1, 158–65. **p. 313**

GENSHAFT, J. L. and HIRT, M. 1974. 'Language differences between black children and white children', *Developmental Psychology* 10, 3, 451–6. **p. 340**

GHUMAN, P. A. S. 1975. *The Cultural Context of Thinking* NFER Pub. Co., Slough. 136 pp. Humanities Press, Atlantic Highlands, NJ.

GINSBURG, H. 1972. *The Myth of the Deprived Child: Poor Children's Intellect and Education*, Prentice-Hall, Engelwood-Cliffs, NJ. 252 pp.

GOLDEN, M. and BIRNS, B. 1968. 'Social class and cognitive development in infancy', *Merrill-Palmer Quarterly* 4, 2, 139–49. **p. 116**

GOLDEN, M., BIRNS, B., BRIDGER, W. and MOSS, A. 1971. 'Social class differentiation in cognitive development among black preschool children', *Child Development* 42, 1, 37–45. **p. 313**

GOLDEN, M., BRIDGER, W. H. and MONTARE, A. 1974. 'Social class differences in the ability of young children to use verbal information to facilitate learning', *American Journal of Orthopsychiatry* 44, 1, 86–91.

GRAY, S. W. 1974. 'Children from three to ten: the early training project', in S. Ryan (ed) *A Report on Longitudinal Evaluations of Preschool Programs. Vol I. Longitudinal Evaluations*, DHEW Publication No. (OHD) 74–24, US Department of Health, Education and Welfare, Washington, DC. 61–7.

GRAY, S. W. and KLAUS, R. A. 1970. 'The early training project; a seventh year report', *Child Development* 41, 4, 909–24.

GREEN, R. B. and ROHWER, W. D. 1971. 'SES differences on learning and ability tests in black children', *American Educational Research Journal* 8, 4, 601–9. **p. 313**

HAGGARD, E. A. 1954. 'Social status and intelligence: an experimental study of certain cultural determinants of measured intelligence', *Genetic Psychology Monographs* 49, 2, 141–86.

HALSEY, A. H. (1972a) 'The national pre-school experiment' in A. H. Halsey (ed) *Educational Priority. Vol I: EPA Problems and Policies*, HMSO, London. 86–100. **p. 390**

HALSEY, A. H. (ed) (1972b) *Educational Priority. Vol 1: EPA Problems and Policies*, HMSO, London. 209 pp.

HANEY, J. H. and HOOPER, F. H. 1973. 'A developmental comparison of social class and verbal ability influences on Piagetian tasks', *Journal of Genetic Psychology* 122, 235–45. **p. 314**

HARVEY, S. and LEE, T. R. 1974. 'An experimental study of educational compensation', in C. M. Morrison (ed) *Educational Priority, Vol 5: EPA – A Scottish Study* HMSO, Edinburgh. 124–66. **p. 391**

HAWKINS, P. R. 1969. 'Social class, the nominal group and reference', *Language and Speech* 12, 2, 125–35 (also re-printed in B. Bernstein (ed) 1973 *Class, Codes and Control, Vol 2*, Routledge and Kegan Paul, London). 81–92; Schocken Books, New York. **p. 340**

HEIDER, E. R. 1971. 'Style and accuracy of verbal communications within and between social classes', *Journal of Personality and Social Psychology* 18, 1, 33–47. **p. 341**

HERTZIG, M. E., BIRCH, H. G., RICHARDSON, S. A. and TIZARD, J. 1972. 'Intellectual levels of school children severely malnourished during the first two years of life', *Pediatrics* 49, 6, 814–23.

HERTZIG, M. E., BIRCH, H. G., THOMAS, A. and MENDEZ, O. 1968. 'Class and ethnic differences in the responsiveness of preschool children to cognitive demands', *Monographs of the Society for Research in Child Development*, Serial no. 117, 33, 1. 69 pp. **p. 314**

HERZOG, E., NEWCOMB, C. H., and CISIN, I. H. 1974. 'Double deprivation: the less they have the less they learn' in S. Ryan (ed) *A Report on Longitudinal Evaluations of Preschool Programs. Vol I. Longitudinal Evaluations* DHEW Publication no. (OHD) 74–24, US Department of Health, Education and Welfare, Washington, DC. 69–93.

HESS, R. D. and SHIPMAN, V. C. 1965. 'Early experience and the socialization of cognitive modes in children', *Child Development* 36, 4, 869–86.

HESS, R. D. and SHIPMAN, V. C. 1967. 'Cognitive elements in maternal behavior', in J. P. Hill (ed) *Minnesota Symposia on Child Psychology, Vol 1*, University of Minnesota Press, Minneapolis. 57–81.

HESS, R. D., SHIPMAN, V. C., BROPHY, J. E. and BEAR, R. M. 1968a. *The Cognitive Environments of Urban Pre-school Children*, University of Chicago. 381 pp. **p. 365**

HESS, R. D., SHIPMAN, V. C., BROPHY, J. E. and BEAR, R. M. 1968b. 'Mother's language and child's cognitive behavior', chapter 7 in R. D. Hess, V. C. Shipman, J. E. Brophy and R. M. Bear, *The Cognitive Environments of Urban Pre-school Children*, University of Chicago. 147–70. **p. 366**

HINDLEY, C. B. 1965. 'Stability and change in abilities up to five years: group trends', *Journal of Child Psychology and Psychiatry* 6, 2, 85–99.

HOROBIN, G., OLDMAN, D. and BYTHEWAY, B. 1967. 'The social differentiation of ability', *Sociology* 1, 2, 113–29.

HOROWITZ, F. D. and PADEN, L. Y. 1973. 'The effectiveness of environmental intervention programs', in B. M. Caldwell and H. N. Ricciuti (eds) *Review of Child Development Research, Vol III*, University of Chicago Press, 331–402.

HOUSTON, S. H. 1970. 'A reexamination of some assumptions about the language of the disadvantaged child', *Child Development* 41, 947–63. **p. 342**

HUNT, J. McV. 1975. 'Reflections on a decade of early education', *Journal of Abnormal Child Psychology* 3, 4, 275–330.

HUNT, J. McV., KIRK, G. E. and LIEBERMAN, C. 1975a. 'Social class and preschool language skill: IV. Semantic mastery of shapes', *Genetic Psychology Monographs* 92, 1st half, 115–29.

HUNT, J. McV., KIRK, G. E. and VOLKMAR, F. 1975b. 'Social class and preschool language skill: III. Semantic mastery of position information', *Genetic Psychology Monographs* 91, 317–37. **p. 317**

INNER LONDON EDUCATION AUTHORITY, 1972. *Literacy Survey: 1971 Follow-up Preliminary Report*, ILEA, London. 11 pp.

JENCKS, C. 1973. *Inequality: A Reassessment of the Effect of Family and Schooling in America*, Allen Lane, London; Harper & Row, New York, NY.

JENSEN, A. R. 1969. 'How much can we boost IQ and scholastic achievement?' *Harvard Educational Review* 39, 1, 1–123.

JENSEN, A. R. 1973. 'Level I and Level II abilities in three ethnic groups', *American Educational Research Journal* 10, 4, 263–76.

JENSEN, A. R. 1974. 'Interaction of Level I and Level II abilities with race and socio-economic status', *Journal of Educational Psychology* 66, 1, 99–111. **p. 315**

JENSEN, A. R. and FREDERIKSEN, J. 1973. 'Free recall of categorized and uncategorized lists: a test of the Jensen hypothesis', *Journal of Educational Psychology* 65, 3, 304–12. **p. 316**

JONES, P. A. 1972. 'Home environment and the development of verbal ability', *Child Development* 43, 3, 1081–6. **p. 367**

JONES, P. A. and McMILLAN, W. B. 1973. 'Speech characteristics as a function of social class and situational factors', *Child Development* 44, 1, 117–21. **p. 343**

KAGAN, J. and KLEIN, R. E. 1973. 'Cross-cultural perspectives on early development', *American Psychologist* 28, 11, 947–60.

KAMIN, L. J. 1974. *The Science and Politics of IQ*, Halsted Press, New York. 183 pp.

KARNES, M. B. 1973. 'Evaluation and implications of research with young handicapped and low-income children', in J. C. Stanley (ed) *Compensatory Education for Children, Ages 2 to 8*, Johns Hopkins, Baltimore. 109–44.

KARNES, M. B., TESKA, J. A., HODGINS, A. S. and BADGER, E. D. 1970. 'Educational intervention at home by mothers of disadvantaged children', *Child Development* 41, 4, 925–35.

KARNES, M. B., ZEHRBACH, R. R. and TESKA, J. A. 1974. 'The Karnes' preschool program: rationale, curricula offerings and follow-up data', in S. Ryan (ed) *A Report on Longitudinal Evaluations of Preschool programs, Vol I. Longitudinal Evaluations*, DHEW Publication no. (OHD) 74–24, US Department of Health, Educational and Welfare, Washington, DC. 95–108.

KELSALL, R. K. and KELSALL, H. M. 1971. *Social Disadvantage and Educational Opportunity*, Holt, Rinehart and Winston, New York, 217 pp.

KINNIE, E. J. and STERNLOF, R. E. 1971. 'The influence of nonintellective factors on the IQ scores of middle- and lower-class children', *Child Development* 42, 6, 1989–95.

KIRK, G. E. and HUNT, J. McV. 1975. 'Social class and preschool language skill: 1. Introduction', *Genetic Psychology Monographs* 91, 2, 281–98. **p. 317**

KIRK, G. E., HUNT, J. McV. and LIEBERMAN, C. 1975a. 'Social class and preschool language skill: II Semantic mastery of color information', *Genetic Psychology Monographs* 91, 2, 299–316. **p. 317**

KIRK, G. E., HUNT, J. McV. and VOLKMAR, F. 1975b. 'Social class and preschool language skills V: Cognitive and semantic mastery of number', *Genetic Psychology Monographs* 92, 1st half, 131–53.

KOGAN, K. and WIMBERGER, H. C. 1969. Interaction patterns in disadvantaged families', *Journal of Clinical Psychology* 25, 4, 347–52.

KRAUS, R. M. and ROTTER, G. S. 1968, 'Communication abilities of children as a function of status and age', *Merrill-Palmer Quarterly* 14, 161–73.

LABOV, W. 1969. 'Some sources of reading problems for Negro speakers of nonstandard English', in J. C. Baratz and R. W. Shuy (eds) *Teaching Black Children to Read*, Center for Applied Linguistics, Washington DC. 29–67.

LABOV, W. 1970. 'The logic of nonstandard English' in J. E. Alatis (ed) *Report of the Twentieth Annual Round Table Meeting on Linguistics and Language Studies*, Georgetown University Press, Washington DC. 1–39 (also in F. Williams (ed) 1970. *Language and Poverty*, Markham, Chicago. 153–89.) **p. 343**

LAWSON, A. and INGLEBY, J. D. 1974. 'Daily routines of pre-school children: effects of age, birth order, sex and social class and developmental correlates', *Psychological Medicine* 4, 4, 399–415.

LAWTON, D. 1968. *Social Class, Language and Education* (especially chapter 6: 'An experimental study of the speech and writing of some middle- and working-class boys'), Routledge and Kegan Paul, London. 181 pp. **p. 344**

LAYZER, D. 1972. 'Science or superstition: a physical scientist looks at the IQ controversy', *Cognition* 1, 2–3, 265–99.

LAYZER, D. 1974. 'Heritability analyses of IQ scores: science or numerology?', *Science* 183, 29, 1259–66.

LESSER, G. S., FIFER, G. and CLARK, D. H. 1965. 'Mental abilities of children from different social-class and cultural groups', *Monographs of the Society for Research in Child Development*, Serial no. 102, 30, 4, 115 pp. **p. 318**

LEVENSTEIN, P. 1970. 'Cognitive growth in preschoolers through verbal interaction with mothers', *American Journal of Orthopsychiatry* 40, 3, 426–32.

LEVENSTEIN, P. and SUNLEY, R. 1968. 'Stimulation of verbal interaction between disadvantaged mothers and children', *American Journal of Orthopsychiatry* 38, 1, 116–21.

LEWIS, M. and GOLDBERG, S. 1969. 'Perceptual-cognitive development in infancy: a generalized expectancy model as a function of the mother-infant interaction', *Merrill-Palmer Quarterly* 15, 1, 81–100. **p. 117**

LEWIS, M. and WILSON, C. D. 1972. 'Infant development in lower-class American families', *Human Development* 15, 112–27. **p. 54**

LEWONTIN, R. 1970. 'Race and intelligence', *Bulletin of the Atomic Scientist* 26, 2–8.

LIANG, P. K., HIE, T. T., JAN, O. H. and GIOK, L: T. 1967. 'Evaluation of mental development in relation to early malnutrition', *American Journal of Clinical Nutrition* 20, 12, 1290–4.

LING, D. and LING, A. H. 1974. 'Communication development in the first three years of life', *Journal of Speech and Hearing Research* 17, 1, 146–59. **p. 55**

LOBAN, W. 1966. *Language Ability. Grades Seven, Eight and Nine*, Co-operative Research Monograph No. 18 (OE–30018), US Department of Health, Education and Welfare, Office of Education, Washington, DC.

LOEHLIN, J. C., LINDZEY, G. and SPUHLER, J. 1975. *Race Differences in Intelligence*, W. H. Freeman, San Francisco, Calif. (especially chapter 5).

McFIE, J. and THOMPSON, J. A. 1970. 'Intellectual abilities of immigrant children', *British Journal of Educational Psychology* 40, 3, 348–51.

MARJORIBANKS, K. 1972a. 'Ethnic and environmental influences on mental abilities', *American Journal of Sociology* 78, 2, 323–37. **p. 319**

MARJORIBANKS, K. 1972b. 'Environment, social class and mental abilities', *Journal of Educational Psychology* 63, 103–9. **p. 368**

MENSING, P. M. and TRAXLER, A. J. 1973. 'Social class differences in free recall of categorized and uncategorized lists in black children', *Journal of Educational Psychology* 65, 3, 378–82. **p. 319**

MERMELSTEIN, E. and SHULMAN, L. S. 1967. 'Lack of formal schooling and the acquisition of conservation', *Child Development* 38, 1, 39–52.

MESSER, S. B. and LEWIS, M. 1972. 'Social class and sex differences in the attachment and play behavior of the year old infant', *Merrill-Palmer Quarterly* 18, 4, 295–306. **p. 94**

MIDWINTER, E. 1972. *Priority Education. An Account of the Liverpool Project*, Penguin, Harmondsworth. 191 pp.

MILLER, G. W. 1971. *Educational Opportunity and the Home*, Longman, London. 162 pp; Humanities Press, Atlantic Highlands, NJ.

MILLER, L. B. and DYER, J. L. 1975. 'Four preschool programs: their dimensions and effects', *Monographs of the Society for Research in Child Development*, Serial no. 162, 40, 5–6, 170 pp.

MOELY, B. E., OLSON, F. A., HALWES, T. G. and FLAVELL, J. H. 1969. 'Production deficiency in young children's clustered recall', *Developmental Psychology* 1, 1, 26–34.

MOORE, C. L. and RETISH, P. J. 1974. 'Effect of the examiner's race on black children's Wechsler Preschool and Primary Scale of Intelligence IQ', *Developmental Psychology* 10, 5, 672–6.

MORTON-WILLIAMS, R. 1967. 'The 1964 national survey: survey among parents of primary school children', in Central Advisory Council for Education (England) *Children and Their Primary Schools. Vol 2. Research and Surveys* (Chairman Lady Plowden), HMSO, London. 93–178.

MOSS, H. A., ROBSON, K. S. and PEDERSEN, F. 1969. 'Determinants of maternal stimulation of infants and consequences of treatment for later reactions to strangers', *Developmental Psychology* 1, 3, 239–46. **p. 57**

MURRAY, R. 1974. 'Overcrowding and aggression in primary school children', in C. M. Morrison (ed) *Educational Priority. Vol 5: EPA – A Scottish Study*, HMSO, Edinburgh. 116–23.

NAZZARO, J. N. and NAZZARO, J. R. 1972. 'Associative and conceptual learning in disadvantaged and middle-class children', *Journal of Educational Psychology* 3, 341–44.

NELSON, G. K. and KLAUSMEIER, H. J. 1974. 'Classificatory behaviors of low-socioeconomic status children', *Journal of Educational Psychology* 66, 3, 432–8.

NEWSON, J. and NEWSON, E. 1968. *Four Years Old in an Urban Community*. Allen and Unwin, London (especially chapter 14: 'Verbalization and the question of truth', 430–76); Aldine Publishing Co., Chicago, Ill.

NURSS, J. R. and DAY, D. E. 1971. 'Imitation, comprehension and production of grammatical structures', *Journal of Verbal Learning and Verbal Behavior* 10, 68–74. **p. 345**

OSSER, H., WANG, M. D. and ZAID, F. 1969. 'The young child's ability to imitate and comprehend speech: a comparison of two subcultural groups', *Child Development* 40, 4, 1063–75. **p. 346**

OVERTON, W. F., WAGNER, J. and DOLINSKY, H. 1971. 'Social-class differences and task variables in the development of multiplicative classification', *Child Development* 42, 6, 1951–8. **p. 320**

PACE, A. 1973. 'Conservation of identity and equivalence among children from varying socio-economic backgrounds', *Scientica Paedagogica Experimentalis* 10, 1, 58–69.

PALLISTER, R. and WILSON, J. 1970. 'Parents' attitudes to education', *Educational Research* 13, 1, 56–60.

PALMER, F. H. 1970. 'Socioeconomic status and intellective performance among Negro preschool boys', *Developmental Psychology* 3, 1, 1–9. **p. 321**

PARASKEVOPOULOUS, J. and HUNT, J. McV. 1971. 'Object construction and imitation under differing condition of rearing', *Journal of Genetic Psychology* 119, 301–21. **p. 119**

PAYNE, J. 1974. 'The survey of parents' in J. Payne (ed) *Educational Priority, Vol 2. EPA Surveys and Statistics*, HMSO, London. 79–122.

PEAKER, G. F. 1967. 'The regression analyses of the national survey' in Central Advisory Council for Education (England) *Children and Their Primary Schools. Vol 2. Research and Surveys* (Chairman Lady Plowden), HMSO, London. 179–221.

PEISACH, E. 1974. 'Relationship between knowledge and use of dimensional language and achievement of conservation', *Developmental Psychology* 9, 2, 189–97.

RADIN, N. 1972b. 'Three degrees of parental involvement in a pre-school program: impact on mothers and children', *Child Development* 43, 4, 1355–64.

RAVEN, R. J. 1967–8. 'The development of classification abilities in culturally disadvantaged children', *Journal of Research in Science Teaching* 5, 224–9.

RESNICK, L. B. and LEINHARDT, G. 1975. 'Commentary' in J. Stallings 'Implementation and child effects of teaching practices in Follow Through classrooms', *Monographs of the Society for Research in Child Development*, Serial no. 163, 40, 7–8. 123–33.

REX, J. 1972. 'Nature versus nurture: the significance of the revived debate', in K. Richardson, D. Spears and M. Richards (eds) *Race, Culture and Intelligence*, Penguin, Harmondsworth. 167–178.

RHODES, P. 1973. 'Obstetric prevention of mental retardation', *British Medical Journal* i, 5850, 399–402.

RICHARDSON, K., CALNAN, M., ESSEN, J. and LAMBERT, L. (1976) 'The linguistic maturity of eleven year olds; some analysis of the written compositions of children in the National Child Development Study', *Journal of Child Language* 3, 1, 99–115.

RICHMAN, N. 1976. 'Depression in mothers of pre-school children', *Journal of Child Psychology and Psychiatry* 17, 1, 75–8.

ROBINSON, W. P. 1965. 'The elaborated code in working-class language', *Language and Speech* 8, 243–252.

ROBINSON, W. P. and CREED, C. D. 1968. 'Perceptual and verbal discriminations of "elaborated" and "restricted" code users', *Language and Speech* 11, 3, 182–93 (also re-printed in B. Bernstein (ed) 1973 *Class, Codes and Control, Vol 2*, Routledge and Kegan Paul, London 120–32; Schocken Books, New York). **p. 346**

ROHWER, W. D. JNR. 1971. 'Learning, race and school success', *Review of Educational Research* 41, 3, 191–210.

ROHWER, W. D. JNR. and AMMON, M. S. 1971. 'Elaboration training and paired associate learning efficiency in children', *Journal of Educational Psychology* 62, 5, 376–83.

ROHWER, W. D. JNR., AMMON, M. S., SUZUKI, N. and LEVIN, J. R. 1971. 'Population differences and learning proficiency', *Journal of Educational Psychology* 62, 1, 1–14.

ROTHENBERG, B. B. 1969a. 'Conservation of number among four and five year old children: some methodological considerations', *Child Development* 40, 2, 383–406.

ROTHENBERG, B. B. 1969b. 'Preschool children's understanding of the coordinated concepts of distance, movement, number and time', *Journal of Genetic Psychology* 115, 263–76.

ROTHENBERG, B. B. and COURTNEY, R. G. 1969. 'Conservation of number in very young children', *Developmental Psychology* 1, 5, 493–502.

ROTHENBERG, B. B. and OROST, J. H. 1969. 'The training of conservation of number in young children', *Child Development* 40, 3, 707–26.

RYAN, S. (ed) 1974. *A Report on Longitudinal Evaluations of Preschool Programs. Vol I. Longitudinal Evaluations*, DHEW Publication No. (OHD) 74–24, US Department of Health, Education and Welfare, Washington, DC. 140 pp.

SCARR-SALAPATEK, S. 1975. 'Genetics and the development of intelligence', in F. D. Horowtiz (ed) *Review of Child Development Research. Vol IV*, University of Chicago Press.

SCARR-SALAPATEK, S. and WEINBERG, R. A. 1975. 'The war over race and IQ: when black children grow up in white homes', *Psychology Today* 9, 7, 80–2.

SCHACHTER, F. F., KIRSHNER, K., KLIPS, B., FRIEDRICKS, M. and SANDERS, K. 1974. 'Everyday preschool interpersonal speech usage: methodological, developmental and sociolinguistic studies', *Monographs of the Society for Research in Child Development*, Serial no. 156, 39, 3, 88 pp.

SCHWARTZ, M. and SCHWARTZ, J. 1974. 'Evidence against a genetical component to performance on IQ tests', *Nature* 248, 84–5.

SCROFANI, P. J., SUZIEDELIS, A. and SHORE, M. 1973. 'Conceptual ability in black and white children of different social classes: an experimental test of Jensen's hypothesis', *American Journal of Orthopsychiatry* 43, 4, 541–53. **p. 321**

SIGEL, I. E., ROEPER, A. and HOOPER, F. H. 1966. 'A training procedure for acquisition of Piaget's conservation of quantity: a pilot study and its replication', *British Journal of Educational Psychology* 36, 3, 301–11.

SINCLAIR-DE-ZWART, H. 1969. 'Developmental psycholinguistics', in D. Elkind and J. H. Flavell (eds) *Studies in Cognitive Development*, Oxford University Press. 315–36.

SITKEI, E. G. and MEYERS, C. E. 1969. 'Comparative structure of intellect in middle- and lower-class four year olds of two ethnic groups', *Developmental Psychology* 1, 5, 592–604.

SKEELS, H. M. 1966. 'Adult status of children with contrasting early life experiences: follow up study', *Monographs of the Society for Research in Child Development*, Serial no. 105, 31, 3, 65 pp.

SMEDLEY, D. A. 1969. 'Language and social class among grammar school children', *British Journal of Educational Psychology* 39, 2, 195–6.

SMITH, G. 1975a. 'Pre-school: the main experiment', in G. Smith (ed) *Educational Priority. Vol 4. The West Riding Project*, HMSO, London. 97–120. **p. 392**

SMITH, G. 1975b. 'Pre-school: the home visiting project', in G. Smith (ed) *Educational Priority, Vol 4. The West Riding Project*, HMSO London. 135–66. **p. 393**

SMITH, G. 1975c. 'Reception class: the individual language follow-up programme' in G. Smith (ed) *Education Priority, Vol 4. The West Riding Project*, HMSO, London (section iii in Chapter 'Pre-school – primary school: further developments') 175–83. **p. 394**

SMITH, G. (ed) 1975d. *Educational Priority, Vol 4. The West Riding Project*, HMSO, London. 282 pp.

SMITH, G. 1975e. 'Pre-school: a further year and the teachers' view' in G. Smith (ed) *Educational Priority, Vol 4. The West Riding Project*, HMSO, London. 121–34.

SMITH, G. and JAMES, T. 1975. 'The effects of preschool education: some American and British evidence', *Oxford Review of Education* 1, 3, 223–40.

SOLKOFF, N. 1972. 'Race of experimenter as a variable in research with children', *Developmental Psychology* 7, 1, 70–5.

SONSTROEM, A. M. 1966. 'On the conservation of solids', in J. S. Bruner, R. R. Oliver and P. M. Greenfield, *Studies in Cognitive Growth*, Wiley, New York. 208–24.

SPRIGLE, H. 1974. 'Learning to learn program', in S. Ryan (ed) *A Report on Longitudinal Evaluations of Preschool Programs. Vol I. Longitudinal Evaluations*, DHEW Publication No. (OHD) 74–24, US Department of Health, Education and Welfare, Washington, DC. 109–24.

SROUFE, L. A. 1970. 'A methodological and philosophical critique of intervention-oriented research', *Developmental Psychology* 2, 1, 140–5.

STALLINGS, J. 1975. 'Implementation and child effects of teaching practices in Follow Through classrooms', *Monographs of the Society for Research in Child Development*, Serial no. 163, 40, 7–8, 133 pp.

STREISSGUTH, A. P. and BEE, H. L. 1972. 'Mother-child interactions and cognitive development in children', in W. W. Hartup (ed) *The Young Child. Reviews of Research, Vol 2*, National Association for Education of Young Children, Washington, DC.

STEVENSON, H. W., WILLIAMS, A. M. and COLEMAN, E. 1971. 'Interrelations among learning and performance tasks in disadvantaged children', *Journal of Educational Psychology* 62, 3 179–84.

STEVENSON, J. 1975. 'The nursery school language work', in J. Barnes (ed) *Educational Priority, Vol 3. Curriculum Innovations in London's EPAs*, HMSO, London. 69–98. **p. 395**

STEWART, W. A. 1969. 'On the use of Negro dialect in the teaching of reading', in J. C. Baratz and R. W. Shuy (eds) *Teaching Black Children to Read*, Center for Applied Linguistics, Washington, DC. 156–219.

SUMNER, R. and WARBURTON, F. W. 1972. *Achievement in Secondary School*, NFER Pub. Co., Slough. 208 pp; Humanities Press, Atlantic Highlands NJ.

THOMANECK, J. K. A. 1972. 'A sociolinguistic study of adjective and adverb', *Language and Speech* 15, 1, 8–13.

TIZARD, B. 1973. 'The environment and intellectual functions', Paper given at Institute of Biology Symposium.

TIZARD, B. 1974. 'IQ and race', *Nature* 247, 5349, 316.

TIZARD, B. 1975. *Early Childhood Education. A Review and Discussion of Research in Britain*, NFER Pub. Co., Slough. 142 pp. Humanities Press, Atlantic Highlands, NJ.

TIZARD, B. and REES, J. 1974. 'A comparison of the effects of adoption, restoration to the natural mother, and continued institutionalization on the cognitive development of four year old children', *Child Development* 45, 1, 92–9. **p. 322**

TIZARD, B., PHILPS, J. and PLEWIS, I. 1976. 'Staff behaviour in pre-school centres', *Journal of Child Psychology and Psychiatry* 17, 1, 21–33.

TIZARD, J. 1974. 'Early malnutrition, growth and mental development in man', *British Medical Bulletin* 30, 2, 169–74.

TOUGH, J. 1970. *Language and Environment: An Interim Report on a Longitudinal Study*, University of Leeds, Institute of Education (Unpublished).

TOUGH, J. 1973. 'The language of young children: the implications for the education of the young disadvantaged child', in M. Chazan (ed) *Education in the Early Years*, Faculty of Education, University College of Swansea, 60–76. **p. 346**

TULKIN, S. R. 1968. 'Race, class, family and school achievement', *Journal of Personality and Social Psychology* 9, 1, 31–7. **p. 323**

TULKIN, S. R. 1973. 'Social class differences in attachment behaviors of ten month old infants', *Child Development* 44, 1, 171–4. **p. 102**

TULKIN, S. R. and KAGAN, J. 1972. 'Mother-child interaction in the first year of life', *Child Development* 43, 1, 31–41. **p. 62**

TULKIN, S. R. and KONNER, M. J. 1973. 'Alternative conceptions of intellectual functioning', *Human Development* 16, 33–52.

VERNON, P. E. 1969. *Intelligence and Cultural Environment*, Methuen, London. 264 pp; Barnes and Noble Books, New York.

WACHS, T. D., UZGIRIS, I. C. and HUNT, J. McV. 1971. 'Cognitive development in infants of different age levels and from different environmental backgrounds: an explanatory investigation', *Merrill-Palmer Quarterly* 17, 4, 283–317. **p. 122**

WALBERG, H. J. and MARJORIBANKS, K. 1974. 'Social environment and cognitive development: toward a generalized causal analysis', in K. Marjoribanks (ed) *Environments for Learning* NFER Pub. Co., Slough. 259–73.

WATSON, P. 1972. 'Can racial discrimination affect IQ?' in K. Richardson, D. Spears and M. Richards (eds) *Race, Culture and Intelligence*, Penguin, Harmondsworth. 56–67.

WEDGE, P. and PROSSER, H. 1973. *Born to Fail?* Arrow Books in association with National Children's Bureau, London. 64 pp. **p. 368**

WEENER, P. D., 1969. 'Social dialect differences and the recall of verbal messages', *Journal of Educational Psychology* 60, 3, 194–9.

WEI, T. T. D., LAVATELLI, C. B. and JONES, R. S. 1971. 'Piaget's concept of classification: a comparative study of socially disadvantaged and middle-class young children', *Child Development* 42, 3, 919–27.

WEIKART, D. P. 1972. 'Relationship of curriculum, teaching and learning in preschool education', in J. C. Stanley (ed) *Preschool Programs for the Disadvantaged: Five Experimental Approaches to Early Childhood Education*, Johns Hopkins, Baltimore. 22–66.

WEIKART, D. P., DELORIA, D. J. and LAWSOR, S. 1974. 'Results of a preschool intervention project' in S. Ryan (ed) *A Report on Longitudinal Evaluations of Preschool Programs. Vol 1. Longitudinal Evaluations*, DHEW Publication no. (OHD) 74–24, US Department of Health, Education and Welfare, Washington, DC. 125–33.

411

WHALLEY, G. E. 1970. 'Guided parental choice', *Trends in Education* 18, 28–34.

WHITE, B. L. and WATTS, J. C. 1973. *Experience and Environment: Major Influences on the Development of the Young Child, Vol I*, Prentice-Hall, Engelwood-Cliffs, NJ. 522 pp.

WHITEMAN, M. and DEUTSCH, M. 1968. 'Social disadvantage as related to intellective and language development', in M. Deutsch, I. Katz and A. R. Jensen (eds) *Social Class, Race and Psychological Development*, Holt, Rinehart and Winston, New York. 86–114.

WHITMORE, K. and RUTTER, M. 1970. 'General medical examination of intellectually retarded and reading retarded children', in M. Rutter, J. Tizard and K. Whitmore (eds) *Education, Health and Behaviour*, Longman, London. 75–101.

WILLERMAN, L., NAYLOR, A. F. and MYRIANTHOPOULOS, N. C. 1974. 'Intellectual development of children from interracial matings: performance in infancy at four years', *Behavior Genetics* 4, 1, 83–90.

WILLIAMS, F. and NAREMORE, R. C. 1969a. 'On the functional analysis of social class differences in modes of speech', *Speech Monographs* 36, 2, 77–102.

WILLIAMS, F. and NAREMORE, R. C. 1969b. 'Social class differences in children's syntactic performance: a quantitative analysis of field study data', *Journal of Speech and Hearing Research* 12, 778–93.

WISEMAN, S. 1967. 'The Manchester survey' in Central Advisory Council for Education (England) *Children and their Primary Schools. Vol 2. Research and Surveys* (Chairman Lady Plowden), HMSO, London. 347–400.

WOODHEAD, M. 1976. *Intervening in Disadvantage: A Challenge for Nursery Education. A Review of British Research into Pre-school Education for Disadvantaged Children*, NFER Pub. Co., Slough. 129 pp; Humanities Press, Atlantic Highlands, NJ.

WOOTTON, A. J. 1974. 'Talk in the homes of young children', *Sociology* 8, 2, 227–95. **p. 369**

YARROW, L. J. 1963. 'Research in dimensions of early maternal care', *Merrill-Palmer Quarterly* 9, 101–14. **p. 125**

YOUNG, M. and McGEENY, P. 1968. *Learning Begins at Home: A Study of a Junior School and its Parents*, Routledge and Kegan Paul, London. 166 pp; Humanities Press, Atlantic Highlands, NJ.

ZIGLER, E. and BUTTERFIELD, E. C. 1968. 'Motivational aspects of changes in IQ test performance of culturally deprived nursery school children', *Child Development* 39, 1, 1–14.

412

Addendum

The Newsons (1977),* in their latest report of children growing up in Nottingham found a significant relationship between the children's verbal-reasoning-ability scores at eleven and the extent to which the home environment complemented the school when the child was seven. Both within the middle and working classes, families which were more involved in the cultural activities of the wider society and those which provided a home more supportive of school activities (especially where the parents followed up their children's interest in school topics, using newspapers and books if necessary) tended to have children with higher ability scores. Social-class differences were also striking. Not only were working-class, particularly unskilled working-class, parents less well-equipped in knowing how to pursue their children's interests but they tended to be hampered from making cultural 'visits' with them by the financial outlay involved.

* Newson, J. and E. 1977. *Perspectives on school at seven years old*, George Allen and Unwin, London. 216 pp.

Author Index